作者:乔治·沃尔什

主译:方华文

译者:李亚秋　李　青

英汉对照
**Great Books You Should Have Read
(and probably didn't)**

50+1部

最

值得的

阅读书

巨著

安徽科学技术出版社

Encouragement Press, LLC

图书在版编目（CIP）数据

50+1部最该阅读的巨著 ／（美）乔治·沃尔什（Walsh，G.）
著；方华文等译. —合肥；安徽科学技术出版社，2009.6
ISBN 978-7-5337-4438-0

Ⅰ. ①5… Ⅱ. ①沃… ②方… Ⅲ. ①文学－作品－简
介－世界 Ⅳ. ①I106

中国版本图书馆CIP数据核字（2009）第079288号

50+1部最该阅读的巨著

(美)乔治·沃尔什(Walsh,G.)著 方华文等 译

出 版 人：黄和平
责任编辑：姚敏淑 孙立凯 余登兵
封面设计：朱 婧
出版发行：安徽科学技术出版社(合肥市政务文化新区圣泉路1118号
出版传媒广场，邮编：230071)
网 址：www.ahstp.net
E－mail：yougoubu@sina.com
经 销：新华书店
排 版：安徽事达科技贸易有限公司
印 刷：合肥瑞丰印务有限公司
开 本：787×1092 1/16
印 张：16.5
字 数：455 千
版 次：2009 年 6 月第 1 版 2022 年 1 月第 2 次印刷
定 价：46.00 元

译 者 序

　　一位西方的政治家在演讲时说：一本好书可以造就一位圣人。当时台下就有人哄笑，笑他在说痴话。那位政治家也许有夸大其词之嫌，但优秀书籍对人类精神世界之影响力的确非常巨大，它可以使恶徒"放下屠刀立地成佛"，可以使普通人见识高远、情操高尚。一本好书就是一泓具有神奇功效的清澈的泉水，它可以涤荡我们思想里的污垢；一本好书犹如春风，给我们带来姹紫嫣红；一本好书仿佛良药，可以医治我们精神的病痛；一本好书恰似望远镜，帮我们看见远方的"无限风光"；一本好书像一面明镜，使我们认清自我；一本好书如人间妙音，激励我们上进……好书记载了人类的历史，好书解读错综复杂的社会现实，好书展望似画如诗的未来锦绣世界。它是我们的益友，给我们以精神的抚慰；它是我们的良师，为我们把握人生的航向。这部《50+1部最该阅读的巨著》讲述的就是"好书"的故事……

　　《圣经》是最具有震撼力量的好书！此书于公元前1445年由摩西开始书写，其《旧约》部分完成于公元前450年。这部书成为人类最经典的思想指南，也是西方文学艺术的源泉。在《圣经》的感召下，人类文明迈上了一个新的台阶，每一发展阶段都会有"圣人"出现，他们传播友谊与和平。其影响力之大，超过了任何一部其他的书。当联合国大厦立基的时候，举行了一个仪式，将一本《圣经》放在瓶中，置于地下的基穴里，表示《圣经》才真正是世界和平的基础。当人类违背经训的时候，战争与痛苦就必来临；人类遵从《圣经》的时候，人们必定和睦相处。欧美的总统和君王就位之时，要把手按在《圣经》上宣誓：根据上帝的意愿，为人民谋福利。《圣经》的作用是多方面的，其中之一是教人弃恶从善。葡萄牙有一个制造假币的罪犯，他造的假币非常逼真，几乎没有人可以认出来。当警察带他去受审时，他闭口不讲实情。由于缺乏证据，只好将他关在牢里。坐牢期间他偶然得到一本《圣经》，于是从头到尾仔细阅读，但他阅读的目的不是要信仰基督，而是要证明《圣经》是虚假的。可是当他读到耶稣因"博爱"而被钉上十字架时，他大受感动，决定接受耶稣做自己的主。再次接受审判时，他说出了自己所有的罪行，当众认罪悔改，并且规劝听众相信耶稣。

　　英国作家狄更斯的小说《远大前程》的影响力也振聋发聩。当时有一种说法：19世纪中期的英国，不仅风行维多利亚时代的火车，也风行《远大前程》，其风行程度几近家喻户晓。毫不夸张地说，从王公贵族到平民百姓，几乎都是狄更斯小说的读者。他的小说以白描的手法阐释人生，揭示金钱的力量和由此而产生的罪恶；它讥讽由贪婪的秉性所导致的堕落；它歌颂真爱的欢乐，痛惜爱心受挫或被侮辱之后的痛苦。狄更斯之前，大不列颠这个产生了文豪莎士比亚的国度，极度注重传统文化，文学崇尚古典，弥漫着巴洛克气息。不妨做一想象，当时的文坛恐怕是这番情景：但凡文坛涉足者，或头戴礼帽，手拿文明棍,身着燕尾服,一副绅士做派;或曳长裙,插翎毛,完全淑女姿态。他们出入沙龙,谈论古典主义、英雄主义和理想主义,面对波澜壮阔的社会现实却熟视无睹,对平民生活更不屑一顾。狄更斯的小说则开批判现实主义之先河,用大量的笔墨描写"小人物"的喜怒哀乐。他的小说有着鲜明的情感色彩,颂扬正义和善良,抨击丑陋和邪恶。在他的笔下,好人不光有一颗善良的心,而且禀赋极优,从容貌仪表到言谈举止都端庄得体,显得那么可信可靠、可亲可爱。此类人物中,男性或者像父亲一般慈祥,或者像兄弟一般值得信赖;女性大多善良美丽,人们不由自主要对她们倾心与呵护。《远大前程》中那一个个鲜活的人物就生活在我们周围,这大概就是它不朽的原因之一吧。

　　一本好书,展卷时读者情不自禁地受感动,思想插上翅膀随作者的一管笔翱翔;掩卷后,读者遐思不已,深悟人生哲理。要攀登人生的高峰,需以好书为台阶;要探究事物的真理,需用好书作敲门砖;要加快进步的步伐,需用好书作动力。好书益处多多,而本书是一个好书的集锦!

方华文

2009年4月于苏州大学

方华文简介

　　方华文,男,1955年6月生于西安,现任苏州大学外国语学院英语教授,著名学者、文学翻译家及翻译理论家,被联合国教科文组织国际译联誉为"the most productive literary translator in contemporary China"(中国当代最多产的文学翻译家,Babel.54:2,2008,145–158)。发表的著、译作品达1 000余万字,其中包括专著《20世纪中国翻译史》等,计200余万字;译著《雾都孤儿》《无名的裘德》《傲慢与偏见》《蝴蝶梦》《魂断英伦》《儿子与情人》《少年维特之烦恼》《红字》《从巅峰到低谷》《马丁·伊登》《套向月亮的绳索》《君主论》《社会契约论》以及改写本的《飘》《汤姆叔叔的小屋》《查特莱夫人的情人》《大卫·科波菲尔》《苔丝》《高老头》《三个火枪手》《悲惨世界》等;主编的译作包括《基督山伯爵》《红与黑》《简·爱》《汤姆·索亚历险记》《茶花女》《金银岛》《鲁滨孙漂流记》《巴黎圣母院》《莎士比亚戏剧故事集》《精神分析引论》《论法的精神》和《国富论》等;并主编了多部英汉对照读物。以上均为单行本著作,所发表文章不计在内。

Simple words have had the most profound effect on the world—its history,literature,art,science,religion and economics.To know and to have read the great masters is to understand and appreciate the complex interaction of world events as they unfold.*50 plus one Great Books You Should Have Read* (*and probably didn't*) is the first attempt to organize the great literature,both fiction and non-fiction,in such as way as to demonstrate their world-wide impact.

Every attempt has been made to introduce readers to books and literature that is international in scope and spans the centuries.The works chosen are not necessarily the most famous—nor are their authors.Rather, they represent seminal works,masterpieces that every educated individual should have at least some familiarity with.

In a few short pages,you will learn about the authors,their background and influences,as well as a good deal about the works themselves.In many ways we have provided a very sophisticated book with many important topics—but it is presented to you in an easy-to-read reference style.While not being simplistic by any means,every effort has been make to ensure basic understanding of the authors and their works.

Please remember that we are trying to channel some of the greatest minds and the greatest works into a few pages—which is a trick in itself! Nevertheless,readers will get a treat of their intellectual lifetimes when they begin sampling the many and the variety of writers and books.

For your own enjoyment,to impress others or to improve your trivia skills,this is a wonderfully enjoyable book filled with information and insight.

Savor it; enjoy it and cherish the authors as we do.Happy reading.

George Walsh

简单的词语对世界历史、文学、艺术、科学、宗教和经济产生了最深远的影响。了解并阅读这些伟大的著作就是去理解并体会世界上各种事件的相互影响。《50+1部最该阅读的巨著》首次尝试以这种方式来组编文学作品(包括小说和非小说)以展现其在世界范围的影响。

努力把国际范围的、各个时期的书和文学作品介绍给读者。所选择的作品并不一定是最著名的,作者也不一定是最著名的。然而,它们是具有影响力的作品或巨著的代表,是每一个受过教育的人应该有所熟悉的。

在短短的几页里,你会对作者、他们的背景和影响,以及作品本身有所了解。从各方面来讲我们提供了一本良好的书,书中涉及许多重要的话题,但本书是以易读的参考书的形式展现给你的。努力确保读者能对作者及其作品有基本的了解。

请记住我们努力把一些伟大思想和伟大作品写在几页纸上,这本身是一种戏法!不管怎样,当读者开始品读这许多不同的作家和作品时,他们将会享受他们的知识人生。

满足你自己的乐趣,影响他人或提高你小小的技能,这是一本非常不错的书,书中有大量的信息和真知灼见。

像我们一样,品读、享受它,珍爱作者们吧。阅读愉快。

乔治·沃尔什

Table of Contents

目　录

1

Table of Contents

目　录

2

Table of Contents

目 录

3

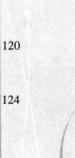

Table of Contents

目　录

4

Table of Contents
目　录

5

扩展视野，以知识影响亲朋
时影响世界的书进行评论
阅读世界一流文学作品，提高文化素质
了解它们为什么是划时代的巨著

The Bible:
Old and New Testaments

The Bible

The complete Bible, both the "Old Testament" (which comprises of 66 books) and the "New Testament" (which comprises of 27), is the effort of many different authors who wrote over a period of time estimated to be about 1,600 years.

The first five books of the "Old Testament" (Genesis, Exodus, Leviticus, Numbers, and Deuteronomy) are, by tradition, believed to have been written by the Jewish prophet and leader Moses. Moses began his writings sometime prior to 1445 B.C. and finished them approximately 40 years later with the completion of Deuteronomy around 1405 B.C. The last book of the "Old Testament" was written by the prophet Malachi; it was completed some time around 450 B.C.

The books of the "New Testament" were written by the followers and apostles of Jesus Christ. The first four books of the "New Testament" (the gospels of Matthew, Mark, Luke, and John) are perhaps the best known, because they chronicle the life, teachings, death and resurrection of Jesus Christ. The apostle Paul is credited as the author of thirteen of the books in the "New Testament." The book of Galatians was written in 49 A.D. and is one of, if not, the earliest books in the "New Testament."

Religious dogma credits the inspiration of the Biblical authors to the divine influence of the Holy Spirit, not to conventional human wisdom. Historic events and interpretation as a result of the personal experiences of the Biblical authors were probably just two of the many factors that shaped the writings that collectively became known as *The Bible*.

The Bible has variously been called *Holy Writ* or *Divine Scripture* or *The Good Book*—among many hundreds of descriptions. These exalted descriptions convey its importance to the world in general.

Since its creation in the centuries before and after the birth of Christ, it has been endlessly organized and reorganized. It is generally described as being in three parts: "The Old Testament," "The New Testament," and "The Apocrypha." "The Apocrypha" is not always included in modern versions, but it was translated and included in the famous King James translation of *The Bible* (1611), which is still the standard in the English-speaking world 4 centuries after it was created.

The three parts are organized by "books" (often, though not always, thought to be the work of one person); these books are subdivided into "chapters," and the chapters are divided into "verses"—not, as the name implies, poetry, but rather numerically designated sequences of a single sentence or two. This organization—thus, Matthew 4:16—was devised to make finding individual passages of *The Bible* simple and easy for readers.

Originally written in Hebrew and Greek, *The Bible* has been translated into more than 2,000 different languages—more than any other book in history. As well, *The Bible* is the world's runaway best-seller. Since the early 19th century, when accurate publishing records started being kept, it is believed to have sold more than five billion copies.

《圣经》
旧约和新约

《圣经》

完整的《圣经》,"旧约"(包括66书)和"新约"(包括27书),是许多不同作者们的努力成果,在大约1 600年内写成。

"旧约"的前五书(创世纪、出埃及记、利未记、民数记和申命记)传统上被认为是犹太人预言家和领袖摩西所著。摩西大约在公元前1445年之前开始写作,大约40年后,于大约公元前1405年完成申命记。"旧约"最后一书由预言家玛拉基所著,大约公元前450年写成。

"新约"中的书是由耶稣基督的追随者和使徒所著。"新约"前四书(马太福音、马克福音、路迦福音和约翰福音)或许是最著名的,因为它们记载了耶稣基督的生活、学说、死亡和复活。使徒保罗被认为是"新约"十三书的作者。加拉太书写于公元49年,是"新约"最早的书之一(如果不是最早的)。

宗教教义把圣经作者的灵感归于圣灵的感召而不是正常的人类智慧。历史事件和圣经作者们根据个人经历而得出的解释可能只是形成这些共同被称作《圣经》的作品的许多因素中的两个。

《圣经》有成千上万种叫法,被叫做神圣的文书、神圣的著作或好书。这些崇高的叫法体现了它对整个世界的重要性。

自从《圣经》问世以来,不管是耶稣基督诞生前还是诞生后,人们都不断地编写和重新编写《圣经》。《圣经》通常有三个部分:"旧约""新约"和"外典"。现代版的《圣经》并不总是包含"外典",但钦定版《圣经》中翻译并包括了"外典"。钦定版《圣经》在《圣经》问世的4个世纪后仍然是英语国家的标准版本。

《圣经》的三个部分是按"书"(通常被认为是一个人的作品)编写的。书下面是"章",章又分为"节"。节并非诗中的诗节,但却是一两个句子用数字表示的序列。这一编写方法(如马太福音4:16)是为了让读者能够容易地找到《圣经》具体的某一页。

《圣经》最初是用希伯来语和希腊语写的,已经被翻译成2 000多种语言,是历史上翻译成语言最多的书。同时,《圣经》也是世界上最畅销的书。自19世纪早期开始准确记录以来,《圣经》已经销售了50多亿本。

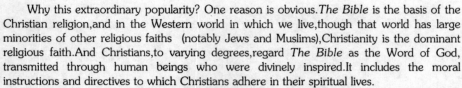

Why this extraordinary popularity? One reason is obvious.*The Bible* is the basis of the Christian religion,and in the Western world in which we live,though that world has large minorities of other religious faiths (notably Jews and Muslims),Christianity is the dominant religious faith.And Christians,to varying degrees,regard *The Bible* as the Word of God, transmitted through human beings who were divinely inspired.It includes the moral instructions and directives to which Christians adhere in their spiritual lives.

Some people would argue that,within the Western world,as well as those portions of the world in which Christianity is a minority faith,the Christian religion is dying.In Protestant countries—for example,England—most people no longer attend church or profess any Christian affiliation.In Catholic countries—for example,France—the same indifference to organized Christianity is growing.Even in the United States—the most religious country in the Western world—a good percentage of the population is secular,though not necessarily immoral or unethical:it is simply that their standards are based on philosophies other than those of traditional Christianity.

Such statistics are misleading.A belief in Evangelical Christianity and its practices is growing—in all parts of the Western world.Thus Bible study—and,particularly,interpretation of that study—is also increasing.

Even if one remains secular in his or her beliefs,there are still compelling reasons for modern man to be familiar with *The Bible*.The great conflicts of the new 21st century so far have been based on religion—conflicts between adherents of Christianity,Judaism,and Islam.*The Bible* affects,is involved in,all three of these great world religions.The "Old Testament" recounts the story of the peoples of the ancient Near East,most notably those people we now call Jews.The "New Testament" concerns the life of Christ and commentary on that life.

Still,the seeds of each religion,to a greater or lesser degree,are obviously all contained within this one great book.And anyone wishing to understand the modern world and its conflicts should begin by reading *The Bible*,then perhaps reading specific accounts of Christianity,Judaism and Islam to see how *The Bible* has been variously interpreted over the centuries from the time these religions were founded and how *The Bible* became for each either the primary or a subsidiary religious guide.Part of the lesson here is that all three religions,despite occasionally painting God as wrathful or vengeful,primarily believe in a God of Love.He is not a God who asks us to destroy the Twin Towers or take revenge against its perpetrators,or,because of that revenge,plot the destruction of Israel.All three religions currently diverge from the teachings of their prophets,and reading *The Bible* shows us the extent of our misdeeds in the name of God.

Even if one has no interest in religion or in current affairs,there are still other reasons to be familiar with *The Bible*.In purely literary terms,the King James Bible is one of the world's great literary works,and,as well as the beauty of the writing contained in that translation,*The Bible*,in whatever version,contains sections—or books—acknowledged by literary scholars to be among the world's most notable literary works.The "Book of Job" is a beautifully written tragedy of loss and redemption—so fine in literary terms that it is consistently assigned in high school and college English classes. "The Psalms" are among the most beautiful lyric poems in any language.The four "Gospels" (the story of the Life of Christ) are superb novels-in-miniature.Not just the story they tell,but the way in which they tell it,has inspired writers throughout the ages.Anyone who aspires to have a well-rounded

为什么如此受欢迎呢？一个原因是明显的。《圣经》是基督教的基础，并且基督教在我们所生活的西方是主导的宗教信仰，尽管其他少数宗教信仰的人数也很多（如犹太教徒和穆斯林）。基督教徒在不同程度上都认为《圣经》是上帝的语言，是由受上帝感召的人们传达的。《圣经》中包含了基督教徒精神生活所遵循的道德教诲和指令。

一些人会争论说，在西方世界和那些基督教是小教派的地方基督教正在消亡。在新教国家，如英格兰，大多数人不再去做礼拜或宣称信仰基督教。在天主教国家，如法国，对基督教的冷漠同样也在增长。甚至在美国这个西方最有宗教信仰的国家，相当一部分人是没有宗教信仰的，尽管不一定是不道德的或不合乎伦理的。他们的标准是以哲学为基础而不是传统的基督教。

这些统计是有误导性的。在西方世界信仰福音派基督教的人数在增加，因此《圣经》研究特别是对研究结果的阐释也在增加。

尽管一个人可以没有宗教信仰，但由于某些原因现代人还是不得不对圣经有所熟悉。21世纪的巨大冲突至今还建立在宗教基础上：基督教徒、犹太教徒和伊斯兰教徒之间的冲突。《圣经》影响着这三大世界宗教。"旧约"讲述的是古代近东人们的故事，很可能就是我们现在所说的犹太人。"新约"是关于基督生平及有关评论的。

每一个宗教的种子都或多或少包含在这一伟大的书中。每一个渴望了解当今世界及其冲突的人都应该先读一下《圣经》；然后再分别读一下关于基督教、犹太教和伊斯兰的叙述，来看一下这些宗教建立以来的几个世纪里《圣经》是怎样被解释的以及《圣经》是怎样成为每一个宗教的宗教向导的（或是主要的或是次要的）。这里可以得出一个结论是：这三个宗教基本都信仰爱神，尽管上帝偶尔会被描写成是愤怒的或谋复仇的。上帝没有让我们去摧毁世贸中心大楼，没有让我们去向罪犯复仇，也没有让我们利用复仇谋划推翻以色列。三个宗教目前在预言家们的学说上有分歧，所以阅读《圣经》我们可以知道我们以上帝为名义所做的不良行为。

即使一个人对宗教和当今时事都不感兴趣，也有其他原因使你需要熟悉《圣经》。纯粹从文学方面来说，钦定版《圣经》是世界著名文学作品之一，译作也保留了原作之美。《圣经》，不管是什么版本，都分为许多个部分（或书）；被学者们列为世界著名文学作品。"约伯记"是个关于损失与偿还的悲剧，写得很好以至于一直在中学和大学英语课中使用。"诗篇"是所有语言中最美的抒情诗。四个"福音"（基督生平故事）是极好的微型小说。不仅是他们讲述的故事，而且讲述的方式启迪了各个时代的作家。任何渴望获得全面教育的人必须要阅读《圣经》：因为它是人类创造的最伟大艺术作品之一。

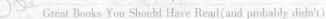
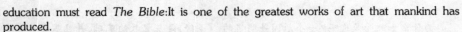
education must read *The Bible*:It is one of the greatest works of art that mankind has produced.

Yet,even supposing that a person has no interest in religion,in current events,or in literary art,there is still one more compelling reason why any person who lives in the Western world should have read *The Bible*.It is the single most important influence in the culture in which we live.

Our most important holidays are based on the stories and instructions of *The Bible*; so are the rituals we follow at birth,marriage and death.It is impossible to understand the great art of the West—not just our literary art,also our visual art—without a knowledge of *The Bible*—much of our greatest painting and sculpture is based on stories related in *The Bible*.

It is difficult—no,it is impossible—to understand the great historical conflicts in Europe, and the great explorations that led to the discoveries of the Americas and their subsequent settlement,without understanding the ways in which these events were responses to the ways in which people of the time interpreted *The Bible*.What were the Dark Ages?—why were they dark? What was the Inquisition? What was the Enlightenment? What inspired the great revolutions in America and in France? What is the Protestantism of the North of Europe—and how is it different from the Catholicism of Southern Europe?

Or,move to the modern world:Why are so many Christians agitated about prostitution or the failure of marriage or homosexuality or abortion? These moral notions are based upon the precepts of *The Bible* and the ways in which they are interpreted by various people.What does *The Bible* actually say about these and any other matters? Anyone wishing to understand the modern culture in which he or she lives should know the answer to these questions.It will interest many people to know that Jesus never mentions any of these matters—why then do so many Christians,particularly more radical Christians,feel so strongly about them? They would answer:The reasons are in *The Bible*.

Not just the modern world but so much of what has come before us,so much that mankind has done for good or bad,is based on this one book—*The Bible*.

　　然而,假设一个人对宗教、当代时事和文学艺术都没有兴趣,还有另外一个西方人必须读《圣经》的原因:它是影响我们的文化的唯一重要因素。

　　我们的重要节日是以《圣经》故事和教导为依据的,出生、婚礼和葬礼所进行的仪式也是如此。不了解《圣经》就不可能了解西方的伟大艺术,不只是文学艺术还包括视觉艺术,许多伟大的绘画和雕塑都是以《圣经》中的故事为基础。

　　如果不知道这些事件的发生是当时人们对《圣经》不同解释的结果,就很难,不,不可能理解欧洲的重大历史冲突和发现美洲新大陆并定居的重大探索。什么是黑暗时代?为什么时代是黑暗的?什么是宗教法庭?什么是启蒙运动?什么引发了美国和法国的重大革命?什么是北欧的新教,它和南欧的天主教有什么不同?

　　或者,看一下当今世界:为什么如此多的天主教徒对卖淫、婚姻失败、同性恋和流产感到不安?这些道德观念都是以《圣经》戒律和人们对戒律的不同解释为基础。关于这些以及其他事情,《圣经》中到底是怎么说的呢?任何一个人如果想要了解他或她生活于其中的现代文化就应该知道这些问题的答案。令很多人觉得有趣的是,耶稣并未提及这些事情,为什么许多天主教徒,尤其是激进天主教徒如此坚信这些戒律?他们会这样回答:原因在《圣经》中。

　　不只是当今世界,许多已经发生的事情,许多人类所做的好事或坏事,都与这本书——《圣经》有关。

Homer:
The Iliad & The Odyssey

Who Was Homer?

No precise or verifiable biographical information exists about Homer. His dates of birth and death are unknown, as are the locations where these events took place. He is believed to have lived in Ionia, subsequently a part of the Greek Empire, now the modern—day country of Turkey.

Any information that we have about Homer's personal history, background, family, education, religious beliefs, or political affiliations are pure conjecture and opinion—we have to accept that there are really no known facts about him.

All that we have are myths and legends. During the Greek and Roman eras, people took a great interest in his life because of the fame of his works. There are no fewer than 10 different accounts of his life from classical times (and probably many more that are lost to us). Each one involves contradictions of the continuities of the others and even glaring discrepancies within themselves. Some commentators believe that he was blind; others think that he was a wandering minstrel; others go so far as to claim that Homer never existed or, if he did, that he was not the author of the works that we now attribute to him.

Modern scholars believe that he did exist, that he wrote somewhere about the 8th century B.C. (the Trojan War and its aftermath, his subject, happened, if it happened at all, in the 12th century B.C.). The references to Homer in other written works establish these dates.

Homer's writings, *The Iliad* and *The Odyssey*, were immensely popular with the people of Classical Greece; indeed, many subsequent literary works of the Greeks and Romans are based on these two epic poems. In more modern times, they have become the cornerstones of a classical education in the Western world.

The Iliad & The Odyssey

No one knows who Homer really was. Yet, except for Shakespeare, more is written about Homer each year than any other writer in history. Traditionally, he was imagined to be a blind minstrel, a singer of stories who was probably a retainer in the court of one of the kings of pre-classical Greece. The first writer of the Western world whose works survive, Homer may have lived at any time between the 7th and 13th centuries B.C. Obviously, if he were blind, someone else must have written down the stories that Homer sang from memory.

Scholars of the 19th and early 20th centuries tampered with that story-Homer was not one person but, instead, he was many people who lived over many different centuries: that is, his great works, *The Iliad* and *The Odyssey*, are, like The Bible, the work of many hands. More recently, scholars have pointed out that diverse sections of these two works-unlike The Bible—are remarkably similar in both style and diction; as well, they involve well-organized

荷马
《伊利亚特》和《奥德赛》

荷马

关于荷马，没有准确的、可以考证的传记资料存在。不知道他出生及去世的时间和地点。人们认为他生活在爱奥尼亚，后来是希腊帝国的一部分，即现在的土耳其。

我们现有的关于荷马的任何资料，他的过去、背景、家庭、教育、宗教信仰和政治信仰，都纯粹是猜测。我们必须承认关于荷马确实没有已知的事实。

我们所拥有的全是神话和传奇。在希腊罗马时代，由于他的作品非常出名，人们对他的生平非常感兴趣。古典时代至今，关于荷马的生平至少有10种不同的叙述（可能许多已经遗失了）。各种叙述之间存在着矛盾之处，甚至同一叙述中也有明显的不同。有些评论家认为他是盲人；有些人认为他是四处流浪的游吟诗人；有些人竟然声称荷马根本就不存在，即便是存在，他也不是作品的作者。

现代学者认为荷马是存在的，他描述的是大约公元前8世纪（特洛伊战争及战后时期，如果战争确实爆发了，那是在公元前12世纪）。这些时间来自于其他关于荷马的书。

荷马的著作，《伊利亚特》和《奥德赛》深受希腊古典时代人们的欢迎。确实，希腊、罗马许多后来的文学作品都以这两首史诗为基础。在近现代，它们已成为西方古典教育的奠基石。

《伊利亚特》和《奥德赛》

没有人知道荷马到底是谁。然而，除了莎士比亚，每年关于历史上作家的文章，写荷马的是最多的。传统上，人们猜想他是一个失明的游吟诗人（吟唱故事的人），很可能是希腊古典时代前期某个国王王宫里的侍从。西方第一个作品保留下来的作家荷马可能生活在公元前13世纪至公元前7世纪。显然，如果他是盲人，一定是另一个人写下了荷马吟唱的故事。

19世纪和20世纪初的学者篡改了上面的说法：荷马不是一个人，而是生活在不同世纪的许多人；他的伟大著作，《伊利亚特》和《奥德赛》像《圣经》一样是许多人的成果。近来，学者们指出两部作品的不同部分在文体和用词上惊人地相似（与《圣经》不同），它们的情节也组织得很好。因此，大多数人现在又认为荷马很可能是一个人，他（或她）生活在

plots.For these reasons most people now again accept that Homer was probably one person,that he (or she) lived in the 8th century B.C.(in other words: 4 centuries before the glory days of Athens),that he recorded and organized the stories and myths of the Greek world,that he probably did speak these myths—recite or sing them in some king's court or at public events and festivals—and that at some point (probably long after his death),these stories were written down in something resembling the form in which they have come down to us.

Does it matter? Asking such a question is like asking: Was Shakespeare really a basically uneducated man from Stratford-upon-Avon,an itinerant actor,and did this same Shakespeare really write the greatest poetry and plays in the English language? We'll probably never be able to answer the question: "Who was Homer"? Just as we may never be able to answer the question: "Did the historical Shakespeare really write the plays that we now attribute to him?" All that finally matters are the works themselves.

The Iliad,usually translated as verse,tells the story of the Trojan War: Paris,Prince of Troy,falls in love with Helen,wife of Menelaus,king of Sparta,and abducts her to Troy.The other kings of Greece—notably Agamemnon,king of the Achaeans (the most powerful of the kings)—rally to avenge Meneleus,sail to Troy in "a thousand ships," and there wage a war that lasts for 10 years,because,despite all their efforts,the Greeks are unable to scale the walls of Troy and conquer the city.The Iliad happens in the 10th year of the war-the Greeks are thwarted—their greatest warrior,Achilles,refuses to fight.At last provoked to fight,Achilles kills Paris' older brother Hector,and The Iliad ends with Hector's funeral. From The Odyssey and from The Aeneid,the continuation of the Trojan story by Virgil,the greatest of Roman poets,we learn that,after killing Hector,Achilles is himself killed—and the remaining Greeks pretend to abandon Troy,leaving in their stead a great wooden horse,a homage to the monumental battle that the two sides have just fought.The Trojans bring the horse inside their walls.The horse is filled with a small contingent of Greeks,who,during the night,while most of Troy is sleeping,leave the horse,open the city gates,and admit the vast legions of Greek soldiers (who have only pretended to leave the area).The Greeks destroy the city and massacre Hiram,king of Troy and Paris' father.

The Odyssey,in modern times usually translated as prose,not only describes the fate of Troy; it also tells of the fates of the various kings as they return home to Greece.Yet it focuses primarily on one of those kings,Odysseus,notable for his wisdom and cunning,who, after the sack of Troy,wanders the earth for another 10 years before he is allowed by the Gods to return to his own kingdom of Ithaca.The Odyssey is his story and that of the wife and son who he left behind,who have lived without him for 20 years.

Both stories are epics—that is,stories of cataclysmic events rendered in exalted language.Besides Homer and Virgil,other great epic writers have been Dante (The Divine Comedy) and Milton (Paradise Lost).Most of these other notable epics have what we would call agendas—either religious or political or both.Homer is unique in merely telling the most important historical story of his people (rather as an American poet might tell objectively the story of the Civil War).In its emphasis on character and the motivations of character, The Odyssey is now also widely regarded as the first novel.

Did Troy actually happen? For centuries,scholars thought it was only a myth.In the early 19th century a city,now called Troy,was discovered on the western coast of Turkey.It is a city that has existed in different forms at different times—but one that was definitely

公元前8世纪(即雅典繁盛时期四个世纪之前)。他记录并编写了希腊的神话和故事,可能也确实在王宫里或公共活动和节日时吟诵了这些神话,并且在某个时候(可能在他去世很长时间以后)这些故事以类似于现在我们看到的形式记录下来。

　　这很重要吗? 问这样的问题就像是问:莎士比亚是来自埃文河畔斯特拉特福德基本没有受过教育的巡游演员吗? 就是这个莎士比亚写了英语中最伟大的诗歌和戏剧吗? 我们可能永远不能回答这个问题:荷马是谁? 就像我们永远也不能回答"历史上的莎士比亚真的写了我们所说的那些戏剧吗? "。最终,重要的是作品本身。

　　《伊利亚特》通常被翻译成诗节的形式,讲述的是关于特洛伊战争的故事。特洛伊王子帕里斯爱上了斯巴达国王墨涅拉斯的妻子海伦,并将她诱拐到特洛伊。希腊的其他国王们,主要是阿凯亚国王阿伽门农(最强大的国王),召集一千艘船驶向特洛伊为墨涅拉斯报仇;掀起了一场历时10年之久的战争。战争之所以持续10年之久是因为不管希腊人怎么努力他们也无法登上特洛伊城墙并占领这个城市。《伊利亚特》中讲述的是战争第10年的故事:希腊人战败,因为他们的第一勇士阿基里斯拒绝参加战斗。最后阿基里斯的战意被激发,杀死了帕里斯的哥哥赫克托尔。《伊利亚特》以赫克托尔的葬礼结束。从罗马著名诗人维吉尔的《奥德赛》和《埃涅阿斯记》(特洛伊故事的续篇),我们得知在杀死赫克托尔后阿基里斯他自己也被杀了;剩下的希腊人假装离开了特洛伊,留下了一个巨大的木马以向双方所进行的不朽战争致敬。特洛伊人把木马搬到城内。木马里是一小批希腊人,夜间大部分特洛伊在入睡时,希腊人离开木马,打开城门,大量希腊军团(他们假装离开了特洛伊)进入城内。希腊人摧毁了特洛伊城,杀死了特洛伊国王,帕里斯的父亲海勒姆。

　　《奥德赛》现在通常翻译成散文,不仅描述了特洛伊的命运,还讲述了国王们回到希腊后各自的命运。然而主要讲述的是其中的一个国王,奥德修斯他以其智慧和智谋而闻名。攻陷特洛伊之后,奥德修斯又漫游世界10年直到天神们允许他返回自己的故乡伊塔克。《奥德赛》讲述的是奥德修斯和他离开了20年的妻子和儿子的故事。

　　这两个故事都是史诗,用典雅语言描述的灾难性事件。除了荷马和维吉尔,著名的史诗作家还有但丁(《神曲》)和弥尔顿(《失乐园》)。大部分其他著名史诗都有我们可以称为待议事项的内容,宗教的或是政治的或者两者皆有。荷马不同,他仅仅讲述了人们最重要的历史故事(而不是像一个美国诗人那样客观地讲述美国内战)。《奥德赛》注重人物和人物动机的描写,因而现在被广泛认为是第一部小说。

　　特洛伊战争真的发生了吗? 几个世纪以来,学者们认为这只是一个神话。19世纪早期,在土耳其西海岸发现了一个现在叫做特洛伊的城市。这个城市在不同时期有着不同的境况,但有一个时期,大约是公元前1200年,这个城市的确被摧毁了(重建之前)。许多

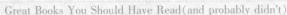

destroyed (before being rebuilt) about 1200 B.C.Many scholars now feel that that is approximately the time that the war Homer was describing probably happened.Whether or not the particulars were as Homer describes them,a conflict within the world of the eastern Mediterranean,between those countries that we now call Greece and Turkey,actually happened.

The Importance of Homer

Does that matter either? Not really.Homer used the occasion of this war,whether or not it actually happened,as a means of telling the most popular stories of his people-and produce d works of the imagination so powerful that they have been avidly read for thousands of years.But they have virtues beyond the literary—and they deserve our attention for reasons other than that they tell stories that have enthralled people throughout history.

They influenced the Greece that came after Homer: virtually all of the Greek plays that we know are variants on the themes of Troy.Virtually all of the great philosophers of Greece (notably those of Plato and Aristotle) are steeped in Homeric values.As the power of Greece faded,its place as the dominant power in the Western world was assumed by Rome,and Rome appropriated all of these stories and values as its own.Between them— their art,their philosophy,their accomplishment in the various academic disciplines,their laws,their science and technology—Greece and Rome have been the greatest single influence on the Western world—and in a very real sense *The Iliad* and *The Odyssey* are The Bible of the ancient classical world in whose shadow we still live.

Anyone wishing to understand his or her culture must understand the Greeks,the first of the Western world's great civilizations,and the clue to that understanding is in Homer. Every reader will recognize incidents,characters and especially sayings/expressions that are part of our common heritage—"The Face That Launched a Thousand Ships,A Trojan Horse,Achilles Heel and Scylla and Charybdis."

Yet it is the moral teachings of Homer that are even more important to us.The Renaissance in Europe,the awakening that ended the Middle Ages,essentially has to do with Europe's rediscovery of the Greeks,their myths in the service of their philosophy and their morality.The spirituality of Homer,combined with the tradition of Judeo-Christianity,is the heritage with which we live today.We are all the children of Homer and the world he both recorded and created.The Bible provides for many of us our religious faith,but *The Iliad* and *The Odyssey* offer the moral standards by which men and women,on a day-to-day basis,still live.

学者现在认为那个时候可能是荷马描述的战争发生的时间。不知道细节是否像荷马描述的那样,东地中海地区国家之间(现在的希腊和土耳其)确实发生过冲突。

荷马的重要性

那也重要吗?真的不重要。荷马利用战争场合(不管战争是否发生)作为一种手段来讲述最受人们欢迎的故事,创作了如此充满想象的作品,以至于数千年来一直为人们所阅读。但它们还拥有文学方面以外的优点。它们值得我们去关注不是因为讲述了吸引人的故事。

它们影响了荷马时代之后的希腊。实际上我们所知道的所有希腊戏剧都是以特洛伊为主题的变体。实际上希腊所有的伟大哲学家(主要是柏拉图和亚里士多德)都沉浸于荷马的价值观。随着希腊势力的衰弱,希腊在西方世界的主导地位由罗马取代,罗马将所有的故事和价值观视为已物。希腊和罗马的艺术、哲学、它们在各个学科的成就、它们的法律、科学和技术,希腊和罗马对西方世界产生了未有的巨大影响,确切地说《伊利亚特》和《奥德赛》是古代古典世界的《圣经》,我们仍然活在古代古典时代的阴影之下。

任何一个人如果想要了解他或她自己的文化,必须了解希腊文化这个西方伟大文明中的第一个文明,了解希腊文化的线索就是荷马。每个读者都会发现一些事件、人物,特别是一些谚语和表达方式也是我们文化的一部分:"能使一千艘船起航的美貌,特洛伊木马,阿基里斯的脚后跟(致命弱点)及西拉和克里布迪斯(进退维谷)"。

然而对我们更重要的是荷马的道德教导。欧洲的文艺复兴(这一觉醒结束了中世纪)主要是欧洲重新发现希腊文化,服务于哲学和道德的神话。荷马的精神及犹太教和基督教共有的传统是我们今天所赖以生存的文化。我们是荷马及他所记录和创造的世界的孩子。《圣经》给我们很多人提供的是精神信仰,而《伊利亚特》和《奥德赛》提供的是男人和女人日常生活所遵循的道德标准。

Two

Confucius: The Analects

Who Was Confucius?

Much of what we know about the life of Confucius is almost certainly fiction—a good deal of it is probably legendary (his name is more often rendered in Chinese as the equivalent of Kong Fuzi or Kung-fu,meaning Great Master Kong; Confucius is the Latinized, Western,version of his name).We think that he lived in the 6th-7th centuries before Christ (probably 551-479 B.C.),that he was born in the state of Lu in what is now Shandong Province,China.He may have married at an early age; he had one son and two daughters.

The story is also that his family,once noble,became poor; yet,despite his impoverished early life,he rose to positions in China of great prominence.More certain—we know these facts from his writings—is that he was a thinker,a philosopher,possibly a political figure,an educator,and the founder of what is now called the Ru school of Chinese thought.

What is without question is the position that he holds in the history of Chinese thought.In much of the Western world,Jesus is regarded as the great spiritual and religious teacher; Socrates,as conveyed to us by Plato,is the great philosophermoralist,the person in the West who has been most influential in describing how a man should live his life-in society,in this world.Confucius has had the same influence in the Far East.He is the Socrates of China.

The Analects

As the "dialogues" of Plato provide us with the thought of Socrates,so do what we now call *The Analects* give us the thought of Confucius (*The Analects* are probably his writings and sayings,collected by his followers after his death).The subjects of his thought are these:The proper education of a man; how he should behave—that is,how he should act not just on his own but in his interactions with others; the form of government that is ideal-that which a ruler should strive for.Put another way:Confucius can be said to have three topics:1) How a man should be educated; 2) how he should behave in society; and 3) how he should govern others.

Education

Confucius emphasizes the importance of education,but it is education that is anything but passive:he does not believe in any kind of schooling that involves just study.Yes,real study does involve finding a good teacher,imitating that person,listening to what he says and recommends.But equally important is reflecting on what one has learned.In other words:Confucius would disapprove of that modern student who does nothing but write down on a pad what his professor has said in a lecture.Instead,he recommends reflection He says:"He who studies but does not also think is lost." Education,then,as we might say,is an interactive process.Confucius as well talks about "six arts," or "six subjects," that are important in education,but he obviously regards morality (how we behave) as the most

孔子

　　关于孔子的生平,我们所知道的大部分都是虚构的,很大一部分是传奇。(他的名字在汉语中通常被叫做孔夫子,意思是孔大师;Confucius是他名字的拉丁文,西方人的叫法。)我们认为他生活在公元前7世纪至公元前6世纪(公元前551年~公元前479年),出生在鲁国,今中国山东省。他可能结婚较早,有一个儿子和两个女儿。

　　据说他家曾经是个贵族,后来没落了。然而尽管早年生活很贫穷,他还是上升到了中国显贵地位。比较确定的是(从他的文章中得知)他是一个思想家、哲学家、政治家、教育家和儒家学派的创始人。

　　毫无疑问的是他在中国思想史上的地位。大部分西方世界,耶稣被认为是伟大的精神和宗教导师;苏格拉底,如柏拉图所说,是个伟大的哲学家和道德家。他描述了一个人在社会中、世界上应该怎样生活,这在西方非常有影响力。孔子在远东有着同样的影响力,他是中国的苏格拉底。

《论语》

　　正如柏拉图对话录告诉我们的是苏格拉底的思想,我们现在称作《论语》的告诉我们的是孔子的思想。(《论语》是孔子去世后由他的弟子们整理的孔子言论。)他的主题思想是:人的良好教育;如何做人,即不以己为中心,如何在与他人交往中做人;统治方式,只是理想的,统治者应该努力采取的。换一种方式说,孔子的3个话题是:1)如何受教育;2)如何在社会中做人;3)如何统治他人。

教育

　　孔子强调教育的重要性,但教育却是被动的。他不提倡仅仅包括学的各种教育。真正的学习是包括找到一个好老师,模仿他,听取他的言论和建议。但同等重要的是要思考所学过的。换句话说,孔子不赞成只在本子上记下老师课堂上所说的。相反,他提倡思考。他说:"学而不思则罔。"教育,如我们所说,是个互动的过程。孔子也谈到"六艺",是教育中重要的部分,但他认为学习中最重要的是道德(如何做人)。

important subject for study.

His teaching methods are also interesting.He believes that a teacher should pose questions,cause students to understand the classic works of history—but his most important directive is that students should participate—with the teacher—in the learning process.His goal,as a teacher,is to create gentlemen in the old-fashioned sense-people who have poise, who speak correctly,but who—this is most important result—behave with integrity in all aspects of life.The purpose of education,in other words,is that students learn to be virtuous.

Behavior

Confucius believes that certain limits on man are imposed by both his creator and by nature itself.Yet,with in these boundaries,men are responsible for their actions and, particularly,for their treatment of others.This is a philosophy not very different from one that says:God creates the world; Nature imposes limits; but both God and Nature then leave man to fend for myself.How he "fends" is supremely important to Confucius.We can do nothing to change our fate in such matters as our "allotted time" on earth—but we ourselves are responsible for what we accomplish; we are responsible,too,for how others remember us.

This philosophy of behavior has to do with the concept of ren—which means "compassion for" and "loving" others.Practicing ren often involves putting others—whether family or friends—before oneself,and such altruism can be accomplished only by those who have learned self-discipline.One should behave in a way that gains the respect and admiration of others.

Government

Confucius's ideas about who should govern and how is really an extension of his views about the ordinary individual's day-to-day behavior.A ruler should learn self-discipline,should govern his subjects (his constituents) by being himself an example of virtue,should treat those that he governs with love and concern.Even in Confucius's own time,the idea—to which we in the West now mainly subscribe—that government should be that which enforces laws—was gaining the ascendancy.Yet,Confucius believed an emphasis on "legalism" was wrong,that rulers should rule by example—that they should attempt to be more virtuous than the people they governed.So that the ruler was admired,so this admiration inspired loyalty in those he ruled,so that force of any kind was never needed.

Confucius was interested in the language of the governor,the name that he and others used to describe himself,the process by which a governor was constantly attempting to "rectify," to adjust his behavior to make it correspond to the grandeur of the name.A modern example would be the presidency of the United States.Any president-could Confucius comment upon the modern presidency—must strive to live up to the best of that office,not the worse; any president must constantly "work on" (rectify) himself to achieve an ideal of the presidency.

None of these ideas seem foreign to a western reader.Confucius's notions of education are similar to our own notions of what a classical education ought to accomplish.His notions of behavior sound like a variant of the Golden Rule.He ideas about government remind us of Plato's ideas of what a philosopher-king can accomplish—or Shakespeare's notions of what an ideal ruler should be.We can say that they add up to a kind of virtuous humanism,and,in so saying,realize,from reading *The Analects*,that perhaps not so much separates East and West as previously we may have thought.

他的教学方法也很有趣。他认为老师应该提出问题,引导学生去理解历史经典作品,但他主要的指导思想是学生应该和老师一起参与到学习过程中。作为一个老师,他的目标是培养出君子:举止得当,言谈得体,最重要的是为人正直。换句话说,教育的目的是使学生成为有道德的人。

行为

孔子认为造物主和大自然将某些限制强加于人类。然而,在这些限制里,人应谨慎行事,尤其要善待他人。这个哲理与一个说法大致相同:上帝创造了世界;自然强加了限制;但上帝和自然让人类独立生活。怎样去生活,这对孔子尤其重要。我们无法改变命运,如无法改变寿命;但我们可以左右我们的作为,也可以左右别人怎样记住我们。

这一行为哲学与"仁"有关,"仁"就是同情、爱护他人。"仁"是要求先人(家人或朋友)后己,这种利他主义只有自律的人才能做到。一个人应该做到其行为可以得到他人的尊重和敬仰。

统治

孔子关于谁来统治以及怎样统治的思想是他个人日常行为思想的发展。统治者应该学会自律,应该以德治民,爱护和关心子民。在孔子生活的时代,实行法治的思想(现在西方赞同的思想)占主导地位。然而孔子认为强调"法律条文"是不正确的;他认为统治者们应该树立榜样以治国,即应该试图比他们所统治的人民更有道德。这样统治者会得到敬仰,敬仰会激发起人民的忠诚,因此任何武力都是不必要的。

孔子对统治者的语言、统治者自己以及他人对统治者的称呼和统治者不断修正和调整自己的言行以符合庄严的称呼的过程感兴趣。一个当代的例子就是美国的总统职务。如果孔子能够评论当今的总统,任何一个总统都必须尽力履行职责,任何一个总统都必须不断修正自己以实现最佳统治。

对西方读者来说,所有这些思想并不陌生。孔子的教育思想与我们的传统教育思想相似。他的行为思想像是黄金法则的变体。他的统治思想让我们想起了柏拉图关于哲学家国王的观点或者莎士比亚理想统治者的构想。我们可以说他们构成了善良人道主义,所以通过阅读《论语》,我们可以发现或许东西方的差异不是我们原来想象的那么大。

Three

Aeschylus:
The Oresteia

Who Was Aeschylus?

Aeschylus (525-456 B.C.) was the earliest and the greatest of the three major playwrights of Ancient Greece:the other two are Sophocles and Euripides.Little is known for certain about his life,little that is not legend:tradition says that he was born into a prominent family in Eleusis,near Athens.We know that he fought at the battle of Marathon (against the Persians—the great victory in Greek history),and that he won several prizes for his plays.He wrote more than 70 plays,yet only a handful survive; of these the most famous are *Agamemnon,The Libation Bearers,*and the *Eumenides*,which together comprise the trilogy Oresteia.The trilogy is arguably the greatest play to come to us from Ancient Greece—and it is generally regarded,as well,as one of the great works of world literature.

The Oresteia

The Orestia involves a plot that originates with Homer; it was almost certainly embellished by those writer/composers of epics who came after Homer (most of whose works are unknown to us).It is story of the House of Atreus.

That story is this:Atreus and Thyestes,the sons of the former king of Argos,were in dispute; Atreus claimed the throne; Thyestes not only disputed his claim,but had as well seduced his brother's wife.Thyestes lost the battle between them,was banished,yet returned years later,with his children,to beg forgiveness.Pretending to be reconciled,Atreus invited Thyestes to a feast.He killed all of Thyestes's children but one,served them as the main course at the feast,and Thyestes ate the flesh of his own dead children.Thyestes put his curse on his brother's house,and fled with his surviving son,Aegisthus.The sons of Atreus, Agamemnon and Menelaus,eventually inherited the kingdom of Argos,and married, respectively,Clytaemestra and Helen,who were themselves sisters.Clytaemestra and Agamemnon had three children—Iphigeneia,Electra,and Orestes.Paris,one of the princes of Troy,seduced Helen,took her back to Troy,and the brothers vowed revenge.They convinced the other kings of Greece to join them in the destruction of Troy,and the "1,000 ships" of the Greek kings gathered for the voyage to Troy at Aulis,where they were held by wind and weather—until Agamemnon,told by his seer to do so,sacrificed his daughter,Iphigeneia.The fleet was then allowed to set sail for Troy.

In the 10th year of battle the Greeks captured and destroyed the city and enslaved those of its people they did not kill.On the way back to Greece,the Greeks encountered a great storm at sea,and all their ships were sunk or lost to sight (subsequently,in other Greek stories,we learn that some of the ships survived—for example,those of Odysseus). Agamemnon returned to Argos with a single ship,carrying not only what remained of his troops but also enslaved Trojans and,as well,Cassandra,princess of Troy,who had become his mistress.It is at this point that the play Agamemnon begins.

Aegisthus, has seduced Clytaemestra.The lovers now rule Argos as dictators, Clytaemestra

3

埃斯库罗斯
《奥瑞斯忒斯》

埃斯库罗斯

埃斯库罗斯(公元前525年~公元前456年)是古希腊三大剧作家中最早、最伟大的剧作家,另外两人是索福克勒斯和欧里庇得斯。埃斯库罗斯的生平不详,几乎都是传奇。一般认为他出生在雅典附近厄琉西斯城的一个富裕家庭。我们知道他曾参加马拉松战役(与波斯人的战争,希腊历史上的伟大胜利),他的剧本也获得了几项奖章。他写了70多部剧本,而只有几个幸存下来了,其中最著名的是《阿伽门农》《奠酒人》和《复仇神》,这三部合称为《奥瑞斯忒斯》三部曲。这三部曲被认为是古希腊流传下来的最伟大的剧本,同时也被认为是世界文学名著之一。

《奥瑞斯忒斯》

《奥瑞斯忒斯》的情节源于荷马,是由荷马之后的史诗作家们(他们的大部分作品我们都不知道)润色而成的,讲述的是阿特柔斯家族的故事。

故事是这样的:阿戈斯前国王的儿子,阿特柔斯和堤厄斯忒斯,争夺王位。阿特柔斯要求继承王位,堤厄斯忒斯不仅阻止他继承王位,还诱拐了他的妻子。堤厄斯忒斯在这场争夺中失败了,被驱逐出国门。几年后,他带着孩子们回来乞求原谅。假装要和解,阿特柔斯邀请堤厄斯忒斯共进盛宴。阿特柔斯杀死了堤厄斯忒斯的孩子们,仅留下一个,把他们的肉作为盛宴的主菜;堤厄斯忒斯吃了他自己孩子们的肉。堤厄斯忒斯诅咒他哥哥的家庭,带着他幸存的儿子埃癸斯托斯逃走了。阿特柔斯的儿子,阿伽门农和墨涅拉俄斯,最终继承了阿戈斯国,并分别娶了克吕泰墨斯拉特和海伦姐妹。克吕泰墨斯拉特和阿伽门农有三个孩子:依菲琴尼亚,伊莱克特拉和奥列斯特。特洛伊王子帕里斯诱拐海伦,并把她带回特洛伊。阿伽门农兄弟发誓要报仇,他们说服其他国王加入他们去摧毁特洛伊。希腊国王们的"一千艘船"在奥列斯会师远征特洛伊,但由于逆风,无法出航。阿伽门农的预言家告诉他需要杀死他的女儿依菲琴尼亚献祭神灵,以获得顺风。阿伽门农杀死女儿献祭神灵后,船队才得以起航驶往特洛伊。

战争的第十年,希腊人占领并摧毁了特洛伊城,俘获了没被杀害的特洛伊人。在回希腊的途中,希腊人在海上遇到了巨大的暴风雨,他们所有的船只都沉没不见了(后来,在其他的希腊故事中,我们知道有些船幸存了,如奥德修斯的船)。阿伽门农乘坐着唯一的一艘船回到阿戈斯,船上不仅载着剩下的士兵,还有特洛伊俘虏和他的情妇特洛伊公主卡珊德拉。戏剧《阿伽门农》就是由此开始的。

埃癸斯托斯,勾引了克吕泰墨斯特拉。他们两个人现在是阿戈斯的统治者。由于奥列

having banished Orestes, who has vehemently opposed his mother's actions; his sister Electra, powerless, remains in Argos. Clytaemestra, waiting until her unsuspecting husband is unarmed and in his bath, stabs Agamemnon to death, then, as well, murders Cassandra. Because of the power of the despots, their subjects acquiesce, accept them as legitimate rulers.

In *The Libation Bearers*, which takes place many years after the close of *Agamemnon*, Orestes returns, disguised as a traveler bringing news of his own death, makes contact with Electra, and together they plan to avenge their father. He gains access to the palace and kills his mother and her lover. He believes that the cycle of bloodshed is at an end, but that is not possible; his view is hopelessly optimistic. Almost immediately, the Furies (also called Eumenides), which are symbols of society's demand for retribution for his murder of his mother, appear to him, torment him, drive him out of Argos. He takes refuge with Apollo, the God of the arts and intellect (Apollo symbolizes the best that human beings can attain), who purifies him.

In *The Eumenidies*, Orestes, still pursued by the Furies, is referred to Athens and to its patroness, the greatest (after Zeus himself) of the divinities, Athena, goddess of wisdom and justice. The Furies argue for Orestes's destruction; Apollo argues for his acquittal. Athena, reserving to herself any deciding vote, refers the matter to what we would call a "jury," a group of mortal men. Their vote is tied, and Athena casts the deciding vote in Orestes's favor, and placates the Furies by placing them in a new role, minor gods in Athens. With this episode, *The Oresteia* ends.

It is necessary to stand back from the great panorama of *The Oresteia* and consider what it means. Aeschylus is considering the moral code, the legal code, of the ancient Greek world—which is not so different from that of the ancient world we know from The Bible; an eye for an eye, a ceaseless cycle of vengeance in the name of justice. The single most obvious fact of the story of the House of Atreus is that it is a story of never-ending revenge: Atreus kills the children of Atreus except for Aegisthus; Aegisthus, avenging his father and his siblings, with Clytaemestra, who is avenging the death of her daughter Iphigeneia, kills the son of Atreus, Agamemnon; Orestes, the son of Agamemnon, with his sister, plot the death of, then kill, their mother—as revenge for their father's death; then the Furies taunt Orestes for his crime, pursue him until they can destroy him. In the background the Trojan War looms-which is itself is a lesson in revenge begetting revenge begetting revenge, ending in not only the destruction of Troy but, as well, that of most of the young men of Greece, the victors. In these stories, violence never ends, no one ever wins.

Finally, the matter—this case, which involves not just Orestes but is also the story of what passes for "justice" in Ancient Greece-the never—ending cycle of retribution- is referred to Athena, the symbol to the Greeks of an eternal wisdom to which no individual mortal may aspire. Athena says and does two things; in effect, she says: The Furies are always with us-the barbarous inclination of man cannot be destroyed; it exists, and exists forever. Man cannot become Apollo—he may aspire to be, but the Furies are part of his nature. They must be recognized as such, given the status of minor gods—acknowledged to be part of human nature, just as Apollo, the god of man at his best, is part of our mortal nature. Yet, the civilized will triumph over the barbarous (Apollo will win over the Furies) only if man agrees to laws in the ultimate service of the good-and shows that agreement by accepting the decision of mortal "juries" in matters such as the saga of the House of Atreus. Only by the rule of law can the Furies in us be kept at bay and the Apollo in us cultivated—because the law is in the service of Athena (wisdom) herself.

斯特强烈反对其母克吕泰墨斯特拉的做法而被流放;他毫无权力的姐姐继续留在阿戈斯。克吕泰墨斯特拉等到她毫无疑心的丈夫手中没有任何武器时,在浴缸中,把阿伽门农刺死;然后杀死了卡珊德拉。由于专制君主掌握着权力,国民们默认他们为合法的统治者。

《奠酒人》发生在《阿伽门农》之后的许多年。奥列斯特伪装成一个旅行者回来,带来他自己去世的消息。他与伊莱克特拉取得联系,共同计划为父亲报仇。奥列斯特进入宫殿杀死了他的母亲及其情人。他认为流血的循环就此结束了,但那是不可能的。他想得太乐观了。随即,复仇女神孚里厄斯(也叫做欧墨尼得斯),社会要求的象征,要他为杀害他母亲而受到报偿。复仇女神出现在他面前,折磨他,把他驱逐出阿戈斯。他逃到艺术和智慧之神阿波罗(阿波罗是人类优点的象征)那里避难,阿波罗净化他的心灵。

《复仇神》中,奥列斯特,仍然被复仇女神所追逐,来到雅典向它的守护女神雅典娜求助。雅典娜,智慧和公正女神,是宙斯之后最伟大的神。复仇女神要求处死奥列斯特,阿波罗要求豁免他。雅典娜保留了她决定性的一票,把这件事交由一群凡人决定,相当于我们现在的"陪审团"。投票结果是平局,雅典娜投了决定性的一票,解救了奥列斯特;为了安抚复仇女神,雅典娜让她们成为雅典的神。《奥瑞斯忒斯》就此结束。

现在需要离开《奥瑞斯忒斯》的盛大场面来考虑一下它的寓意是什么。埃斯库罗斯考虑的是古希腊的道德和法律法则:以眼还眼,以正义的名义进行无休止的报复;这与我们从《圣经》中了解到的古代世界相差不大。阿特柔斯家族故事最明显的事实就是这是一个无休止的复仇故事:阿特柔斯杀死了堤厄斯特斯的所有孩子,除埃癸斯托斯以外;埃癸斯托斯为他的父亲和兄弟们报仇,克吕泰墨斯特拉为她死去的女儿依菲琴尼亚报仇,共同杀死了阿特柔斯的儿子阿伽门农;阿伽门农的儿子奥列斯特和他的姐姐一起谋划,杀死了他的母亲来为他们的父亲报仇;然后复仇神因为奥列斯特的罪恶而折磨他,追赶他,直到她们可以将他毁灭。故事发生的背景是特洛伊战争,这个战争的教训就是复仇不断地导致复仇。特洛伊战争不仅以特洛伊的毁灭而告终,也以希腊许多年轻人,胜利者们的毁灭而告终。在这些故事中,暴力从未结束,也没有人赢得胜利。

最后,这件事情,不仅是奥列斯特,还有这个在古希腊被认为是"公正"的故事,报偿的无休止循环,交由希腊永恒智慧的象征雅典娜来处理。雅典娜说了并做了两件事。实际上,她说:复仇神永远与我们同在,人类的野蛮倾向是不能被毁灭的,它是存在的,而且永远存在。人类不能变成阿波罗,他可能渴望成为阿波罗,但复仇神是他本质的一部分。必须给她们以神的地位,承认她们是人类本质的一部分,就像人类之神阿波罗是我们道德本质的一部分。然而,只有当人类赞同服务于正义的法律,并接受凡人"陪审团"在诸如阿特柔斯家族传奇事件的决定,文明才能战胜野蛮(阿波罗才能战胜复仇女神)。只有通过法治,我们心中的复仇神才能得到控制,我们心中的阿波罗才能得到教化,因为法律服务于雅典娜(智慧)。

Four

Herodotus:
The Histories

Who Was Herodotus?

Herodotus—sometimes called Herodotus of Halicarnassus,after the city where he was born—lived during the 5th century B.C.(484-424 B.C.),the "glory days" of Ancient Greece, and we know more about his life than we do about many of the lives of his famous contemporaries,possibly because,strictly speaking,he wasn't really Greek at all.Halicarnassus is a city of Asia Minor,now Bodrum in southwestern Turkey:during his lifetime it was part of the Persian,not the Greek,empire.But Herodotus,it seems,wished to be Greek,the dominant "intellectual" power of the time.After his exile from Halicarnassus (he had been involved in an unsuccessful attempt to depose its rulers),he spent most of his life traveling throughout the Greek Empire,recording what he saw of daily life.Most notably,recording the great battles between the two empires,which finally involved the triumph of the Greeks over the Persians,a triumph that made the Greeks the dominant power in the Western world.

The Histories

Herodotus's monumental work concerns the rise of the Persian Empire,the Persian invasions of Greece in 490 and 480 B.C.,and the Greek's battles with and final victory over the Persian Empire,which made the Greeks the dominant power in the Western world.For this achievement,he has been called the "Father of History."

Isn't Homer equally deserving of the title? True,Homer recorded not contemporary events,but he did compose epics about momentous events that had transpired centuries before his time.Or,couldn't the same things be said about the great playwrights who borrowed Homer's stories and those of the epic writers who came after him,adding their own embellishments,to create the great Greek tragedies? The accomplishment of Herodotus is very different from those of these other men,however notable their accomplishments may have been.

Homer,and the great playwrights who came after him,were,in reality,recycling the great legends and myths of their people,much as Shakespeare did many centuries later.In reading Homer and later scribes,we must ask ourselves:Was there really a Trojan War? Did the Greeks defeat the Trojans and destroy Trojan civilization? Did the Trojans,as the great Roman poet Virgil claimed in *The Aeneid*,really go on to found the Roman Empire? Such questions are similar to those we might ask about Shakespeare:Did Hamlet,Prince of Denmark,really exist? Did he try to avenge his father? Was there a medieval king of Scotland called Macbeth whose wife spurred him to murderous acts in an attempt to gain the crown? Such questions merely beg other questions:What in our literature,and the literature of the ancients,is really fact? What is fiction? Will we ever know the answer to such questions? Probably not.

Herodotus is very different.He called what he produced "historie," meaning,in his own time and in his own language,an "inquiry." The word passed into the Latin of the Romans

4

希罗多德
《历史》

希罗多德

希罗多德,有时叫做哈利卡纳索斯的希罗多德(以他出生的城市命名),生活在公元前5世纪,古希腊的繁盛时期。与他同时代的名人相比,我们对于希罗多德的生活了解更多,可能是因为从严格意义上说希罗多德不是真正的希腊人。哈利卡纳索斯是小亚细亚的一个城市,即现在土耳其西南部的博德鲁姆。在希罗多德生活的时代,哈利卡纳索斯是波斯帝国而不是希腊帝国的一部分。但似乎希罗多德希望自己是个希腊人,那个时代主导的智慧力量。希罗多德被从哈利卡纳索斯流放后(参加废黜统治者的活动,活动失败),余生的大部分时间都在游历希腊帝国,记下日常所见。最主要的是,记下了两个帝国之间的大战,战争以希腊战胜波斯而告终。这一胜利使希腊成为西方世界的主导力量。

《历史》

希罗多德的巨作讲述的是波斯帝国的崛起,于公元前490至公元前480年间侵略希腊,希腊最终战胜波斯,成为西方世界的主导力量。他的这一成就使他被称为"历史之父"。

荷马也同样应该得到这个称号吗?的确,荷马不仅记载了他那个时代的事件;也创作了史诗,史诗是关于发生在几个世纪之前的重大事件。或者,那些借用荷马故事的伟大剧作家们,荷马之后的史诗作者们增加了自己的修饰以创作伟大的希腊悲剧,他们可以得到同样的称号吗? 不管他们的成就是多么伟大,希罗多德的成就与他们的成就截然不同。

荷马和他后来的伟大剧作家们事实上是在重复着人们伟大的传奇和神话,就像许多世纪之后的莎士比亚。在阅读荷马和后来抄写员的作品时,我们必须要问自己:真的有特洛伊战争吗?希腊人打败了特洛伊人,并摧毁了特洛伊文明吗?特洛伊人,真的像罗马伟大诗人维吉尔在《埃涅阿斯记》中所说,建立了罗马帝国吗?关于莎士比亚,我们可能也会问类似的问题:丹麦王子汉姆雷特真的存在吗?他试图为父亲报仇了吗?他的妻子唆使他谋杀以获得王位的苏格兰中世纪国王麦克白存在吗? 这些问题会引发其他问题:在我们的文学及古代文学中,什么是真的呢? 什么是小说? 我们将会知道这些问题的答案吗? 很可能不会。

希罗多德完全不同。他称他所写的是"历史",在他那个时代,他的语言中是"调查"的意思。这个词进入罗马人的拉丁语中,成为"故事"的意思。3个世纪后,罗马伟大诗人西塞

and came to mean a "story" —in our sense of the word "history." It was 3 centuries later that the great Roman writer Cicero referred to Herodotus as the "Father of History."

What, precisely, did Cicero mean? He was referring to what had passed for "history" before Herodotus began to write—for example, that Paris had abducted Helen, the wife of a Greek king, that the Greeks had avenged this insult by sailing in their 1,000 ships to Troy, then battling Troy for 10 years until they had defeated that kingdom, which battle in turn gives us the story of Agamemnon and Achilles and Odysseus. These stories may or may not be true. Herodotus, very differently, was trying to record what he actually saw in his travels and what he actually knew of the actual events of contemporary Greek life and the immediate past history of the Greeks.

To modern readers that difference is hard to grasp—simply because we take such a difference for granted. If we read a novel, we know that the plot of the novel is the invention of the novelist, even though it may involve a certain kind of "truth"-yes, we might say: this story is contrived by the novelist, yet this novelist's rendering of his characters is consistent with what we know about people of that kind. But if we read an account of current or past events—a conflict or any event in which our country is or was involved or other countries are or were involved—if we read it in a newspaper or magazine, see it portrayed on television or on the Internet, or read it in a book that claims to be "history"—we expect that all particulars are true, not "made up," even if we make allowances for media distortions.

The body of his work is known as *The Histories*, and these works were published between 430 B.C. and 424 B.C.—within the space of 6 years, in other words. Later editors divided his work into nine books. All of them, besides offering observations gleaned from his travels, document the growth of the Persian Empire, its defeat at Marathon, its attempt to avenge that defeat, 10 years later, by absorbing Greece into its empire, leading to its eventual defeat, in 479 B.C., at the Battle of Plataea.

In 431 B.C., the Polyponnesian War broke out-between the two main kingdoms of Greece, Athens and Sparta. Herodotus may have been provoked to publish his works, beginning the year after—to inspire Greece not to destroy itself in a Civil War, by reminding his readers of the glory days of the empire, when they had defeated the seemingly invincible Persian Empire.

In this goal, too, he seems like a modern man-as, say, a contemporary American historian might write about World War II as a wake-up call to modern America, to remind it of the sacrifice of that time, its people coming together, forgetting their differences, in a noble effort to defeat oppressors and free the world's peoples-as to way of inspiring America to be at its best again.

For the beginnings of history as a discipline, and to understand how the profession came to be, and to understand what historians try to accomplish—as well as to be given a glimpse of what the ancient Greek world was really like—any informed reader will want to have sampled The *Histories* of Herodotus.

罗把希罗多德称为"历史之父"。

西塞罗的确切意思是什么？他所指的是希罗多德开始写作之前被当做"历史"的事情吗？例如，帕里斯诱拐了一个希腊王的妻子海伦，希腊人驾驶一千艘船前往特洛伊以雪耻，战争进行了10年希腊人才打败了特洛伊人。这一战争转而又给我们带来了阿伽门农、阿基里斯和奥德赛的故事。这些故事或许是真实的，或许不是。希罗多德则不同，他尽量记下旅途中自己的真实所见，他所知道的当时希腊人生活的真实事件和刚刚过去的希腊人的历史。

对于现代的读者们，这一不同是很难体会的，仅仅是因为我们认为这一不同是理所当然的。如果我们读一本小说，我们知道小说的情节是小说家的发明，尽管其中可能包含一定的真实性。是的，我们会说：这个故事是小说家的构想，然而小说家描写的人物与我们所了解的那类人是一致的。但是如果我们读的是对现在或过去事件的叙述，如我们国家或其他国家现在或曾经陷入的冲突或其他事件，如果我们在报纸或杂志上读到，电视或因特网上看到，或在称作"历史"的书中读到，尽管我们允许媒体歪曲，我们还是期待所有的细节都是真实的，而不是编造的。

他的主要作品是《历史》，这些作品出版于公元前430年~公元前424年6年的时间内。后来的编辑们把他的作品分成9本书。所有这些书，除了记载了他旅途中所见，还都记载了波斯帝国的发展：马拉松战役战败，然后试图雪耻；10年后，公元前479年，企图吞并希腊帝国，在普罗提亚战役中最终战败。

公元前431年，伯罗奔尼撒战争爆发，战争是发生在希腊两个主要王国雅典和斯巴达之间。可能是战争促使希罗多德开始出版他的作品，使读者们回想起打败不可战胜的波斯帝国后希腊的繁盛时期，以启迪希腊不要在内战中摧毁自己。

在这一点上，他似乎像一个现代人。一个美国当代历史学家可能会描写第二次世界大战以呼吁现代的美国觉醒，使它想起那时候的牺牲；启迪美国重现辉煌。人们忘记不同，团结在一起，共同打败侵略者，解放世界各族人民。

历史如何成为一门学科，历史学家如何成为一种职业，历史学家们要做什么，以及古希腊世界到底是什么样子的，想要了解这些，读者们需要品读一下希罗多德的《历史》。

Five

Plato:
The Republic

Who Was Plato?

Everyone knows Plato,or at the very least,knows of him.Of course we also know of Pericles of Athens or Nero of Rome,as well as many other people of the ancient worlds of Greece and Rome whose fame continues to the present day-Aristotle or Cicero,Sophocles or Virgil.They are as much a part of our history as are the great figures of the Jewish/ Christian world.But,among the well-known "stars" of the Greek and Roman worlds,Plato is by far the most famous.

Most of us know at least a few facts about him—that he was born into a wellto-do-family and lived in Athens,the greatest of Greek cities,in the 4th century B.C.(he lived from 427 to 347 B.C.); that he was a student of the great teacher,Socrates; that at the age of 40 he founded the Academy,one of the most renown schools in history; and that he continued to teach at the Academy for the rest of his life,where he was the teacher of Aristotle,one of the pre-eminent philosophers in human history.Some of us may also know that Plato was himself a great philosopher.One of his best-known philosophers of more recent times has said: "All subsequent philosophy is a footnote to Plato." In other words,there is a very strong case for regarding Plato as the father of philosophy,if not its greatest practitioner. Literary scholars might add:Plato was one of the greatest creative writers who ever lived.

The Republic

Plato was obviously the most prominent teacher at the Academy he founded,but his lectures notes,like those of most illustrious teachers from the past,have not survived.What we have instead is his writings.All of his thought is there,rendered in such a way that we must admit:this is not cold philosophical theory presented in textbook form; this a first and foremost a series of dramatic stories that are truly excellent of their kind.His writings do, however,also convey what Plato regarded as philosophical truths—much as Jesus conveyed what he regarded as the certainties of human life and eternity via the literary device of parables.One of the generally accepted facts about Plato is that he started out as a playwright—and he was obviously a skillful one—he conveys his philosophy through the devices of the drama (setting,characters,conflict).One of the facts/legends about Plato was that he was inspired to change from drama to philosophy as a result of Socrates's influence on his early life.

Yet,most of us,nowadays,do not experience what used to be called a "classical education." It is very likely that most of us (unlike people before the advent of the modern world) have not read the ancient writers and philosophers:we know Plato only by reputation.

His greatest works are "dialogues" ("plays," we might call them),a form that he employed for all of his life.In them,his hero,Socrates,is found in a variety of situations— lecturing his disciples in a public forum or meeting with them,for conversation,at a dinner

柏拉图
《理想国》

柏拉图

每个人都熟悉柏拉图，或至少听说过他。当然，我们也听说过雅典的伯里克利或罗马的尼禄，还有许多至今还很有名的古希腊人和古罗马人，如亚里士多德、西塞罗、索福克勒斯和维吉尔。他们跟犹太教和基督教人物一样是我们历史的一部分。但在古希腊和古罗马的著名"明星"中，柏拉图是最著名的。

大部分人对柏拉图都有一些了解：他出生在一个富裕的家庭，公元前4世纪（他生活在公元前427年~公元前347年）居住在希腊著名城市雅典；他是苏格拉底的学生；在40岁时创办了阿卡得米，历史上最著名的学校之一；他的后半生一直在阿卡得米任教，就是在此他是人类历史上卓越哲学家之一——亚里士多德的老师。有些人也知道柏拉图本人也是伟大的哲学家。近代的一个哲学家曾说过："后来的一切哲学都是对柏拉图的补充。"换句话说，柏拉图如果不是哲学的伟大实践者，完全可被称作是哲学之父。文学家们会说：柏拉图是最富创造力的作家。

《理想国》

柏拉图是他所创建的阿卡得米学院里最杰出的老师；但他的授课笔记，像过去其他杰出老师们的笔记一样，没有保存下来。我们所拥有的是他的文章，他所有的思想都在其中。他的文章不是教科书里冰冷的哲学理论，而首先是一系列真正优秀的戏剧故事。然而，柏拉图的文章的确传达了他所谓的哲学真理，就像耶稣以寓言的形式传达了他所谓的人类生活的确定性与永恒。关于柏拉图，大家普遍认为他是剧作家出身，并且显然是善于写作的，他通过戏剧（背景、人物和冲突）的形式传达他的哲学。据说，柏拉图由戏剧转向哲学是苏格拉底对他早年生活影响的结果。

然而，当今，我们大多数人都没有体验过过去所谓的"古典教育"。很可能我们大多数人（不同于古代的人们）都没有阅读过古代作家和哲学家的作品，我们知道柏拉图只是因为他的名声。

他的伟大作品都是"对话"（我们也可称作"戏剧"），他一生都采用对话形式写作。在他的作品中，他的主人公苏格拉底出现在各种场合：在公共广场上向他的信徒们演讲，或

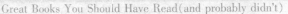

party or strolling with friends outside the walls of Athens.All the evidence is that Socrates actually lived,that he was a kind of itinerant teacher (unconnected with any formal "institution"),that he was put to death (by being forced to drink hemlock) for "impiety" (not accepting the received religion of the time) and for "corrupting" the youth of Athens-giving them notions of which the government of Athens disapproved.So much we know.But whether he actually thought and said everything that Plato attributes to him is open to dispute.Because Socrates,unlike Plato,was not also a writer,we can only conjecture what,in Plato,about Socrates,is real and what is not.Most scholars feel that the early dialogues of Plato,following the death of Socrates (he died in 399 B.C.; Plato was then about 30 years old) are fairly accurate transcriptions of what Socrates thought and said.As Plato continued writing,as he got further and further away from the time of Socrates's death,he more or less becomes his own man.The dialogues increasingly become reflections of his own thought,even though Socrates continues to be his hero,even though Plato's thoughts continue to be attributed to Socrates (as a character,he is missing from only Plato's last work,Laws).

What exactly did Socrates have to say? His thought is so complex,involves so many ruminations on human life,that it is perhaps best to make a few generalizations.In the Western world,our notions of the devine,of the condition and nature of God,are those of the great Jewish thinkers (if we are Jews),Jesus Christ (if we are Christians),or Muhammad (if we are Muslim).Our notions of morality-of what is right and wrong in human behavior,of what our intellectual goals as men and women should be-are all traceable to Socrates-as he is created for us by Plato.Socrates says:The proper pursuit of men should be refinement of the intellect,so that we are able to see the "truth" in life,so that we are able to behave in our own lives (or in our interactions with others) according to the truths we gain.Yet Socrates,in offering these notions,says,I myself know nothing; I merely ask constant questions.

The search for truth (which is also the ultimate in "beauty") is a life-long pursuit-just as, say,the search for grace,for pleasing God,is a lifelong pursuit in Christianity.We come to Socratic truth by a constant searching of our assumptions,by admitting when we are wrong, by admitting too that we are more often wrong than right—and do so via the device of conversing and testing our assumptions with like-minded companions.It is only gradually that we come to truth."The unexamined life is not worth living," said Socrates; our notions, even those ideas we already regard as true,must be constantly re-examined,constantly challenged.

Any of Plato's dialogues will provide the reader with a sense of what Plato and his hero,Socrates,were preaching:any one will serve to demonstrate the method of constant questioning of assumptions to arrive at larger,abiding truths.But The Republic is probably the most profound of all of Plato's works.

In The Republic (probably written about 390 B.C.),Plato most clearly defines what he has been driving at all along.Here he offers his belief in "forms," that there exists,in the universe,a perfect example of anything we know,from our senses,on earth—a universal.The ultimate of these is the Form of the Good (in effect,Plato's God).We strive,in human life,to know what unchanging perfection would be like,but we see these universals only dimly,if at

在晚会上与他们一起谈天说地，或与朋友们一起漫步在雅典城墙外。关于苏格拉底，比较清楚的是：他确实存在，是一个巡游教师（不属于任何一个正式"学院"）；因为不虔诚（不接受当时广为接受的宗教）和"腐化"雅典青年（向雅典青年灌输雅典政府反对的思想）而被处死（被迫服毒）。我们只知道这些。但他的思想及言论是否与柏拉图描述的一样还有待争议，因为苏格拉底不同于柏拉图，他不是作家；关于苏格拉底，我们只能从柏拉图的作品中推测哪些是真实的，哪些不是。多数学者认为柏拉图的早期对话，写在苏格拉底去世之时（苏格拉底死于公元前399年，柏拉图当时30岁左右），是对苏格拉底思想及言论较为准确的记录。随着柏拉图写作的继续，随着苏格拉底逝世时间的远去，他逐渐成为他自己。尽管苏格拉底仍然是主人公，尽管柏拉图把自己的思想继续归属于苏格拉底（作为作品中的人物，苏格拉底只是没出现在柏拉图的最后一部作品《法律篇》中），对话逐渐成为他自己思想的反映。

苏格拉底到底想要说什么呢？他的思想非常复杂，包含许多对于人类生活的反思，所以最好还是概括一下。在西方世界，我们对于神圣及上帝的处境和本质的看法都是伟大犹太思想家们（如果我们是犹太教徒）、耶稣基督（如果我们是基督教徒）或穆罕默德（如果我们是穆斯林）的看法。我们对于道德的看法——人类行为的对与错，男人和女人应有的学术目标——都可追溯到苏格拉底，因为柏拉图为我们创造了苏格拉底。苏格拉底说：人类应该追求智力的精炼，这样我们才能看到生活的"真理"，才能按照所得到的真理生活（或与他人相处）。然而，苏格拉底在提出这些看法时说，我自己什么也不知道；我只是提出永恒的问题。

探索真理（也是美的终极）是一生的追求，就像基督教中探索优雅、取悦上帝是一生的追求一样。通过不断探索我们的设想，通过承认我们的过错，承认我们的错误多于正确，（与志趣相投的朋友们谈论检验我们的设想）我们得出苏格拉底的真理。我们是逐渐地得出真理的。苏格拉底说"未经检验的生活是没有价值的"。因而我们的看法，即便是那些我们已经认为是正确的观点，必须得到不断反复的检验，必须得到不断的挑战。

柏拉图的任何一个对话都会让读者了解到柏拉图和他的主人公苏格拉底所宣扬的：任何人都应该通过反复质疑设想来得出更深刻、永恒的真理。但《理想国》很可能是柏拉图的作品中最深刻的一部。

《理想国》中（大概写于公元前390年），柏拉图明确指出了他一生的追求。书中讲述了他对"形式"的信仰，他认为我们可以感知的任何事物在宇宙中都有一个完美的典范—共相。这一切最终都是上帝的形式（实际上是柏拉图心中的上帝）。人类一生都努力想知道不变的完美是什么样的，但如果看到的话，也只是模糊地看到这些共相，因为我们是通过

all,because we know the world only through our senses,not through our minds.Those "dim glimpses" become less dim,more real to us,the greater the refinement of our mind,our intellect and our understanding.For example (to take a simple example):a table.All tables we create,in human life,are attempts to emulate the "form" of the universal table,and we strive, with each table we create,to get nearer to the perfect table.Of course,what Plato is most concerned about is what we would call abstractions:what is courage,what is sincerity,what, finally,is perfect love? *The Republic* is Plato's most vivid rendering of what he regards as the most important goal in human life—to bring ourselves closer and closer,through self-knowledge,to these elusive "forms" of perfection.This is the ultimate virtue,and this is the activity that Plato recommends as a means for human beings to "live well."

But *The Republic* is something more.Plato is also examining the institutions we create as a result of self-knowledge,and his interest is in the most important of human institutions-the ways in which we choose to govern ourselves.Those who have achieved the greatest knowledge—the "philosopher king" is an expression that has entered our language—those who are,in other words,most like Socrates—are those who should rule.They are disinterested persons who rule not for their personal benefit for the good of everyone else-in them,the gift for ruling,for the exercise of power,and the gift for philosophy,for the exercise of thought about perfection in human behavior,entirely coincide.Just as the most advanced person should run a family,or the most advanced person should be the principal of a school,or the most gifted executive should run a company.

Of course,Plato,in *The Republic*,in all of the dialogues,is talking about ideals,ideals of conduct,or ideals of intellectual inquiry,or ideals of government—they remain always out of our reach.Raise that objection,and Plato would respond: The striving for that goal of perfection is the business of human life; there is no other,whether you succeed or not-and you will not ultimately succeed.The striving is everything,the distance you move your greatest reward.

We should all be aware of the ideals of *The Republic*—and these goals-which 2,500 years later are still,if we are honest,our most precious goals,that for which,in our best moments,all human beings still strive.

感官而不是思想来认识世界的。那些模糊的所见变得越发模糊、真实,我们的思想、智力和理解力就可以得到更好的锤炼。举一个简单的例子,桌子。我们人类所创造的所有桌子都是试图模仿共相桌子的"形式",并且尽力使所创造的每个桌子更贴近完美的桌子。当然,柏拉图最为关心的是抽象概念:什么是勇气?什么是真诚?什么又是完美的爱情?《理想国》中,柏拉图对他所认为人生最重要的目标作了生动的论述:通过丰富自己的知识,向这些完美的不定形式不断靠近。这是最终的善,柏拉图建议这是人类更好地生活的一种方式。

但《理想国》讲述的不只是这些。柏拉图还探析了我们为了丰富自己知识而建立的机构,他的兴趣在于人类机构的最重要部分——我们选择什么样的方式管理自己。那些已经获取伟大知识的人们(哲学家国王,这一说法已进入我们的语言),换句话说,那些像苏格拉底一样的人们,他们应该是管理者。他们是无私的,他们管理不是为了个人利益而是为了每一个人的利益。管理、行使权力、哲学和实践人类完美行为构想,这些方面的天赋完全集中在他们身上。就像最先进的人应该掌管家庭、应该是校长;最有天赋的执行官应该掌管公司一样。

当然,在《理想国》中,在所有对话中,柏拉图都谈论理想,理想的行为、理想的智力询问和理想的政府。它们永远是我们无法达到的。提出这一不同意见,柏拉图会这样回答:人类生活就是要为完美这一目标努力奋斗,别无其他;不管你成功与否,你将不会最终成功。努力奋斗是重要的,你取得的进展就是最大的回报。

我们应该知道《理想国》中的理想,目标,在2 500年后仍然是我们比较珍惜的目标,人类在壮年时期也仍为之努力奋斗。

Six

Aristotle: Metaphysics

Who Was Aristotle?

Aristotle is one of the most famous men who ever lived. Everyone knows his name, and, unlike many of the most prominent of the ancient Greeks, we know the facts of his life—most are documented, few are legend. After a childhood in Macedonia (he was born in 384, died in 322 B.C.), where his father was the court physician, Aristotle, at age 18, went to Athens to study with Plato at Plato's Academy. He remained there until Plato's death in 347 when he was himself 37 years old. Passed over as Plato's successor (this happened twice in his lifetime), Aristotle traveled, eventually arriving at the court of Philip of Macedonia, where he became tutor to young Alexander the Great (when Alexander was 13 years old). He remained Alexander's tutor for 5 years, until Alexander was a man and had himself ascended the throne of Macedonia and went off on his campaigns of conquest in Asia.

At that point, Aristotle returned to Athens, founded the Lyceum (a school in the style of Plato's Academy), and from then until his early death at the age of 62, he continued to teach and to do most of the writing for which we now remember him. Ironically, his work was not published in his lifetime. It languished in one of the great libraries of Athens until the 1st century B.C. when Athens was sacked, and its treasures taken back to Rome-where Aristotle's works were at last published. As a result of that publication, his fame spread to all corners of the Roman Empire.

Metaphysics

Everyone is aware that Aristotle was a great philosopher. But that is not the entire story. With Plato, he is now regarded as one of the two greatest philosophers produced by ancient Greece. But there is even more to his accomplishment than that—Plato can be said to have created the Idealistic School of philosophy; Aristotle is credited with creating the Empirical School of Philosophy—distinctions in philosophy that persist until this day. Plato's reputation went into a decline (it has recovered in modern times); Aristotle's views dominated western thought for more than 15 centuries. Aristotle's thought was the only accepted thought for longer than any other thinker has ever held sway in the history of the Western world. His influence, obviously, has now waned.

Aristotle spent only 13 years at the Lyceum, but his writings were voluminous. Aristotle did not understand the "term" philosopher in quite the same way that we do—as someone who studies human knowledge and develops systems for understanding human experience. Aristotle, almost certainly, thought of himself as what we mean by a scientist, someone who examines the facts and laws of the physical world and tries to understand the workings of nature as a way to develop the facility of human reasoning. He studied, and wrote about, virtually every subject that existed in his time—from anatomy to geography, from geology to zoology. Unlike Plato, he did not write imaginative literature. Most of his writings are almost certainly lecture notes and treatises created for the consumption of his students (what we

6

亚里士多德
《形而上学》

亚里士多德

亚里士多德是人类历史上最著名的人物之一。每个人都知道他的名字，并且与其他古希腊著名人物不同的是，我们知道他的生平事实。多数都是有记载的，很少是传奇故事。亚里士多德(公元前384年~公元前322年)童年生活在马其顿，父亲是宫廷医生，18岁时到雅典柏拉图的学院从师于柏拉图。柏拉图去世于公元前34年，当时亚里士多德37岁，直到那时他一直在学院。成为柏拉图的继承人后(此事在他的一生中出现过两次)，亚里士多德开始巡游，最后到达马其顿腓力宫廷，成为青年亚历山大大帝的私人教师(此时亚历山大13岁)。他教导亚历山大5年之久，直到亚历山大长大成人，自己登上马其顿王位并开始了他征服亚洲的战役。

就在那个时候，亚里士多德回到雅典，创建了吕克昂(与柏拉图的阿卡米得形式相同的学校)。从此一直到他早逝于62岁，他一直从事教学并写作，写下了让我们铭记他的作品。滑稽的是，他的作品在他在世时并没有出版；一直被冷落在雅典的一个著名图书馆里。直到公元前1世纪，雅典遭洗劫，所有的财富都被带回罗马，亚里士多德的作品才最终在罗马出版。作品的出版使他闻名于整个罗马帝国。

《形而上学》

每个人都知道亚里士多德是个伟大的哲学家，但这并不全面。他和柏拉图现在被认为是希腊最伟大的两大哲学家。但他的成就不仅是这些：如果说柏拉图开创了哲学的理想学派，那么亚里士多德就开创了哲学的经验学派。哲学上的这一区分至今仍然存在。柏拉图的声望下降(在现代已经恢复)，亚里士多德的观点统治西方思想长达15个世纪之久。在西方历史中，亚里士多德的思想被人们接受的时间最久。现在，显然，他的影响也有所减弱。

亚里士多德在吕克昂仅仅13年的时间，却写出了大量作品。我们认为哲学家研究人类知识并创建体系以理解人类经验，亚里士多德却不这么认为。亚里士多德认为他自己是我们所称为科学家的人，探索物质世界的现象与规律并尽力理解自然的规律以开发人类思维能力。他研究那个时代所存在的几乎每一个学科，并著有著作：从解剖学到地理学，从地质学到动物学。与柏拉图不同，他不创作虚构文学。他的作品大部分都是他的授课笔记和便于学生理解而写的专著(我们可以称为"教科书")。这些作品很可能是在他死后由他的学生和后来的学者和编辑编写的。亚里士多德的作品既非虚构的，也不是为了出版，所以现代读者可能很难理解。然而，公正地说，就他的作品所涉及的范围，亚里士多

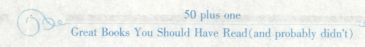
might call "textbooks"); they were probably "organized" by his students after his death and by scholars and editors of later generations.As it is neither imaginative nor,initially,written for publication,Aristotle's writings can be tough going for the modern reader.Yet,it is fair to say that,in the breath of his writing,Aristotle virtually created an encyclopedia of what was known,and what was surmised,by the ancient Greeks.

Why read him if his influence has largely waned? Yes,it has waned—in the sense that Aristotle is no longer regarded by modern readers as the repository of all knowledge.But his reliance on empiricism—hypothesis offered,then tested as to its reliability,whether it holds true in experiments-remains the basis,more than 2,000 years after his death,of modern scientific method.And he continues to be influential in other ways—one of the most persistent schools of modern literary scholarship,for example,is based on principles of composition set out by Aristotle in his *Poetics*—and literary scholars still refer to the Aristotelian "unities" of time,place,incident in discussing not just the drama (his immediate subject) but other forms of literary composition.And to cite another example:In our behavior,in our ethics,we still refer to the Aristotelian "mean," meaning a life that is lived in the avoidance of excess,striving for balance and the middle way (for example:Boastfulness and bashfulness are both excesses; the goal is modest self-confidence).

So many of Aristotle's writings remain influential that it is difficult to choose one on which the modern reader should focus—but perhaps *Metaphysics* would provide an appropriate introduction.Again,it is important to understand-despite modern connotations of the word "metaphysics"—just what Aristotle was talking about.He means "after physics," and by "physics" he means the observable world.In other words:What conclusions do we reach about life after we have observed its physical manifestations? What conclusions do we reach about the meaning of life? In these concerns-indeed,in all of his philosophical writings—he differs from his mentor.Simply:Plato strived to understand universal ideals—for example,truth,justice,courage,love—and from his conclusions to extrapolate about human life;Aristotle,conversely,closely observes both human life and the natural world in which it exists,and from his conclusions about human activity and motivation attempts to construct ideals.His *Metaphysics*,then,has to do with his conclusions about "meaning," after he has long observed the world of man,not the world of ideals.

In *Metaphysics*,he asks:What are the essential attributes of man's existence,his being-are there,in other words,universal truths about man's existence that can be known?

Obviously,he believes the answer to this question is yes.He argues,too,that true being, our selfhood,is not an abstraction; it is concrete,it exists in this world.Put another way:He asks himself-and asks us to consider—what is the final end for which some aspect of life is created? What causes it to happen? What is its final purpose?

Aristotle,in short,is no longer the "be all and end all" of western thought,yet his thought remains potent to this day,part of our mental equipment whether we know it or not.The questions he asks,in the *Metaphysics* and elsewhere,are questions we are all still asking.

德的确创作了一部百科全书,记录了古希腊人的所知所想。

既然他的影响已经减弱,为什么还要读他的作品呢?是的,影响减弱了,现代读者不再认为亚里士多德是所有知识的宝库。但他所相信的逻辑实证论(先提出假设,然后验证它的可靠性,在实验中是否成立),在他去世2000多年后仍然是现代科学方法的基础。他也仍然影响着其他方面,如现代文学中一个最执著的学派仍然以亚里士多德在《诗学》中提出的创作原则为基础,并且在讨论戏剧(他的主要体裁)及其他文学创作形式时,文学工作者仍然会提及亚里士多德所谓的时间、地点和事件的"统一"(三一律)。还有一个例子:谈及行为道德,我们还是会提到亚里士多德的"适度",意思是说生活要避免过度,努力追求平衡和中间道路(如自夸和羞怯是过度,目标是谦虚的自信)。

亚里士多德的许多作品都仍有影响力,很难选出一个供现代读者品读;但可能《形而上学》是个合适的简介。最重要的是,我们应该撇开metaphysics(形而上学)的现代含义,去理解亚里士多德所谈论的metaphysics。他所说的metaphysics是"after physics","physics"的意思是可观察的世界。换句话说:在我们观察了生活的外在表现之后,关于生活我们得出什么样的结论呢?关于生活的意义我们又得出什么结论?在这些方面,在他的所有哲学作品中,他不同于他的导师。简单地说:柏拉图努力了解普遍理想,如真理、公正、勇气和爱,并从这些结论中推断人类生活;亚里士多德则相反,他密切观察人类生活及其存在其中的自然界,通过得出的有关人类活动和动机的结论试图构建理想。他的《形而上学》是关于"意义"的结论,长期观察人类世界而不是理想世界而得出的结论。

《形而上学》中,他问道:人类存在的重要属性是什么?换句话说,是否有人类可以理解的普遍真理存在?

显然,他认为问题的答案是肯定的。他说,我们自我的真正存在不是抽象的;它是具体的,存在于这个世界上。换个方式:他让他自己,也让我们考虑,生活某些方面存在的最终目的是什么?什么使之发生,最终目的又是什么?

简言之,亚里士多德不再是西方思想的全部,然而他的思想至今仍具影响力;不管我们知道与否,他的思想仍是我们思想的组成部分。他在《形而上学》及其他地方提出的问题是我们至今仍在问的问题。

Seven

Mahabharata

Mahabharata

Most people in the Western world are aware of at one time or another having heard of the *Mahabharata* or of having read about it in some history or literary text,but most of us could not actually define what it is.Or even how to pronounce it.It is Ma-ha-barr-a-ta,with emphasis on the third syllable.

The *Mahabharata* is one of the two major Sanskrit epics of India.It is,as well,one of the longest epic poems in the world; it is about 2.5 million words long.Although it is traditionally ascribed to the ancient sage Vyasa,also a character in the story,it is one of those ancient works,probably begun about 500 B.C.,that tells popular and legendary stories of Gods and kings and their adventures,and it is almost certainly the work of many hands-from writers to priests to minstrels to actors.Later,in the 4th century A.D.,it came to be a unified text,written down in Sanskrit.With the Ramayana,it constitutes the cultural memory of the Indian people,much as Homer was the cultural memory,the history and tradition,of the Greeks.Yet even though it is now more than 2,000 years old,it still exerts enormous cultural influence throughout India and Southeast Asia.

A full reading of the Mahabharta is probably daunting to most modern readers; it is, after all,a very long work.But there are a few compelling reasons for any reader to have sampled it:

It is,like the works of Homer,a powerful and compelling tale.It presents a sweeping panorama that includes Indian ideas of both the cosmos and of humanity and of the divinities that are part of Indian culture.It is,too,one of those works so ambitious in its storytelling and in its definitions of the life and history of humanity that it seems to transcend its time and place—much as The Bible,the Greek tragedies,the Iliad and the Odyssey and the works of Shakespeare transcend theirs; it is one of the comparatively few literary works produced by mankind that can be said to be "eternal." To sample it is to understand something of the culture of a vast world that is not our own.Though,in some ways,it will seem familiar to Western readers,who know that our literature starts with the Greeks and Romans.In its mixture of the divine and the secular,in its dazzling and fantastic plot,relieved by moments of poignant encounters between mortal individuals,it reminds us of the works of Homer and Virgil.

The central story of the work is that of a dynastic struggle—and great war—for the throne of the kingdom of Hastinapura.Two collateral branches of the family participate in the struggle:the Kauravas and the Pandavas.It is a struggle (attended by Gods on both sides) that is not unlike the struggle of the sons of Argos and the sons of Troy,in the Trojan War, for the soul of Greece.

Much will seem familiar to the reader-not least the character of Krishna,a participant in the battle,who is yet a son of God,born to a mortal woman.Later in the story,he returns to heaven to be united with God.

The *Mahabharata*,in other words,is also a religious work.Besides being one of the literary triumphs of mankind,it is also a core text of the Hindu religion—one of the great

7

《摩诃婆罗多》

《摩诃婆罗多》

　　在西方，许多人曾听说过《摩诃婆罗多》或者在某个历史或文学作品中读到过，但我们大多数人的确不知道它到底是什么。或者甚至不知道这个词(Mahabharata)该怎么读，读作Ma-ha-barr-a-ta，重读第三个音节。

　　《摩诃婆罗多》是印度两大梵文史诗之一，也是世界最长的史诗之一，大约250万字。传统上认为它是古代圣人毗耶婆所作，毗耶婆也是故事中的一个人物。《摩诃婆罗多》大概开始写于公元前500年，讲述的是神和国王们广为流传的传奇故事和奇遇。此书由许多人写成，包括作家、牧师、游吟诗人和演员。

后来，于公元4世纪，才用梵文写成一部统一完整的书。它和《罗摩衍那》一起构成了印度人们的文化记忆，就像荷马是希腊人的文化记忆、历史和传统一样。尽管此书已有两千多年的历史，它在印度乃至东南亚仍有巨大的文化影响。

　　通读《摩诃婆罗多》可能会让大多数读者望而却步，毕竟篇幅比较长。但仍有几个原因要求读者必须品读一下。

　　与荷马的作品一样，《摩诃婆罗多》是个有巨大影响力的故事。它呈现了一个全面的景象，包括印度人对于宇宙、人性和神圣的看法，这些都是印度文化的一部分。此书也属于那些敢于大胆讲述故事、对人生下定义和描述历史的书，所以它似乎超越了时空限制，就像《圣经》、希腊悲剧、《伊利亚特》、《奥德赛》和莎士比亚作品也超越了时空限制。此书是人类创作的文学作品中可以被称为是"永恒"的较少数作品之一。品读它，可以了解我们生活以外的广阔世界的文化。认为西方文学开始于希腊、罗马人的西方读者们还是熟悉《摩诃婆罗多》中的某些内容的。此书中宗教与非宗教统一在一起，情节悬惑奇异，凡人的出现又使情节有所缓和；这些使我们想起了荷马和维吉尔的作品。

　　本书的主要故事是个王朝战争，争夺哈斯提那普拉王国王位的战争。参加战争的是家族的两个旁系分支：俱卢和般度。这一战争(双方都有神仙参加)与特洛伊战争中阿戈斯的儿子们和特洛伊的儿子们争夺希腊的战争不同。

　　读者对大部分内容都很熟悉，不只是其中的人物克里希纳。克里希纳是上帝的儿子，由一个凡人妇女所生；他也参加了战争。故事中，他后来回到天堂与上帝连为一体。

　　《摩诃婆罗多》也是一部宗教作品。它不仅是文学上的成功，也是印度教的主要著作。印度教是世界伟大的宗教之一，大部分西方人对其几乎一无所知。

religions of the world and one about which most Westerners know virtually nothing.

If readers read nothing else, they should read one of its chapters, the "Bhagavad Gita," which puts forth, in concise terms, the basic principles of Hinduism.

The *Mahabharata* is, like most of the world's great literary works, concerned about how a man should live—his values, his morality. Just as in Greek literature, the Trojan War is seen not to have accomplished anything but death, destruction and chaos, which in their wake beg all sorts of questions, so in the *Mahabharata* the cessation of the great battle is only a kind of prelude to the overwhelming moral questions that follow. In a sense, the resolution of the war is to no one's satisfaction—all anyone is left with is a sense of futility and horror.

The characters, troubled by what has happened, seek meaning—either by trying to find justification for what has happened on a grand scale or by coming themselves to some sort of inner peace, living ascetic, quiet lives. A central character, Yudhishthira, tries both ways- trying to find some justification for what has happened, at the same time that, assured by good counselors that the war was just and necessary, he searches to find personal equilibrium. The *Mahabharata* ends charmingly: Yudhishthira arrives at the gates of heaven with his dog—he refuses to leave the dog behind, and the dog is revealed to be a god. Then, in a final test, he is told that his brothers are not in heaven but in hell, and he insists on joining them there. This, too, is revealed to be an illusion—and a test for him-his brothers are really in heaven with him.

For all of its battles and bloodshed, the *Mahabharata* ends on a quieter note, one of all-encompassing love. The *Mahabharata* provides an insight into one of the great civilizations of the East, a civilization that is growing increasingly important in world affairs—and an insight into that civilization's religion and philosophy. Yet, ironically, it shows us, in its main and abiding emphasis, that it upholds values with which we are familiar from our own literature, from its beginnings to the present, and from our own religion. If it is both the Indian Bible and the Indian Homer, it is not so unfamiliar to us as we might suppose and provides us with a reminder that the greatest literary minds-of whatever time and whatever part of the world—have come to many of the same religious and ethical conclusions as has our own civilization.

读者最应该读的一个章节是"薄伽梵歌",这一章简要阐述了印度教的基本教义。

《摩诃婆罗多》与大多数世界文学名著一样,也关注人应该怎样生活:他的价值观和道德观。希腊文学中,特洛伊战争带来的只是死亡、毁灭和混乱,进而又引起了各种问题;《摩诃婆罗多》也是如此,不停的战争只是更多道德问题的序幕。从一定意义上说,战争不能使任何人满足,留给每个人的是徒劳和恐惧感。

书中人物受所发生事情的困扰而寻找意义:或者尽力为所发生事情寻找正当理由;或者使自己达到某种内在的平静,过着禁欲平静的生活。主人公俞德西斯尝试了这两种方式,一方面尽力为发生的一切寻找正当理由,同时好的顾问使他确信战争是正义的和必要的之后,他努力寻求个人平衡。《摩诃婆罗多》的结局很完美。俞德西斯和他的狗来到天门,他拒绝抛弃狗;结果狗是个神。在最后一个考验中,他被告知他的兄弟们不在天堂而在地狱,他坚持要到地狱去和他的兄弟们在一起。这也是一个假象,是对他的考验;其实他的兄弟们在天堂。

尽管《摩诃婆罗多》中有很多战争和流血事件,但结局很平和,体现了包容一切的爱。《摩诃婆罗多》给我们提供了了解东方伟大文明的机会,了解这一文明的宗教和哲学。这一文明在世界事务中起着越来越重要的作用。滑稽的是,这一文明所主要强调和坚持的价值观我们并不陌生,在我们从古至今的文学中,在我们的宗教中。《摩诃婆罗多》是印度的圣经和荷马,我们对它也不陌生;因为我们可以由此发现任何时代任何地方的伟大文学家,可以得出许多相同的宗教和道德结论。

Eight

Euclid of Alexandria: The Elements

Who Was Euclid of Alexandria?

So little is known of Euclid the mathematician that he is always referred to as Euclid of Alexandria to differentiate him from Euclid of Megara,a Socratic philosopher who lived roughly a century earlier.We know a few facts about Euclid of Alexandria,that he was born about 325 B.C.,which means that he was born about 22 years after the death of Plato,3 years before the death of Aristotle.In other words,he lived during the time of Plato's immediate successors,and there is some evidence that he studied at Plato's Academy in Athens.He spent most of his life in Alexandria,in Egypt,during the reign of Ptolemy I (though Egypt was then not so much the great civilization that it had once been as it was a part of the Greek Empire,a Hellenistic state.He probably worked at the great library in Alexandria (the greatest library of antiquity);   he was probably head of his own school of mathematics there (at least,he was the leader of a team of notable mathematicians and the students who attended them as acolytes and students);   and he died in Alexandria,probably about 265 B.C.

The Elements

What is extraordinary about his obscurity is that Euclid of Alexandria wrote the most famous work of antiquity on the subject of mathematics-indeed,*The Elements*,a comprehensive 13-volume work,became the standard for work in mathematics,particularly geometry,for more than 2,000 years until it began to be supplanted by non-Euclidian geometry in the 19th century.More than that,having endured for those 2,000 years,*The Elements* could be said to be the most famous textbook ever written.Some scholars have estimated that only The Bible has gone through more editions and more translations.*The Elements* was known to mathematicians in all times and in virtually all the civilized countries of the world.Given the prominence of this textbook over 2 millennia,Euclid of Alexandria can be said to be the most famous teacher of mathematics that the world has ever known.

Its composition is something of a mystery.Was Euclid an historical figure who single-handedly composed *The Elements* and the other works that have been attributed to him? Or was he the leader of a group of mathematicians,working under his supervision,very possibly teachers and students at his school,or scholars who had gathered around him,who "published" under his name-and continued doing so even after his death? Or did he never exist at all? Is Euclid of Alexandria simply a pseudonym for a group of mathematicians, based in Alexandria,connected to its library (a kind of university in antiquity) who took the name Euclid because it was a popular name of the time?

No one knows the answer for sure,but most scholars would now say that Euclid of Alexandria existed;   that he brought together all known mathematical knowledge of the time;   that he set it out in comprehensible terms that others,for centuries after his death

亚历山大里亚的欧几里得
《几何原本》

亚历山大里亚的欧几里得

    对于数学家欧几里得,我们知之甚少。他通常被叫做亚历山大的欧几里得,以区别于早他一个世纪的苏格拉底学派哲学家米加拉的欧几里得。关于亚历山大的欧几里得我们还是有所了解的,他出生在约公元前325年,也就是柏拉图去世22年后,亚里士多德去世前3年。也就是说,他与柏拉图的继承人们生活在同一时期,并且有证据表明他曾在雅典柏拉图的学院学习过。他一生大部分时间都生活在埃及的亚历山大里亚,托勒密一世统治时期(此时的埃及已不是过去的伟大文明,是希腊帝国的一部分,一个希腊化的王国)。他可能在亚历山大里亚的著名图书馆(著名文物图书馆)工作,可能是数学学校的校长(至少是一群数学家以及追随他们的学生们的领导者)。他大约于公元前265年在亚历山大里亚去世。

《几何原本》

    使亚历山大里亚的欧几里得如此闻名的是他写出了古代数学方面最著名的作品《几何原本》。《几何原本》总共13卷,2 000多年里一直是数学,尤其是几何研究的标准,直到19世纪开始被非欧几里得几何所代替。《几何原本》可以说是最著名的教科书。有些学者估计只有《圣经》的版本和译本超过了《几何原本》。各个时代的数学家和几乎世界上所有文明国家都熟悉《几何原本》。《几何原本》这一教科书闻名了2 000年,欧几里得可以说是世界上最著名的数学老师。

    《几何原本》的创作是个谜。欧几里得是历史上的一个人物吗?是他一个人写了《几何原本》和其他作品吗?一群数学家们在他的指导下工作,他是引导者吗?这群数学家很可能是他学校里的老师和学生,或者是追随他的学者。这些学者以他的名字发表文章,甚至在他去世后也是如此。他到底是否存在呢?欧几里得是不是只是一群数学家的笔名呢?他们都生活在亚历山大里亚,并与那里的图书馆(文物图书馆)有联系,他们选用欧几里得这个名字是因为它当时比较流行。

    没有人知道确切的答案,但现在多数学者都认为欧几里得是存在的。他把当时所知道的所有数学知识汇集在一起,然后用较易理解的术语系统整理出来。他所使用的术语在他去世后的几个世纪仍能为人们所理解。编撰《几何原本》的巨大工作得到了他所信赖

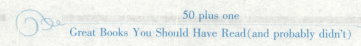
could follow and that he was aided in the enormous task of compiling *The Elements* by trusted fellow mathematicians,students,scholars and editors—the intellectual class that was attracted to Alexander and its reputation for research and scholarship.

Very few readers,especially non-mathematicians,or non-historians of antiquity,non-classicists,are likely now to plow through and absorb all 13 volumes of Euclid's Elements. But most people who wish to understand human intellectual history should at least do a sampling of this mighty work,to see what it accomplished as a work of synthesis.

Most of us acknowledge that the "beginnings" of most intellectual disciplines come to us from the Greek World.Euclid is not an original thinker; rather he is a compiler,one of the greatest who ever lived.That is,Euclid did not emerge out of thin air; other mathematicians of note had preceded him.He took their work,proved that it was correct or showed that it had to be modified to be proved.In all of this,he could be said to be a Platonist; that is,he wished to show that certain "forms" were eternal,were subject to rules that could in fact be demonstrated to be true.In a sense,he was also an Aristotelian-believing that we could come to "universals" via our precise observation of and experimentation with the observable phenomena of the known world.

The accomplishment of *The Elements* is that,within this work,Euclid describes the properties of geometrical objects,which he deduces from a relatively narrow set of axioms. He thereby defines,anticipates,and inspires the axiomatic method of modern mathematics. The book is best known for its comments on geometry,but it as well includes various conclusions about the theory of numbers-for example,the connection between perfect numbers.Yes,some of his results originate with earlier mathematicians (in some cases we don't even know who they were),but his great triumph was to present them in a single framework that made sense to those who read it—his contemporaries and those who came after him,those who studied mathematics for the next 2,000 years.

Even to non-mathematicians-to those who will never make the entire journey through *The Elements*—Euclid of Alexandria provides an example of the kind of thought that we inherited from the Greeks,that guides our studies-and our attempts to reason—even now.It was well worth any reader's taking the time to sample Euclid of Alexandria's intellectual rigor,to allow it to become,as it should be,an inspiration.

的数学家、学生、学者和编辑们的帮助。这些知识分子们因亚历山大里亚以研究和学术著称而被吸引到此。

现在很少有读者,特别那些不是数学家、历史学家和古典主义者的人们,会仔细完整地阅读欧几里得长达13卷的《几何原本》。但想要了解人类知识历史的人们至少还是应该品读一下这一伟大巨著,看一下这部综合之作的成就。

我们多数人承认大部分知识学科都开始于希腊世界。欧几里得不是最初的思考者,他是最著名的编撰者之一。也就是说,欧几里得不是毫无参照的,在他之前还有著名的数学家。他拿来他们的作品,证明它是正确的或表明它必须得到修改以待证明。这可以说明他是个柏拉图主义者。他想证明某些"形式"是永恒的,并受规则的制约,而规则是可以证明是正确的。从某种意义上说,他也是个经验主义者。他相信通过准确观察可知世界的可观察现象并对其进行实验来获得"普遍特质"。

《几何原本》的成就在于欧几里得讲述了几何物体的特性,这些特性是他从有限的公理中推断出来的。因此他界定、预料和启发了现代数学得出公理的方法。此书以它对几何的评述而著名,但也包括数字理论的各种结论,如完全数之间的关系。当然,他的某些结论是源于早期数学家(我们甚至不知道他们是谁),但他的伟大成功在于把它们用一套体系陈述出来,读者可以理解的体系,他同时代的人以及后来乃至2000年后研究数学的人们都可以理解的体系。

甚至对于不是数学家的人们,对于那些没有完整地读过《几何原本》的人们,欧几里得也提供了某种思想典范。这种思想是我们从希腊人那里继承的,它指导我们的研究和推理。每个读者都应花时间品读欧几里得的知识力量,使它发挥它应有的启迪作用。

Nine

Cicero:
On the Good Life

Who Was Cicero?

Marcus Tullius Cicero (106-43 B.C.) was an orator and statesman of ancient Rome; he was,as well,one of the most influential writers in Latin literature as well as the greatest of Roman orators.Cicero's work reflected his command of Latin,and his precision in choice of words,his attention to grammar and his skillful use of narration and prose rhythm created a standard of Latin that served as the universal language of intellectual and scientific communications for hundreds of years.

Cicero was born in Arpinum,Italy,of the well-to-do family Tullii.Because he was an excellent student,he was given the opportunity to study Roman law,which was considered to be a great honor.Nevertheless,he expanded his interests beyond the law and also studied poetry,philosophy and Greek literature.

After successfully prosecuting a corrupt former governor of Sicily,he won the approval of the Roman aristocracy.With its support,Cicero became consul,Rome's highest elected political office at the time.The lawyer had also become a politician.

It was politics,unfortunately,that hastened his downfall.The First Triumvirate of Julius Caesar,Gnaeus Pompey and Marcus Licinius Crassus expelled Cicero from Rome in 58 B.C.because he opposed their government.He was,however,permitted to return the following year.The Second Triumvirate of Octavian (later Emperor Augustus),Marcus Aemilius Lepidus,and Mark Antony,on the other hand,refused to tolerate Cicero's opposition after he wrote the Philippics in which he attacked Mark Antony as ruling Rome with absolute power.In 43 B.C.this Second Triumvirate had him assassinated.

During his lifetime,Cicero was a prolific writer.He wrote more than 100 orations, several of which endorse the Republican form of government; he remained staunchly opposed to any kind of one-man rule.In later years he wrote philosophical works in which he drew heavily on the moral ideas of the Greek philosophers.These works later became an important part of the education of 18th century Europeans and Americans,including most of the writers of the American Declaration of Independence and Constitution.

On the Good Life

Everyone has heard of Cicero of ancient Rome.He is so famous that we tend to call him by only his "last name," as if he were Greek,not Roman.In fact his last name wasn't Cicero but Tullius.Cicero is a nickname,derived from the Latin word for "chickpea." One of the Cicero's ancestors had a cleft in the tip of his nose,hence the nickname,which Cicero, even when he became prominent statesman,refused to change.So,we've all heard of this man,so famous that we call him by the nickname that he himself used,even though it wasn't really his name.

But why is he famous?

西塞罗
《论美好生活》

西塞罗

马尔库斯·图利乌斯·西塞罗是古罗马演说家和政治家。他既是最著名的演说家,也是拉丁文学中最具影响力的作家之一。西塞罗的作品体现了他精通拉丁文、用词准确和注意语法。他还熟练运用记叙和散文韵律,这为拉丁文创造了一个标准。拉丁文作为学术和科学交流的世界语言达几百年之久。

西塞罗出生在意大利阿尔皮努姆一个富裕家庭。他因成绩优秀而有机会学习罗马法律,这在当时被认为是一大荣誉。然而,他的兴趣不只局限于法律,还学习了诗歌、哲学和希腊文学。

他成功调查了西西里一名前政府腐败官员,这使得他赢得了罗马贵族的信任。在贵族的支持下,西塞罗成为一名领事,当时罗马选举产生的最高政治官员。律师也成了一名政治家。

不幸的是,正是政治加速了他的衰落。尤利乌斯·恺撒、格奈乌斯·庞培和马卡斯·李西尼·克拉苏组成的前三雄执政因西塞罗反对他们的统治而于公元前58年将他驱逐出罗马。然而,次年就允许他回到罗马。西塞罗写了《腓力比克》攻击安东尼对罗马的独裁统治,这使由屋大维(后来的奥古斯都大帝)、马尔库斯·埃米利乌斯·雷比达和马可·安东尼组成的后三雄执政无法再容忍他的反对意见。公元前43年,后三雄执政派人暗杀了西塞罗。

西塞罗是个多产的作家。他写了100多篇演说词,其中有几篇提出共和政府形式,他坚决反对任何形式的个人统治。后来,他还写了哲学作品,主要阐述希腊哲学家们的道德思想。这些作品成为18世纪欧洲人和美洲人,包括美国独立宣言和宪法起草者们所受的教育的一个重要部分。

《论美好生活》

大家都听说过古罗马的西塞罗。他如此出名以至于我们直接叫他的"姓",似乎他是希腊人而不是罗马人。实际上,他的姓不是西塞罗而是图利乌斯。西塞罗只是个绰号,来自于拉丁文"鹰嘴豆"一词。西塞罗一个祖先的鼻尖上有个裂缝,所以即使在西塞罗成为显要政治家时也不愿放弃。我们都听说过这个人,他如此出名我们都叫他的绰号。尽管那不是他的名字,他也仍然使用。

但他为什么出名呢?

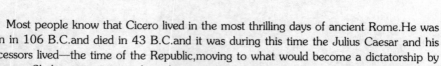

Most people know that Cicero lived in the most thrilling days of ancient Rome.He was born in 106 B.C.and died in 43 B.C.and it was during this time the Julius Caesar and his successors lived—the time of the Republic,moving to what would become a dictatorship by emperors.Shakespeare immortalizes this period in his plays "Antony and Cleopatra" and "Julius Caesar." Cicero was one of that period's most prominent statesmen.

Even as a student Cicero was already known throughout Rome for his brilliance. Although he studied law,he was also particularly fond of great writing and absorbed the works of the great literary figures of Greece.Although Cicero's family were landed gentry rather than aristocrats,Cicero achieved a career that the vast majority of men of his social class could not.He served as a magistrate (a "quaestor") in Western Sicily; thereafter,he created a very successful law practice in Rome and enjoyed more than his share of triumphs as an advocate.Then,despite the fact that his family was neither noble nor patrician,that no Tullius had ever been a consul before him,Cicero was elected a consul of Rome,and during the year he served in office he suppressed the "Catiline Conspiracy," a plot to overthrow the Republic-which brought him even more fame.Because he was responsible for putting the conspirators to death without trial (actually,a Senate decision,but Cicero was directly responsible for making it happen),he was subsequently exiled for a year,then he came back to Rome as a hero.He supported Pompey against Caesar,then,after the assassination of Caesar,he supported the claims of Octavian,Caesar's heir,against Antony's attempts to grab power.Cicero became the voice of the Senate of Rome (in which he continued to serve) against the dictates of Antony,who was Caesar's executor.Cicero became more and more a hero of the people.Cicero,despite initially praising him,also distrusted Octavian.When Antony and Octavian reconciled,and (with Lepidus) formed the Second Triumvirate,they named Caesar as an "enemy of the state," a traitor,and he was pursued,subsequently captured,beheaded,and his head displayed in public.An ignominious end to an illustrious public life.

Yet,the fame of Cicero lived on,not so much for his part in these historic events as for his words.Even after his death,and the end of the Republic,his memory survived—not as a statesman but as a great orator and writer.Those writings were so revered that they caused him to be declared a "righteous pagan" by the early Roman Catholic Church—therefore his works were regarded as worthy of preservation.St.Augustine and other church fathers quoted liberally from Cicero—one reason why so many recreations of his works (many of which survived only in fragments) were possible.

Despite what seems like an action-filled life,Cicero still managed to write as extensively as someone who was a professional,full-time writer.Six of his books on rhetoric and (parts of) seven of his books on philosophy have survived.Just 58 of his speeches (either as advocate or senator) survive,as do some 800 of his letters.His literary output was vast; even what survives is impressively large.

Cicero is now acknowledged to be the greatest prose stylist that Rome produced (he is also acknowledged to have been a great orator,but of course we have no way of judging that reputation except by the testimony of those who heard him speak).Students of Latin still read his work to see the Latin language at its most stylish,its most elegant—much as we might lionize the great essayists/stylists in English such as Dr.Johnson or Thomas Jefferson.

多数人都知道西塞罗生活在古罗马最繁盛时期。他出生于公元前106年,于公元前43年去世,正是尤利乌斯·恺撒和他的继承人统治时期,由共和国逐步转向独裁统治。莎士比亚的戏剧《安东尼与克莉奥佩特拉》和《恺撒》就发生在这一时期。西塞罗是当时最著名的政治家之一。

甚至在西塞罗还是学生的时候,他就因他的聪明才智而闻名于罗马。虽然他学的是法律,他也尤其喜欢名著,阅读希腊著名文学家的作品。虽然西塞罗的家庭属于中上阶层而非贵族阶层,他的成就是同一社会阶层大多数人所不能达到的。他曾任西西里的地方法官(度支官),后来,他成功地创造了一套罗马法律惯例,成为一名成功的律师。另外,尽管他的家庭并非贵族,图利乌斯家族也没有人做过领事,西塞罗当选为罗马的领事。在他任职期间,他镇压了企图推翻共和国的"喀提林阴谋",这使他更加出名。他因未通过审判将阴谋者处死(实际上是议会的决定,但由西塞罗来承担责任)而被流放一年,后来回到罗马后成了一名英雄。他支持庞培反对恺撒;后来恺撒被暗杀后,他又支持恺撒的继承人屋大维反对安东尼企图夺取政权。西塞罗成为罗马议会(他仍是议会成员)反对恺撒的执行者安东尼独裁统治的代言人。西塞罗更成为人民的英雄。尽管西塞罗最初赞同屋大维,后来也不信任他。安东尼和屋大维讲和,并(与雷比达)形成后三雄执政后,他们认为西塞罗是"国家的敌人",叛国徒。他遭到追捕,被捕后被砍首,头颅示众。卓越的公众人物却落个耻辱的结局。

然而,西塞罗的名声依存,不是因为他参与历史事件而是因为他的言论。甚至在死后,在共和国结束后,人们仍然记着他,不是作为一个政治家而是作为一个伟大的演说家和作家。他的作品受到极大尊重,他被早期罗马天主教堂宣布为"正义的异教徒",并认为他的作品是值得保存的。圣·奥古斯丁和其他教父都直接引用西塞罗的作品,这就是他的作品可能不断地被再创造的原因之一(许多只有部分还存在)。

尽管西塞罗一生似乎从事的活动很多,他仍然像职业、全职作家一样广泛写作。现在保存下来的有6本修辞方面的书和7本(部分)哲学方面的书;还有58篇演说词(作为律师或议员)和大约800封信。他的文学产出巨大,甚至保留下来的也相当多。

西塞罗现在被认为是罗马最伟大的散文文体学家。(他也被认为是伟大的演说家,但我们无法评判,只有那些听过他演说的人才能证明。)学习拉丁语的学生仍然阅读他的作品来学习时尚优雅的拉丁语,就像我们崇拜英语论说文作家或文体学家,如约翰逊和托马斯·杰斐逊一样。

But there is something more to Cicero than just his mastery of Latin.Cicero was,in a sense,the conscience of Rome.He wrote about abstract concepts of human rights,based both on law and custom,as well drawing on the wisdom of the writers/philosophers who had preceded him,and in so doing,he often suggests various of the goals and virtues enshrined in such much later documents as the "Declaration of Independence" or "The Rights of Man." Cicero also wrote about such subjects as duty,friendship,the training of leaders,what it meant to be moral (a person of integrity),and the conditions by which a person might be happy.

We think of Greece as having established various of our intellectual disciplines- and even the concept of government for,by and of the people to which we subscribe.When we are not contemplating the Romans as world-conquerors or tyrants flinging Christians to lions,we acknowledge that it is,from them,that we inherit more modest but just as enduring values-our laws (the notion of the rule of law) and our ideas of what constitutes domestic virtue and happiness.Cicero is the prime Roman voice of such virtues—of notions of how a man should live his life.It is Cicero who is often credited with being the voice of the Italian Renaissance when it happened centuries later,when thinkers of the Renaissance turned again to the writings of ancient Greece and Rome.

Cicero never wrote a book called *On the Good Life*.It is compilation of various of his writings,compiled and translated by Michael Grant,and published in the 1970s,but it helps us to see the breadth and flavor of his writings.The "good life" for Cicero was two kinds of lives:A life of moral value and a life of contentment (of happiness),and the two were intertwined.A person cannot have contentment,in Cicero's view,unless he lives a life that is virtuous.Moral integrity,in other words,is the means to human happiness.Cicero talks of friendship,of our duty to our friends,our family,our country—and he offers a kind of extended lesson in ethics; his lesson is simple,it is universal; it is,of course,very difficult to live up to.

We should all sample and savor Cicero via this excellent anthology of his works- for Cicero espouses values that,since the time he articulated them,have never died as ethical guideposts for mankind.

但西塞罗不只是精通拉丁语。一定意义上说，西塞罗是罗马的良知。他以法律和习俗为基础，并利用先辈作家和哲学家的智慧，讲述了人权的一些抽象概念。他所提倡的各种目标和德善在后来如《独立宣言》和《人权》的文件中被奉为神圣。西塞罗还讲述了职责、友情、领导者的培养、怎样才是道德的(正直的人)和人快乐的条件。

我们认为希腊建立了各种学科，甚至"民享、民治、民有"的统治观念。如果我们不考虑罗马人是世界的征服者或迫害基督教徒的暴君，我们承认从他们那里继承了比较谦逊的永恒的价值观念(法律、法治的观念)和有关内在善和快乐的观点。西塞罗是善以及人该如何生活在罗马的主要代言人。西塞罗也常被认为是发生在几个世纪后的意大利文艺复兴的代言人，文艺复兴时期的思想家重新回到古希腊罗马作品。

西塞罗从来没写过叫做《论美好生活》的书。此书汇编了西塞罗的各类文章，由迈克尔·格兰特编写翻译而成，出版于20世纪70年代。此书使我们了解西塞罗文章的广度和特色。对于西塞罗来说，"美好生活"有两种：有道德意义的生活和满足(愉快)的生活，并且两者是交织在一起的。西塞罗谈到了友谊、对朋友的责任、家庭和国家；他还谈到了伦理学方面的问题。他的见解是简单、普遍的，但当然很难做到。

我们应该通过这一作品集来品读西塞罗，因为西塞罗所拥护的道德标准自从他提出至今一直是人类的道德路标。

Ten

Lucretius:
De Rerum Natural
(On the Nature of Things)

Who Was Lucretius?

Lucretius (99-55 B.C.),whose full name was Titus Lucretius Carus,was a Roman poet and philosopher.His only surviving work is the epic poem *De Rerum Natura (On the Nature of Things)*.

Little is known about Lucretius's life.Because of his name,he was thought to be from the noble family of Lucretii,although it is possible that he was a former slave who had been freed by that family.His command of language and the depth of learning reflected in his work support the idea of his having been an aristocrat.

All that is certain is that he was a poet devoted to the teachings of the philosopher Epicurus,and that he evidently died before completing his epic poem.But *De Rerum Natura* itself reveals Lucretius to be not only an accomplished poet,but also a gifted philosopher,critic of religion,social commentator,and observer of culture.

Despite the obscurity of his life,Lucretius had great literary influence,especially among such poets as Virgil,John Milton and Walt Whitman.In addition to being one of the primary sources of Epicurean ideas,his work was the forerunner of Western scientific thought-he anticipated modern theories in biology,geology,sociology,and medicine.To the Spanish poet and philosopher George Santayana (1863-1952),for example,Lucretius was the creator of scientific materialism.Some scholars also believe that Lucretius's ideas influenced Charles Darwin,although Darwin claimed not to have read *De Rerum Natura*.One influence is certain,however,in advocating the material basis of the human mind as a collection of atoms,Lucretius prepared the groundwork for modern neuroscience and its reliance on molecular processes.

De Rerum Natura

Mention Lucretius (Titus Lucretius Carus) to most educated people and,unless they are philosophers or classicists,they probably won't know whom you are talking about.Yet philosophers would say that he is one of the most innovative and profound of the philosophers of ancient Rome.Classicists and literary scholars would say that he is one of the greatest of Roman poets-some have said that his only known work,*De Rerum Natura* (On the Nature of Things or,as sometimes translated,On the Nature of the World/the Universe),is greater than Virgil's "Aeneid," that it is the masterpiece of Latin verse.Even those who would not go that far would admit that *De Rerum Natura* is very important for its influence on Virgil and other of the Roman poets.Perhaps its greatest achievement is in the excellence of its verse combined with the innovation of its philosophy.Yet,to modern readers,Lucretius remains an unknown person,*De Rerum Natura* virtually an unknown work.

10

卢克莱修
《物性论》

卢克莱修

卢克莱修(公元前99年~公元前55年)全名为提图斯·卢克莱修·卡鲁斯,罗马诗人和哲学家。他唯一现存的作品是史诗《物性论》。

卢克莱修的生平基本不得而知。根据他的名字,人们认为他出身于贵族家庭卢克莱,当然他也可能是卢克莱家释放的奴隶。作品中反映他精通语言、学识渊博,这证明他还是贵族出身。

可以确定的是,卢克莱修是一名诗人,致力于哲学家伊壁鸠鲁的学说,未完成他的史诗就去世了。但《物性论》表明卢克莱修不仅是一位卓越的诗人,还是有天赋的哲学家、宗教批评家、社会评论家和文化观察家。

尽管卢克莱修的生平不为人知,但他的文学影响是巨大的,尤其是对诗人维吉尔、约翰·弥尔顿和沃特尔·惠特曼的影响。他的作品除了是伊壁鸠鲁学说的主要来源之一,还是西方科学思想的先导。他较早提出了生物学、地质学、社会学和医学方面的现代理论。西班牙诗人、哲学家乔治·桑塔雅那(1863~1952)认为卢克莱修是科学唯物主义的创始人。尽管达尔文声称没有读过《物性论》,有些学者认为卢克莱修的思想影响了达尔文。然而,有个影响是确定的,卢克莱修认为人类思想的物质基础是大量原子,这为现代神经系统科学及其所依赖的分子过程奠定了基础。

《物性论》

跟大部分受过教育的人提起卢克莱修,他们可能不知道你在说谁,除非他们是哲学家和古典文学艺术研究者。而哲学家们会说卢克莱修是古罗马最具革新精神、最有造诣的哲学家之一。古典文学艺术研究者和文学工作者认为他是罗马最伟大的诗人之一,有些人还认为他的唯一作品《物性论》胜过拉丁诗的杰作——维吉尔的《埃涅阿斯记》。那些不会如此夸大的人也承认《物性论》的重要性,因为它对维吉尔和其他罗马诗人有着一定的影响。或许它最伟大的成就在于它把诗的精华与哲学革新结合在一起。然而,现代读者还是不知道卢克莱修是谁,不知道《物性论》是怎样的一本书。

There are perhaps two reasons for this dual obscurity.Almost nothing is known about Lucretius—even the dates of his birth and death (possibly he lived from 99 B.C.to 55 B.C.) are conjecture,provoked by other people's references to him,particularly those of St. Jerome.Jerome claims that Lucretius lived to be age 44,that he had drunk a love potion and was insane for most of his life,writing his poem only during moments of lucidity,and that he committed suicide during a period of madness.Jerome,who would have objected to Lucretius's anti-religious stance,may well have been trying to discredit Lucretius.It is hardly possible that a lunatic could have composed a poetic masterpiece; besides,a rather engaging and rational personality shines through the lines of *De Rerum Natura*.About all that Jerome has to say that might be reliable is that Cicero "amended" the work,which could mean that Cicero edited it,was responsible for its publication.

Further,it is impossible to know what in the philosophy of Lucretius is original.He is a spokesman for Epicurus (a philosopher of ancient Greece,of the 4th century B.C.; Epicuris is said to have produced a vast number of works,but only a very small fraction of them survive:Epicurus really comes to us by way of Lucretius,much as Plato is a spokesman for Socrates.And as with Plato and Socrates it is impossible to know how much of Lucretius is a "reproduction" of Epicurus,how much is Lucretius himself.

Yet,these reasons for Lucretius's obscurity don't really hold up to scrutiny.Almost nothing is known of Homer,yet Homer is one of the most popular poets the world has ever produced.And Plato endures—it hardly matters whether Socrates,as conveyed by Plato,is real or mainly imagined.Plato remains the most influential philosopher the Western world has ever produced.

There might be an even better reason for Lucretius's obscurity—his philosophy (whether it is entirely that of Epicurus or not)—the Epicurean philosophy—is one that entirely discounts religious belief as irrelevant.We know from earliest recorded history in the West that the ancient civilizations believed in deities,in a variety of gods and goddesses. Simultaneously,the ancient world of the Jews accepted a universe in which one God ruled. From the time of Constantine,Christianity was the official religion of the West,and so it remains to the present day.Meanwhile,all other countries of the world have a religious faith (Hinduism,Islam,Buddhism,etc.).Yet,Lucretius posits a Godless universe; he has always been the odd man out.

Indeed,the main message of his work is that he wishes to free man of his superstitions and of the fear of death.By "superstition" Lucretius means the notion that God (or,in his case,the Gods) created the world and continue in some way to direct what happens to that world and to our lives.Belief in God (the Gods) can be abolished,Lucretius says,by pointing out that natural forces rule our world,that we and everything around us are simply comprised of atoms that exist in empty space; our actions,the actions of the world,have nothing to do with the intervention of deities.As for fear of death what,Lucretius argues,is to be feared about annihilation; the nothingness of death is neither good nor bad; we are not there to experience it—just as we were not there to experience all the time that occurred before our births.We should fear only that which is tangible.

Why does he offer such a point of view in verse? To make it more palatable.Like the great religions and their beliefs,the beliefs of Lucretius have endured as a kind of eternal

　　大家不知道卢克莱修及其《物性论》可能有两个原因。关于卢克莱修，几乎一无所知；就连他的生卒日期(可能是公元前99年~公元前55年)也是推测，根据其他人对他的描述，主要是圣·哲罗姆。哲罗姆说卢克莱修活到44岁，他曾服用春药，大部分时间精神错乱；他的诗是在清醒的片刻写的；他在精神错乱时自杀而亡。哲罗姆曾反对卢克莱修的反宗教立场，他可能试图诋毁卢克莱修。一个疯子几乎不可能写出杰出的诗篇，另外《物性论》的字里行间闪耀着迷人、理智的个性。哲罗姆所说的有一点或许是可信的，西塞罗"修订"了这一作品，也就是说西塞罗编辑出版了这一作品。

　　另外，很难弄清楚卢克莱修哲学思想中哪些是他个人的。他是伊壁鸠鲁(公元前4世纪古希腊哲学家)的代言人。据说伊壁鸠鲁创作了大量作品，但只有一小部分保存了下来。我们是通过卢克莱修了解伊壁鸠鲁，就像柏拉图是苏格拉底的代言人。就像柏拉图和苏格拉底一样，很难知道哪些是卢克莱修对伊壁鸠鲁思想的再创造，哪些是他自己的思想。

　　然而，这些卢克莱修不出名的原因是经不起推敲的。对于荷马，人们几乎一无所知；然而他是世界著名诗人之一。不管柏拉图所描述的苏格拉底是真正存在的，还是完全出于想象，柏拉图还是永垂不朽。柏拉图仍是西方最有影响力的哲学家。

　　卢克莱修不出名更好一点的原因可能是他的哲学（不管是否完全是伊壁鸠鲁的思想）——伊壁鸠鲁哲学，完全否定宗教信仰。我们从最早有记载的西方历史知道古代文明信仰神，各种各样的神。同样，古犹太人认为宇宙是上帝主宰的。从君士坦丁时代至今，基督教一直是西方的法定宗教。世界上所有其他国家也都有宗教信仰(印度教、伊斯兰教、佛教等)。而卢克莱修提出宇宙是没有上帝的，他是个游离在外的人。

　　的确，他的作品主要是想把人类从迷信中，从对死亡的恐惧中解放出来。卢克莱修所谓的"迷信"是认为上帝(或诸神)创造了世界并在某些方面掌控着世界及我们的生活思想。卢克莱修说，自然力量控制着我们的世界，我们周围的事物都是由存在于空间的原子构成的；我们的行为、世界的行为与神的干预毫无关系，所以我们可以废除对上帝的信仰。卢克莱修认为恐惧死亡就是恐惧毁灭，死亡的虚无没有好坏可言，我们的存在不是为了要经历死亡，就像我们不是要经历出生前的事情。我们只应该恐惧那些看得见摸得着的。

　　他为什么在诗中表达这样一种观点？为了使之更受欢迎。
　　和伟大宗教及其信仰一样，卢克莱修的信仰永远是少数人的观点。想一想卡尔·马克

minority viewpoint.One need only think of Karl Marx and his statement that "religion is the opiate of the people," or listen to the arguments of a modern atheist,or observe the actions of modern men and women who live only for the gratifications of this life,to realize the justice of that statement.Yet,Lucretius differs from Marx in that he takes a very jaundiced view of social strife and political violence/struggle; Karl embraced them.And Lucretius has been misunderstood:"Epicureanism" has come to mean a life devoted to pleasure rather than one devoted to the contemplation of God.But,in proposing a life that rejects God,that sees life as an end in itself,Lucretius is not recommending hedonism as an alternative life-style.Lucretius's goal is the pursuit of intellectual pleasure (in fact,he takes a dim view of sexual pleasure or romantic love),which will in turn lead to a tranquility of mind,once superstition is banished.Lucretius,in his views,suggests the ways in which the universe may have been formed,the atomic structure of matter and the ways in which the various life forms would have emerged—in which views he predates modern science.In other words,he recommends not the pleasures of the flesh but the pleasures of the mind—and he was as good as his own recommendations.He offered speculations about the physical world that we now know to be true.

Every reader should have sample Lucretius and *De Rerum Natura* to understand where this atheistic view of the universe comes from in the first place-then to realize that Lucretius is something more than a proponent of mindless sensual gratification,that he aims for much higher goals than those of many of the "godless" men who followed him.He offers the most perfect expression of the Epicurean worldview in the literature of the West.

思及其"宗教是人们的麻醉剂"的论述,听一听现代无神论者的观点,观察一下只追求今生满足的现代人的行为,就可以意识到这一论述的正确性。然而与马克思不同的是,卢克莱修对社会冲突和政治暴力或斗争的观点较为偏激;马克思却可以接受它们。卢克莱修还被误解,认为伊壁鸠鲁学说提倡生活致力于享乐,而不是对上帝的冥想。但卢克莱修提倡拒绝上帝的生活,把生活本身看成目的,并不是提倡快乐主义是一种生活方式。卢克莱修的目标是追求学术上的乐趣(实际上,他对性快乐和浪漫爱情持悲观态度);一旦迷信得到废除,这将会带来心灵的平静。卢克莱修指出了宇宙是怎样形成的,物质的原子结构和各种生活形式是怎样出现的。他的这些观点使他领先于现代科学。换句话说,他提倡的不是肉体的快乐而是精神的快乐。他也致力于自己所提倡的精神快乐。他对现实存在的物质世界进行了思辨。

品读卢克莱修和《物性论》首先可以了解宇宙无神论的来源,其次可以知道卢克莱修不是支持盲目的肉体上的满足,他的目标远高于他的那些"无神论"追随者。在西方文学中,他的作品最完美地阐述了伊壁鸠鲁学说的世界观。

Eleven

Saint Augustine: Confessions

Who Was Saint Augustine?

Saint Augustine (354-430)-also known as Augustine of Hippo or by his Latin name Aurelius Augustinus-was one of the most important philosopher-theologians in the development of the early Christian church.His most notable writings are his autobiographical *Confessions* and The City of God,a Christian interpretation of history. Although he is a saint in the Roman Catholic church,his influence on Western theology has been so significant that both Roman Catholic and Protestant theologians consider him one of the founders of Western theology.His ideas have influenced the teachings of John,Calvin, Martin Luther and other Protestant reformers and his thinking is reflected in the work of such Western philosophers as Immanuel Kant and Blaise Pascal.

Augustine was born in the Roman provincial city of Tagaste (in what is now Algeria in North Africa) of a devout Catholic mother,Monica,and a pagan father,Patricius.Augustine studied Latin literature as a child and later traveled to Carthage to study rhetoric and philosophy.During his stay in Carthage,he became a teacher and established a relationship with a young woman with whom he had a son.He also lived a hedonistic life-style and embraced the Manichaean religion for a time.Manichaeism was a dualistic philosophy that advocated the principle of conflict between good and evil and a rational interpretation of Scripture.Its moral code was not strict.

Eventually,Augustine became disillusioned by his inability to reconcile contradictory Manichaeist beliefs,and he began to search for other theological doctrines.During this time he left Carthage for Rome and later Milan,where he met Ambrose,the distinguished Catholic bishop of Milan.Under the influence of Ambrose,Augustine turned to Christianity. In 391 he was ordained as a priest,and in 395 became bishop of Hippo Regius in northern Africa.He remained in Hippo as the leader of African Catholicism until his death in 430.

Confessions

St. Augustine is one of the four great fathers of the Roman Catholic Church; the others are Ambrose,Jerome,and Gregory the Great.Mention these three others,however,and most non-Catholics would have difficulty identifying them; even most Catholics would have trouble remembering the details of their lives.But though he lived from the 4th to 5th centuries A.D.,Augustine is still,16 centuries later,one of the most famous men who ever lived.Even those who do not know his writings know the details of his life-for the reason that he has come to be regarded as the classic example of the man who struggles against the demands of the flesh only to emerge as the champion of the life of contemplation.

Augustine's education was in philosophy and rhetoric—the art of persuasion and public speaking.He then became a teacher of these subjects in both Tagaste and Carthage,but eventually he headed for Rome,where he believed the best rhetoricians were to be found. He quickly became disillusioned with Rome,and,through a stroke of good luck,became

11

圣·奥古斯丁
《忏悔录》

圣·奥古斯丁

圣·奥古斯丁(354~430),也称作希波的奥古斯丁或拉丁文名字奥雷里乌斯·奥古斯提奴斯,是早期基督教会形成中最著名的哲学家兼神学家之一。他的著作主要是自传体形式的《忏悔录》和基督教对历史的阐释《上帝之城》。虽然他是罗马天主教会的圣徒,但他对西方神学有着巨大的影响,罗马天主教和新教神学家都认为他是西方神学的创始人之一。他的思想影响了约翰、加尔文、马丁·路德和其他新教改革者们的学说,他的思想也反映在诸如伊曼努尔·康德和布莱斯·帕斯卡西方哲学家们的作品中。

奥古斯丁出生在罗马塔加斯特城(今北非的阿尔及利亚),母亲莫尼卡是虔诚的天主教徒,父亲帕特利修是异教徒。奥古斯丁从小开始学习拉丁文学,后来到迦太基学习修辞和哲学。在迦太基期间,他成为一名教师并与一年轻女子生下一子。他曾一度追求享乐主义的生活方式并信奉摩尼教。摩尼教是二元论哲学,提倡善与恶的对立,还提倡理性地阐释《圣经》。它的道德准则不够严格。

最后,奥古斯丁因无力调和摩尼教矛盾的信条而绝望,并开始寻找其他神学教义。此时他离开迦太基前往罗马,后来又到了米兰。在米兰他遇到了米兰杰出的天主教主教安布罗斯。在安布罗斯的影响下,奥古斯丁皈依了基督教。391年,他为委任为牧师;395年成为北非希利基乌斯的主教。直到他430年去世,他一直留在希波,是非洲天主教的领袖。

《忏悔录》

圣·奥古斯丁是罗马天主教四大创始人之一,其余三人为安布罗斯、哲罗姆和格列高利。然而,说起其余三人,许多非天主教徒都不知道,甚至许多天主教徒也记不清他们的详细生平。尽管奥古斯丁生活在4世纪至5世纪,在16个世纪后他仍然很著名。即便那些不知道他的作品的人们也知道他的生平事迹,因为他被认为是反对肉体需求而拥护冥想生活的典范。

奥古斯丁学的是哲学和修辞——劝说和公众演说的艺术。后来在塔加斯特和迦太基他成了这两门课的教师。后来他前往罗马,相信在那可以找到最好的演说家。他很快对罗马失望了,却一时走运成了米兰王室的修辞学教师;当时他年仅30岁。米兰的学术领袖在帝国中是最具声望、最著名的,所以他很可能可以走上政治道路(这经常发生在有威望的

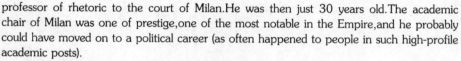

professor of rhetoric to the court of Milan. He was then just 30 years old. The academic chair of Milan was one of prestige, one of the most notable in the Empire, and he probably could have moved on to a political career (as often happened to people in such high-profile academic posts).

Augustine continued his wayward, party-boy ways. Monica followed him to Milan, urged him to get married to a prominent woman of her choosing. He abandoned his mistress, then realized he would have to wait 2 years until his bride-to-be came of age—so took up with another woman. It is at this time that he uttered the famous prayer for which, across the centuries, he is best known: "Grant me chastity and continence, but not yet."

Much of Augustine's writing survives, for example, we have many of his sermons; many of them of course involve religious controversies that have long since died away. But one of his works—*Confessions*—retains an enduring popularity (as, for religious thinkers, does his City of God). In *Confessions* Augustine describes his wayward youth and his spiritual rebirth: it is the first and most influential religious autobiography that we know of, almost certainly the first "sinner saved" story, and it has delighted people for centuries. It has been a "standard" ever since Augustine wrote it, and many commentators have noted that, after The Bible, it is the most popular and enduring work of the Christian religion.

In both this work and in City of God—and this is their interest for us today—Augustine is a great synthesizer. His reading was immense, and he was greatly influenced by Platonism and Neoplatonism; he legitimized the philosophy of the Greeks as part of Christian intellectual thought and tradition. In describing his mother, he not only gives us a portrait of a kind of ideal Christian woman; as well, he suggests the role of women in the early church, a prominent role in a world we tend to think of as a patriarchy. He was, as well, instrumental in establishing the notion of original sin and its partner, the human will. He also commented on more worldly matters—for example, he is largely responsible for the notion that there can be a "just war"—to prevent wholesale destruction and slaughter.

Besides establishing certain doctrines that we now regard as inherent in Christianity (as if they were there from the beginning), Augustine offered views that now seem strikingly modern. He argued that, though the Bible was sacred, that it was the voice of God coming to us through the agency of man, it was not infallible—for the reason that its agency was human compositors who had written it centuries earlier. He argued: If something in the Bible contradicts what we know from science or from the exercise of our reason (a gift from God), then we must opt for the dictates of science and reason. For example: In considering the creation story in the Bible, Augustine says that he believes that everything was created simultaneously by God—not in 7 days.

Confessions should be read by everyone because it is a stimulating work from one of the greatest minds that ever lived. What he struggles against (the temptations of the flesh) are the struggles of every Christian, of everyone who tries to live, if not a religious life, at least a life of the mind—right against wrong, good against evil, the struggle to find truth in human life. But, in reading *Confessions*, readers should remember that much that we take for granted—in the Christian religion, in our view of the world, and in the best syntheses between religion and science-comes from this remarkable man.

www.ahstp.net

学术人物身上)。

奥古斯丁继续着他不稳定的政治生活。莫尼卡跟随他到了米兰,并劝说他与她所选的优秀女士结婚。他抛弃了他的情人;后来才知道他要等两年,等他的未婚妻成年后才能结婚,所以他开始与另一个女人开始来往。就是在这个时候他说出了著名的祈祷文"赐予我纯洁与节欲吧,只是现在不要"并因此而闻名。

奥古斯丁的许多作品都保存了下来,如很多布道,当然其中很多涉及早已不存在的宗教争议。但他的作品《忏悔录》却一直很受欢迎(就像他的《上帝之城》一直受宗教思想者们的欢迎)。《忏悔录》中,奥古斯丁讲述了他年轻时的不稳定生活和他精神的重生。它是第一部也是最有影响力的宗教自传,大概也是第一个"罪人得救"的故事。几个世纪以来,它一直使人们得到快乐。自从奥古斯丁写出此书,它一直是"范本"。许多评论家指出,它是继《圣经》之后不朽的、最受欢迎的基督教作品。

在此书以及《上帝之城》中,奥古斯丁是个伟大的综合者(这就是它对我们有用的地方)。他博览群书,深受柏拉图主义和新柏拉图主义的影响。他使希腊哲学合法化,成为基督教学术思想和传统的一部分。在讲述他母亲时,他不仅描绘了一个理想的基督教妇女形象,还提出了早期教会中妇女的地位问题,妇女应该在这个类似于父权制社会的这个世界里占重要地位。在确立原罪及人类欲望观念上,奥古斯丁也起了重要作用。他还评述了一些世俗的事情,如他提出可以存在"正义战争",以阻止大规模的毁灭和屠杀。

奥古斯丁确立了基督教的一些教义,我们现在认为其是本来固有的(好像一开始就存在)。除此之外,他还提出了现在看来比较现代的观点。他说,尽管《圣经》是神圣的,但上帝的声音是通过人传达给我们,它不是毫无差错的;因为它的媒介是人类作家,他们在几个世纪以前创作了《圣经》。他说,如果《圣经》与科学或我们的理智相矛盾,我们必须选择科学和理智。例如,关于《圣经》中上帝创造万物的故事,奥古斯丁认为一切都是上帝同时创造的,而不是七天内创造的。

每个人都应该阅读《忏悔录》,因为它是伟大思想家写的一部激励性的著作。他所努力摆脱的(肉体的诱惑),正是每一个基督教徒,每一个要生存的人要摆脱的;即使不是在宗教生活中,至少是在思想生活(正确战胜错误,正义战胜邪恶,努力找到人类生活的真理)中要摆脱的。但阅读《忏悔录》时,读者们应记住许多我们所认为理所当然的——基督教中、我们的世界观中和宗教与科学的最佳综合中——都来自于此位杰出人物。

Twelve

Muhammad:
The Koran

Who Was Muhammad?

Muhammad (his name is sometimes spelled Mohammed; there are other variants) is the founder and greatest prophet of the Muslim religion, also called Islam, to which he has the same relation as Jesus does to Christianity. There are two important differences between the two men—although Muslims accord all conceivable earthly glory to Muhammad (his name in Arabic means "the praised one") and, though claims are made for his God-like nature, he is not in fact claimed to be divine or the son of Allah (the Muslim God); also, Muhammad was born about 600 years after Christ, and much more is known about the events of his life than we know about the events of the life of Jesus Christ.

He was born about 570 in Mecca and died in 632 in Medina. Both cities are in what we now call Saudi Arabia, and both are the holiest cities of Islam—all Muslims try to make a pilgrimage at least once in their lives to Mecca. Muhammad's family was fairly affluent, successful merchants and traders, and Muhammad, in his 20s and 30s, was a widely-traveled merchant himself. He married one of the clients, and together they had six children; after her death, he married other women and was not monogamous. But Muhammad was also monk-like in some of his habits: during the years that he was a merchant he often retreated to a cave near Mecca for quiet evenings of contemplation. In 610, when he was 40, Muslims believe, he was visited in the cave by the Angel Gabriel. Gabriel commanded him to listen to, then record, the words of Allah—rather as, in the Christian/Jewish tradition, God commands Moses to record the Ten Commandments. A crucial difference is that Moses received the Commandments in one solitary retreat; Muhammad continued the process of recording the words of Allah for 23 years after the first visitation from Gabriel, until the time of his own death.

The Koran

These words of God that Muhammad transcribed later became part of the *Qur'an* (or Koran), the Muslim bible (those parts of the *Qur'an* not written by Muhammad are the work of other Muslim prophets and scribes).

There is a great difference between Judaism and Christianity (the two great religions of the Western world) and Islam (the most prominent religion of the East. By 750, it had emerged as equal in world importance to the two other monotheistic religions). Judaism and Christianity, even though the latter borrows from the former as well as from pagan traditions, both claim to be the one true religion. Muhammad rejected neither of these religions—he regarded such people as Moses and Jesus as great prophets, accepted many of their essential teachings (in 620 he told his followers that he had been on a miraculous journey, had toured Heaven and Hell, and had spoken with earlier prophets such as Abraham. Muslims believe that he ascended to heaven for this experience from the mosque on Temple Mount in Jerusalem, hence the holiness of Jerusalem to Muslims as well as to

穆罕默德
《古兰经》

穆罕默德

　　穆罕默德是穆斯林教(也叫伊斯兰教)的创始人和伟大预言家,他与穆斯林的关系相当于耶稣与基督教的关系。但他们有两大不同之处:尽管穆斯林把所有可以想象的尘世荣耀都归于穆罕默德(他的名字在阿拉伯语中的意思是"被称赞的人"),尽管人们声称他是神一般的人物,实际上他不是神,也不是安拉(穆斯林所信奉的神)的儿子;穆罕默德出生于基督之后600年,关于他的生平事迹,我们知道的远多于耶稣基督。

　　他于大约570年出生在麦加,于632年在麦地那去世。这两个城市都在我们今天的沙特阿拉伯,也都是伊斯兰的圣城,穆斯林们都尽量在有生之年至少去麦加朝圣一次。穆罕默德的家庭非常富裕,是成功的商人;他自己在二三十岁时也是个到处游历的商人。他同他的一个顾客结婚并生有六个孩子;他的妻子去世后,他又同其他女人们结婚,不是一夫一妻。但穆罕默德的有些习惯又像个和尚:在他是商人的时候,他经常隐居在麦加附近的山洞,在寂静的夜晚沉思。1610年,他40岁时,穆斯林认为,他在山洞里受到了安吉尔·哲布勒伊来的拜访。哲布勒伊来命令他听并记下安拉的话,就像基督教或犹太教中上帝命令摩西记下十条戒律一样。主要的不同是,摩西是在一次静修时接受戒律的;而穆罕默德是在哲布勒伊来第一次拜访之后23年内一直记录安拉的话,直至他去世。

《古兰经》

　　穆罕默德记下的神的话后来成为《古兰经》的一部分,《古兰经》是穆斯林的圣经(《古兰经》中不是穆罕默德所写的部分是其他穆斯林预言家和抄写者的作品)。

　　犹太教、基督教(西方两大宗教)和伊斯兰教(东方最著名的宗教,至750年,它在世界的重要性与其他两个一神教相同)之间有个很大的不同。犹太教和基督教都声称是一个真正的宗教,尽管后者借鉴了前者和异教徒传统。穆罕默德拒绝这两个宗教,他把诸如摩西和耶稣这样的人看做是伟大的预言家,并接受他们许多重要的学说(620年,他告诉他的追随者,他曾进行过一次奇迹般的旅行,游历了天堂和地狱并同早期预言家谈话,如亚伯拉罕。穆斯林认为他是从耶路撒冷圣殿山上的寺庙升天去旅行,因此耶路撒冷成为穆斯林以及基督教徒和犹太教徒的圣地)。但是,尽管穆罕默德敬仰犹太预言家和耶稣,他声称是上帝派他去补充、完善和升华他们的学说。

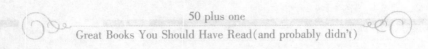
Christians and Jews).But,despite his reverence for the Jewish prophets and for Jesus, Muhammad claimed that he had been sent by God to complete,perfect and refine their teachings.

Islam was born in conditions of strife,rather than in the destruction of its leader. Muhammad,after his first vision of the Angel Gabriel,became (like Jesus) a preacher.Many of the religious and political leaders of Mecca persecuted him and his followers (the traditions of Islam claim that there were various attempts to assassinate Muhammad); they believed that they were trying to uphold an old and stable order of tribal rule and the sanctity of a multiplicity of gods.This persecution continued until the situation for Muhammad and his followers became so dangerous that in 622 he moved his community from Mecca to Medina (that journey is known to Muslims as the "Hijra"),where,with his followers,he formed the first Muslim community.For almost a decade this "state" was attacked by the forces of Mecca,bent on destroying it.Muhammad,with far fewer troops at his disposal,always prevailed in these battles (the battles themselves are regarded as holy in Muslim tradition),and in the end Muhammad and his followers took control of Medina.Other Arabian tribes (from different sectors of that country) began to send ambassadors to Medina,and gradually Arabia united under Muhammad's leadership.After Muhammad's death,Islam spread throughout what we now call the Middle East,and then to India,China and throughout the Far East.

Readers of the *Qur'an*,even those who only sample it,learn that,like Christianity,Islam is both an ethical and humane religion.Much of Muhammad's teachings will seem familiar to Christians or Jews—that the laws of man are superseded by the laws of God,that we are all responsible to God for the conduct of our own lives,that love is the ideal by which we must try to interact with other people.Sometimes we must fight for our religion,but only to defend ourselves and that religion; we must never be attackers,never the ones who instigate strife and war.The *Qur'an* says:"Fight those who fight you."

To conform to Muslim teachings,bin Laden claims to be defending Islam in a holy war—a jihad-against Western aggressors bent on destroying the Islamic world.Whether Muhammad would agree that the West had as its mission the destruction of Islam is an open question.

What is not in question is that Muhammad is one of the great prophets of history,who substituted a humane,monotheistic religion of love and respect for divine law for a pagan system of dog eat dog,and violence begetting violence.His message is as positive,for humans,as that of Jesus.And Christians are not unaccustomed,in the 2,000 years since his death,to corruptions of the teachings of Jesus,particularly the ways in which those words and teachings have been used to justify making war on others with whom the aggressor did not agree.

伊斯兰教是在争斗中而不是在领导者的毁灭中诞生。穆罕默德在第一次见到安吉尔哲布勒伊来后成为传教士(像耶稣一样)。麦加的许多宗教和政治领袖都迫害他及他的追随者(伊斯兰教传说有很多人企图暗杀穆罕默德),因为他们认为穆罕默德及其追随者竭力拥护旧的稳定的部落统治和多神论。这一迫害一直持续,直到622年,形势对于穆罕默德及其追随者极其危险,他把他的社区从麦加搬到麦地那(穆斯林称之为"逃亡")。在麦地那,他同他的追随者一起建立了第一个穆斯林社区。在大约10年的时间里,麦加的军队一直攻击这一"领土",并企图摧毁它。穆罕默德拥有绝对少数的军队,却在战争中占上风(伊斯兰教称这些战争为圣战),最终穆罕默德及其追随者占领了麦地那。其他阿拉伯部落(来自国家的不同地方)开始向麦地那派驻大使,在穆罕默德的领导下阿拉伯逐渐走向统一。穆罕默德去世后,伊斯兰在现在的中东传播,后来传到印度、中国和远东地区。

读过《古兰经》的人,甚至仅仅浏览过的人,就会得知伊斯兰教跟基督教一样是个道德的仁爱的宗教。穆罕默德的学说在基督教徒和犹太教徒看来也是熟悉的:上帝的法则替代人类的法则;我们的生活要对上帝负责;爱是理想,我们必须通过它与他人交往。有时我们必须为宗教而战,但只是捍卫我们自己和宗教;我们永远不能成为进攻者,不能挑起战争和冲突。《古兰经》中说:"同侵犯你的人战斗。"

为了符合穆斯林教义,本·拉登声称是在圣战(护教战争)中捍卫伊斯兰,抵抗致力于毁灭伊斯兰世界的西方侵略者的圣战。至于穆罕默德是否会认为西方把毁灭伊斯兰作为使命,还有待讨论。

毫无疑问的是,穆罕默德是历史上伟大的预言家之一,他用充满爱和对神圣法则尊重的仁爱的一神宗教代替了狗咬狗、暴力引起暴力的异教。他的学说像耶稣的学说一样对人类有积极意义。在耶稣去世2 000年后,基督教徒也不能接受对耶稣学说的歪曲,尤其是利用这些学说来证明侵略别人的战争是正当的。

Thirteen

The Arabian Nights

The Arabian Nights

Like many works of antiquity or the Middle Ages, *The Arabian Nights* (also sometimes called *One Thousand and One Nights*) is a work by multiple authors, a compilation of stories, some of which are realistic, most of which are fantastic.

During the 8th century, Baghdad had become an important trading center for merchants from the Middle East, from Asia, Europe and Africa—and in turn it had become a very cosmopolitan place. During this time many different stories, originally folk stories, what we might today call fairy tales, from the various countries represented in Baghdad, were collected orally over a considerable period of time. A century later they were collected into a single book and translated into Arabic. Many people have been credited with that accomplishment; the person most often mentioned is the famed storyteller Abu abd-Allah Muhammed el-Gahshigar. The framing story—of Queen Scheherazade—probably dates from the 14th century, and in this instance the author is unknown. But the authorship of *The Arabian Nights* has never been so interesting to the world as has the book itself.

The framing device of *The Arabian Nights* is perhaps its most famous story of all. During the Sassanid era a Persian king, Shahryar (who rules a country, an island, "between India and China"), is not necessarily an evil or malevolent person: he is made so by events. He discovers that his wife and her lover are plotting to kill him—his wife is not just faithless, she is also guilty of treason; he has her and her lover executed, and thereafter believes in the universal faithlessness and treachery of women. Shahryar instructs his grand vizier (his most trusted adviser and the greatest administrative official in his kingdom) to find him a new wife every day. After spending the night with the wife, he has her executed. This practice continues for some time (the story never says how long), until the vizier's beautiful but also ingenious daughter Scheherazade devises a scheme to outwit the king and, in doing so, stop the killings. She herself offers to become Shahryar's next wife, and is accepted. Every night, in their marriage chambers, Scheherazade tells Shahryar stories, but she is careful to stop at dawn before ending the story—and she stops with a cliffhanger—the king spares her life, so that, the following night, he may hear the rest of the story. Having finished one story halfway through the evening, she starts another—until, years hence, she has given birth to three of their sons. Convinced of the faithfulness of Scheherazade (a woman he loves, as she loves him), he revokes his decree, at her request pardons her. From malevolence, and through his wife's inspired trickery, he comes to find love. All's well that ends well.

But if this is the most famous story of *The Arabian Nights*, there are others—such as "Ali Baba and the Forty Thieves" or "Sinbad the Sailor"—that are almost as famous. Most of *The Arabian Nights* is a hodge-podge-of love stories and comedies and tragedies and historic legends; also included are even some famous religious myths. Some of the stories involve magic and the supernatural; yet within legendary places and fables there are accounts of those we know to have been real people. But, as there were multiple authors with multiple agendas, there cannot be said to be a discernible theme.

The stories were first brought to the West in the early 18th century when they were

13

《天方夜谭》

《天方夜谭》

像许多古代或中世纪作品一样,《天方夜谭》(有时也叫做《一千零一夜》)是由多个作者编写而成的故事集。其中有些故事是现实的,但大部分都是想象的。

8世纪时,巴格达成为重要的贸易中心,来自中东、亚洲、欧洲和非洲的商人汇集于此,巴格达进而成为国际化的大都市。在此期间,许多来自不同国家的故事,最初是民间故事(我们现在称为神仙故事)汇集在巴格达。相当长一段时间内,人们口头收集这些故事。一个世纪后,这些故事被编成一本书并翻译成阿拉伯语。这一成就归功于很多人,最经常提起的是有名的讲故事者阿布·阿布德·阿拉·穆罕默德·艾尔盖希伽。框架故事,山鲁佐德女王的故事,大概可以追溯到14世纪,所以作者不得而知。但《天方夜谭》的作者远没有书本身有趣。

萨桑王朝时期,波斯国王沙赫尔亚尔(统治着在中国和印度之间的一个岛国)本不是一个邪恶、恶毒的人,是现实让他变得如此。他发现他的妻子及其情人要谋害他,认为他的妻子不只是不忠,而且犯有背叛罪;所以他将她及其情人处死,并认为所有的女人都是不忠的和容易背叛的。沙赫尔亚尔命令他的维齐尔(他最信任的进言人及王国最重要的行政官员)每天给他找一个新妻子。跟每个妻子度过一晚之后,就把她处死。这样持续了一段时间(故事中没说到底持续了多长时间),直到维齐尔漂亮聪明的女儿山鲁佐德想出一个计谋来智胜国王,这才结束了杀戮。她自己主动提出要成为沙赫尔亚尔的妻子并被接受。每天夜里,在他们的婚房中,山鲁佐德给沙赫尔亚尔讲故事,但她小心地在黎明时,或是在故事结束前停下来,或是在讲到扣人心弦的地方停下来。国王没有处死她,以便在下一个夜里可以听到剩下的故事。在半夜里讲完一个故事,她又继续讲另一个故事,直到几年后她生下了3个儿子。他相信了山鲁佐德(他所爱的女人,她也爱他)的忠实,并在她的请求下取消了法令,赦免了她。通过她妻子具有启发的计谋,他由敌意开始找到了爱。结果好就是一切好。

但如果这是《天方夜谭》中最著名的故事,其他的故事也同样著名,如"阿里巴巴和四十大盗"和"水手辛巴德"。《天方夜谭》是个大杂烩,有爱情故事、喜剧、悲剧和历史传奇,还有一些著名的宗教神话。有些故事中有魔法和超自然现象,然而在传奇的地点和故事中所讲述的有些人物也是现实中的。但是,许多不同的作者都有不同的意图,很难说本书有一个清晰的主题。

这些故事是在18世纪早期以法语译本出版时传到西方的;第一个英语版本是在19世

published in a French translation.The first substantial version in English was published in the late 19th century.It has become one of the world's most popular literary works.

What is its significance? If by a significant book we mean one that changed the world, changed the way at least some people think and feel,then it must be said that *The Arabian Nights* has virtually no significance whatsoever.But to say so is to lose sight of a more subtle distinction.The stories have inspired countless movies and TV specials; they have even inspired some composers of music.Movies based on *The Arabian Nights* will be released in 2006 and 2007.The gifted playwright and director Mary Zimmerman has presented her own staged version of many of the stories,and her play has been popular throughout the country.

Perhaps the more interesting question to ask is why *The Arabian Nights* endures and why it continues to inspire those who make our movies and television programs,compose our music,and write our plays.

For some reason,most people like stories of the exotic,the legendary,the supernatural. But there have been many such stories in the history of the world,and only a handful endure (the stories of Homer would be a good example).Something about the stories of *The Arabian Nights* attracts people to them.The psychologist Jung might have said that they touch on our collective memories as humans,the myths about human behavior that,over the centuries,we have come to accept.

Whatever the reason,*The Arabian Nights*,written centuries ago in lands most of us do not know,continue to intrigue and delight modern readers—and reading them can provoke the reader to ask the same kind of questions:what here touches on what is universal in all of our experience?

纪末出版。它已成为世界最著名的文学名著之一。

它的重要性在哪儿呢？如果我们说一本重要的书就是一本改变世界或至少改变人们思维方式的书，那么《天方夜谭》实际上就没有重要性可言了。但如果这样说就忽视了一个更细微的重要之处。这些故事促成了无数部电影和电视特别节目；甚至还启发了一些作曲家。基于《天方夜谭》的电影将在2006和2007年上映。天才剧作家和导演玛丽·齐默曼已经把许多故事搬上戏剧舞台，她的剧作在全国备受欢迎。

或许更有趣的问题是，为什么《天方夜谭》可以永垂不朽；为什么它可以启发那些制作电影和电视节目、作曲和写剧本的人们？

大概是因为多数人都喜欢具有异国情调、传奇色彩和超自然现象的故事。但世界历史上这样故事很多，却只有几部是永垂不朽的(荷马写的故事就是一个很好的例子)。《天方夜谭》故事中的某些东西吸引着人们。心理学家荣格曾说过，它们触及了人类共同的回忆；讲述了有关人类行为的神话，我们经历了几个世纪才得以领悟的行为。

不管是什么原因，《天方夜谭》这部写于几个世纪前我们大多数人所不知道地方的书仍然启发和愉悦着现代读者；并且读这些故事会激发读者问同样的问题：这里所谈及的，哪些是在我们生活中普遍存在的？

$\mathcal{F}ourteen$

Muraski Shikibu:
The Tale of Genji

Who Was Murasaki Shikibu?

It should be very unlikely that Murasaki Shikibu—she is sometimes called Lady Murasaki by her modern admirers—would be remembered by the world today.She lived in the 10th and 11th centuries (around 974 to around 1014 or 1025) in the imperial court of Japan during what is now called the Heian Period.Her father was an official of that court,and she was,therefore,a Japanese aristocrat.Because her mother had died young (it was the custom of the time for children to be raised by their mother; married couples lived separately), Murasaki was raised by her father.It was obvious to her father that she was very intelligent; so he gave her an education considered at the time more appropriate for a man than for a woman.She,too,when she was no longer a child,was also a servant of the court:she served as a lady-in-waiting to the Empress.

What saves Murasaki from obscurity-from disappearing into the mists of history-is that she was also a notable novelist and poet.Although much of her verse still exists ("The Murasaki Shikibu Collection," published after her death,is a collection of 128 of her poems),it is her novel,*The Tale of Genji*,that has brought her immortality.Everyone acknowledges that it is the first novel of which we know that was written by a woman.Some critics go further,discounting the claims of Homer and other Greeks and Romans,as well as those who wrote prose narratives during the early Middle Ages,and say that *The Tale of Genji* is very likely the first modern novel.It is,the first book that is recognizably what modern readers would call a novel.Quite an accomplishment for an obscure female servant of the Japanese court who lived three centuries before Chaucer!

The Tale of Genji

The tradition is that the Lady Murasaki wrote *The Tale of Genji*,and her poems,for other ladies of the aristocracy-to amuse them,to give them a diversion in what was otherwise a rather sedentary life.Then,as now,women were thought to like love stories,and the novel is the story of the aristocratic Genji,his life and (most of all) his loves.Some literary commentators have noted that *The Tale of Genji* has no plot,that the story covers Genji and his life,as well it tells us what happens to his descendants after his death,but the events unfold not so much through a series of plot devices (there are no cliff-hangers in Genji) but rather as a sequence of events that happen because the characters are growing older, moving through life.But to a contemporary reader,this method seems very modernist-the great novel of Proust,Remembrance of Things Past,and those of the novelists he influenced, are not very different.We follow characters as they live their lives; they don't really move from one plot contrivance to the next.That is the method of second-rate modern fiction-not the greatest works of our greatest novelists.

Despite the fact that she was writing in a kind of void (as far as we know,there were no predecessor novels to guide her),Murasaki maintains remarkable consistency.Even

14

紫式部
《源氏物语》

紫式部

当今世界还能记着紫式部(她的现代崇拜者有时称她为紫式部女士)本应是很不可能的。她生活在10世纪至11世纪(974~1014/1025年)平安时期的日本皇宫内。她的父亲是朝廷官员,因而她就是一名日本贵族。紫式部的母亲很早就去世了(那个时候的传统是,已婚夫妻要分开生活,孩子由母亲抚养),所以她由父亲抚养长大。她的父亲发现她非常聪明,让她接受了在当时看来更适合于男人的教育。长大后,她也是朝廷的一名官员:皇后的一名女官。

使紫式部不再默默无闻,免于消失在历史的迷雾中的是,她还是一个著名的小说家和诗人。尽管她的很多诗还存在(《紫式部集》,收集了她的128诗,在她去世后出版),但让她不朽的是她的小说《源氏物语》。大家都承认这是第一部由女作家写的小说。有些评论家甚至无视荷马和其他希腊罗马作家以及中世纪早期散文记叙文作家,说《源氏物语》很可能是第一部现代小说。它是第一本被现代读者称为小说的书。对于早于乔叟3个世纪,日本宫廷一个默默无闻的女官来说,这是多么伟大的成就。

《源氏物语》

据说,紫式部女士的《源氏物语》和诗是为其他女贵族们而写的,为了供她们消遣,为了让她们看到她们沉寂生活以外的世界。同现在一样,当时女人们都喜欢看爱情故事,所以小说《源氏物语》讲述的是贵族源氏的生活及其爱情故事。一些文学评论家认为《源氏物语》没有情节;故事讲述了源氏的生活及他死后他的后代的情况,但事件不是通过一系列的情节手法展现的,而一系列事件的发生只是因为人物在成长,在变老。但对当代读者来说,这一手法是现代主义的手法。普鲁斯特的著名小说《追忆逝水年华》以及受他影响的小说家们的小说都属于这一类。故事是按照人物的生活经历展开的,而不是从一个阴谋情节发展到另一个。这是二流现代小说的写作方式,不是伟大小说家的伟大作品。

尽管紫式部的写作是在空白中进行的(据我们所知,没有先辈的小说指导她),但她惊人地保持了作品的整体统一性。尽管小说中有400多个人物,她主要描写源氏及次主要

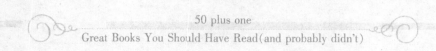
though there are more than 400 characters in her novel,she focuses on Genji,on her subsidiary major characters,and they are recognizably the same people throughout the novel.Even though,as was traditional in polite society of the time,characters are rarely named,are known only by their professions,their position in society.

Genji is a son of the Japanese emperor,and *The Tale of Genji* is the story of how he ascends to the greatest honor in the land.He never becomes the emperor himself,but the emperor knows that he is the illegitimate son of Genji and the great love of his life,Lady Fujitsubo-Genji's stepmother who secretly becomes his mistress-a woman he continues to love throughout his life,despite his adventures with other women.His son,the emperor,at what might be called the dramatic conclusion of the novel,raises Genji's rank to the highest possible in the court of Japan.

The Tale of Genji is still regarded by the Japanese as the greatest novel of their culture,and,though Murasaki's language is difficult (Heian Japanese is exalted,classical and grammatically complex),therefore difficult to translate into other languages,the novel does exist in notable English and other language translations.In its translations into various languages,both Eastern and Western,it continues to fascinate the world.Not just for its interesting story—which is epic-like in its breadth.It fascinates us,too,for its glimpse into a feudal world that most of us can barely comprehend; the potency of that long-ago world is increased,not diminished,by its being set in the Japanese Imperial Court,by its concentration on the ruling class of its time.This world is as "foreign" as anything could be to the modern reader.And,yet the novel grips us—we care what happens to Genji and to his compatriots.

The secret of *The Tale of Genji* continued hold on modern readers is almost certainly traceable to Lady Murasaki's genius in conveying the psychological truth of her characters and of their actions.Her story is compelling because we recognize personality traits in her characters not that different from our own—even though they are men and women of the 11th century,living in a world most of us can't even begin to imagine.They seem to be like us,and,in saying that,we recognize that we are in the hands of a master.The novel,first and foremost,is the art form in which we examine not so much the adventures of human beings,or the events,real or imagined,of their lives-as it is the form in which the greatest novelists show us man's reactions,what he learns or fails to learn from those life adventures and events.The novel,we might say,is the form in which we trace the ways in which man develops his consciousness of the world and of himself.

In this kind of artistic effort,Lady Mursaki may be said to be our first novelist of the consciousness and,by any measure,one of the greatest.Any reader should have sampled her work to understand what other definers of the human soul have had as their example of the supreme mastery of their craft.

人物;这些人物在小说中都是同一类人。根据当时社会的礼貌传统,小说中人物很少有姓名,只是以他们的职业和在社会的地位来称呼。

源氏是日本皇帝的儿子;《源氏物语》讲述他如何获得最高荣誉。他自己从来没成为皇帝,但皇帝知道自己是源氏和其一生最爱藤壶的私生子。藤壶是源氏的继母,却秘密地成为他的情人。尽管源氏后来又与其他女人在一起,但他一生一直爱着藤壶。他的儿子,皇帝,使他在日本宫廷的地位达到了他所能达到的最高位置。这可谓是戏剧性的结局。

日本人仍然认为《源氏物语》是日本最伟大的小说。尽管紫式部的语言比较难懂(平安时代的日语比较高雅、古典,而且语法复杂),难以翻译成其他语言;但小说还是翻译成了英语及其他语言。在被翻译成其他语言(东方和西方语言)的过程中,它继续吸引着整个世界。吸引我们的不只是它史诗般的有趣故事;它还可以让我们认识一下我们多数人几乎不能理解的封建社会。小说以日本皇宫为背景,着重描写当时的统治阶级;这使得那一遥远世界的势力增强了,而不是减弱了。这一世界对现代读者来说可能是非常陌生的。然而,小说吸引着我们,我们想知道源氏及其同胞们到底发生了什么。

《源氏物语》仍吸引现代读者的奥秘是紫式部善于表达人物及其行为的真实心理。她的故事引人入胜是因为我们发现故事中人物的性格特点与我们差别不大;尽管他们生活在11世纪,生活在我们多数人难以想象的世界。他们似乎很像我们;这就是说,我们认识到我们是受统治者控制的。首先,小说这一艺术形式更多的是伟大小说家们向我们展示人类的各种反应,从生活历程及事件中学到的和没学到的;而不只是供我们欣赏人类的生活历程及事件(真实的或虚构的)。我们可以说,通过小说这一艺术形式,我们追寻人类对世界及自身的觉悟过程。

从这一艺术成就来说,紫式部可以说是一个觉悟小说家,并且也是最伟大的之一。每个读者都应品读她的作品,以了解其他人类灵魂界定者们如何把握他们的作品。

Fifteen

Turold:
The Song of Roland

The Song of Roland

The Song of Roland (in French:La Chanson de Roland-song/chanson in the sense of ballad; it is likely that,originally,it was composed to be sung) is a French epic poem (it dates from about 1050) that was probably written by someone called Turold.His name is mentioned in the last line of the poem,though it could well be that Turold is simply the person who brought together a host of variants on the Roland story.It is the first great work of French literature and is universally regarded as the greatest "chanson de geste," one of a series of epic poems that helped to create the legend of Charlemagne during the period that we now call the Late Middle Ages.

These works commemorate Charlemagne's life many centuries after that life,and the various poems,though largely fictional,do contain a basic core of historic truth.In this way, they are like the British stories of King Arthur—except that Arthur lived earlier than Charlemagne,and the most famous work about Arthur was written 3 centuries after Turold compiled *The Song of Roland*.

There is one other,even more crucial,difference.Scholars are divided about whether or not King Arthur actually lived—or whether he was a war lord who was elevated,in myth,to kingly stature-or whether he is a composite who,in legend,became one person,a necessary hero to the British nation,which required some sense of itself as a distinct people with a glorious past.

Charlemagne may serve the same function for the French and Germans,the peoples of Central Europe,but no such controversy exists about whether or not Charlemagne actually existed.He did exist.He lived from 742 to 814.He was King of the Franks from 768 until his death,King of the Lombards from 774 until his death,and in 800 he was appointed (by Pope Leo) the first Holy Roman Emperor.Charlemagne,assisted by his grandfather and father before him,conquered most of Western Europe; his family established the first great and stable kingdom after the Fall of the Western Roman Empire.Charlemagne is an authentic hero,the greatest figure of what we sometimes call the Dark Ages and at other times call the Early Middle Ages.Because he was so notable an historic figure,legends about him continued to develop centuries after his death.

The Song of Roland tells an interesting story.Much as The Iliad deals with an historic (though perhaps mythical) battle in Greek history,so *The Song of Roland* deals with a battle in French history—the Battle of Roncesvalles (Roncevaux) in 778,which was really an insignificant encounter between the French and the Basques-Turold makes it an earth-shattering event.Charlemagne and his army have been fighting in Spain for 7 years; they have conquered all of Spain except for Saragossa.Roland,one of the 12 senior knights of the court,and Charlemagne's nephew,proposes that Charlemagne send his stepfather, Ganelon,to negotiate peace terms.Incensed that Roland has proposed him for what is actually a very dangerous task (previous ambassadors have been murdered by the Saracens)

15

杜洛杜斯
《罗兰之歌》

《罗兰之歌》

　　《罗兰之歌》(民歌,可能最初是用来吟唱的)是一部法国叙事史诗(可以追溯到大约1050年),可能是一个叫做杜洛杜斯的人所写。诗的最后一行提到这个名字,当然杜洛杜斯可能仅仅是把各种罗兰故事汇编在一起。《罗兰之歌》是法国文学中第一部伟大作品,并被公认为是最伟大的"纪功歌",讲述了中世纪晚期查理曼的传奇故事。关于查理曼传奇故事的史诗还有很多,《罗兰之歌》是其中一部。

　　查理曼去世许多世纪后,这些作品讲述了他的事迹以纪念他。尽管这些诗大都是虚构的,但其中也的确有一定的历史真实性。在这方面,它们很像英国亚瑟王的故事;除了亚瑟生活在早于查理曼的时代,而关于亚瑟的最著名作品却写于杜洛杜斯编写《罗兰之歌》的3个世纪之后。

　　还有另外一个更为重要的不同。亚瑟王是否的确存在;他是否像传说中说的那样,曾是军团的首领,后来成为国王;他是否是多个人物的综合体,而在传奇中被认为是一个人,是英国这个自认为有着光荣过去的优秀民族所必须的英雄;学者们对此有着不同的看法。

　　对于法国人和德国人,中欧的各民族,查理曼起着同样的作用;但关于查理曼是否确实存在并无异议。他确实存在,生活在742年至814年间。他768年起成为法兰克国王,774年起成为伦巴第国王,直至他去世。800年他被(教皇利奥)加冕为第一个神圣罗马帝王。

　　在祖父和父亲的帮助下,查理曼征服了西欧的大部分地区;西罗马帝国灭亡之后,他的家族建立了第一个稳定的伟大王国。查理曼是真实存在的英雄,我们所称为黑暗时代或有时候称为中世纪早期的伟大人物。他是一个如此著名的历史人物,所以在他去世许多世纪后,仍有关于他的传奇故事。

　　《罗兰之歌》讲述了一个有趣的故事。就像《伊利亚特》讲述了希腊历史上的一个有历史意义的战争(当然也可能是神话),《罗兰之歌》讲述的是法国历史上的一个战争,发生在778年的龙塞斯瓦列斯战役。这个战争是法国人与巴斯克人之间不太重要的冲突,杜洛杜斯却使它成为震撼世界的事件。查理曼和他的军队在西班牙征战7年之久,他们占领了除了萨拉戈萨以外的整个西班牙。王宫中12圣骑士之一,查理曼的侄子罗兰建议查理曼派他的继父冈隆去讲和。冈隆得知罗兰推荐他去完成这一实际上非常危险的任务(先前的大使们都被撒拉森人谋杀了),他非常生气,并谋划杀害他的继子。查理曼的军队穿越比利牛斯山脉时,军队的后卫队(罗兰及其他圣骑士)被大量撒拉森人的军队包围。罗兰

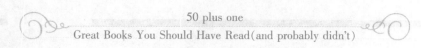
Ganelon plots his stepson's destruction.As Charlemagne's army crosses the Pyrenees,the rear guard of that army (which includes Roland and his fellow senior knights) is surrounded by a huge and overwhelming Saracen force.Roland is the commander of this rear guard,and he fights nobly and heroically,even as he is certain to be defeated.His motivation is that he lives according to a code of honor,that he cannot admit defeat even in the face of overwhelming odds-and he can revel in the glory of his future renown—and in doing so he refuses the advice of his best friend Oliver (another of the 12 senior knights) to call Charlemagne to his aid.As a result of Ganelon's conniving,the rear guard is essentially decimated,and Roland and his comrades die.Charlemagne avenges his men.When he returns to France,he breaks the news to Roland's fiancée,Aude,Oliver's sister,and she dies of grief and shock.*The Song of Roland* ends with the execution of Ganelon for his treason.

A rollicking good story to be sure,and it is told in a clear and direct style that engages the reader.Besides well-rendered scenes of conflict,it involves compelling stories of betrayal (Ganelon and Roland) and stories of friendship (Roland and Oliver) and of love (Roland and Aude).But these are not the only reasons to read *The Song of Roland*.More than any other work from the continent of Europe during the Middle Ages,it gives us the basic tenets of chivalry that was to flower in the centuries after its composition.The world,we are shown,is corrupt; there is selfishness everywhere; betrayal of one human being by another is commonplace—yet there are those who,like Charlemagne and his knights,behave with honor and honesty,who attempt to love,who strive for a perfection of behavior-who try to be true servants of Christ.As being such a servant often involves battles and bloodshed,and as the men (and their women) are knights and servants of God's appointed master on earth, the king.Some modern readers will have difficulty reconciling the kind of morality involved with their own lives.One must accept the battles and bloodshed as givens of the time-just as they are givens of the time in which we live.

Readers coming to The Song of Roland for the first time are likely to be entranced by its story-just as all of us are captivated by the legends of Arthur.But within the grandeur and nobility of the story,there is a kind of longing,and striving,to live life well.The Song of Roland was enormously popular from the time of its writing until the 14th century—a space of 200 years; and,since then,it has endured.Readers should remember that this book,The da Vinci Code of its day,is most of all interesting for the ways in which it shows different men learning the appropriate ways for a man to live—it implicitly asks:What are appropriate actions and attitudes and beliefs? As so many of these questions survive to the present day,it is instructive for any reader to learn the ways in which they were asked nearly a millennium ago and what the world of chivalry actually involved.

是后卫队的将军,即使在注定要战败的时候,他还是英勇战斗。他的动力是,他崇尚名节,甚至在强大的困境中他也不能承认失败;他可以尽享将来的荣誉。因此,他的好朋友奥利弗(12圣骑士之一)建议他向查理曼求助时,他拒绝了。由于冈隆的谋害,后卫队被基本歼灭,罗兰及他的战友们都牺牲了。查理曼为他的战士们报仇雪恨。查理曼回到法国,把这个消息告诉罗兰的未婚妻奥德(奥利弗的妹妹),她在悲伤和打击中死去。最后冈隆以背叛罪被处死,《罗兰之歌》就此结束。

　　这的确是一个有趣的故事,而且叙述方式清楚直接,吸引着读者。除了叙述良好的冲突场景,还有吸引人的有关背叛(冈隆和罗兰)、友情(罗兰和奥利弗)和爱情(罗兰和奥德)的故事。但这些都不是要阅读《罗兰之歌》的唯一原因。与中世纪欧洲大陆的其他作品不同,它告诉我们了骑士精神的基本信条,这些信条在之后的许多世纪一直盛行。展现在我们面前的世界是腐化的:到处充斥着自私,人与人之间的背叛也是家常便饭。然而也有像查理曼及他的骑士们那样崇尚名节和诚实的人,热爱和为善良的人服务的人,追求行为完美的人。作为这样一个仆人通常会遇到战争和流血冲突,并且这些人是骑士和上帝任命的统治者——国王的仆人们,因此现代的读者很难使他们的这种道德符合他们自己的生活。我们必须认为战争和流血冲突是当时的正常现象,就像也是我们这个时代的正常现象一样。

　　首次阅读《罗兰之歌》的读者很可能沉浸在它的故事情节中,就像我们被亚瑟王的传奇故事所吸引。但在故事的宏伟与高贵之中,会渴望和追求美好生活。《罗兰之歌》从写成至14世纪(跨越200年)一直深受欢迎,并从此永垂不朽。读者应该记住这本书——当时的达·芬奇密码——最有趣的是,它展示了不同人是怎样寻求正确生活方式的。它间接地提出了这样的问题:什么样的行为、态度和信仰才是正确的?许多此类问题至今仍然存在,所以对于读者们了解大约1 000年前提出的问题以及骑士世界到底是什么样的是很有帮助的。

Sixteen

St. Thomas Aquinas: Summa Theologica

Who Was St. Thomas Aquinas?

St. Thomas Aquinas (1225-1274) was a prominent churchman of the 13th century, and he lived the typical life of such a figure—except in some very important respects: his parents were Italian aristocrats, and his uncle was abbot of the Benedictine monastery at Monte Cassino; he had very auspicious beginnings. The only conflict of his early life was that, while studying at the University of Naples, he was drawn to, then completely attracted to, the new order of the Dominicans, and engaged in a rather serious fight with his family about his decision to become a Dominican monk (he was held captive in one of his family's castles—to make him see reason; it was his family's expectation that he would one day succeed his uncle as abbot at Monte Cassino).

Once Aquinas had began life as a Dominican, when he was 17, he went on to an illustrious career. His superiors realized that he showed unusual promise as a theologian, and they sent him to Cologne to study with Albertus Magnus, the great theologian/philosopher of the time. For several years he stayed with Albertus, both as student and then as acolyte. Aquinas was designated a Doctor of Theology in 1256, and from then until his death in 1274 he never stopped working. He traveled throughout Western Europe teaching and lecturing; he also traveled constantly on the business of his Order, to which he became increasingly valuable. Despite all of this activity, Aquinas still found time to write, and, given his learning and his reputation, he was often consulted about affairs of state and matters of theology by the reigning powers of the Church, including the Pope himself.

Summa Theologica

During his lifetime St. Thomas Aquinas was considered a great philosopher as well as a great theologian. He worked on his best-known work, *Summa Theologica*, during the period 1266-1273, leaving it unfinished at the time of his death. He claimed to have had a mystical vision in late 1273. He said of it, "I cannot go on…All that I have written seems to me like so much straw compared to what I have seen and what has been revealed to me." Despite his learning and accomplishments, Aquinas remained a model of Christian humility.

If anything his fame became even greater after his death. His fellow theologians elevated him to a position within the historic Church comparable to that of Paul and Augustine; he was canonized in 1323. At the Council of Trent (1545-63), *Summa Theologica* was put on the altar next to the Bible; in 1567, Pope Pius V compared him in importance to the four great Latin fathers of the Church; and in 1880, Aquinas was declared patron of all Roman Catholic educational institutions. No one doubts his renown as a theologian; some people might even say that he is the greatest theologian the Roman Catholic Church has ever produced.

But, Aquinas lived in the 13th century—even Roman Catholics might ask what relevance he has to us today. And, Protestants are even more likely to ask such a question.

16

圣·托马斯·阿奎那
《神学大全》

圣·托马斯·阿奎那

　　圣·托马斯·阿奎那(1225～1274)是13世纪著名的教士。他过着教士特有的生活,某些重要的方面除外:他的父母是意大利贵族,他的叔叔是蒙特卡西诺峰的本笃会修道院院长。他年轻时非常顺利,遇到的唯一一次争论是:在那不勒斯大学学习时,他接触到了多明我会的新教义,而后完全被之吸引并与他的家人展开了激烈的斗争,决定成为多明我会修道士(他被关在他家的一个城堡里,让他找回理智。他的家人期望他将来继承他叔叔成为蒙特卡西诺峰的修道院院长)。

　　阿奎那17岁时开始成为多明我会修道士,从此就开始了他光辉的职业生涯。他的指导者们发现他具有成为神学家非同寻常的资质,他们派他到科隆拜当时伟大的神学家、哲学家阿尔伯图斯·马格努斯为师学习。他与阿尔伯图斯一起的几年里,既是学生后来又是侍僧。1256年他被任命为神学家,从此直至他于1274年去世,他从未停止工作。他走遍整个西欧,教导人们;他还不停地因修道会的事务而外出,进而他对修道会越来越重要。尽管阿奎那要进行各种活动,他仍然抽出时间来写作。由于他的学识及名望,教会的掌权者们,包括教皇,经常向他请教国家事务及神学问题。

《神学大全》

　　圣·托马斯·阿奎那在世时被认为是伟大的哲学家和神学家。他的伟大著作《神学大全》写于1266～1273年,去世时并未完成。他声称1273年底有过人神灵交的幻觉。他说:"我不能继续……与我所看到的和所领会的相比,我所写的一切在我看来似乎像是稻草一样。"尽管阿奎那学识渊博、成就巨大,他仍是基督教谦逊的模范。

　　他在去世后更具威望。神学家们称赞他的教会是有历史意义的教会,可以与保罗和奥古斯丁的教会相媲美。他于1323年被载入圣者名册。在特伦托议会,《神学大全》紧挨着《圣经》被放在祭坛上;1567年,教皇庇护五世把其重要性与教会四大拉丁神父相提并论;1880年,阿奎那被宣布为所有罗马天主教教育机构的圣职授予人。对于他是著名的神学家,没有人有所疑问;有些人甚至说他是罗马天主教最伟大的神学家。

　　但是,阿奎那生活在13世纪;就连罗马天主教也会问他和今天的我们有什么关联。新教徒更有可能会问这个问题。

Perhaps too much is made in our time of the differences between Catholics and Protestants.At the time that Aquinas lived there was only one Church,the one that he served so brilliantly.And the "protest" of Martin Luther (who lived almost 3 centuries later) had much to do with what Luther saw as the corruption of the Church.More important for us,Luther regarded certain Catholic beliefs,particularly those involved in various of the sacraments,as too mystical.Luther believed that the individual must come to some truths on his own,not always follow the dictates of a priesthood he did not believe had been ordained by God.But the core beliefs themselves were not challenged—the essentials of Christianity are the same in either church.For example,in the mass,during communion,Catholics believe that their priest achieves mystical union with Christ; Protestants believe only that they are remembering Christ at the Last Supper.But both kinds of Christian churches regard that sacrament,whatever actually happens in its practice,as crucial to their faith.Aquinas's skill,in defining the core tenets of Christianity,is relevant to any kind of Christian.

Aquinas did not write the Summa for his fellow theologians and philosophers.He set out to write a manual—what we would today call a textbook-of the main theological teachings of his time; he attempted to give the reasons for all components of the Christian faith.Because,by any measure,he was a genius,he did not just offer the accepted wisdom but refined and reworked it to such a degree that his explanations exist as if for the first time.It can truly be said that he sums up Christianity—and does it so brilliantly that his words resonate with us even at the present time.The Summa is in three parts:1) The Nature of God and the Universe That He Created; 2) Human Activity and Ethics; and 3) Christ and the Sacraments.

In presenting his explanations and definitions,Aquinas also attempts to encompass the philosophy of the Greeks.He lived at a time when the scholarly world was beginning to discover such philosophers from the past as Aristotle.Aquinas believed that knowledge of God was through revelation—God's revealing of Himself to an individual when that individual is in a state of grace—that is,has practiced right behavior pleasing to God.But, bringing in Aristotle,he believed that grace (the moving by man toward God) can happen as a result of an examination of God's created order.The Christian says:Certain aspects of God can be revealed to us only by the Bible.the Aristotelian says:The "condition" of God's creation is revealed to us only by study of that creation.Aquinas attempts to reconcile these two views,and,in this,he is the great synthesizer-and his synthesis survives to the present day.

Anyone,whether Christian or not,who wishes to understand Christianity—one of the world's great religions,perhaps its most influential religion—must read the Summa,to understand the remarkable description of Christianity,an amalgam of the classical and medieval world views,that Aquinas created.

　　或许我们今天太多地强调天主教与新教的不同。阿奎那生活的时代只有一个教会，他服务于这一教会并且成就卓越。马丁·路德(生活在大约3个世纪后)之所以"抗议"是因为他看到了教会的腐败。对于我们来说更重要的是，路德认为某些天主教信仰，尤其是有关各种圣礼的信仰，太神秘。路德认为，个人应该自己发现真理；而并非总是听从上帝所任命的他所不信任的牧师的支配。但主要的信仰并没有受到挑战，基督教的本质在两个教会中是一样的。例如，做弥撒时，圣餐中，天主教认为牧师可以与基督进行人神灵交；新教徒认为只有在最后的晚餐时为基督祈祷的人们才能与之进行人神灵交。但两个基督教会都认为圣礼是他们重要的信仰，不管圣礼实际上是如何进行的。阿奎那解释了基督教的核心信条，这与任何一种基督教都是有关的。

　　阿奎那写《神学大全》不是给神学家和哲学家们看的。他是要写一本有关当时主要神学学说的手册，我们今天称为教科书；他试图解释基督教的所有信仰。他是个天才，不仅仅阐述了已经被人们所接受的智慧，还对此进行升华和重新解释，似乎他的这种解释是第一次出现。的确可以说，他对基督教进行了总结，他的总结如此精彩至今仍回响在我们耳边。《神学大全》分3个部分：1)上帝的本质及其所创造的宇宙；2)人类活动和道德；3)基督和圣餐。

　　在陈述他的解释和定义的时候，阿奎那还试图阐述希腊哲学。他所生活的时代，当时学术界正开始从过去发现诸如亚里士多德之类的哲学家。阿奎那认为通过默示才能了解上帝，个人的德行——令上帝高兴的正确行为才能使上帝将自己默示给个人。但引入亚里士多德，他认为通过检验上帝所创造的法则可以达到德行(人类向上帝靠近的行动)。天主教徒说：上帝的某些方面只有通过《圣经》才能默示给我们。亚里士多德学派说：上帝造物的"条件"只有研究了之后才能默示给我们。阿奎那试图调和这两种观点，所以他是个伟大的综合者。他的综合至今仍然存在。

　　不管是不是基督教徒，任何想了解基督教(世界伟大宗教之一，也可能是最具影响力的宗教)的人都必须阅读《神学大全》，以了解阿奎那对基督教的精彩描述，古典教派和中世纪观点的综合。

Seventeen

Marco Polo:
The Adventures of Marco Polo

Who Was Marco Polo?

Marco Polo (1254-1324) was a Venetian trader and explorer who was one of the first Westerners to travel the Silk Road to China or, as he called it, Cathay. He wrote a book, *The Travels of Marco Polo (Il Milione)* describing his travels, which offered Europeans some of their earliest information about Cathay.

Born in Venice into a family of merchants and traders, Marco Polo accompanied his father, Nicolò, and his uncle, Maffeo, on their second trading mission to eastern Asia. Earlier, before Marco's birth, the two brothers had traveled to Asia where they had met the Mongol ruler, Kublai Khan, in China. The Khan invited them to return; they prepared for another expedition that included Marco, then 17 years old. The trio set out across the deserts and mountains of Asia, and after more than three years they reached Kublai Khan's summer palace in Shangdu.

For almost 20 years the Polos, Marco in particular, served the Khan as diplomats and aides. Eventually, they started worrying about returning home safely—the Khan was aging, and if he died, the Polos were afraid that his enemies might capture them. The Khan finally agreed to their leaving in 1292, provided they escorted a Chinese princess who was to marry a Persian king.

Their return trip began on a ship from China to Singapore; they went north of Sumatra, around the southern tip of India, and across the Arabian Sea and the Gulf of Oman. The Polos left the wedding party and traveled overland to a port on the Black Sea from which they sailed to Istanbul and then traveled on to Venice.

Upon their arrival home in 1295, Marco joined the Venetian Army in its fight against Genoa. In 1298 he was captured and imprisoned in Genoa. During his 2 years in custody, Marco dictated his accounts of his travels to a fellow inmate, Rustichello of Pisa, who translated the book into Old French, the literary language of the time in Italy, and entitled it Le divisament du monde (The Description of the World). Later the book was translated into other languages, including an English edition, *The Travels of Marco Polo*; it was distributed throughout Europe. The book enjoyed instant popularity.

In January of 1324, Marco Polo died and was buried in the Church of San Lorenzo.

The Travels of Marco Polo

Marco Polo's account of his travels to Cathay and throughout Asia is divided into four books: Book One describes the Middle Eastern and Central Asian lands through which the Polos traveled on their way to China; Book Two depicts China and the court of Kublai Khan; Book Three provides secondhand accounts of some of the Far Eastern coastal regions, including Japan, India, Sri Lanka, Southeast Asia, and the east coast of Africa; and Book Four recounts wars among the Mongols and describes some of the far northern

马可·波罗
《马可·波罗游记》

马可·波罗

马可·波罗(1254~1324)是威尼斯商人和探险家,是早期通过丝绸之路到达中国的西方人之一。他写了一本书,叫做《马可·波罗游记》,讲述了他的旅行经历。该书使欧洲人对中国有了最初的了解。

马可·波罗出生在威尼斯一个商人家庭,他曾同他的父亲尼科洛及叔叔马泰奥一起到东亚完成第二次贸易任务。马可出生之前,他的两个哥哥也到过亚洲,他们在中国见到了蒙古的统治者忽必烈可汗。可汗邀请他们再次来蒙古,所以他们就准备了另一次远行。马可加入了这一次远行,当时他17岁。他们三人穿越亚洲的沙漠和山脉,经过3年多的时间最终到达忽必烈可汗在上都的宫殿。

波罗氏,特别是马可,一直作为外交家和助手服务于可汗达20年之久。后来,随着可汗逐渐变老,他们开始担心是否能够安全地回国。波罗氏担心如果可汗去世,他们的敌人可能会将他们抓起来。1292年,可汗最后同意他们离开,条件是他们必须护送要嫁给波斯王的公主。

他们乘船由中国到新加坡,经过苏门答腊北部,环绕印度南部,穿过阿拉伯海和阿曼湾。波罗氏离开婚礼,经由陆路到达黑海的一个港口,由此乘船到伊斯坦布尔,然后最终回到威尼斯。

他们于1295年回国后,马可加入威尼斯军队参加反对热那亚的斗争。1298年,马可被捕,监禁在热那亚。在被监禁的2年期间,马可向他的狱友比萨的普鲁蒂谦口述了他的旅行经历。普鲁蒂谦把此书翻译成古法语(意大利当时的文学语言),并命名为《讲述世界》。后来该书被翻译成其他语言,其中翻译成英语的叫做《马可·波罗游记》。该书在整个欧洲流传,立即受到了人们的欢迎。

1324年1月,马可·波罗辞世,被埋葬在圣洛伦佐教堂。

《马可·波罗游记》

马可·波罗记述其到达中国并穿越亚洲之行的书分为四册:第一册描述了波罗氏中国之行途中经过的亚洲中部和中东部地区;第二册描述了中国及忽必烈可汗王朝;第三册提供了有关远东沿海地区的二手材料,包括日本、印度、斯里兰卡、东南亚和非洲东岸地区;第四册记述了蒙古人之间的战争,还描述了北部的一些地区,如俄罗斯。每本书,除了描述了该地区的地理情况,还讲述了该地区的政治、农业、经济、军事力量、葬礼制度、宗教信仰和文化习俗。

regions such as Russia. Each book, in addition to being a geography of the region, describes the politics, agriculture, economy, military capability, burial system, religious beliefs, and cultural practices of the region.

Marco was receptive to new ideas and marveled at some of the Asian practices that had never been seen in Europe. He described the Kublai Khan's prosperous and advanced empire. He discussed the Khan's postal system of courier stations and horseback riders across the kingdom, relaying messages from one station to another. He commented on many Chinese and Asian customs, including the mining and use of coal as fuel (Marco called coal "black stones"), Chinese paper money bearing the seal of the emperor, credit systems, iron manufacturing, salt production, papermaking, printing, and a canal-based internal transportation system. At that point in history, China had greater wealth and a much more complex social structure than any country or region in Europe.

Because many of Marco Polo's stories of what he discovered in Asia seemed so far-fetched to many of his readers, many Europeans doubted his veracity. Some even questioned whether he had even traveled to China. Many thought that he probably gathered information from Arabs who were Silk Road travelers. There was a flourishing trade between the Middle East and the Far East, and merchants and travelers were known to enjoy relating stories of their adventures in great detail. Although Marco's reference to Japan by its Chinese name, "Zipang" or "Cipangu," is considered to be the first mention of Japan in Western literature, many scholars thought that Marco could have learned about Japan from fellow merchants on the trade routes. In the 18th and 19th centuries, however, travelers to Asia confirmed what he had written.

Regardless of such questions about its authenticity, *The Travels of Marco Polo* had an enormous impact when it was first published. Even though the Polos were not the first Europeans to reach China, Marco's book was acknowledged to be the most important account of the world beyond Europe at the time. Marco's skill in conveying new or unknown cultures, plus his willingness to travel through uncharted areas in unknown weather to unfamiliar lands, gave his travelogue credence and appeal to most European readers. Today, the book has become a useful account of the history, geography, politics, and social customs of 13th century China.

Marco Polo introduced Europe to paper currency, coal as fuel, a courier postal system, papermaking, printing, and the compass. On a more domestic level, legend has it that Marco introduced new Chinese products to Italy, namely, ice cream and spaghetti and other pastas. *The Travels of Marco Polo* also exerted tremendous influence on geographic exploration by suggesting new possibilities for Western explorers.

The book and its tales of wealth and adventures also captured the imagination of explorers. Marco's description of the Far East and its riches inspired Christopher Columbus two centuries later to seek a western route to those lands. Christopher Columbus owned a copy of The Travels to which he added numerous annotations. Even today *The Travels of Marco Polo* is one of the most complete records of geographic exploration in Asia and the Far East, and many geographers and topographers call Marco Polo's work the precursor of scientific geography.

马可不断接受新思想并惊叹亚洲的一些习俗，这些习俗是他在欧洲从来没见到过的。他描述了忽必烈可汗繁荣而先进的帝国。他谈到了可汗的邮政体系，包括信使站和骑马的信使；信使骑马穿越整个王国，向每一个信使站传送信件。他评述了许多中国和亚洲的习俗；包括采矿和使用煤作燃料（马可把煤叫做"黑石头"），中国纸币上有国王的印章，信贷制度，炼铁，制盐，造纸，印刷和以运河为基础的内部运输体系。当时的中国比欧洲任何一个国家和地区都富有，社会体系也更复杂。

由于马可·波罗讲述其在亚洲发现的许多故事在许多读者看来似乎有点牵强，所以许多欧洲人怀疑其真实性。甚至有人怀疑他是否真的到过中国。许多人认为他很可能是从经常往返于丝绸之路的阿拉伯人那里搜集信息。当时中东和远东之间的贸易往来繁盛，商人和旅行者们喜欢详述他们的旅途经历。尽管马可提到日本时使用的是其在汉语中的名字，但"Zipang"或"Cipangu"被认为是西方文学中首次提到日本。许多学者认为马可可能是在贸易途中从其他商人那里了解日本的。然而，18、19世纪，到亚洲的旅行者证实了马可作品的真实性。

且不说《马可·波罗游记》的真实性，它在刚出版之时产生了巨大的影响。尽管波罗氏不是最早到达中国的欧洲人，但马可的书被认为是当时描述欧洲以外世界的最重要的书。马可善于传播人们所不知道的新的文化；加上他愿意不顾天气情况，穿越地图上没有标记的区域到达不熟悉的领土；这些使他的游记更为可信，对欧洲读者更有吸引力。今天，这本书中对13世纪中国历史、地理、政治和社会习俗的叙述变得非常有用。

马可·波罗把纸币、燃料煤、信使邮政体系、造纸术、印刷术和罗盘传入欧洲。在家庭方面，传说马可把中国食物传入意大利，即冰淇淋、意大利实心面条和其他意大利面食。《马可·波罗游记》对地理学上的探索也产生了巨大的影响，为西方探险家提供了新的可能。

本书及其对财富和探险的陈述使探险者们为之神往。马可对远东及其财富的描写2个世纪后促使克里斯托弗·哥伦布寻找到达那些地方的西方航线。克里斯托弗·哥伦布有一本《马可·波罗游记》，并在上面加了很多注解。直至今天，《马可·波罗游记》仍是完整记载亚洲和远东地理探索的书之一。许多地理学家和地形学者把马可·波罗的作品称为科学地理学的先兆。

Eighteen

Dante:
The Divine Comedy

Who Was Dante?

Dante (1265-1321),whose full name was Dante Alighieri,was born into an aristocratic family in Florence,Italy.At age 12 Dante was promised in marriage to Gemma Di Manetto Donati,a common practice at that time—he did eventually marry her,and they had four children.At age 9,however,Dante had met 8-year-old Beatrice Portinari; she became the central figure in an unrequited love affair from afar—she was,as well,the inspiration of his poetry.

Although little is known about his education,Dante later revealed a knowledge of music,painting,Tuscan poetry,Provencal minstrels,and of Latin culture,particularly the work of Virgil.In 1295 he became a member of the Guild of Apothecaries as a doctor and pharmacist,because Florentine law required that a noble wishing to enter politics and assume public office had to belong to the *Corporazioni de Arti e Mestieri*.Dante never had any intention of pursuing those professions,but his membership served its purpose:for several years he held various important public offices and participated in the civic and cultural life of Florence.

During this time Florence was undergoing political turmoil because two factions were competing for control of the city.Dante allied himself with the Guelfs,the faction that endorsed Florentine political autonomy and supported the papacy.The opposition,the Ghibellines,were backed by the Holy Roman Emperor.After defeating the Ghibellines,the Guelfs,driven by economic and family interests,split into two groups:the White Guelfs,the group to which Dante belonged,and the Black Guelfs.By the end of the 13th century the Pope was backing the Black Guelfs,who were in turn more strongly committed to the Pope than were the moderate White Guelfs.The White Guelfs were forced into exile,and for the next 20 years Dante lived in various Italian cities but never returned to Florence,the city to which he had devoted a great deal of public service.In 1319 he moved to Ravenna where he completed *The Divine Comedy* before his death in 1321.

The Divine Comedy

Although Dante was a prolific writer,*The Divine Comedy* (La divina commedia) is considered his greatest work and has been called the primary epic of Italian literature. Dante's epic (a long narrative poem told in dignified and exalted style) is composed of three books—Inferno (Hell),Purgatorio (Purgatory),and Paradiso (Paradise)—of 33 cantos each with a single introductory canto for a total of more than 14,000 lines.The cantos have an internal rhythm because of their three-line terza rima stanzas,a verse form Dante developed. In this verse form the first and third lines of each stanza rhyme with the middle line of the preceding stanza.

The Divine Comedy is a first-person account of the poet's travels through the three realms of the dead; it all takes place during Holy Week in the Spring of 1300.The Roman

但丁
《神曲》

但丁

　　但丁(1265~1321)，全名为但丁·阿利盖利，出生在意大利佛罗伦萨一个贵族家庭。他12岁时被迫答应娶杰玛·迪马涅托·多纳提，这在当时是常事。他最后确实同她结婚，并生有4个孩子。而但丁9岁时遇到了8岁的贝阿特丽齐·坡提纳里，她从此成为他单恋爱情中的中心人物，也是他诗歌创作的灵感。

　　但丁的教育情况我们基本不得而知；但后来显露出他通晓音乐、绘画、托斯卡纳诗歌、普罗旺斯游吟诗人和拉丁文化，尤其是维吉尔的作品。1295年，他成为药师协会的成员，成为一名医生和药剂师；因为佛罗伦萨法律规定想要进入政界并承担公共职务的贵族必须是艺术协会的成员。但丁从来没有刻意要从事那些职业，但他的成员身份发挥了它的作用。他曾担任各种要职，并参加佛罗伦萨的公共文化生活。

　　由于两个派别争夺对佛罗伦萨的统治权，佛罗伦萨处在政治动荡中。但丁加入归尔甫派，此派赞同佛罗伦萨的政治自主并支持教皇统治。反对派，吉伯林派受神圣罗马帝王支持。战胜吉伯林派后，受经济和家庭利益的驱使，归尔甫派分裂成两派：白归尔甫派(但丁属于此派)和黑归尔甫派。到13世纪末教皇支持黑归尔甫派，因为黑归尔甫派比温和的白归尔甫派更效忠于教皇。白归尔甫派被流放，接下来的20年里，但丁居住在意大利的其他各城市，但从未回到佛罗伦萨这个他付出巨大努力的城市。他于1319年搬到拉纳，在此他完成了《神曲》并于1321年离开人世。

《神曲》

　　但丁是个多产的作家，《神曲》被认为是他的最伟大作品，同时也被认为是意大利文学的主要史诗。但丁的史诗(长叙事诗，文体高贵、优雅)包括三部分：地狱、炼狱和天堂。每部分33章，加上一个介绍章节，总共14 000多行。所有章节有个内在的韵律，因为是三行隔句押韵诗节。这一诗节形式是但丁发明的。在这类诗节中，每一节的第一行和第三行与前一节的中间一行押韵。

　　《神曲》以第一人称讲述了诗人游历死亡三界的经历，一切都发生在1300年春天复活节前一周。罗马诗人维吉尔引导但丁游历地狱和炼狱；贝阿特丽奇，但丁理想的女人、纯

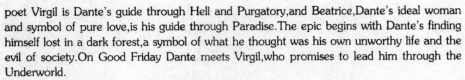

poet Virgil is Dante's guide through Hell and Purgatory,and Beatrice,Dante's ideal woman and symbol of pure love,is his guide through Paradise.The epic begins with Dante's finding himself lost in a dark forest,a symbol of what he thought was his own unworthy life and the evil of society.On Good Friday Dante meets Virgil,who promises to lead him through the Underworld.

Dante begins this journey by passing through the Gate of Hell and crossing the river Acheron into Hell itself.Virgil then steers Dante through the nine concentric circles of Hell, each one representing a progressively greater evil and each one punished appropriately. Each circle is populated by crowds of individuals,some of whom are from the past but most of whom are from Dante's time,who are being punished for their sins.The journey culminates in the center of the earth at the seat of Satan.

The poets escape the Inferno by riding Lucifer though the center of the earth into the southern hemisphere on Easter Sunday.Virgil now guides Dante through the seven terraces of Purgatory,which purges each of the representative sins.The seven terraces correspond to the seven deadly sins:pride,envy,wrath,sloth,avarice,gluttony,and lust.At the top of the terraces is the Garden of Eden where,because he is a pagan,Virgil is denied access and where Beatrice becomes Dante's guide.Beatrice leads Dante through the concentric spheres of Heaven.Beatrice leaves Dante at one of the levels after which he ascends beyond physical existence to a plane of existence where he meets God and receives an understanding of divine and of human nature.

Although in some sense *The Divine Comedy* is a love poem extolling Beatrice's innocent beauty and her moral power to lead Dante to supreme goodness,it is also a personal account of Dante's spiritual development and of the preoccupation of the 13th and 14th century Christianity with life after death.Dante's goal was to create a poem that reflected the world of the Christian God of his time.Part of his philosophical approach was influenced by his belief in the reconciliation between Aristotelian thought and Christian faith espoused by St.Thomas Aquinas.

For many scholars,*The Divine Comedy* is significant in that it is thought to be the last great work of literature in the Middle Ages-indeed,it is often cited as a summary of medieval thought-as well as the first great work of the Renaissance.Scholars have lauded the work not only for its innovative and magnificent poetry but also for its immense learning.

As an important thinker and writer,Dante exerted a great deal of influence on later writers:Geoffrey Chaucer and John Milton imitated Dante's works.Interest in *The Divine Comedy* and Dante's other writings languished during the Enlightenment of the 18th century.The Enlightenment was a historical intellectual movement that advocated rationality as the basis of aesthetics,ethics,and logic.The intellectual leaders of this movement proposed to lead the world out of the period of irrationality,tradition,and superstition that they called the Dark Ages and into a world of progress.Dante seemed irrelevant.

The romantic writers of the 19th century re-discovered Dante.Dante and his work influenced the thinking and work of many 19th century writers,including William Blake, Longfellow,Byron,Shelley,Tennyson,Victor Hugo,and Friedrich Schlegel,the German poet and critic.Dante also influenced such 20th century writers as T.S.Eliot,Ezra Pound,Samuel Beckett,and James Joyce.

洁爱情的象征,引导他游历天堂。史诗开篇但丁发现自己迷失在黑暗的森林里,他认为这是自己平凡生活的象征,是社会罪恶的象征。受难节那天但丁遇到维吉尔,维吉尔承诺带他游历地狱。

但丁此行穿越地狱之门和冥河到达地狱,然后维吉尔引领但丁穿越地狱的九层,每一层代表着逐渐严重的罪恶,并且每种罪恶都得到应有的惩罚。每层都有很多人,有些是过去的人,但大部分都是但丁那个时代的人,因罪过而受到惩罚。此段旅行结束在地球之心撒旦之位。

诗人复活节那天乘坐明亮之星穿过地心,逃离地狱进入南半球。维吉尔现在带领但丁游历炼狱的7层,每层都清除其所代表的罪恶。7层对应着7大致命罪恶:傲慢、忌妒、愤怒、怠惰、贪财、贪食、贪色。顶端是伊甸园,维吉尔是异教徒,所以他不能进入,就由贝阿特丽奇带领但丁游历天堂的九重天。贝阿特丽奇离开,但丁脱离物质存在在天府见到上帝,并获得对神圣和人类本质的理解。

尽管从某种意义上说,《神曲》是首爱情诗,歌颂贝阿特丽奇纯洁的美和她引领但丁达到极善的道德力量;也叙述了但丁的精神历程和13、14世纪基督教对来生的神往。但丁的目标是创作一首反映当时基督教世界的诗。他的哲学观受圣·托马斯·阿奎那提倡的亚里士多德思想与基督教信仰调和论的影响。

许多学者认为《神曲》之所以意义重大是因为它被认为是中世纪最后一部伟大著作(它的确常被认为是中世纪思想的总结),也是文艺复兴时期第一部伟大著作。学者们不仅赞扬它是具有革新意义的宏伟诗篇,也赞扬其中广博的知识。

作为伟大的思想家和作家,但丁对后来的作家产生了巨大的影响:杰弗里·乔叟和约翰·弥尔顿都模仿但丁的作品。18世纪启蒙运动时期,人们对《神曲》及但丁其他作品的兴趣开始萎缩。启蒙运动是历史上的知识分子运动,提倡理性作为审美、道德和逻辑的基础。这一运动的知识分子领袖们建议把世界从非理性、传统和迷信的黑暗时代引向一个进步的世界。但丁似乎是不相干的。

19世纪浪漫主义作家们重新发现了但丁。但丁及其作品影响了19世纪许多作家的思想和作品,有威廉·布莱克、朗费罗、拜伦、雪莱、丁尼生、维克多·雨果、弗里德里希·施莱格尔以及德国诗人和批评家。但丁还影响了20世纪作家,如:T.S.艾略特、庞德、塞缪尔·贝可特和詹姆斯·乔伊斯。

Nineteen

Petrarch: Canzoniere

Who Was Petrarch?

Francesco Petrarch (1304-1374) was an Italian scholar,poet,and humanist; he was,as well,a major cause of the flowering of what we now call the Renaissance.As a scholar, Petrarch rediscovered and emphasized the greatness of classical literature:he was responsible for the first Latin translation of Homer,and he found some undiscovered manuscripts of the Latin writers Cicero and Livy.His interest in classical literature inspired him to collect these and other ancient manuscripts that had been forgotten in monastic and cathedral libraries and to build a private library that became the model for such famous libraries as the Laurentian in Florence,St.Mark's in Venice,and that of the Vatican in Rome.

He displayed his displeasure about the neglect of ancient manuscripts when he said: "Each famous author of antiquity whom I recover places a new offense and another cause of dishonor to the charge of earlier generations,who,not satisfied with their own disgraceful barrenness,permitted the fruit of other minds,and the writings that their ancestors had produced by their toil and application,to perish through insufferable neglect.Although they had nothing of their own to hand down to those who were to come after,they robbed posterity of its ancestral heritage."

Born in Arezzo,Italy,Petrarch spent his early years in a village near Florence,because his father,Petracco,a clerk of one of the courts of justice in Florence,had been expelled from Florence by the conquering Black Guelph political faction,the same group that had exiled Dante during the same period.After a short time in Arezzo,Petracco took the family to Pisa,then to Avignon,France.At his father's insistence,Petrarch studied law at Montpelier and Bologna,but his interests were really focused on writing and on Latin literature.This interest so infuriated his father that he burned a number of his son's favorite ancient manuscripts.When his father died,Petrarch abandoned his law studies and turned to writing and his real scholarly interests.

Petrarch returned to Avignon and took minor offices in the Church.He thus received a small income from the Church while enjoying the social life of Avignon.It was during this time that he encountered Laura for the first time.In 1327 in the church of Sainte-Claire d'Avignon,Petrarch saw a woman named Laura with whom he fell in love-at a distance. Although it is not known whether Laura actually existed as a person,many scholars have speculated that she may have been Laura de Noves,the wife of Hugues de Sade.Petrarch's realistic portrait of Laura in his poems expresses his joy in her presence but also his pain in their unrequited relationship.In his "Letter to Posterity," Petrarch wrote, "I struggled constantly with an overwhelming but pure love affair…"

彼特拉克

　　弗朗西斯科·彼特拉克(1304~1374)是意大利学者、诗人和人文主义者,他也是文艺复兴的主要倡导者。作为一个学者,彼特拉克重新发现并强调古典文学的伟大之处;他首先将荷马的作品翻译成拉丁文,他还发现了拉丁作家西塞罗和李维一些未被发现的手稿。他对古典文学的兴趣促使他收集这些手稿和其他被遗忘在寺院和天主教图书馆的古代手稿,然后创建了一个私人图书馆。著名图书馆,如佛罗伦萨的劳伦图书馆,威尼斯的圣马克图书馆和罗马的梵蒂冈图书馆,就是按照这一模式建立的。

　　他对于人们忽视古代手稿表示极为不满:"我每重新发现一个古代著名作家就避免了一个新的冒犯和使先辈们不履行其职责的原因。先辈们因自己没写出作品而羞愧,却让别人的成果和祖先们经过辛苦努力而写出的作品在遗忘中消失。他们没有任何自己的作品流传给后代,却使后代丧失了祖先们的遗产。"

　　彼特拉克出生在意大利的阿雷佐,早年生活在佛罗伦萨附近的一个村庄;因为他的父亲彼特拉克,佛罗伦萨一个低级法院的职员,被黑归尔甫派驱逐出佛罗伦萨。但丁也是在同一时期被黑归尔甫派流放。在阿雷佐住了很短一段时间后,彼特拉克家搬到比萨,后来又搬到法国的阿维尼翁。在他父亲的坚持下,彼特拉克在蒙彼利埃和波伦亚学习法律,但他的兴趣却在写作和拉丁文学上。他的这一兴趣激怒了他父亲,烧毁了许多他喜爱的古代手稿。他父亲去世后,彼特拉克放弃了法律学习,开始从事写作及他真正的学术兴趣。

　　彼特拉克回到阿维尼翁并在教堂里担任一些不重要的职务,这样他可以从教堂获得一点收入,享受着阿维尼翁的社会生活。就是在这期间他这一次遇到了劳拉。1327年在阿维尼翁的圣克莱尔教堂,彼特拉克从远处看到了一个叫劳拉的女子,然后就爱上了她。尽管不知道是否真的有劳拉这个人存在,许多学者推测她可能是萨德·休斯的妻子诺微司·劳拉。彼特拉克在诗中对劳拉的现实主义描写表现了他因她的存在而高兴也表现了他单相思的痛苦。在"致后代的信"中,彼特拉克写到:"我不断地在强烈而纯洁的爱中挣扎……"

Canzoniere

Petrarch wrote most of his works in Latin,but Latin did not allow him to express his personal thoughts and observations.More important are his works in Italian,particularly his love lyrics to the mysterious Laura,which are collected in the Canzoniere (Book of Songs).

The Canzoniere is a chronological account of Petrarch's passion for Laura.The tone alternates between physical pleasure and religious feeling,mirroring the individual's uneasiness when faced with both spiritual love and physical desire.There are 366 poems, including sonnets,odes,songs,madrigals,and ballads,divided into two parts:The first part includes 263 poems written during Laura's lifetime and offers a chronological account of the poet's continuing passion for her.The second part consists of poems written after Laura's death—it portrays Laura as a guide,leading her lover toward God and salvation.Throughout the work there is a sense of juxtaposition of spiritual love and human physical pleasure.

Canzoniere is often regarded as the first work to portray modern man emerging from a medieval world into the Renaissance period,because it shows human uncertainties,frailties, and indomitable spirit.

The Canzoniere is one of Europe's most influential works.Petrarch perfected the verse forms of the sonnet and the ode,and he expressed the joy and pain of human love in a sequence of related poems.Many subsequent European poets and writers drew on Petrarch's legacy of the courtly representation of spiritual yet human love for an exalted and unattainable woman.The work of Chaucer,Shakespeare,Pope,Byron,and Rossetti reflect Petrarch's influence.These poets,as well as Renaissance poets Thomas Wyatt and Edmund Spenser and the Romantic poet Lord Byron,demonstrate in their work the extended metaphors introduced by Petrarch.Spenser and Wyatt were early translators of Petrarch's sonnets and songs.

One of Petrarch's primary contributions to literature was his use and refinement of Italian in his verse—despite the fact that he knew Latin well and did much of his writing in Latin,particularly his scholarly treatises and letters.He understood that the use of Italian would permit more personal expression of his feelings and infuse his love poetry with an immediacy and significance that he could not achieve with Latin.The Italian language allowed him to portray Laura as a real woman,not just a spiritual symbol,and to define true emotions rather than medieval conventions.

Petrarch was also a noted scholar.His interest in classical writings led him to realize that Platonic thought and Greek studies provided a cultural framework for his own thinking; he believed it could help other men as well.He became a student and commentator on ancient Greek and Roman works that emphasized the pre-Christian concept of man as the central focus of life.These studies were instrumental in his becoming an active participant in the development of Christian humanism as an outcome of the Italian Renaissance.Often called the father of humanism,Petrarch believed that the human individual could lead a life of self-reliance and meaning.He did not minimize nor ignore Christian belief,but neither did he see a contradiction between faith and human individualism.His defining and espousing humanism during the flowering of the Italian Renaissance was the beginning of a movement that had a profound effect on the Renaissance,the Reformation,the Enlightenment,and on the American Revolution.

《歌集》

彼特拉克的作品大都是用拉丁语写的，但是拉丁语不能表达他个人的思想和所见。用意大利语写的作品更为重要，尤其是写给神秘的劳拉的爱情诗，这些诗收集在《歌集》中。

《歌集》按时间顺序叙述彼特拉克对劳拉的感情。诗的格调在物质享受和宗教感情之间变换，反映了人在面对精神恋爱和肉欲时的不安。《歌集》共有366首诗，包括十四行诗、颂歌、歌曲、抒情短诗和民歌。《歌集》分为两部分：第一部分包括写在劳拉在世时的263首诗，以时间顺序讲述了诗人对她的持久的爱；第二部分包括写在劳拉去世后的诗，描写了劳拉作为向导引领她的爱人向上帝靠近并获得拯救。整部作品中，精神恋爱和人类物质享受交织在一起。

《歌集》通常被认为是第一部描写现代人从中世纪进入文艺复兴时期的作品，因为它表现了人类的不确定性、脆弱性和不可战胜的精神。

《歌集》是欧洲最具影响力的作品之一。彼特拉克完善了十四行诗和颂歌的诗节形式，并在诗中表达了人类爱情的乐与痛。后来许多欧洲诗人和作家借用彼特拉克的这一主题，表述对高贵而难以获得的女人的精神恋爱。乔叟、莎士比亚、蒲柏、拜伦和罗塞蒂的作品反映了彼特拉克的影响。这些诗人、文艺复兴时期诗人怀亚特和埃德蒙·斯宾塞及浪漫主义诗人拜伦在其作品中使用了彼特拉克介绍的扩展比喻。斯宾塞和怀亚特较早地翻译了彼特拉克的十四行诗和歌曲。

彼特拉克对文学的主要贡献之一是在诗中使用并完善了意大利语。他精通意大利语，他的多数作品都是用意大利语写的，尤其是学术论文和信件。他认为使用意大利语更能充分表达个人情感，使爱情诗更直接、重要，而用拉丁语却无法做到。意大利语可以让他描绘出一个真实的劳拉而并非仅仅是精神上的象征；还可以让他表达真正的感情而并非中世纪惯例。

彼特拉克也是著名的学者。他对古典作品的兴趣使他意识到柏拉图思想和希腊研究为他个人思想提供了文化框架，他认为这也会帮助其他人。他开始学习并评论古希腊和罗马作品，这些作品强调前基督教思想认为人是生活的核心。这些研究有助于他积极参加意大利文艺复兴，发展基督教人文主义。彼特拉克常被称作人文主义之父，他认为个人可以过着自立而有意义的生活。他既不贬低和忽视基督教信仰，也不认为信仰和个人主义是冲突的。他对人文主义的定义和赞同是意大利文艺复兴的开始，这一运动对文艺复兴、宗教改革、启蒙运动和美国革命产生了深远的影响。

Twenty

Geoffrey Chaucer:
The Canterbury Tales

Who Was Geoffrey Chaucer?

Geoffrey Chaucer (1340-1400),the English poet,was also a civil servant and a diplomat.Chaucer was born in London into a well-do-do family of wine merchants,and during the course of his life he made a significant contribution to English literature by writing in English during a time when most court poetry was being written in Anglo-Norman or Latin.

Chaucer served the crown or the nobility,beginning in 1357 when,through his father's connections,he became a page to Elizabeth de Burgh,the Countess of Ulster.In 1359 he served in King Edward III's Army when Edward invaded France at the beginning of the Hundred Years' War.During the siege of Reims,Chaucer was captured by the French,but Edward III valued Chaucer's military skills so much that he personally ransomed him.Later, during the reigns of both Edward III and Richard II,Chaucer held a number of positions at court,including the posts of Comptroller of the Customs and Clerk of the King's Works (the institution that maintained and repaired governmental buildings).He was subsequently appointed Justice of the Peace in Kent and was elected to Parliament.As well,he went on diplomatic missions to the Continent during the 1370s,including some missions to Italy where he may have come into contact with medieval Italian poetry for the first time.It is even possible that in 1372 he met Petrarch or even Giovanni Boccaccio,the Italian humanist poet who was Petrarch's friend.Critics have noted that Chaucer's own work seems to have been inspired from his exposure to Italian verse and Italian poets.

By 1366 he had married Philippa Roet,a lady-in-waiting to Edward III's queen,and they had two sons.After Philippa's death in 1387,Chaucer re-entered the crown's service.It was also a period of creativity for Chaucer; he wrote many of his great poems during this time, including Troilus and Cressida.Much of the inspiration for his work came from the poetry of Ovid and Virgil and the work of such Italian authors as Dante and Petrarch.Scholars believe that Chaucer's early writing were also influenced by French literature:Chaucer could read French,Italian,and Latin.

Chaucer was buried without fanfare in Westminster Abbey in a spot at the entrance to St.Benedict's Chapel.In 1556,in recognition of his reputation as one of the great English poets,his tomb was moved to its present location in the south transept in that area now known as Poet's Corner.

The Canterbury Tales

Chaucer is best known for his epic work,The Canterbury Tales.Written primarily after 1387,the unfinished The Canterbury Tales is a collection of stories about 30 pilgrims (one of whom is the impartial narrator Chaucer) who gather at the Tabard Inn at Southwark across the Thames River from Central London and travel to the shrine of St.Thomas à Becket at Canterbury.The pilgrims,representing a cross-section of 14th century English

杰弗里·乔叟
《坎特伯雷故事集》

杰弗里·乔叟

杰弗里·乔叟(1340~1400),英国诗人,也是公务员和外交家。乔叟出生在伦敦一个富裕的酒商家庭。在大多数宫廷诗人都用英国法语或拉丁语写诗的时代,乔叟用英语写诗,对英国文学做出了巨大的贡献。

1357年,通过他父亲的各种关系,乔叟成为阿尔斯特女爵伊丽莎白·蒂伯的侍从,开始了服务于王室和贵族的生活。1359年,国王爱德华三世侵略法国,在这个百年战争的初期,乔叟在爱德华的军队中服役。在围攻兰斯时,乔叟被法军俘虏;但爱德华三世非常重视他的军事才能,亲自赎回了乔叟。后来,在爱德华三世和理查德二世统治时期,乔叟在宫廷担任过许多职务,有关税督察和廷臣(维护和修理政府建筑的机构)。他后来被任命为肯特郡的治安法官并当选为议会成员。14世纪70年代,他还因外交事务到欧洲大陆,这其中包括意大利;在那乔叟可能第一次接触中世纪意大利诗歌。甚至可能是在1372年,他遇到了彼特拉克和彼特拉克的朋友意大利人文主义诗人乔万尼·薄伽丘。许多学者发现乔叟的作品似乎受意大利诗歌和诗人的启发。

1366年,乔叟与爱德华三世王后的女官菲利帕结婚并生下两个儿子。1387年菲利帕去世后,乔叟重新服务于王室。这也是乔叟发挥其创造性的时期,他的许多伟大诗歌都是在这段时间里创作的,包括《特洛伊罗斯和克雷达西》。他创作的灵感主要来自于奥维德和维吉尔的诗及意大利作家但丁和彼特拉克的作品。学者们认为乔叟的早期作品也受法国文学的影响,因为乔叟懂法语、意大利语和拉丁语。

乔叟被悄悄地埋葬在威斯敏斯特教堂的本尼迪克特教堂的入口处。1556年,乔叟被认为是英国著名诗人之一,他的坟墓被移到现在所在的位置,威斯敏斯特教堂南部现在被称为"诗人之角"的地方。

《坎特伯雷故事集》

乔叟以他的叙事诗《坎特伯雷故事集》而著名。《坎特伯雷故事集》并未写完,主要写于1387年后,是关于30名朝圣者(其中之一是客观叙述者乔叟)的故事集。30名朝圣者聚集在南华克的泰巴旅馆,从伦敦中部穿过泰晤士河前往坎特伯雷圣托马斯·贝克特的圣地。朝圣者们,代表着14世纪英国社会不同阶层,互相讲故事以打发时间。朝圣者中有骑士、牧师、庄稼汉、磨坊主、办事员、商人和来自于巴斯的妇女。许多评论家认为骑士、牧师

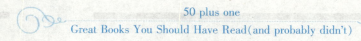

society,tell each other stories to pass the time on the journey.Among the pilgrims are a knight,a priest,a ploughman,a miller,a clerk,a merchant,and a wife from Bath.Many critics view the knight,the priest,and the ploughman as exemplars of the three estates of the Middle Ages—the nobility,the clergy,and the workers.The other characters are drawn from the middle class of 14th century English society.

The diverse stories are divided into separate sections of one or more tales with links to intervals in which the characters converse with each other and reveal medieval attitudes and customs from all social points of view;   common themes are love,marriage,and domestic harmony.

Chaucer's plan,outlined in the general prologue,was to have each traveler tell two tales on the way to Canterbury and two tales on the way home.Chaucer completed only 24 tales,four of which are themselves incomplete.The pilgrimage is therefore one-way.

Chaucer wanted to portray the pilgrimage as an intimation of the human journey from earth to heaven.

The significance of Chaucer rests not only on his skill as a storyteller in The Canterbury Tales but also on his innovations in its rhyming verse.Chaucer was one of the first English poets to use the seven-line stanza in iambic pentameter—the five-stress line-known as rhyme royal;   as well,he uses the heroic couplet in his work.He also helped increase the prestige of English as a literary language and to standardize Middle English dialect.Chaucer was not afraid to write in regional dialects to improve the story or add humor.His skill in doing so makes Chaucer one of the earliest satirists in the English language,and his work later influenced the greatest of English satirists,Jonathan Swift.The Canterbury Tales is often considered the forerunner of subsequent satiric travel narratives, such as Swift's Gulliver's Travels in the 18th century or even Vladimir Nabokov's Lolita in the 20th century.

Chaucer's influence dominated the thinking and work of subsequent 15th century writers,but thereafter a major change in the English language resulted in a diminished understanding of Chaucer's language.Much of his verse depended on sounding a final e;   it has become silent or has disappeared in modern English.Yet,though Middle English differs from today's English,most readers can,with a little effort,understand Chaucer's stories-often after reading them aloud.Many linguists consider the modern Scottish accent the closest to that of Chaucer,which explains the popularity of Chaucer in Scotland,both in the centuries immediately following Chaucer's death and today.

Many writers have imitated Chaucer's style and techniques.Shakespeare borrowed the plot from Chaucer's "Troilus and Cressida" for his own play of that name.The comic and light humor of other Shakespeare plays also reflect the spirit of Chaucerian wit.The 16th century poet Edmund Spenser looked up to Chaucer as an inspiration and a mentor. Alexander Pope and John Dryden in the 18th century rewrote and modernized some of the tales.Dryden alluded to Chaucer's timelessness in his "Preface to the Fables" in 1700:"He must have been a man of a most wonderful comprehensive nature,because,as it has been truly observed of him,he has taken into the compass of his Canterbury Tales the various manners and humors (as we now call them) of the whole English nation in his age."

和庄稼汉分别代表了中世纪的三大阶层—贵族、牧师和劳动人民。其他人物来自于14世纪英国的中产阶级。

各种不同的故事分成单独的部分,每个部分有一个或几个故事;故事中间还有人物互相讨论的内容,反映了中世纪不同阶层的观点和习俗;讨论的主题是爱情、婚姻和家庭和谐。

乔叟在总序言中计划每个朝圣者在去坎特伯雷和回来的路上各讲两个故事。乔叟只写了24个故事,其中有4个还没写完整;因而只写了去朝圣时讲述的故事。

乔叟想将朝圣描述为人类由人间到天堂之行的征兆。

乔叟的重要性不只是在于他在《坎特伯雷故事集》中讲故事的技巧,还在于他在诗节押韵上的创新。乔叟是最早在七行诗节中使用五步抑扬格(称为君王诗体)的英国诗人之一;他还使用了英雄双韵体。他还提高了英语在文学语言中的地位并使中古英语方言标准化。乔叟大胆使用地方方言来完善故事或增加幽默,他的这一技巧使他成为英国最早的讽刺家之一;他的作品后来影响了英国最伟大的讽刺家乔纳森·斯威夫特。《坎特伯雷故事集》通常被认为是后来讽刺游记的先行者,如18世纪斯威夫特的《格列佛游记》和20世纪弗拉基米尔·纳博科夫的《洛丽塔》。

乔叟影响了15世纪作家的思想和作品,但英语的重大变化使乔叟的语言令人难懂。他的许多诗节中词末e发a的音;而现代英语中e要么不发音,要么消失了。然而,尽管中古英语不同于今天的英语,多数读者经过努力(通常是大声朗读后)能够读懂乔叟的故事。许多语言学家认为现代苏格兰音调与乔叟的很接近,这也证明了乔叟在苏格兰很受欢迎,不仅是在他刚刚去世的几个世纪甚至在今天也很受欢迎。

许多作家模仿乔叟的文体和技巧。莎士比亚借用了乔叟《特洛伊罗斯和克雷西达》的故事情节创作了自己的同名剧作。莎士比亚其他剧作中的滑稽轻幽默也反映了乔叟智慧的实质。16世纪诗人埃德蒙·斯宾塞尊崇乔叟为启迪者和导师。18世纪的亚历山大·浦柏和约翰·德莱顿重写了其中的一些故事。1700年,德莱顿在他的《古今故事诗集序》中提到乔叟的永垂不朽:"他一定是个非常博学的人,因为就像我们真正看到的一样,他在《坎特伯雷故事集》中使用了那个时代英国的各种手法和幽默(我们现在的叫法)。"

Twenty-one

Sir Thomas Malory: Le Morte d'Arthur

Who Was Sir Thomas Malory?

Nothing in Malory's life makes sense. How did the well-off knight become the hardened criminal who was finally in the poor house? And how is it possible that Malory could have written *Le Morte d'Arthur*? Such questions are unanswerable. Even more bizarre, all indications in his book are that he wrote the book while in prison or, certain parts were written when he was out of prison, then they were written while he was engaged in his criminal pursuits. Scholars believe that he began to write the book in the 1450s, concluded it in 1470, the year before his death. It was published 14 years later, in 1485, by the famous printer William Caxton.

Le Morte d' Arthur

Because this story is so unlikely, scholars have tried to prove that Malory cannot possibly be the author of *Le Morte d'Arthur*, but most scholars now accept that the criminal-knight was in fact the author.

Malory accomplishes two things in his great work: he brings together all the myths of Arthur and his knights, their adventures and love affairs, and in so doing creates a kind of nationalistic epic for England—as Ancient Greece had, via Homer, the myth of the Trojan War, or Romans, via Virgil, had the myth of the founding of Rome, or the medieval French, via Turold, had the myth of Charlemagne (though Charlemagne was a real, historic figure). Malory's work is written almost a thousand years after Arthur, if there was an Arthur who actually lived; Arthur and his knights are models not of men of their time but ideals of Malory's own time.

If there ever was an Arthur, he was probably a 6th century leader of the Britons, possibly a Roman, who joined with the Celts to fight the invasion of Anglo-Saxons; Arthur is supposed to have won the Battle of Badon Hill (the battle actually took place). He surfaces again in histories of the 12th century. Because nothing about Arthur is "written down" between the 6th and 12th centuries, Arthur was probably a folk hero, whose exploits were told in song or recited by storytellers. By the 12th century, however, his fame had probably also spread to France and northern Italy.

In 1137 Geoffrey of Monmonth's History of the Kings of Britain was published, and in it Arthur plays a prominent part; he is presented as the greatest of Geoffrey's mythical kings-and Geoffrey's work is essentially patriotic. It creates a myth that continues earlier myths-just as Romulus fled from Troy to Rome and founded the Roman Empire, so did Brutus flee to Britain and found that kingdon. Thus, Britain is, like Rome, a descendant of the Greek world, and the greatest of its mythical kings, Arthur, has virtues that rival those of notable warrior—kings of the past.

Arthur became the subject of what we now call the "Breton lays," French poems popular from the mid-12th century onwards. Sir Thomas Malory converted these lays, their

托马斯·马洛礼
《亚瑟王之死》

托马斯·马洛礼

　　关于马洛礼没有一件事是可以讲得通的。一个富裕的骑士怎么变成了无情的罪犯，最后过着贫困的生活？马洛礼怎么能够写出《亚瑟王之死》呢？这些问题都没有答案。更奇怪的是，书中的所有细节表明他的书是在狱中写的，某些部分是出狱后写的，还有些是他后来从事犯罪活动时写的。学者们认为他于15世纪50年代开始写作的，完成于1470年，他去世的前一年。14年后，1485年，著名出版商威廉·卡克斯顿出版了该书。

《亚瑟王之死》

　　因为关于马洛礼的故事太不可能，学者们试图证明马洛礼不是《亚瑟王之死》的作者，但大多数学者现在已经接受罪犯骑士实际上是作者。马洛礼的著作有两大成就：他汇集了有关亚瑟及其骑士们的所有神话，他们的历险和爱情故事；这样就为英格兰创造了一部民族主义的史诗，就像荷马使古希腊拥有特洛伊战争的神话，维吉尔使罗马人拥有罗马建立的神话，杜洛杜斯使中世纪法国人拥有查理曼的神话(尽管查理曼是的确存在的历史人物)。如果亚瑟真的存在的话，马洛礼的作品写于亚瑟之后大约一千年；亚瑟及其骑士们不仅是他们那个时代人们的楷模，也是马洛礼时代人们的典范。

　　如果曾有个亚瑟的话，他可能是6世纪布立吞人的领袖，可能是罗马人，曾加入凯尔特人抵抗盎格鲁撒克逊人的入侵；亚瑟被认为在巴顿山之战(的确爆发过这一战争)中取胜。亚瑟又出现在12世纪的历史中，因为6世纪至12世纪期间关于亚瑟的事情没有记载下来。亚瑟可能是个民间英雄，他的事迹只是在歌中吟唱或由讲故事者们朗诵。然而，到了12世纪，他的名声可能也传到了法国和意大利北部。

　　1137年，蒙茅斯的杰弗里的《不列颠国王史》出版，亚瑟在其中是个重要的部分；亚瑟是杰弗里所描写的神话般的国王中最伟大的一个，杰弗里的作品是显示爱国主义精神的。书中的神话是以前的神话的继续：就像罗穆卢斯逃离特洛伊到达罗马并建立了罗马帝国，布鲁图逃到不列颠建立了不列颠王国。因此，不列颠和罗马一样是希腊的后代；神话般的国王中最伟大的一个，亚瑟，他的美德可以与过去著名的善战的国王们的美德相媲美。

　　亚瑟成为"布列塔尼籁歌"的题材，布列塔尼籁歌是12世纪中期开始流行的法国诗歌。托马斯·马洛礼把这些以亚瑟为题材的籁歌转换成散文体裁的传奇故事，并把收集到

Arthurian subject matter,into what we would now call a prose romance—and gathered into this romance all the extant stories of Arthur and his Round Table that were available to him-a remarkable achievement when one considers he wrote the book while he was a prisoner.

Arthur and his court,though,are no longer Roman/Celtic warriors; they are men of the Late Middle Ages,exemplars of the Chivalric Code—and thus Malory not only creates his national myth but also provides,within this myth,what he sees as a model of human behavior.Malory's world is one of moral behavior,courtesy to others,decorous conversation. More important,it is a world of Christian men and woman,who believe in service to others as the highest virtue,for whom the greatest quest is that for the Holy Grail,the cup from which Christ drank at the Last Supper.For finding that Grail promises to unite the finder with the essence of Christ.It is a world in which Christian virtues actually exist,in which love is the highest of those virtues;   love between individuals (between Knights of the Round Table; between the Knights and their beloved wives and mistresses) is an ideal that must always be upheld-as must the ideals of bravery,loyalty,and honor.

All of this describes the highest goals of Malory's world,the world of Camelot (a modern world synonym for a perfect world).But we,as readers,would not be fascinated by Malory's world if that world was one that had achieved perfection.Perfection,in Malory, remains the ideal.His stories are about the ways in which his characters fail to reach that perfection.It is a world of rivalries,of revenge and selfishness and malice,of quests and battles that go wrong.

The fascination of *Le Morte d'Arthur* for modern readers is that it posits a perfect world,an ideal of human behavior,then shows,in stories that have lasted for centuries,stories that appeal even to children,the ways in which human beings always fall short of their own ideals.It is a common theme of the world's literature,but very few writers have presented the human dilemma as effectively and dramatically as has Malory.

的现存的所有关于亚瑟及其圆桌骑士们的故事加入其中。想到他是在监狱中创作此书，不得不感叹这一伟大的成就。

亚瑟及其朝臣不再是罗马或凯尔特战士，他们生活在中世纪晚期，是骑士守则的典范。马洛礼不仅创作了民族神话，还在神话中提供了人类行为的模范。马洛礼的世界里都是道德的行为、对他人礼貌和得体的谈话。更重要的是，这是个基督教徒的世界，他们认为服务于他人就是最大的德善；对于他们最大的追求就是圣杯，基督在最后的晚餐时所用的杯子。找到圣杯需要把寻找者与基督的精髓统一起来。这是个基督教德行存在的世界，其中爱是最大的德行；个人之间的爱(圆桌骑士们之间的爱，骑士与他们的妻子及情人之间的爱)是必须坚持的努力目标，勇敢、忠诚和荣誉也是必须坚持的努力目标。

所有这些都描述了马洛礼极乐世界(完美世界)的最高目标。但作为读者，我们不会被马洛礼的完美世界所吸引。在马洛礼的世界里，完美只是努力目标。他的故事中的人物都没有达到完美。这个世界充满着对立、报复、自私、敌意，以及不正常的追求和战争。

《亚瑟之死》吸引现代读者的地方是它展现了一个完美的世界—人类奋斗的最终目标；其中的故事已历经几个世纪，这些故事甚至也吸引着孩子们，讲述了人类总是不能实现自己的目标。这是世界文学的常见主题，但很少有作家像马洛礼这样清楚有效地把人类的进退维谷展现出来。

Twenty-two

Leonardo da Vinci: The Notebooks

Who Was Leonardo da Vinci?

Leonardo da Vinci (1452-1519) was a man of the Italian Renaissance and a prime example of what we mean by a Renaissance Man—he was a painter,inventor,architect, sculptor,anatomist,physiologist,engineer,musician,and student.Trained as a painter,he nevertheless took an interest in a wide variety of fields,recording his observations and ideas in notebooks.

Born in the village Vinci near Florence (hence,the appellation "da Vinci" which means "from Vinci"),Leonardo was raised by his father and given the best education obtainable in Renaissance Florence.In 1466 he was apprenticed to Andrea del Verrocchio,the leading Florentine painter and sculptor of his day.Leonardo eventually became an independent artist and accepted commissions for paintings and sculptures at his own studio in Florence.

In 1482 Leonardo left Florence to serve the Duke of Milan; his duties included designing artillery (as a military engineer) and stages for pageants (as a civil engineer).He also continued painting and sculpting.He completed his painting "The Last Supper" about 1497 and began to produce scientific drawings,particularly of the human body.His anatomical drawings,sketched while dissecting human bodies and small animals,are considered the first accurate representations of human anatomy and physiology.

Leonardo left Milan for Florence when the French defeated the Duke.Because of his reputation as a painter,the people of Florence welcomed him,and his work began to influence a new generation of artists.During this period he painted the "Mona Lisa," his famous portrait of a young wife of a Florentine merchant.With this painting he changed the traditional technique of portrait painting by including the woman's hands in her lap,thus giving the subject a more complete appearance.

In his later years Leonardo lived in both Milan and Rome.As he grew older,he painted less and concentrated more on his drawings of machines.His drawings of flying machines, parachutes,hanging gliders,helicopters,and submarines were far ahead of their time and were themselves works of art with their detailed shadowing and illusion of motion.His study of the human body,both structure and function,led to his design of the first known robot and to an explanation of the functioning of the heart's valves,even though he was unaware of the basic facts of blood circulation.

In 1517 Leonardo accepted the invitation of King Francis I of France to move into a large home near Tours.He remained there as the king's guest until his death in 1519 and was buried in the Chapel of Saint-Hubert in the castle of Amboise.

The Notebooks

Throughout his life,Leonardo kept notebooks in which he recorded daily his observations,ideas,and drawings.*The Notebooks* were originally loose sheets of paper of different sizes and types; they were bound together as volumes only after his death.The

22

列奥纳多·达·芬奇
《达·芬奇笔记》

列奥纳多·达·芬奇

列奥纳多·达·芬奇(1452~1519)生活在文艺复兴时期,是文艺复兴理想完人的主要典范。他是画家、发明家、建筑师、雕塑家、解剖学家、生理学家、工程师、音乐家和学生。虽然是专业的画家,但他的兴趣极其广泛,在笔记本上记下他的所见所想。

列奥纳多出生在佛罗伦萨附近一个叫芬奇的村庄 (达·芬奇意思就是来自芬奇),由父亲抚养长大并接受了文艺复兴时期佛罗伦萨最好的教育。1466年,他学艺于安德烈·德尔·韦罗基奥;韦罗基奥是当时佛罗伦萨最杰出的画家和雕塑家。列奥纳多最终成为独立的艺术家,并在佛罗伦萨他自己的画室里接收绘画和雕塑任务。

1482年,列奥纳多离开佛罗伦萨服务于米兰公爵,他的职责是设计大炮(军事工程师)和庆典舞台(土木工程师)。他也继续绘画和雕刻。大约在1497年,他完成其绘画作品"最后的晚餐";并开始进行科学绘画,尤其是人体绘画。他的解剖学的绘画(边解剖人体和小动物,边绘画)被认为是人类解剖学和生理学上最早的精确的代表作。

法军打败米兰公爵后,列奥纳多离开米兰回到佛罗伦萨。因为他是著名的画家,米兰人民都很欢迎他;他的作品开始影响新一代的艺术家们。这一时期,他创作了他的著名作品"蒙娜丽莎",画的是一个佛罗伦萨商人的年轻的妻子。在这幅画中他改变了传统的绘画方式,在她的腰部画上了手,这使人物的形象更加完整。

列奥纳多晚年住在米兰和罗马。他晚年极少作画,更专注于绘制机械图。他绘制的航空器、降落伞、悬挂式滑翔机、直升机和潜水艇远远领先于那个时代;这些图也是艺术品,其中有细致的阴影部分并使人有运动的错觉。他对人体结构和功能的研究使他设计了第一个机器人并解释了心脏瓣膜的机能,尽管他没有注意到血液循环的作用。

1517年,列奥纳多接受法国国王弗兰西斯一世的邀请搬到图尔附近的一座大房子里。他作为国王的客人一直住在那直到他于1519年去世,去世后被埋葬在昂布瓦斯城堡中的圣·于贝尔教堂里。

《达·芬奇笔记》

列奥纳多一生坚持记笔记,记下每天的所见、所想和草图。《达·芬奇笔记》最初是不同大小和类型纸的活页,在他去世后装订成册。笔记中还包括短小的论说文和随笔,全是

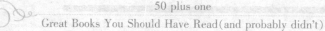
entries also include short essays and notes,all written in Italian and in Leonardo's mirror writing-left-handed and moving from right to left.No one knows why Leonardo never published his notebooks or why he wrote in mirror writing.Some historians believe that Leonard kept *The Notebooks* as a private journal to prevent anyone from using his ideas irresponsibly,such as building military weapons based on his plans.Others think he periodically reviewed his notes to revise,upgrade,or add material.

Leonardo began the first section of The Notebooks in Florence in 1508,but the rest of the notes were written during different periods in his life.The work contains notes and drawings on a variety of subjects from mechanics,hydrodynamics,anatomy,and botany to the flight of birds.Leonardo was interested in the geometry of the patterns of light reflection,in the use of mirrors as sources of heat,human anatomy and physiology (including embryology and pregnancy),architecture,and painting techniques,all of which he discussed or sketched in his Notebooks.

Leonardo's *Notebooks* contain thousands of pages of notes and drawings; they reflect his approach to science and art.Leonardo did not differentiate between art and science but instead described or depicted an object or a subject in great detail as a means of understanding what he was observing.Leonardo was not interested in conducting experiments or formulating theoretical explanations; rather,he explored ideas and topics as a kind of brilliantly informed observer.

His *Notebooks*-in the form of loose pages and jotted notes—were distributed by friends after his death and eventually became part of major collections in the Louvre in Paris,the National Library of Spain,the Ambrosian Library in Milan,and the British Library in London.The Ambrosian Library contains one of the largest collections,the "Atlanticus Codex," which is comprised of 393 folio pages containing more than 1,600 leaves of notes.The British Library's collection is known as the "Codex Arundel," because it was acquired by Thomas Howard,the Earl of Arundel (1586-1646) and later presented by the Earl of Arundel's descendants first to the Royal Society,then to the British Museum,and finally to the British Library.The major scientific work of Leonardo,the "Codex Leicester," written between 1506 and 1510,is the only collection in private hands; it is on loan to major museums for display by its owner,William H.Gates,Ⅲ.

Leonardo remains the prototype of the Renaissance man who was both curious and inventive.That he was also talented allowed him to express his observations in tangible and accessible ways.Although only a few of his paintings survive,his *Notebooks* have preserved the legacy of a man skilled and well-versed in the arts and sciences.

During his apprenticeship under Andrea del Verrocchio,Leonardo was exposed to many forms of artistic expression,including painting and sculpture.His abilities in painting, however,took him beyond the lessons of his teacher.He developed new painting techniques in many of his own pieces.He conceived of and perfected a color technique known as "chiaroscuro," using his own custom-made paints to portray subtle transitions between color areas to emphasize contrast between light and dark.He also developed a technique known as "sfumato," which creates a hazy or smoky effect.

In science and engineering,Leonardo's ideas were far ahead of his time.His fascination with aviation led to his detailed notes and drawings of the flight of birds.He used these

用意大利语反写(用左手,由右向左写)而成。没有人知道列奥纳多为什么不出版他的笔记,为什么反写。一些历史学家认为列奥纳多把笔记作为私人日记是为了避免别人滥用他的思想,例如利用他的计划制造军事武器。另一些人认为他定期复习笔记以修改、改善笔记并增加内容。

列奥纳多于1508年在佛罗伦萨开始写《达·芬奇笔记》的第一部分,但笔记的其余部分写于不同的时期。此书中的随笔和草图涉及许多方面,如机械学、流体动力学、解剖学和植物学以及鸟类的飞行。列奥纳多对光反射类型的几何学、用镜子作为热源、人体解剖学和生理学(包括胚胎学和妊娠)、建筑学和绘画技巧感兴趣,这些他都在《笔记》中有所讨论或画出草图。

列奥纳多的《笔记》有成千上万页的随笔和草图,它们反映了他对科学和艺术的研究。列奥纳多并不把科学与艺术区别对待,相反他把详细描述或勾画一个物体或主题作为理解他所见事物的方式。列奥纳多对做实验和进行理论阐释不感兴趣,他作为一个有见识的观察者来探索思想和论题。

列奥纳多的《笔记》(草草写在活页纸上的记录)在他死后由朋友们分发了,后来主要收藏在巴黎的罗浮宫、西班牙的国家图书馆、米兰的昂布瓦斯图书馆和伦敦的不列颠图书馆。昂布瓦斯图书馆收藏的是《大西洋手稿》,是393页的对开本,大约1,600页的笔记。不列颠图书馆的收藏品是《阿伦德尔手稿》,因为它最初是由托马斯·霍华德和阿伦德尔伯爵拥有,后来阿伦德尔伯爵的后代首先把它交给皇家学会,然后交给不列颠博物馆,最后交给了不列颠图书馆。列奥纳多的主要科学作品《莱斯特手稿》,写于1506年至1510年,是唯一由私人拥有的收藏品。它的主人威廉H·盖茨三世把它借给主要博物馆展出。

列奥纳多仍然是文艺复兴理想完人的典范,他好求知并且善于发明创造。他也很有天赋,这使他能够以明确易懂的方式表达他的观察所得。虽然他的绘画作品保存下来的不多,但《笔记》保存了一个精通于艺术和科学的人的遗产。

在列奥纳多学艺于安德烈·德尔·韦罗基奥期间,他接触了很多艺术表现形式,包括绘画和雕塑。然而,他的绘画能力超越了老师所教内容。他在许多画中使用了新的绘画技巧。他创造并完善了一种色彩技巧"明暗对照法",他用自己定制的色彩画出不同颜色之间细微的转化以强调明暗的对比。他还发明了一种技巧"渲染层次",这种技巧可以创造出烟雾效果。

列奥纳多在科学和工程方面的思想远远超过他所生活的时代。他对飞行的着迷使他详细记录和画出了鸟类的飞行。他利用这些观察所得设计了几个航空器,有人造鸟、悬挂

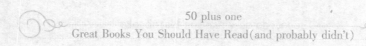
observations to plan several flying machines,including an artificial bird,a hang glider,and a helicopter.He even designed a parachute.He designed bridges (his design in 1502 for a bridge at the mouth of Bosporus was the basis of bridge constructed in Norway in 2001),a submarine,an early calculator,and a robot.His military designs included an armored tank, machine gun,and a cluster bomb.Presciently,given the current need for alternative energy sources,Leonardo studied and suggested industrial uses of solar power by using concave mirrors to heat water.

Most of Leonardo's devices and inventions were not constructed during his lifetime because the technology needed to manufacture the inventions was not yet available.His work did produce,however,in many instances,prototypes of many items used today.

Leonardo's interest in anatomy and physiology began when he was apprenticed to Andrea del Verrocchio,who insisted that all of his students learn anatomy.As his reputation as an artist grew,Leonardo was allowed to dissect human corpses first at a hospital in Florence and later at hospitals in Milan and Rome.Leonardo was the first person to describe the intricacies of the human spine and backbone and to draw cross-sections of the human brain.His drawings of human fetuses in the uterus,as well of the reproductive and urinary tracts,are especially detailed and accurate.Eventually,his interest in anatomy led to study of human physiology,and he was able to describe the flow of blood through the human heart, which inspired later scientists attempting to understand the human circulatory system.

Leonardo's wide-ranging endeavors greatly expanded the scope of knowledge in art, science,and engineering.His early theories and observations have guided scholars through the centuries since the Renaissance.He was more of an intellectual than a philosopher,and his approach was naturalistic and pragmatic.His need to describe and draw his thoughts and observations have left a legacy of valuable knowledge to which subsequent artists,scientists, and thinkers have turned for instruction and inspiration.

式滑翔机和直升机。他还设计了降落伞。他还设计了桥梁(2001年挪威建造的一座桥就是以他1502年为博斯普鲁斯海峡口设计的桥为基础)、潜水艇、早期计算器和机器人。他在军事方面的设计有装甲坦克、机关枪和集束炸弹。鉴于现在需要替代能源,当时列奥纳多很有先见之明,他研究太阳能并建议将其应用于工业,使用凹镜来加热水。

列奥纳多的大多数设备和发明在他在世时并没有生产出来因为生产所需要的技术还不存在。然而,他的作品的确创造了我们今天所使用的许多物品的原型。

列奥纳多对解剖学和生理学的兴趣开始于他学艺于安德烈·德尔·韦罗基奥时,韦罗基奥要求他的每一个学生学习解剖学。作为一名艺术家,随着他的名声越来越大,佛罗伦萨的一家医院第一次允许列奥纳多解剖人的尸体,后来米兰和罗马的医院也允许他解剖人的尸体。列奥纳多是第一个描述了错综复杂的脊椎和脊柱的人,他还首次画了人脑的剖面图。他所画的子宫中的胎儿和尿道都非常细致精确。后来,他对解剖学的兴趣使他开始研究人类生理学;他能够描绘出血液在人的心脏中的流动,这启发了后来的科学家们去研究人的循环系统。

列奥纳多的广泛努力大大扩大了艺术、科学和工程方面的知识范围。他的理论和言论引导了文艺复兴以来的学者们。与其说他是个哲学家,不如说他是个知识分子,他采用自然主义和实用主义的方法。他讲述和描绘他的思想和观察所得时留下了宝贵的知识遗产,后来许多艺术家、科学家和思想家都向这一遗产寻求启迪。

Twenty-three

Sir Thomas More:
Utopia

Who Was Sir Thomas More?

Thomas More (1478-1535) was an English writer,humanist scholar,lawyer,and politician.Because of his association with Henry VIII,he became an extremely influential and powerful figure in English Renaissance politics and humanism.Yet his fall from favor was equally dramatic and significant.His refusal to accept the king as head of the English church established More as a symbol of the individual who places personal conscience above the claims of secular authority.For his stance,More was beheaded by Henry VIII in 1535.Four hundred years later,in 1935,the Roman Catholic Church declared him a saint.

More was born in London,the son of a lawyer.After serving as a page in the service of the Archbishop of Canterbury,More attended Oxford University where he learned Latin and logic.He then studied law with his father and became a barrister in 1501.He considered joining the Franciscan order but instead decided to marry and start a family.He married Jane Colt with whom he had four children; after her death he married a widow with one daughter.He maintained his devotion to Catholicism and observed religious practices in his daily life.

More began his political career as Under-Sheriff of London in 1510.By 1518 he had entered the service of Henry VIII as councilor and ambassador,and after being knighted he became Under-Treasurer in 1521,Speaker of the House of Commons in 1523 (where he established the parliamentary privilege of free speech),and Chancellor of the Duchy of Lancaster from 1525 to 1529.When Henry dismissed Cardinal Wolsey in 1529,More became the first layman to hold the position of Lord Chancellor.

More's first language for his writing was Latin.His most famous work,Utopia,was written in Latin and not translated into English until 1551,years after his death.More did contribute to the growing body of literature in English by writing many of his religious works in English,beginning with his "Dialogues," which were refutations of the principles of the Protestant Reformation.The "Dialogues," including his "Dialogue of Comfort Against Tribulation," written in prison while he was awaiting execution,are important in English literature because of More's use of colloquial English.Despite his scholarly rhetoric,More was comfortable using humor in his written colloquial English,which added interest to his intellectual analyses of issues and his polemics.

Utopia

Utopia was written as a rational critique of English society,as a satire on unrealistic idealism,and as a proposal for an alternative social organization.More coined the title from the Greek roots meaning "not a place" (ou,"not," and topos,place).His readers were to understand that More was employing the humanist's love of irony and paradox.He carried out the irony by avoiding blatant criticism; rather,his protagonists praise Utopian values,thus criticizing More's England by means of negative comparison.

23

托马斯·莫尔
《乌托邦》

托马斯·莫尔

托马斯·莫尔(1478~1535)是英国作家、人文学者、律师和政治家。由于与亨利八世的关联,他成为英国文艺复兴时期政治和人文主义方面极具影响力的人物。然而他的失宠也同样比较戏剧化,有着深远的意义。他反对国王作为英国国教的领袖,这使莫尔成了把个人道德心置于非教会政权要求之上的人的代表。因此,1553年亨利八世将莫尔砍头处死。400年后,1935年,罗马天主教会宣布莫尔为圣人。

莫尔出生在伦敦,父亲是个律师。做过坎特伯雷大主教的侍从之后,莫尔进入牛津大学学习拉丁语和逻辑学。他跟父亲学习法律并于1501年成为一名律师。他曾考虑加入方济各会教会,但还是决定结婚成家。他娶了简·科尔特并生了4个孩子;科尔特去世后,他娶了一个寡妇并生了一个女儿。他坚持忠实于天主教,并在日常生活中遵守宗教习俗。

1510年,莫尔担任代理县治安官,开始了他的政治生涯。至1518年,他做过亨利八世的参赞和大使;被封为骑士后,1521年任代理财政大臣,1523年任下议院议长(他使议会拥有言论自由特权),1525年至1529年任兰开斯特公爵郡大臣。1529年,亨利罢免沃尔西主教后,莫尔担任大法官职务,他是第一个担任此职务的平信徒。

莫尔写作最初使用的是拉丁语。他的著名作品《乌托邦》就是用拉丁语写成,直到他去世后,于1551年才被翻译成英语。莫尔为英语文学的发展作出了贡献,用英语写了大量宗教作品,最早的是一些反驳新教宗教改革原则的"对话"。这些"对话",包括《关于苦难之慰藉的对话》,写于狱中等待上断头台时,因莫尔使用了口语体英语而在英语文学中占有重要的地位。尽管莫尔专门研究修辞,他在口语体英语中能够自如地使用幽默,这给他所分析的问题和他的争辩学增加了趣味。

《乌托邦》

《乌托邦》是对英国社会理性的批评,对不现实的理想主义的讽刺,提供了一个供选择的社会组织形式。莫尔从拉丁词根中创造了这个标题,意思是"不是一个地方"(ou,不是;topos,地方)。读者认为莫尔是在使用人文主义者们喜欢用的反语和矛盾手法。他使用反语以避免公然的批评;他的主人公们赞扬乌托邦的社会准则,进而通过反面的比较来批判莫尔所在的英格兰。

The work is a narration by a traveler,Raphael Hythloday,about his trip to Utopia.As part of his story,he relates the customs and culture of this mythical land.More compared Utopian values-lack of poverty,simple legal code,humane punishments,unselfishness,and abolition of private property—to those of the English social structure,which by contrast he deemed inferior.In Utopia:

- Everyone works everyday to produce food to feed the entire population.
- All activities and social needs,such as caring for the sick and providing family needs, are supervised.
- Money and valuable artifacts are meaningless.
- Laws and lawyers are not needed.
- War is to be avoided.
- Everyone is attuned to doing what is necessary for the greater good of all.
- Everyone worships a single God.
- Everyone believes in the immortality of the soul and life after death.
- Elimination of private property is the foundation of the society.

It is evident that the cultural values of More's Utopia are based on the monastic life,an established way of life at that time despite the humanistic and religious reformation movement.Despite his humanist philosophy,More was a product of orthodox Christian beliefs and a proponent of religious authority.His steadfast religious convictions in the face of his imprisonment and death are proof of his Christian principles.

More has influenced social thinking in the centuries following the appearance of his most famous work.The significance of Utopia extends far beyond 16th century England. More's Utopia has attracted modern socialists who find More a shrewd observer of economic and social exploitation.Thus,Utopia became an important historical reference for the development of early socialist ideas.

Many scholars have speculated that such thinkers as Thomas Hobbes ("Leviathan," 1660), John Locke ("An Essay Concerning Human Understanding," 1699),Thomas Jefferson (U.S. "Declaration of Independence," 1776),Thomas Paine ("The Rights of Man," 1791) and Karl Marx and Friedrich Engels ("The Communist Manifesto," 1848) may have been influenced by More's vision in Utopia.The American transcendentalist Henry David Thoreau may have conceived his own philosophy as set forth in "Walden" after studying More's Utopia.

Actual events that occurred in the years following the publication of Utopia may have received their impetus from the core idea of More's work:The change from a poorly functioning culture to a society working on more rational,egalitarian values.These events include the English Civil Wars of 1642 to 1660,the American Revolution of 1776,the French Revolution of 1789,and the revolt of the Spanish Colonies (Haiti,Venezuela, Colombia,Ecuador,Chile) during the 18th and 19th centuries.

Beyond its social and political impact,Utopia may also be considered an early forerunner of the modern novel.Utopia is prose fiction that supposedly propounds historical truth,yet its satirical tone informs the reader that is it neither real nor true.Utopia is a travelogue,a story,a history,and a satire,all of which are elements of the modern novel. More's skillful use of English vernacular and humor further contribute to the genesis of what has evolved as modern fiction.

本书记叙了旅行者拉斐尔·希斯洛德的乌托邦之旅。故事中讲述了这一神秘土地的习俗和文化。莫尔把乌托邦的社会准则——没有贫穷、简单的法律、人道的惩罚、大公无私和取消私有财产——与英国社会准则相比较,通过对比他认为英国社会制度是低级的。在乌托邦:

● 每个人每天工作,生产出所有人需要的食物。
● 所有活动和社会需要,如照顾病人和满足家庭需要,都得到管理。
● 钱和珍贵的手工艺品都是没有意义的。
● 不需要法律和律师。
● 不再有战争。
● 每个人习惯于做对所有人有好处的事情。
● 大家崇信一个上帝。
● 每个人都相信灵魂的不朽和来生。
● 取消私有财产是社会的基础。

很明显莫尔《乌托邦》中的文化准则是以禁欲生活为基础的;尽管有人文主义运动和宗教改革运动,但这种生活方式已被接受。尽管莫尔宣扬人文主义哲学,他还是信奉正统基督教信条,支持宗教权威。面对监禁和死亡所表现的坚定的宗教信仰就是他信奉基督教信条的证明。

莫尔著作的问世影响了几个世纪的社会思想。《乌托邦》的重大影响远远超出了16世纪的英格兰。莫尔的《乌托邦》吸引着现代社会学家,他们发现莫尔是经济和社会剥削的敏锐观察者。因此,《乌托邦》是早期社会主义思想形成的重要历史参考。

许多学者推测莫尔在《乌托邦》中的洞察力可能影响了思想家托马斯·霍布斯(《利维坦》1660)、约翰·洛克(《人类理解论》1699)、托马斯·杰斐逊(美国《独立宣言》1776)、托马斯·潘恩(《人的权力》1791)及卡尔·马克思和弗里德里希·恩格斯(《共产党宣言》1848)。美国超验主义者亨利·大卫·梭罗可能是在研究莫尔的《乌托邦》之后创造了他自己的哲学,并在《沃尔登》中阐述。

《乌托邦》出版之后发生的一些事件其推动力可能来自于莫尔作品的中心思想:把不起作用的文化变成以理性、平均主义准则为基础的社会。这些事件有1642年至1660年英国国内战争、1776年美国革命、1789年法国革命和18、19世纪西班牙殖民地(海地、委内瑞拉、哥伦比亚、厄瓜多尔和智利)的反抗。

除了其社会和政治影响,《乌托邦》也可被看做是现代小说的先驱。《乌托邦》是散文体小说,当然其中有很多史实;但它的讽刺语气使读者感觉它的内容并不真实。《乌托邦》是游记、故事、传说和讽刺文学,这些都是现代小说的要素。莫尔熟练使用英语方言和幽默为现代小说的形成作出了贡献。

Twenty-four

Martin Luther:
The 95 Theses

Who Was Martin Luther?

It can truly be said of Martin Luther,as it can be said of few other people,that he changed the course of Western civilization.It is also true,however,that many people misinterpret what he actually did.Luther did not intend to found a new kind of Christian church.The concepts we associate with him—"Protestant" or "Reformation"—should really be appreciated for their simplest meaning:to protest,to reform.

Martin Luther was a Roman Catholic priest,who protested against his church,who tried to reform it; he did not imagine himself to be creating,founding,a new religion.

Luther was born in Eisleben,Germany to a family that had been peasants.His father had first worked in copper mines,later he operated such mines—we would say that he had moved from being a working-class man to being a middle-class man.In common with other such self-made men,Luther's father wanted him to have a better beginning that he himself had,and Luther was sent to the University of Erfurt,where he earned both a B.A.and M.A.; he then entered law school at Erfurt.In 1505,at the age of 22,he went through a life-changing experience:he was caught in a violent thunderstorm,prayed to St.Anna that if he managed to avoid the horrendous lightning of this storm,he would become a monk.Because his life was spared,he left law school,and entered Erfurt's Augustinian monastery in 1507. Luther was a dedicated monk,and in 1507 he was also ordained a priest.In 1508 he began teaching theology at the University of Wittenberg.In 1512,he was awarded a Doctor of Theology degree,then was made a member of the Wittenberg Theological Faculty Senate,a position he was thereafter to retain for the rest of his life.

The 95 Theses

Luther was a priest of the Roman Catholic Church—he was,as well,one of its most prominent theologians and teachers.It was his study and research as an academic that caused him to begin to question some articles of dogma of his Church.

As a result of his study,Luther came to feel that the Church had lost sight of,had been diverted away from,some the central truths of Christianity.The most important of his conclusions-in terms of his future and that of his church—was that,in his view,the Church had over time created a hierarchy of regulations and procedures designed to lead man to God.Yet,in Luther's view,The Bible promised that salvation is a gift from God,through His son Jesus—and that that condition of grace,man's preparedness for salvation,can be and should be achieved by man on his own.Luther came to feel that God offers salvation to each individual,that this gift depends on the individual's relation to God through that agency of God that man can understand,namely Jesus Christ.

It was a short step from this point of view to Luther's questioning the legitimacy of the Pope (God's chosen spokesman on Earth,in the view of his Church) and his priests,special individuals (ordained sacramentally) who could guide man,absolve him of sin-only priests,

马丁·路德
《九十五条论纲》

马丁·路德

说起马丁·路德,我们完全可以说,像其他几个人一样,他改变了西方文明的轨迹。然而,许多人也的确曲解了他的行为。路德没有打算要建立新的基督教会。我们把"新教徒"和"宗教改革"这些概念与路德联系在一起,这些概念应该被认为是其最简单的意思:抗议和改革。

马丁·路德是罗马天主教会牧师,他抗议他所在教会的统治并试图对其进行改革;他没有想到自己将要创建新的宗教。

路德出生在德国艾斯莱本一个农民家庭。他父亲起初在铜矿工作,后来自己经营铜矿,我们可以说他由劳动人民变成了中产阶级。和其他靠自己奋斗成功的人一样,路德的父亲想让路德跟自己一样有个良好的开始,便送路德到埃尔富特大学读书。路德在埃尔富特大学获得了文学学士和文学硕士学位,后来又进入埃尔富特的法学院学习。1505年,22岁时,一个经历改变了他的生活:他被困在猛烈的雷暴中;他向圣·安娜祈祷,如果可以躲避可怕的雷电,他将成为一名修道士。他得救了,所以他离开了法学院,1507年进入埃尔富特的奥古斯丁修道院。路德是个忠诚的修道士,1507年被授以牧师职。1508年,他开始在威登堡大学教授神学。1512年,他获得神学博士学位;后来成为威登堡神学院议会的成员,此后他一直是议会的成员。

《九十五条论纲》

路德是罗马天主教会牧师,也是著名的神学家和教师。正是他在学术上的学习和研究使他开始怀疑教会教义的某些条款。

经过研究,路德发现教会忽视并背离了基督教的某些核心真理。从他及教会的未来来看,他最重要的结论是:教会创造了不同级别的规定和程序来把人类引向上帝。而路德认为,《圣经》承诺灵魂得救是上帝通过他的儿子耶稣给予人的礼物;获得恩惠的条件,即人类获得灵魂得救的准备,可以而且应该由人类自己来完成。路德开始认为上帝使每个人获得灵魂得救,这一礼物取决于人类可以理解的上帝的那个代理,即耶稣基督,对每个人的讲述。

路德进而开始质疑教皇(上帝所选的其在人间的代言人,代表教会)及其牧师们的合法性。牧师们是被授以圣职的特殊的人们,他们可以引导人类,免除人类的罪过;但只有当牧师由大主教引导,然后由教皇引导,他们才可以把人类带给上帝。路德越来越相信人

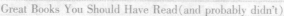
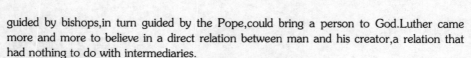
guided by bishops,in turn guided by the Pope,could bring a person to God.Luther came more and more to believe in a direct relation between man and his creator,a relation that had nothing to do with intermediaries.

As well,he questioned the legitimacy of the sacraments,particularly the Eucharist or Communion.Was Communion really an occasion of transubstantiation,in which priests (and priests only) participated in a mystical union with Christ,therefore with God.Or was Communion designed for all men,to renew their allegiance to Christ? It is only Christ,not the priesthood,Luther felt,who can reveal God to mankind.

In addition to his classes as a professor,Luther also was a preacher at Wittenberg's City Church,St.Mary's; as well,he was now and then asked to preach to Wittenberg's Elector and his court at the Castle Church.In all of these activities as speaker,his new views had emerged-yet it was the question of indulgences that brought matters to a head.An "indulgence" was supposed to remove any sin that still remained after absolution-a forgiveness on earth,as well a forgiveness for souls in Purgatory; they were sold by the Church as a way of way of raising funds.Luther saw this trade as one that could mislead people-they would rely on paying their way out of sin,rather than truly repenting.In 1516 and 1517 he preached three sermons against this practice,then,on October 13,1517,he posted *The 95 Theses* on the door of the Castle Church in Wittenberg.In his Theses Luther is actually rather mild-he condemns greed and worldliness in the Church and he asks for further study of what the sellers of indulgences should be allowed to claim.

But the floodgates were open.However unobtrusively,Luther,a priest,had questioned the Church.Within 2 weeks copies of *The 95 Theses* had spread throughout Germany; within 2 months copies were available throughout Europe.Christianity would never be the same again.

The rest of Luther's life was one of conflict.The Pope got involved,ordered one of his advisers to look into the matter of the Theses.This adviser declared Luther a heretic,and denounced his writing and preaching.Luther responded with equal determination,and a heated controversy developed,with Luther's eventually declaring that the papacy had nothing to do with the actuality of Christianity—that the "keys to the kingdom" had been given not to one man but to all of the faithful.In all of this,Luther's fame grew,and students and scholars flocked to Wittenberg to hear Luther preach on what he regarded as the corruption and false teaching of the papacy; instead,Luther emphasized the supreme worth of the individual's relation not to his spiritual advisers but to God.One of this most famous phrases of the time was: "I submit to no laws of interpreting the Word of God." The inevitable took place; 3 years after Luther had posted *The 95 Theses*,the Pope excommunicated him.

The Holy Roman Emperor then got involved.Charles V opened the imperial Diet of Worms in January 1521,and Luther was summoned there to renounce his views.Luther testified and said:"I do not accept the authority of popes and councils—my conscience is captive to the Word of God." Again,the inevitable happened-Luther was declared an outlaw and a heretic,and his writings were banned.Luther was exiled for a year to Wartburg Castle, where he worked on a translation of the New Testament into German,a feat that later directly influenced the King James Bible.Such a task also involved a concentrated study of

类与其造物主之间是直接联系的,与中间人无关。

路德也质疑圣礼的合法性,特别是圣餐。圣餐时真的会出现圣餐变体吗?圣餐中,牧师(并且只有牧师)与基督神秘结合,并与上帝成为一体。圣餐是用来供所有人表现他们对基督忠诚的吗?路德认为只有基督才能将上帝展现给人类,而不是牧师们。

路德除了是学校的老师外,他还在威登堡市政教堂——圣·玛丽教堂布道。他还被请到城堡教堂向威登堡的选帝侯及其侍臣们布道。在这些布道活动中,他的新观点产生了;然而赦罪券是个导火索。赦罪券被认为可以清除赦罪(人间的赦免,炼狱中对灵魂的赦免)后仍然存在的罪过。教会兜售这些赦罪券以筹集资金。路德认为这一交易会误导人们,人们只是花钱赎罪,而不是真正地忏悔。1516年和1517年他曾三次布道反对这一做法;1517年10月13日,他把《九十五条论纲》贴在威登堡城堡教堂的门上。在《论纲》中路德比较和缓,谴责了教会的贪婪和世俗,并要求进一步研究允许赦罪券兜售者们宣扬什么。

但是洪水之门打开了。不管怎么地不鲁莽,路德,一个牧师,对教会提出了质疑。两周内《九十五条论纲》传遍了德国;两个月内传遍了欧洲。基督教不能再同以前一样了。

路德的余生充满了冲突。教皇也参与此事,命令他的顾问调查《论纲》事宜。这个顾问宣布路德为异教徒,并取消他写作和布道。路德同样坚决地回应,宣称教皇与现实中的基督教无关,"天国的钥匙"并不是给一个人而是给所有虔诚的人们。这引起了激烈的争论。路德因此而更为出名,学生和学者们都汇集在威登堡,听路德针对教皇的腐败和虚假说教的布道。路德强调个人向上帝而不是向精神顾问忏悔的重要性。当时最有名的一句话是"我不屈从于任何阐释上帝意旨的法律。"不可避免的事情发生了。路德张贴《九十五条论纲》3年后,教皇把他驱逐出教会。

后来神圣罗马天主帝王也参与此事。1521年1月查理五世召开沃姆斯帝国议会,路德被召到此重新阐述他的观点。路德证明自己的观点并且说:"我不承认教皇及议会的权威,我的良心被上帝意旨停获。"不可避免的事又一次发生了,路德被宣布为犯人和异教徒,他的作品也被禁止。路德被流放到瓦特堡城堡一年,在那他把《圣经新约》翻译成德语,他的这一功绩后来直接影响了金·詹姆斯的《圣经》。早期对《圣经》的研究使他产生了许多观点,这一翻译工作也需要认真研究《圣经》。

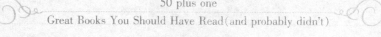
The Bible,his earlier study of which had provoked so many of his ideas.

For the rest of his life Luther continued to refine those ideas-for example:The ordination of a priest is not a sacrament; it is simply an acknowledgement that someone has been "called" to the service of preaching and administering the sacraments to his fellow mortals.

Whether Luther ever thought of himself as a radical,founding a new church,is open to question.But,in the end,his views were sufficiently divergent from those of the Church,which early in his life he had served,that congregations,accepting his views,began to form even during his own lifetime.Whatever his intentions,a new Church did continue to come into being.70 million Christians now call themselves Lutherans,and in the world today there are some 400 million Christians who call themselves Protestants,who trace their history back to Martin Luther.We should all remember that it was *The 95 Theses* that started this phenomenon that changed our civilization-but we should as well remember,whatever our religion affiliations,that Luther's message was at its most basic one that was both simple and that relied on the individual.Luther felt,finally,that man should not live in some kind of spiritual slavery to his own sins,particularly those sins that someone else defined for him,but should instead attempt to live a life of love and service to others.It is a notion that in its time was revolutionary,but readers should remember that it is also a message,whatever its effect,that is truly benign and,in the end,spiritual.

　　路德利用余生继续完善他的观点。例如,授牧师职不是圣礼;只是承认某个人应召进行布道和主持圣礼。

　　路德是否认为自己是个激进分子,创建了新教,这还有待于讨论。但最后,他的观点完全不同于他早年服务的教会的观点;赞同他的观点的教会甚至在他在世时就开始形成。不管他的意图是什么,新的教会逐渐产生了。现在有7,000万基督教徒称自己为路德教徒;有约4亿基督教徒自称是新教徒,把他们的历史追溯到马丁·路德。我们应该铭记是《九十五条论纲》引发了改变我们文明的运动;不管我们的宗教信仰是什么,我们也应该铭记路德的观点是最基本的,既简单又依赖于个人。

　　最后,路德认为人类不应该生活在自己罪过的精神奴役中,尤其是那些别人赋予的罪过;相反应该试图过着充满爱的生活,并服务于他人。这一观念在当时是革命性的,但读者应该记住,不管其影响如何,这也是善意的,最终是精神的启示。

Twenty-five

Michel de Montaigne: Essays

Who Was Michel de Montaigne?

Michel de Montaigne is an important and influential writer of the French Renaissance (he lived in the 16th century:1533-1592).He is the epitome of what we now call the Renaissance Man—he was active as a statesman; he was a scholar and writer; he was interested in a wide variety of subjects.

Montaigne was also what we would now call "privileged." He was born in Perigord,in the family castle,not far from Bordeaux; his family was very rich.Not much is known about his mother,but his father,himself an interesting figure,was an important influence in Montaigne's life.His father served as a soldier; he also served as mayor of Bordeaux; and he had some very liberal notions of education.Montaigne was tutored at home (by a tutor instructed to speak only in Latin),very much according to his father's notions of "home schooling;" he then attended the best boarding school in Bordeaux,then studied law in Toulouse and became a lawyer.From 1557,he served as "counselor" to the Parliament in Bordeaux; from 1561 to 1563 he was employed at the court of King Charles IX.During this period and after he also translated the *Theologia* of the Spanish monk Sebond,and prepared an edition of the works of his friend Boetie.

On his father's death,Montaigne inherited the castle (Chateau de Montaigne) and he moved back there in 1570.In 1571,at the age of 38,he retired from public life; he moved into the Tower of the Chateau de Montaigne,and for nearly 10 years he worked on his *Essays* (in French:Essais).After living like a hermit for all of these years,Montaigne published the result of his work,his *Essays*,in 1580.Thereafter,he seems to have gone back, rather easily,to his life as a public man: he traveled throughout the Continent from 1580-1581;   while visiting Rome in 1581 he learned that he had been elected Mayor of Bordeaux; he returned there and served until 1585.Thereafter,he continued to revise and expand and oversee the publication of his *Essays*-until his death in 1592.

Essays

Montaigne seems to have been that very rare kind of individual who can both pursue a public/professional life at the same time that he can step away from that life and create an enduring work of literary art.

But his accomplishment is not just in his life but in his art itself.Montaigne is credited with almost single-handedly having created the literary form of the essay,with influencing writers and philosophers who came after him (including people as diverse as Shakespeare and Nietzsche),and,with his *Essays*,of having established a tone and method of literary non-fiction that is still the accepted standard even now.Every memoir,biography,autobiography, collections of essays or articles now being published bears his stamp.

His accomplishment was not just the form but what he managed to encompass within that form.He combined the personal with the objective; in his work,casual ruminations co-

米歇尔·德·蒙田
《随笔集》

米歇尔·德·蒙田

  米歇尔·德·蒙田(1533~1592)是法国文艺复兴时期一位重要而有影响力的作家。他是文艺复兴理想完人的典型代表:他是活跃的政治家、学者和作家;他对各个学科都感兴趣。

  蒙田也是我们所称为的"有特权的人"。他出生在佩里戈尔自家的城堡里,离波尔多不远;他的家庭非常富有。关于他的母亲,知道的不多;他的父亲,是一个很有趣的人,对蒙田的一生有着重要的影响。他的父亲曾服过兵役;曾担任过波尔多的市长;关于教育,他有一些非常开明的观念。蒙田是在家里接受教育 (家庭教师奉命只用拉丁文授课),完全按照他父亲的"家庭教学"观念。后来,蒙田进入了波尔多最好的寄宿学校,然后在图卢兹学习法律,成为一名律师。1557年开始, 他担任波尔多议会顾问;1561年~1563年期间,他受雇于国王查尔斯九世的宫廷。在此期间及以后,他翻译了西班牙僧侣塞朋德的《神学》,并且为他的朋友博埃蒂的作品作了准备。

  蒙田的父亲去世后,他继承了城堡(蒙田的城堡),并于1570年搬回此处。1571年,蒙田38岁时,他退出社会生活,搬到了蒙田城堡的塔里;在之后的十年中,一直致力于写作《随笔集》。这些年类似于隐士的生活使蒙田于1580年出版了他的工作成果《随笔集》。之后,他似乎又回到了他作为一个公众人物的生活:1580年至1581年,他游历欧洲大陆;1581年在罗马旅行时,他获悉自己已被选举为波尔多市长,于是他回到波尔多担任市长一职直至1585年。之后,他继续修订、扩充《随笔集》,并监督其在国外的出版直到他于1592年去世。

《随笔集》

  只有极少数人能够在追求社会或职业生活的同时,又能够摆脱这一生活并创作出不朽的文学作品。

  但是他的成就不仅限于他的生活,而且也表现在他的艺术创作方面。蒙田的成就在于他几乎独立地创造了随笔这种文学形式;影响了他之后许多有影响力的作家和哲学家(包括莎士比亚和尼采);他的《随笔集》确立了一种文学非小说文体的格调与手法,至今仍是广为接受的标准。今天所出版的每一本回忆录、传记、自传、随笔集或文章集都带有他的印记。

  他的成就不仅仅是文学形式,而且是文学形式中所包含的内容。他将主观与客观相结合;他的作品中,随意思考与智力沉思并存。在蒙田那个时代,他被尊为政治家和仲裁

exist with intellectual speculation.In his own time,Montaigne,revered as a statesman and arbitrator (particularly of conflicts between Catholics and Protestants and between adherents of one royal faction against the other),was not greatly honored as a writer.People of his own time were confused by what they saw as the lack of the formal in his work.It seemed too personal.Montaigne himself said: "I am the matter of my book"—in other words,I am my own subject.To a 16th century Frenchman,such an attitude was very strange indeed-nonserious,even self-indulgent.The modern reader sees things differently.Montaigne expressed the thoughts of his age,its conflicts and doubts and aspirations,but he did so by relying on the only consciousness he thought valid—his own.Critics ever since have commented that his method (which has become the universally accepted method of literary non-fiction,which is why readers today find Montaigne so "modern")—makes him more honest,more reliable,more human than any other author of the Renaissance.

To have invented a literary genre,to have given it both its characteristic form and tone, and to have that form/tone endure as a standard for more than 5 centuries- these are great accomplishments.

Montaigne can,however,claim yet one more accomplishment:If we had to choose one authentic voice of the Renaissance—one that can best represent that time in history to those of us who live centuries later—it would be the voice of Montaigne.

Montaigne,very much a man of his times,and very much the activist Renaissance man, yet steps back from the pageant,retires for nearly 10 years to his tower,and though it would not be fair to say that he puts a damper on the exuberance of his age,he brings a certain fresh skepticism to this growing belief in human perfectability or superhuman accomplishment.Is there a human nature that can be perfected? He asks.He suggests that first of all we would need to know the most basic characteristics of that nature,and he concludes that,when looking at humans,all he sees is great variety and change—endless change.Moreover,he says,he can't even begin to understand himself; how then is he to understand others? And,if we all suffer from this human myopia,how are we to know of what man is capable?

Montaigne is not a cynic; he is a kind of corrective.He disdains man's pursuit of fame and riches; he wonders why man does not try to detach himself from worldly things—to prepare for the inevitable.He wonders:If we cannot even begin to understand self,how are we to attain true certainty about anything? In all things,should we not favor the concrete of our experience to the abstraction of our theories?

These are but a few of hundreds of examples of his thought,of the subjects of his *Essays*.In all of his writings,he strives to make man more moderate in his ambitions,in his expectations,in what,in life,he can achieve.His view is far from hopeless—he believes that it is possible to live a virtuous life,to live a happy life—but only if man recognizes the limitations of being human and understands that true happiness comes from contentment-not from impossible dreams.

Montaigne's voice comes to us from a time of "great expectations," and seems,in his quiet sermon about moderation,to speak to us now,just as vividly as he spoke to his own century.

人(尤其是在天主教徒和新教徒的冲突以及不同皇族派别的追随者之间的冲突中),却并未被尊为作家。与他同代的人对于其作品缺乏正式内容而感到困惑。他的作品太主观了。蒙田自己曾说:"我本人就是书里所写的内容",换句话说,我就是书的主题。对于一个16世纪的法国人来说,这样的观点的确很奇怪——不严肃甚至有些自我放纵。然而现代读者却不这样认为。蒙田表达了他那个时代的观念、冲突、疑惑和渴望,而且是依赖他认为唯一有效的意识——他本人的意识来实现的。评论家认为他的创作手法(这种手法已成为普遍接受的文学非小说创作手法,也是为什么今天的读者认为蒙田的作品非常"现代"的原因)使他比文艺复兴时期其他任何一个作家都更正直、可信和人性化。

发明了一种文学体裁,确立了其形式特征和格调,并且使其成为5个多世纪以来的文学规范——这些都是蒙田的伟大成就。

然而,蒙田还取得了另外一个成就:如果我们要选出一个最能代表文艺复兴的人——一个能向几个世纪之后的我们最好地讲述那段历史的人,这个人就是蒙田。

蒙田是当时的文云人物,也是激进的文艺复兴完人;而他却退出了这个盛大的场面,隐退在家中的城堡近十年。如果说他在这个繁盛时期扮演了一个令人扫兴的角色似乎有些不公平;可是,对于人类完美和超人成就的信仰,他提出了某种新的疑问。他问到,有没有可以达到完美无缺的人性?他对此提出质疑。他认为我们首先需要知道人性最基本的特征;他得出结论说,观察人类时,他所看到的是多样性和不断的变化。另外,他说他甚至开始不能理解自己;那怎么能够去理解他人呢?如果每个人都这样目光短浅,那我们怎么可以知道人类能够做什么呢?

蒙田并非愤世嫉俗之人;他只是想纠正人们的错误观念。他鄙视人们对名誉和财富的追求;他想知道为什么人们不尝试脱离这些世俗的事物——为不可避免的事情做准备。他想知道,如果我们开始不能理解自我,那如何能够确定其他事情呢?在宇宙万物中,与抽象结论相比,难道我们不应该偏重于具体经历吗?

这些只是他的思想及《随笔集》主题中的一些例子。在他所有的作品中,他努力让人们拥有适当的人生理想和目标,并适度地奋斗。他并非不抱希望——他相信人类可以过上美好、幸福的生活,但人类必须认识到自己的局限性并意识到真正的幸福源于满足,而不是源于不切实际的梦想。

蒙田的声音来自于一个"拥有伟大前程"的时期;他似乎在与我们对话,就适度静静地向我们布道,就如同在与自己时代的人对话一样生动。

Twenty-six

Miguel de Cervantes: Don Quixote

Who Was Miguel de Cervantes?

Spanish poet,playwright and novelist Miguel de Cervantes (1547-1616),best known for his novel *Don Quixote de la Mancha*,wrote what many people regard as the first great modern novel.Although he produced numerous literary works,his entire reputation rests on this one book,which brought him enduring international fame.

Born in Alcalá de Henares,Spain to a poor apothecary surgeon,Cervantes spent his early adult years traveling.After studying in Madrid,he went to Rome where he became acquainted with Italian literature.His life for the most part was one of hardship; one of the reasons for his travels was that he was almost constantly looking for work.He fought in several wars,lost partial use of his left hand in the battle of Lepanto,and after the battle for Tunis,on his return journey home to Spain,he was captured by Turks and was taken by them to Algiers as a slave.

Fortunately for him,the Turks found on him a letter from the Duke of Alba.Because they thought that Cervantes was a man of importance,they tried to sell him for ransom.For 5 years,he was held prisoner before he was finally released.He returned to Spain in 1580, and 4 years later married a woman who was much younger than himself.During their marriage,they had no children,but Cervantes did have a child from another woman with whom he had an affair prior to his marriage.

In the years that followed,his life remained unsettled; it included temporary excommunication and bankruptcy.His plays,poetry,and his first major work "La Galatea" never brought him the financial security he sought.But life changed for him in 1605,when *Don Quixote* was published.

Although Cervantes was never made rich by his book,he did achieve international fame because of it and was able to escape poverty for the first time.He died in 1616,in Madrid,a year after he had completed the second part of *Don Quixote*.

Don Quixote

Miguel de Cervantes is one of the most important writers in Spanish and world literature.His novel,*Don Quixote* de la Mancha,about a gallant knight "with the impossible dream" and his trusty squire Sancho Panza,has become world famous,as have his characters-even to people who have never read the novel.Cervantes is now well loved everywhere,but nowhere so much as in his native Spain,where his face currently appears on Spanish Euro coins.

Who was this man that could generate such respect from readers and endure through the years? What did he offer that other writers didn't?

It is generally believed that Cervantes wrote *Don Quixote* while he was in prison.It was his plan,when he conceived the book,to recreate the manner and speech of the times. This idea was then almost revolutionary.But since he was breaking new literary ground with

26

米盖尔·德·塞万提斯
《堂吉珂德》

米盖尔·德·塞万提斯

西班牙诗人、剧作家和小说家米盖尔·德·塞万提斯(1547~1616)，其代表作《堂吉珂德》被很多人认为是第一部伟大的现代主义巨著。虽然他创作了诸多的文学作品，但其在世界文坛上不朽的荣誉完全来自于这部小说。

作者出生于西班牙阿尔卡拉·德·埃纳雷斯城一个贫寒的家庭，父亲是个外科医生，他年轻时的大部分时间是在旅行中度过的。完成了在马德里的学习，他前往罗马，并在那里了解了意大利文学。塞万提斯大半生是贫困潦倒的，他长期旅行的一大原因就是为了不断地寻找工作。他曾几次参战，在对抗土耳其来犯的勒班陀一战中左手受重伤而残废。打完保卫突尼斯的战役之后，他在返回西班牙的途中，被土耳其人抓获，并作为囚犯被押回了阿尔及尔。

幸运的是，土耳其人在他身上发现了一封来自基督教联军统帅阿尔芭公爵的信，他们便把他当成重要人物，准备勒索巨额赎金。塞万提斯在阿尔及尔整整被囚禁了5年，最终被释放。他于1580年回到了西班牙，4年之后娶了一个年纪比他小很多的女子，他们夫妻二人没有子女，不过塞万提斯在婚前曾有一次风流韵事，当时的情人给他生了一个孩子。

在之后的几年里，塞万提斯仍然流离失所，被临时逐出教会，接着又是遭遇破产。他的剧作、诗歌，还有他第一部重要的作品《伽拉苔亚》都没有带来他所期望的经济上的保证。然而，在1605年《堂吉珂德》的出版，改变了他的人生。

这部小说虽然未能使塞万提斯变得富有起来，却为他赢得了极高的荣誉，并第一次让他摆脱了贫困。1616年，也就是在他完成了《堂吉珂德》第二部写作的次年，塞万提斯在马德里去世。

《堂吉珂德》

米盖尔·德·塞万提斯是西班牙乃至世界文坛上最伟大的作家之一，他的代表作《堂吉珂德·台·拉曼却》，描述了一个怀有不切实际梦想的英勇骑士和他忠实的随从桑丘·潘沙的游侠经历，这部小说因其鲜活的人物形象闻名于世界，甚至没有读过它的人也对其中的人物略知一二。塞万提斯为世界各国人民所喜爱，但都比不上他的祖国西班牙对他的爱戴，他的肖像已经出现在西班牙通用的欧元上了。

那么，这个赢得读者如此高的评价和如此不朽声誉的人究竟是什么样子？他所提供给读者的又有何异于其他作家呢？

人们都普遍地认为塞万提斯是在狱中创作了《堂吉珂德》。他构思这部小说就是为了再现16世纪末17世纪初西班牙封建制度下人们社会生活的现实。这一创作意图在当时可

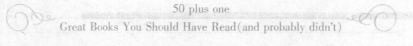
his novel, he also devised many new techniques to tell his story effectively. To make his book "work," Cervantes put aside old story-telling techniques and created new ones.

One of his goals was to create a plot that was believable and realistic and that would give his characters and story the feel of real life.

Unlike the books of his predecessors, his novel displays a mature skill at narration, dialogue and style. There is an excellent definition of characters, which helps make them distinctive, and there is even more realism and believability in his dialogue and plot than what was known in writers who preceded him.

The purpose of his book was to ridicule romantic chivalry, which was very popular during the Late Middle Ages and Renaissance. By creating a provocative character such as *Don Quixote*, Cervantes achieved his goal. Who will ever forget his vivid and believable portrayal of a man who, after reading many questionable stories about knights, decides to become a knight himself and "to right the unrightable wrong."

The general public responded well to his efforts to use the vernacular and to his decision to break away from the more literary style of the past, and they eagerly bought the book, making it a success throughout Europe. Thereafter, the novel became an inspiration to other writers around the world. Translated into many languages, the story of the gallant knight with the impossible dream has been adapted to many media-play, opera, movie, ballet.

Because of Cervantes's many sophisticated literary techniques, *Don Quixote* is not only called the first modern novel, but, as well, it is studied by students, teachers and critics for its style and seemingly effortless humor. Numerous writers through the years have been influenced by Cervantes including Charles Dickens, Herman Melville, and Gustave Flaubert.

Commentators have referred to *Don Quixote* as a prototype of the comic novel. Although the situations sometimes seem to mirror the burlesque in their attempt to create humor, the efforts are generally so refined that the humor never becomes vulgar. Cervantes manages to turn the action into something noble and polished by drawing on his skill as a storyteller. The 20th century French writer Dominique Aubier believes the book to be the first true modern novel developed systematically with structural skill. Unlike the disconnected stories of chivalric romance novels during the medieval period, Cervantes's story fits together well, and it goes beneath the surface of the characters to present in-depth psychological profiles. The reader encounters many firsts—a woman complaining about menopause, another character suffering from eating disorders. Cervantes even uses twists on character perspective to give an added touch of reality.

Anyone who has not read *Don Quixote* will wish to do so—to understand so much that has followed from Cervantes's great achievement.

以说是革命性的,作者利用这部作品开辟了崭新的文学创作的领域,同时他也创造出不同以往的写作手法来有效地讲述他的冒险故事,展现给读者一幅鲜活的社会生活的画面。

作者的创作目标之一就是编织一个现实可信的情节,使其人物形象和故事能使读者感同身受。

有别于前人的作品,这部小说展现了作者在描写记叙、组织人物对白、文体风格方面纯熟的写作功底。作者对剧中人物精彩的刻画,使之个性鲜明,其对白和剧情的描写比以往作家的更显真实、可信。

作者通过刻画堂吉珂德这一以救世英雄自居的荒唐的文学形象来讽刺中世纪晚期及文艺复兴时期盛行一时的带有奇幻色彩的骑士制度。而有的读者在读罢许多值得质疑的骑士故事之后,也极有可能会头脑一热忘了作者生动逼真的人物刻画,打算亲身体验一把骑士的感觉,重蹈覆辙去演绎那些"骑士道的荒唐"。

大众读者对塞万提斯能用白话文写作以及他力图摆脱过去更具文学色彩的写作风格的束缚所做出的努力极为支持,并且纷纷争先购买,使其影响遍及整个欧洲。之后,这部小说激发了世界各国作家们的写作灵感,并被翻译成许多其他语言,这个描述沉浸在幻想之中的英勇骑士的故事被改编成话剧、歌剧、电影和芭蕾舞剧被搬上荧屏。

由于塞万提斯高超纯熟的写作技巧,《堂吉珂德》不仅被称为是第一部现实主义小说,而且其独特的写作风格以及看似不费力所达到的幽默效果一直为很多学生、教师和文学评论家学习研究。不同时期的众多作家都受到了塞万提斯的影响,其中包括查尔斯·狄更斯、赫尔曼·梅尔维尔和古斯塔夫·福楼拜。

评论家们都把《堂吉珂德》视为喜剧小说的一部原型作品。虽然有时在某些剧情中作者为了达到幽默的效果我们似乎能看到滑稽模仿的影子,但作者精炼的笔法并不使这一幽默变得庸俗老套,而是通过讲故事的形式力求美化使其具备贵族气质。20世纪法国作家多米尼克·奥比尔(Dominique Aubier)认为这部作品是第一部真正的具有系统化写作框架的现实主义小说。不同于中世纪那些无条理的荒诞离奇的骑士小说,塞万提斯的作品故事结构缜密,对人物的刻画也是透过表面深入挖掘其内心世界。读者在阅读过程中会碰到许多"新鲜事"——比如某个更年期妇女抱怨绝经,另外还有人苦于饮食紊乱。塞万提斯甚至还运用"曲折"的描述手法对人物进行透视,以进一步反映社会生活的现实。

在此,推荐那些还未曾读过《堂吉珂德》的人们一读,去了解塞万提斯能够取得如此巨大成就的那些背后的故事。

Twenty-seven

William Shakespeare: Hamlet

Who Was William Shakespeare?

William Shakespeare has been called "the greatest" for so many reasons that readers and theatergoers may be forgiven if their heads swim when they come to his work. Shakespeare wrote 38 plays and 154 sonnets; as well, he wrote some occasional poems that are largely forgotten; the plays, and sonnets, are known throughout the world.

His greatness consists of these factors: He is the greatest playwright in English; many critics would argue that he is the greatest in any language. He is also the greatest poet and writer in English; again, many critics would say that he is the greatest writer that mankind has ever produced. It can be said of him that he refined the language of the Middle Ages, turned it into the language that the English-speaking world speaks today. In more literary terms, he perfected blank verse (unrhyming iambic pentameter-though Shakespeare does now and then use rhyme to close a speech or close a scene or to achieve dramatic emphasis); it remains the most exalted form in our poetic language.

In dramatic terms, he created a language that in itself creates drama—thus Romeo spots his lover Juliet at a window, and must tell the listener, the audience, his feelings. He says: "What light through yonder window breaks/It is the East/And Juliet is the sun." Shakespeare invents a language that conveys human feelings in dramatic terms, in terms of an action, an experience, to which the audience can relate. Then, as well, his reader or audience must remember: Shakespeare wrote not for an audience of aristocrats (though it is known that Queen Elizabeth I admired his plays, and he wrote one of them at her request) but for the common people of London, for whom theatre-going was a noisy delight; they did not always pay attention to the play so much as to the activities of other members of the audience—rather like a modern baseball game. Yet Shakespeare triumphed over that audience (all indications are that he was immensely popular), as he triumphs over us.

So great are these accomplishments, and so unlikely that they could all be the doing of one man, that some scholars (for the last 2 centuries) have doubted that the Shakespeare we know about could have been the author of these remarkable plays-better known throughout the world than any other literary works ever created, with the possible exception of The Bible. Surely a more traditional kind of "literary man" must have written the plays.

Shakespeare's life provides ammunition for such prejudices. He was born into a middle-class family in Stratford upon Avon (in what is now England's Warwickshire). His father was a glover and a local alderman. Shakespeare probably attended the King Edward VI Grammar School, which, as far as we know, was probably a good school, if not Eton College. At 18 he married an already pregnant Anne Hathaway. The late 1580s are known as Shakespeare's "lost period," because no one knows what he was doing during that time. By 1592 he was working as a playwright in London, also as an actor, and by 1594 he was part owner of the Chamberlain's Men repertory acting company. He was sufficiently successful as an actor/playwright/producer that toward the end of his life he was able to buy a house, New

27

威廉·莎士比亚
《哈姆雷特》

威廉·莎士比亚

威廉·莎士比亚被誉为最伟大的作家有太多的理由，所以也难怪有的读者和戏迷在欣赏了其作品之后会感到眼花缭乱。莎士比亚一共创作了38部戏剧和154首十四行诗；另外，他还即兴作过很多诗歌，大部分都已被人遗忘了，但其戏剧和十四行诗却闻名全球。

以下就是莎士比亚的伟大之处：他是最伟大的英语剧作家；有批评家认为他是运用所有语言文字写作的作家中最伟大的戏剧天才。他还是用英语写作的最伟大的诗人和作家；同样，也有许多评论家会说他是人类文学宝典上最负盛名的。可以说，是他丰富了中世纪的英语辞藻，使其发展成为当代英语国家所应用的样子。用更专业的文学术语说，他完善了无韵诗（指不押韵的抑扬格五音步诗——虽然莎士比亚也时而用韵脚来结束一组对白、一场戏或者是为了达到更富戏剧性的效果）；这一形式在诗歌语言中至今仍然备受推崇。

用戏剧上的术语来说，莎士比亚创造了一种语言，而这种语言本身就能出产戏剧——如此一来，罗密欧才会在窗前找到了他的恋人朱丽叶，并且必须向听众和观众们倾吐他的满腔激情。他说道："轻声！那边窗子里亮起来的是什么光？那是东方，朱丽叶，你就是我的太阳！"莎士比亚创造了这样一种语言，用戏剧台词表达人类的情感，观众可以从演员的举手投足和遭遇经验上联系到现实的社会生活。那么，同样，读者和观众们也须牢记：莎士比亚并非为贵族阶层写作（虽然我们都知道英国女王伊丽莎白一世很欣赏他的剧作，并且莎士比亚曾遵照其请求为她写过一部剧本），而是为伦敦的普通大众撰写，对他们来说，到剧院看戏就是去凑热闹、寻开心；他们不会像别的观众关注其他活动那样一直保持热情——非常像观看一场现代的棒球比赛。然而，莎士比亚却征服了那些观众（所有的证据都表明他在当时颇受欢迎），正像如今我们为之折服一样。

如此卓越的成就，让人难以相信所有这些杰作会是出自一人之手，致使有的学者（在过去的两个世纪中）提出质疑——就凭我们所了解的莎士比亚何以创作出这般的旷世之作，可能除《圣经》之外，他的剧作比任何现有的文学作品都更闻名于世，肯定是有一位更超凡的传统的"文学巨匠"写就了它们。

莎士比亚的身世将给种种这样的偏见以有力的回击。他出生于英国埃文河畔（今英国沃里克郡）斯特拉特福德镇上一个中层阶级的家庭。他的父亲是当地一个兼营手套生意的政府官员。据我们了解，莎士比亚如若不是就读于伊顿公学，很可能是在英王爱德华六世文法学校读的书，那在当时应该是个很好的学校。18岁时他和已经怀孕了的安妮·海瑟薇结婚。接下来80年代这段时间被认为是莎士比亚"销声匿迹"的时期，因为没有人知

Place,in Stratford.He wrote his last play in 1613,retired to that house and died 3 years later.

Shakespeare was a modestly successful man who lived in the last part of the 16th century,the early part of the 17th century.If it were not for his plays,he would have faded into obscurity—as have millions of people before and after him.That the plays of such renown and brilliance came from so seemingly insignificant a man has baffled many scholars and any non-scholar who has seen or read one of them.But that surprise perhaps has more to do with prejudice than with solid reasoning.What the doubters are actually saying is how could an ordinary man,who did not have the benefit of a university education, who was,after all,a kind of itinerant actor working in conditions no more exalted than 20th century vaudeville or burlesque—how could such a person have created works that continue to astonish the world? The simple answer is genius-which stuns us whenever we encounter it,whether in the music of Mozart or the theories of Einstein.Genius happens not as a result of a university education or an aristocratic background; it just happens.

Hamlet

Even if William Shakespeare's genius is acknowledged,and even if his various accomplishments are noted,something in such an analysis seems missing.Why are so many people,centuries after his death,and everywhere in the world,still mesmerized by his plays? No ordinary theatergoer,encountering his plays,says: Oh yes,he refined our language into what we speak today—or,oh yes,he made iambic pentameter into the prime poetic form in English.Our responses are much more basic.

Examine one of his plays.Though other candidates have been proposed over the years (most notably,King Lear),Hamlet,among his tragedies,is generally regarded as his greatest play-if only because it has been endlessly produced.In theatrical centers such as New York, Chicago,or London,a year does not pass without a new production of Hamlet.

Does Hamlet itself convey Shakespeare's special genius-the one that goes beyond his incredible technical facility as a writer? And if Shakespeare is the world's greatest writer, wouldn't he have special insights into man's fate,the purpose of his life and of life itself; wouldn't he,at the least,have insights,given that purpose,into how a man should live?

To imagine so is to under-estimate Shakespeare.It is very difficult to determine just what it is that Shakespeare believed.There are exceptions to that generalization—he obviously believed that,in general,people are selfish and greedy,that they desire to be powerful,yet power corrupts them,that their battles accomplish nothing,that their idealism often turns to cynicism as they have more experience of the world,that love is as likely to be destructive as fulfilling.Critics have tried to label him; Shakespeare resists them.His sonnets suggest he was homosexual; yet the very same sonnets suggest that Shakespeare,a married man,was involved in an obsessive heterosexual affair,or that he was a royalist—he writes about kings,yes,but they are always corrupt or being corrupted.Anyone reading any Shakespeare play is reading his or her own thoughts into it if he or she comes up with any "philosophy" of life that he or she believes is inherent in the play.

What,then,is Shakespeare's special accomplishment? It is this,that better than anyone else has ever done,Shakespeare says and shows:This is what is; this is the actuality of this

道那段时间他究竟在做什么。直到1592年，他来到伦敦开始一边编写剧本，一边做演员。1594年，他成为"宫内大臣剧团"的股东。无论他作为一名演员、编剧、还是制片人都取得了成功，到晚年时期他终于可以在斯特拉特福德镇买上了自己的房子并取名"新宫"(New Palace)。1613年他写下了最后一部剧作后告老还乡，三年后与世长辞。

莎士比亚是生活在16世纪末17世纪初的一位谦逊的成功人士。如果不是因为他的剧作，他将会像千千万万的前辈和后人一样黯然无光。这样一个看似不起眼的人写就了如此卓越的旷世之作着实令一些专家学者和欣赏过他作品的观众读者们大惑不解。但他们的诧异也许更多的是出于偏见而没有确凿的推论。实际上，那些持有怀疑态度的人就是在狡辩——一个没有受过大学教育的普通人也就是当个巡回演员罢了，都不及20世纪歌舞杂耍或滑稽剧表演，怎么可能创造出享誉天下的巨著？答案很简单，就是天赋——每当我们见识到它的时候必将为之惊叹，不论在莫扎特的曲作中还是在爱因斯坦的《相对论》里，我们都可以领悟到。天赋既不是接受大学高等教育习得的，也非因贵族血统而生，它的发生没有理由。

《哈姆雷特》

即使莎士比亚的天赋已经成为共识，并且他的成就也闻名天下，但对他的研究看上去还有所欠缺。为什么在他故去几个世纪之后，还会有那么多世界各地的读者观众为他的戏剧而痴迷？没有一个普通看戏的观众在看完其剧作之后会说："是的，莎士比亚丰富了我们的语言，使其发展成为今天我们所说的英语"，或者"是啊，莎士比亚使抑扬格五音步诗成为最主要的英语诗作的形式。我们的反映很正常啊！"

鉴赏一下莎士比亚的剧作，虽然在过去几年中有其他候选作品曾被提名(多数是著名的《李尔王》)，但他的悲剧《哈姆雷特》被普遍认为是其最伟大的剧作——仅凭它已经得到了无限的阐释。

在像纽约、芝加哥和伦敦这样的戏剧中心，每年都得上演一场新编的《哈姆雷特》。是否《哈姆雷特》这部作品展现了莎士比亚特殊的戏剧天赋——作为一名作家他的神来之笔令人难以置信？假如他是世界上最伟大的作家，他不是应该具备一种特殊才能能够洞悉人类命运、思考他的人生目标和生命本身的意义吗？若真是天才，至少，他也得能深刻了解人应该怎么个活法？

抱有这样的想法简直就是低估了莎士比亚。我们很难确定究竟莎士比亚信仰什么，但对此推论也有例外——很明显，他相信人基本上都是自私又贪婪的，他们盼着自己变得有权有势，然而权势毁了他们；他们为此争得死去活来，但最终一无所获；随着对世界的感悟，他们的理想主义往往变得玩世不恭；他们的爱心也可能还未满足就付之东流。评论家们曾试图给莎士比亚一个恰当的名分，但遭到他的拒绝。他的十四行诗表明他是同性恋；但同样也是他的十四行诗告诉我们莎士比亚，一个已婚男人，沉醉于儿女情长，或者莎士比亚是个保皇主义者——他的确写的是王公贵族，但他们大都么腐朽堕落要么面临衰败灭亡。倘若读者能从中读出任何"人生哲理"并深信它就是此部作品的哲学内涵，那么读莎士比亚的任何一部剧作就是去解读作者自己对作品的理解。

那么，究竟什么是莎士比亚的特殊贡献呢？它超越了其他任何作家的成就。莎士比亚通过其作品展现给我们的是：世界的本来面目；是人类特殊体验的真实。他提供给读者一

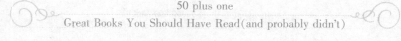
particular human experience.He provides the ultimate "definition," not the meaning of that definition.

The plot of *Hamlet*—though,if presented in its entirety,the play runs for 4 hours-is quite simple.*Hamlet*,a Danish prince,is a university student; his father has died,his uncle has assumed the throne and has married Hamlet's mother,his father's widow.*Hamlet* returns home,to the king's castle in Elsinore,for the coronation.Once home,*Hamlet* is visited by the ghost of his father,who tells him that he has been murdered by the uncle,that his wife, Hamlet's mother,has committed adultery with the uncle—that the throne of Denmark is now corrupt.He enjoins Hamlet to revenge him,and,in so doing,to give peace to his soul. For the remainder of the play,Hamlet deliberates what to do,endlessly vacillates,is always in despair—so much so that readers have christened him the "melancholy Dane." In the end, he acts,but not of his own free will-he is challenged to a duel,which he cannot avoid; in that duel,he,his uncle and his mother all die.

Shakespeare is too wise to tell us what it all means; he is simply but elaborately showing us,defining for us,a common human situation.

Hamlet is not a nerd who can't make up his mind.We learn that he is the ideal of a Renaissance man—handsome,gifted,fashionable,a good student,an intellectual,a lover of the arts-in all ways an admirable human being,someone others look up to.He is,like all young people,an idealist.Shakespeare says in effect:In all young and idealistic lives some event happens that shows us that the world is not as we had supposed,that it is corrupt beyond any expectation we may have had of it.And what is our response? It is depression; it is, more,the coming to a certain crossroads—what do we do to fight that corruption?—which question brings us to another dilemma.In his most famous speech,Hamlet ponders this argument:To be or not to be? By which he means:To live or not to live.He ponders further: If you fight the corruption ("take arms" against it),isn't your death a very real possibility? And don't we all try to avoid that possibility for the reason that none of us knows what death actually means ("no traveler returns" from that particular destination to tell us what the condition of death may be)—thus we avoid action; the contemplation of our own death "makes cowards of us all."

From the depths of his depression,Hamlet is rendered futile,constantly berating himself for not being brave enough to risk his life to avenge his father (save the world?). Shakespeare,with his masterful subtlety,is saying:So are we all such cowards; it is only in our youth that our own behavior appalls us.

But why should the idealist encounter the corruption of the world and be rendered powerless by depression,be tempted to "drop out?" Shakespeare does not answer that question.He simply says:Here is the definition of the Hamlet phenomenon; all young people,as they move from youth to adulthood,experience it.

Every play of Shakespeare involves this kind of definition—of particular human experiences.

To study Shakespeare,to watch and absorb his plays,is thus to contemplate these human situations—more perfectly defined by Shakespeare than by anyone else who has ever lived.To read or watch Shakespeare,therefore,is to define oneself.

个彻底的"诠释",但从不给人们定论。

　　《哈姆雷特》如果全场演满,需要4个小时,但剧情却非常简单。主人公哈姆雷特是一个丹麦王子,在一所大学就读;父亲突然死去,他的叔父篡取王位并娶哈姆雷特的母亲,也就是前任王后为妻。哈姆雷特返回自己的祖国,来到位于厄斯诺的国王的城堡参加新王的加冕仪式。一回国,父亲的鬼魂就来找哈姆雷特,告诉他自己是被其叔父谋杀的,而且其妻,也就是哈姆雷特的母亲,与他的叔父有奸情——丹麦的政权正在腐化堕落。父亲命令哈姆雷特一定要为他报仇,以求灵魂得以安息。本剧的其他情节就是围绕哈姆雷特如何苦思复仇计划,但他又总是畏首畏尾,不断陷入绝望之中——因其多次踌躇难决,读者给他起名"忧郁王子"。最终,他采取了行动,但并非出于自愿——他被迫接受挑战参加决斗;在决斗中,哈姆雷特、他的叔父和母亲全部身亡。

　　莎士比亚如此高明,他不告诉我们此剧作的全部内涵,他的用语言简意赅,但却字斟句酌,展现了人在"生存"与"毁灭"之间挣扎时普遍的心理状态。

　　哈姆雷特并非优柔寡断的"书呆子"。我们知道他是一个典型的人文主义者——他英俊、有天赋、追求时尚、好学、才思敏捷、热爱艺术——方方面面都受人仰慕。像其他年轻人一样,他是一个理想主义者。莎士比亚描述地非常贴切:在所有年轻而充满理想的生命当中,总有些事会发生,告诉我们世界并非期待中的那样,它的腐化超出了我们的任何想象。那么,我们作何反应呢?我们会沮丧;甚至会迷失方向——我们应该如何阻止它的腐化?——这一问题又会把我们带到进退两难的困境。哈姆雷特用他的名言"生存还是毁灭,这真是个问题。"表达了这一冲突,揭示了两者之间的对立,他对此还做了进一步的思考:如果你阻止世道的腐化(采用"武力"予以对抗),那你的毁灭岂不真有可能?而我们不是又会尽力避免这一可能性的发生,因为没有人知道毁灭究竟意味着什么(从未有那样的"冒险者"凯旋而归告诉我们"毁灭"的样子)——因此,我们都不敢采取行动;毁灭的阴影把我们一个个都变成了"胆小鬼"。

　　笔下的哈姆雷特懦弱无能,消沉中他不断地自责为何不敢冒死为父报仇(拯救世界?)。莎士比亚用精湛的笔触告诉世人:其实我们都是这样的"胆小鬼";只有在我们年青的时候,我们的行为才会真正震撼我们自己。

　　然而,为什么理想主义者会遭遇世道的堕落,并且被描绘得消沉而无能,受人迷惑最终"退却"了呢?莎士比亚没有回答这一问题。他只是简单地提到:此作描述的是"哈姆雷特现象";所有的年青人在步入成年的过程中都会有亲身体验。

　　莎士比亚的每一部剧作都涉及这类主题——反映特殊的人类体验。

　　研究莎士比亚,观赏并品味他的戏剧,就如同亲身体验其中人物的遭遇——他精彩的刻画超越了其他任何作家。因此,阅读或者观看莎翁的剧作,就是去认识自我。

Twenty-eight

Galileo Galilei: Dialogue Concerning the Two Chief World Systems

Who Was Galileo Galilei?

Italian physicist, astronomer and philosopher Galileo Galilei (1564-1646) held the controversial view that the sun (heliocentric view), not the earth (geocentric view), was the center of the universe. In his book *Dialogue Concerning the Two Chief World Systems* in 1632, Galileo developed this view, and, as a result of his staunch position on the subject, he found himself in direct conflict with the Roman Catholic Church.

When Pope Urban VIII asked him to write a book on the two different world systems, Galileo was told that he should not in any way advocate heliocentrism. Another request by the pope was that Galileo should also present the pope's view. Despite this request, Galileo presented the pope's view of geocentrism unfavorably and his own view of heliocentrism favorably. By maintaining a strong support for the theories of the Polish astronomer Copernicus (heliocentric view), Galileo succeeded in provoking the church to denounce him. Heliocentrism, according to the Inquisition, was in direct opposition to the "Scriptures." Although most historians agree that Galileo didn't intend to oppose the pope deliberately, Galileo, nevertheless, succeeded at offending the man who had previously been his most powerful supporter.

For his actions, Galileo was placed under house arrest. While under arrest, Galileo once again defied the Roman Catholic Church, which had forbidden him to write and publish; he wrote another important book. This one covered his 30 years' work in physics, *Discourses and Mathematical Demonstrations Relating to Two New Sciences*. Because the church had placed a ban on his writings, he had to have this book published in a country where the church's authority couldn't reach, the Netherlands. Sir Isaac Newton and much later Albert Einstein both agreed that the "Two New Sciences" was one of Galileo's finest books.

Born in Pisa, Italy, Galileo was the son of Vincenzo Galilei, a mathematician. He attended the University of Pisa, where he was eventually hired to teach mathematics, but he soon left the university for a position at the University of Padua where until 1610 he taught geometry, mechanics and astronomy. It was during this period that he began to make scientific discoveries, the result of his own private studies.

His *Dialogue Concerning the Two Chief World Systems*, which was published in 1632, is considered his greatest book. It took him 5 years from 1624 to 1629 to write it, because he was frequently interrupted. The book is a dialogue with three speakers—Salviati, a Copernican like Galileo; Sagredo, a broad-minded man persuaded to Salviati's views; and Simplicio, a staunch defender of the Ptolemaic view (named after the famous Ancient Roman Ptolemy who championed the geocentric view of the world). Simplicio's simplistic dogma (which was associated with the pope) is keenly observed by Salviati. Because of the structure of the book, Galileo was able to claim impartiality; in reality he had weighed the

28

伽利略·伽利莱
《关于托勒密和哥白尼两大世界体系的对话》

伽利略·伽利莱

　　意大利物理学家、天文学家和哲学家伽利略·伽利莱(1564~1642)坚信在当时引起极大争议的宇宙观点：太阳(据日心说)，而非地球(据地心说)是宇宙的中心。他在1632年完成的著作《关于托勒密和哥白尼两大世界体系的对话》中阐述了这一观点，并且巩固了他在此科研领域中的地位，结果发现自己变得和罗马天主教会针锋相对。

　　罗马教皇乌尔班八世要求伽利略写一本关于两种不同世界体系的书，警告他无论如何不能支持日心说，并且让他标明罗马教会的观点。伽利略无视教皇的要求，在书中依然表示反对罗马主教的地心说，而坚持自己的日心说。由于他坚决维护波兰天文学家哥白尼的宇宙理论（日心说），最终招致了教会的告发。据宗教裁判所的审判，日心说直接违背《圣经》。虽然大部分历史学家都认为伽利略并非有意反对罗马主教，然而，他却得罪了此前自己最有势力的支持者。

　　为此，伽利略被强制软禁在家。在这期间，他再次公开反抗曾一度禁止自己写作和发表文章的罗马天主教会，写下了另一部重要著作。这部作品题为《关于力学和位置运动的两种新科学的对话和数学证明》，涵盖了他30年在物理学方面的研究成果。因为教会下令禁止发行伽利略的著作，他不得不在罗马教会权力未及的荷兰出版了此书。艾萨克·牛顿和后来的阿尔伯特·爱因斯坦都认为《两种新科学》是伽利略最优秀的作品之一。

　　伽利略生于意大利比萨市，父亲文森佐·伽利莱是一名数学家。他就读于比萨大学，并且最后受聘留校教授数学，但不久他便离开比萨大学来到了帕图拉大学就职，在那里他任课教授几何、力学和天文学。就是在这段期间，他靠自己的不懈探索开始了他的科学发现。

　　《关于托勒密和哥白尼两大世界体系的对话》于1632年出版，被认为是伽利略最伟大的著作。因创作期间不断受到干扰，作者从1624年到1629年花费5年的时间才完成此作。这本书采用了三人对话的方式——萨尔唯阿蒂同伽利略一样，代表哥白尼的观点；心胸开阔的沙格罗多最终被萨尔唯阿蒂说服；辛普利邱是"托勒密学说"(以拥护宇宙地心说的古罗马著名学者托勒密的名字命名)的忠实捍卫者。辛普利邱的过于肤浅的信条(协同罗马主教)被萨尔唯阿蒂敏锐地察觉到了。因为此书巧妙的写作结构，伽利略得以倡言真理；事实上，他的论证已经偏向了哥白尼的观点。

argument toward the Copernican view.

In 1646,4 years after the publication of "Two New Sciences," Galileo died.Although he never married,he had three illegitimate daughters with his mistress,Marina Gamba.

Dialogue Concerning the Two Chief World Systems

It can be said of few people that they changed the world.That statement is true of Galileo Galilei.

Most people think they know something of the Galileo story,that he was an Italian scientist of the Late Renaissance,a contemporary of Shakespeare (both men were born in 1564,though Galileo lived much longer:Shakespeare died in 1616; Galileo died in 1642). Galileo was one of the great scientists in history,who advanced our knowledge,particularly in physics and astronomy—who,because of his insistence on scientific truth,got himself into serious trouble with the authorities who ruled the Italy of his time.

Ironically,given the almost universal acceptance of the story,this version of Galileo's life is only partially true.

Galileo was a native of Pisa,the first of seven children of what we would now call a lower-middle-class family.Because of his obvious intelligence,he was tutored during his boyhood,then attended the University of Pisa,but was forced to withdraw because he didn't have enough money to continue his studies.When he was 25,though,he was offered a faculty position there,to teach mathematics.That same year he was hired by the University of Padua,again to teach mathematics,also astronomy,and he taught there until 1610,when he was 46.Throughout this period he continued to study science,to make various important if not earth-shattering discoveries—but,apart from his great brilliance,there was nothing in this kind of life of teaching and research that was in any way unusual.

Galileo's quiet life was about to change.

In 1612 he joined the faculty of the Accademia dei Lincei in Rome,and almost at once he became involved in a controversy.The Church had become concerned about the theories of the Polish astronomer Copernicus.The most insidious of these theories,from the Church's point of view,was that the solar system did not revolve around the Earth; rather, the Earth was merely one of many planets and their satellites that revolved around the sun. The sun,not the Earth,was the center of the universe.Copernicus wasn't around to defend himself; he had died 20 years before Galileo was born.But Galileo took up this challenge, defending himself and Copernicus,finally publishing in 1632 *The Dialogue Concerning the Two Chief World Systems*,which offered the two arguments—that of the Church,that of Copernicus.The book is rather loaded; the Church comes off as absurd.Galileo was severely punished and ordered to appear before the Holy Office in Rome,where he refused to retract his beliefs.The court condemned him and his writings,and it forced him to retire, essentially confining him to his villa for the rest of his life.

What man people fail to realize is that Galileo's greatness may well be in the meaning of that life story—rather than in any of his scientific discoveries.Much of his scientific work is now known to be compromised.Copernicus,and his champion Galileo,were wrong in their rightness.True,the planets obit around the sun,rather than around the Earth,but the sun itself is not the center of the universe—it,too,is in orbit,and it is one of countless stars in

1642年,也就是《两种新科学》出版四年后,伽利略与世长辞。尽管他未曾结婚,但他与恋人玛丽娜·贾玛生了三个非婚子女。

《关于托勒密和哥白尼两大世界体系的对话》

可以说极少有人能够改造世界,但伽利略·伽利菜却做到了。

大部分人都觉得自己多少知道关于伽利略的故事——他是一个文艺复兴晚期的意大利科学家,和莎士比亚处在同一时代(两人都生于1564年,但伽利略更长寿一些:莎士比亚在1616年辞世;伽利略故于1642年)。伽利略是历史上最伟大的科学家之一,尤其在物理学和天文学方面做出了突出的贡献,因为对科学真理的执著追求,他陷入了与当时意大利统治集团斗争的漩涡之中。

可笑的是,这些已近乎成为全世界人民的共识,但如果以此为依据的话,那么,本篇关于伽利略生平的介绍只能算部分属实了。

伽利略是意大利比萨郡人,出生在一个中下层阶级的家庭里,家中兄妹七个,他排行老大。因为他天资聪慧,孩童时期家里就找了家庭教师辅导他,后来他就读于比萨大学,但因为没钱支付学费中途被迫辍学。25岁的时候,他受聘在比萨大学教授数学。同年,他又被帕图拉大学聘用,还是教数学,此外他还担任几何课教师。他在那里执教一直到了1610年,那时他46岁。在此期间,他不断地搞科研,即使没有震惊世界的大发现,但他的不少成果还是非常重要的——不过,除了他非凡的才华之外,这样的教学和科研生活并没有任何波澜。

就这样,伽利略平静的生活面临着转变。

1612年,他加入了罗马猞猁学院,但马上便陷入了进退两难的境地。教会早已开始关注波兰天文学家哥白尼的宇宙学说。在他们看来,这些理论中最具破坏性的就是提出了太阳系并非绕地球旋转;地球仅仅是众多环绕太阳旋转的行星和卫星之一。整个宇宙的中心是太阳,而不是地球。哥白尼并没有为自己的学说进行辩护,在伽利略出生前20年他就去世了。但是伽利略承担起了为自己和哥白尼学说辩护的使命,最终于1632年发表了题为《关于托勒密和哥白尼两大世界体系的对话》的专著,在书中他提出了两个论点分别代表了教会一方和哥白尼的观点。此书的论述饱含深意,教会一方的论调显得颇为荒谬。伽利略为此受到了严厉的制裁,并被传唤上了罗马宗教法庭,但即使在那里他也拒绝背叛自己的信仰。法庭谴责他以及他的著作,并下令强制他引退,软禁在家度过余生。

许多人可能没有意识到伽利略的伟大之处在于他实现了生命的价值,而不是他的任何一项科学发现。他的有些科研成果现在已被证实有欠妥当。哥白尼及其拥护者伽利略的理论在正确性上存在偏颇。诚然,行星是绕太阳,而非地球旋转,但太阳本身也不是宇宙的中心——它同样有自己的运行轨道,也是银河系中无数恒星之一,而银河系又是我们所谓宇宙的众多星系之一。

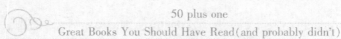

the Milky Way,which itself is one of countless galaxies in what we now call the universe.

Galileo did not invent the telescope—as many people claim.He refined that invention; it already existed,though he did invent the first workable microscope.The story of his dropping stones from the Leaning Tower of Pisa (testing motion theories) is probably mythological.He did,though,make a variety of useful observations in astronomy; he did advance study of the first and second laws of motion—but none of these accomplishments would necessarily have assured him a exalted role in history-or made him an inspiration to scientists and to artists (his life and struggle have been the subject of various plays and movies).

Why then is Galileo held in such reverence? There are three reasons:

Galileo did not invent what we now call "scientific method"—the notion that scientific advance involves the scientist positing an idea about the world (hypothesis),then objectively testing this idea through controlled observation and experimentation.But Galileo was the first great champion of this idea.

Galileo also emphasized,and demonstrated,that the language of science is not human logic (as Aristotle had insisted,and as scientists,following Aristotle,had long maintained)—but that its true language was mathematics.

The third reason is the most telling.Galileo believed that the proofs of science ought to supersede the dictates of Church and State (which,in his time,were virtually the same thing.) Galileo,we're told,was a devout Roman Catholic—he obviously recognized no conflict between his religious and scientific views.His prosecutors had obviously forgotten their Aquinas; Galileo,just as obviously,had not—that there are the revelations that come directly from God,but there are also revelations that come from a study of God's creation.

Galileo would probably be depressed,were he alive today,that the conflict of his time still exists today.Creationists today insist that the universe was created by God in 6 days (because that's what *The Bible says*)—and was created exactly as it exists now; man,formed in the image of his Creator,has always been as he is now.Galileo would stand up to say:The universe was created over billions of years; man has evolved over millions of years to what we see now—and this process is unending.The universe continues to create itself; man continues to evolve.Galileo would marshal the scientific evidence for believing what he does, but would not imagine that,in any way,the scientific view detracted from the glory of God. He would doubtless argue that it should instill in us a greater awe of the majesty and power of God.

Two World Systems will give any reader insight into this remarkable man—and to the basics of an argument that persists from his time until our own.As much as anyone who has ever lived,Galileo may be regarded as the champion of freedom of thought-who,by his example and quiet martyrdom,made us look at the human mind,and what we ought to mean by intellectual freedom,in a new and different way.

正如许多人所言,伽利略并未发明望远镜,他只是进行了改良。尽管他确实是发明了第一台可应用显微镜,但望远镜早在他之前已经存在了。他曾经从比萨斜塔上扔石头(用来验证力学理论)很可能只是道听途说,但他肯定在天文学方面做过很多实际的观测;他还开创性地提出了运动第一定律和第二定律——但这些成就都没有为他赢得卓越的历史地位,也未曾激发科学家或是艺术学家们的灵感(许多戏剧和电影都以他的人生经历和奋斗历程作为题材)。

那么,为什么伽利略如此备受尊敬呢?原因有三点:

伽利略没有发明我们今天所谓的"科学的方法"——科学的进步应该包括科学家们首先对世界提出一个设想(假说),然后经过可操作的观测和实验给以客观的证实。但是,伽利略第一个打破了这一思想的束缚。

伽利略还强调并论证了科学语言不是逻辑(正如亚里士多德所倡导的,和后来者一直维护的那样),——真正的科学语言是数学。

第三点原因是当中最显著的。伽利略认为科学的论证应该代替教会或是政府的强制命令(事实上,在他所生活的年代,教会和政府代表同一股势力)。据我们所知,伽利略是一个虔诚的罗马天主教教徒——很明显,他并未发现他的宗教信仰和科学观点之间存在冲突。控告他的人也显然忘记了他们所信奉的阿奎那(意大利神学家);伽利略没有忘记——有些神旨是上帝直接明示的,但也有些是来自于对上帝所造之物的研究。

如果伽利略现在还活着的话,他应该会很失望,因为在他生活的年代中的冲突至今还存在着。信奉上帝的人依然坚持宇宙万物是上帝在6天之内创造出来的(因为《圣经》中就是这样记载的),并且和当今世界万物一模一样;按照上帝的旨意创造而成的人类也一直是现在的样子。伽利略将会站出来宣称:宇宙是在几十亿年之前就被创造出来的;而人类历经几百万年的进化才变成今天的样子,并且这一进化是永无止境的。宇宙会继续创造自身;人类也将不断进化下去。伽利略会为自己的信仰提供科学的证据,但他无论如何都想象不到科学的观点正是在减损"上帝的光辉"。他还会辩解我们应该更加深信上帝的威严和力量。

读者可以通过阅读《两大世界体系》这一著作深入了解非同寻常的伽利略和从作者生活的年代持续至今的论战。人们都把伽利略视为获得思想解放的胜利者——他用一种崭新的、与众不同的方式,展现给我们一幅人类思想的画卷;他身体力行,本着为科学献身的精神,让世人了解思想自由的真正意义。

Twenty-nine

Rene Descartes:
Discourse on the Method

Who Was Rene Descartes?

French philosopher,mathematician and scientist René Descartes (1596-1650) played an important role in the scientific revolution that was occurring in Western civilization during his lifetime by developing a philosophical base for the natural sciences.Much of what he wrote profoundly influenced western philosophy.

Each subject about which he wrote he approached "as if no one has written on these matters before." Many elements of Aristotelianism,Stoicism and the work of such philosophers as Augustine are evident in his works.His most famous statement is "Je pense, donc je suis" ("I think,therefore I am").To Descartes,the most certain knowledge we have is what we know of our self or from our own mind.He believed that what we experience through our senses can be deceiving; the only thing of which we can be certain is that which we know from our rational minds.

Descartes was born in Indre-et-Loire,France.His father,who was a judge,enrolled him at 10 in the Jesuit Collège Royal Henry-Le-Grand in La Flèche and later in the University of Poitiers,where Descartes received a solid education in mathematics,law,and the classics. When he left the university,the only knowledge Descartes wanted to pursue was that which he would learn from examining himself or the world in general.

He said:"I spent the rest of my youth traveling,visiting courts and armies,mixing with people of diverse temperaments and ranks,gathering various experiences,testing myself in the situations which fortune offered me,and at all times reflecting upon whatever came my way so as to derive some profit from it."

The Dutch philosopher and scientist Isaac Beeckman was responsible for interesting Descartes in mathematics and physics,which led Descartes to think about ways of using mathematics for solving problems in physics.Since he found traditional philosophy and religion disappointing,Descartes believed that only logic,geometry,and algebra could provide the certainty he needed to understand reality.Unfortunately,though,the "certainty" learned through this method could not tell him what was real,for these disciplines all depended on hypotheses.For answers,he needed a new method of thought to determine the validity of the reality that he experienced,one that would provide him with the certainty that mathematics offered.

In *Discourse on the Method*,Descartes first published work,he identified four essential rules for validating information.

Descartes died in 1650 in Stockholm,where he worked as a teacher for Queen Christina of Sweden.The exact cause of his death is uncertain.Letters,though,indicate that he might have been poisoned.Over the years his remains have had several "final" resting places.Presently his tomb is located in the church Saint Germain-des-Pres,Paris.

勒内·笛卡儿
《方法论》

勒内·笛卡儿

著名的法国哲学家、数学家和科学家勒内·笛卡儿(1596~1650)为自然科学提供了哲学基础，在西方文明史上起到了推动科学革命向前发展的重要作用。他的许多著作深刻影响了西方哲学的发展。

他在触及每一个写作题材的时候，"就像是前人都未曾涉猎过一样"。亚里士多德哲学、斯多葛哲学，以及像奥古斯丁等哲学家所著作品当中的许多元素都在笛卡儿的作品中有鲜明的体现。他最有名的哲言就是"我思故我在"。对笛卡儿来说，人们所拥有的最确定的知识莫过于人们对自身的了解，或者它就来源于我们的思想。他认为我们通过感官所体会到的事物可能是虚假的；真正可以确定的是经过理性思考所认识到的。

笛卡儿出生于法国的安德尔·卢瓦尔。他的父亲是一名法官，在笛卡儿十岁的时候父亲就把他送去了由耶稣会士创办的拉·弗莱舍(La Fleche)公学学习，后来他就读于普瓦提·埃大学，在那里笛卡儿受到了良好的数学、法律和古典学教育。大学毕业的时候，笛卡儿唯一想探求的知识就是那些他即将要在检验他自身和整个世界的过程中所习得的。

笛卡儿声称："我要趁着年纪还轻的时候去游历，访问各国的宫廷和军队，与气质不同、身份不同的人交往，搜集各种经验，在碰到的各种局面里考验自己，随时随地用心思考面前的事物，以便从中取得教益。"

是荷兰哲学家和科学家依萨克·比克曼引起了笛卡儿在数学和物理学方面的兴趣，使他受到启发开始探寻如何用数学的方法来解决物理学问题。自从他发觉传统的经院哲学和宗教极其令人失望之后，他便相信只有逻辑推理、几何和代数学才能提供他所需要的了解现实世界的确定的知识。然而，不幸的是，通过这些方法所得到的"确定的知识"并不能告诉他什么是真实的，因为这其中的规则都是依据假设才成立的。为了找到问题的答案，他需要一种新的思维方式去验证他所体验到的现实世界的可靠性，这种新思维将提供给他经过数学验证的确定的知识。

在笛卡儿第一部发表的题为《方法论》的著作中，他提出了验证信息有效性的四项基本原则。

1650年，笛卡儿在斯德哥尔摩去世，他曾在那里做过瑞典克里斯蒂娜女王的私人教师。笛卡儿确切的死因还不甚清楚，但信件上显示，他有可能是被人投毒致死。他的遗体在几年内迁了好几处"安息"的地方，现在，他的墓冢安在巴黎圣杰曼德佩区(Saint Germain-des-Pres)的教堂里。

Discourse on the Method

Change swept through Europe beginning in 14th century Italy,which allowed man to step out of the Dark Ages and experience a new world,a rebirth of interest in the classics.It began in Italy,with what we now call the Renaissance movement,and it reached its apex in France from 1515 to 1559.The Renaissance movement was followed in the 17th Century by a major intellectual awakening,popularly labeled the Age of Reason.It is generally accepted that if it hadn't been for the Renaissance and the revival of interest in classics,the Age of Reason would probably never have happened.

What made the 17th Century (and the periods before and after it) so important was that it was then that man opened his mind to new possibilities—new ways of viewing the world and the universe.Among the great thinkers of this time were such men as Nicholaus Copernicus,John Locke,Isaac Newton,Francis Bacon,Galilei Galileo,and,of course,René Descartes.These great minds began to plant the seeds of wisdom on which modern man has since built.

During most of René Descartes's life,a powerful change was occurring in France.The death of Henry IV was followed by disorder.This unrest would have never have become so significant if it weren't for the Renaissance movement.During the Renaissance,man had started to move away from the old views of life and began to make new discoveries.But like all significant social and intellectual change,this one immediately resulted in the conflict between the old world and the emerging new world.

Descartes lived in this changing new world,dedicating his life to his studies,and he began to defy conventional thinking with brilliant new breakthroughs in thought and research.Much of what occurred in philosophy after him was a reaction to what he had written during this period.He developed four primary precepts in his *Discourse on the Method* that to this day many thinkers respect and avoid violating:

1.Never accept anything as true unless it is obviously true.

2.Divide a problem into as many parts as possible to make it easier to solve.

3.Arrange thoughts in a logically connected order from the simplest to the most complex.

4.Make conclusions complete and general,omitting nothing.

Any time Descartes had doubts he would immediately reject his hypothesis.A humanist who refused to accept anything on faith,he believed the only thing that we can know for certain is what we think. "I think,therefore I am" became the most important words in philosophy-and the foundation for everything that followed.

These words had their roots in the experiences of Descartes's youth.During his early years,Descartes spent considerable time traveling—and like a wise traveler he would test his experiences by reflecting on them.From these experiences,he learned and wrote.And in his writings,Descartes set forth the methodology for what would come after him.

Descartes believed that the only thing that man can know for certain is what he thinks and knows of himself.He believed that what we experience through our senses can be deceiving.By doubting everything,he was able to reconstruct a new system of philosophy from scratch.This led Descartes to believe that only man was capable of thought.Everything else in nature reacted to stimuli mechanically.

《方法论》

14世纪发起于意大利的变革席卷了整个欧洲大陆,使人们走出了"中世纪的黑暗",开始体验一个崭新的世界,人们对文学经典的兴趣得以重生。这场运动兴起于意大利,我们今天称之为文艺复兴,它于1515年至1559年间在法国达到了运动的高潮。继文艺复兴之后,17世纪又出现了一场由当时主要思想家发起的启蒙运动,标志着理性主义时代的到来。我们都普遍地认为,如果没有文艺复兴,没有对文学经典兴趣的再生,那么,崇尚理性主义的时代很可能不会出现。

17世纪(及其之前和之后的阶段)之所以如此重要,是因为正是在这个时期人们开始敞开思维去想象一切新的可能——认识世界和宇宙万物的新方法。这一时期伟大的思想家包括尼古拉·哥白尼、约翰·洛克、艾萨克·牛顿、弗兰西斯·培根、伽利略·伽利莱,当然还有勒内·笛卡儿。他们自那时起就开始为现代人播下了智慧的种子。

在勒内·笛卡儿大部分的人生当中,一次重大的转折发生在法国。亨利四世死后,法国社会紧接着动荡起来。如果没有文艺复兴运动的影响,这一动荡本来也不会那么至关重要。文艺复兴期间,人们已经开始摆脱旧有的人生观,并且开始重新认识世界。然而,像所有重大的社会和思想变革一样,这一动荡立刻导致了新旧世界之间激烈冲突。

笛卡儿生活在这个变革之中的新世界,他倾注了一生的精力进行科学探索,并且利用他在思考和研究当中取得的新突破去反抗传统思想的束缚。在他之后的很多哲学研究都是针对他在这一时期所写的作品展开的。他在《方法论》一书中提出了四项基本原则,直到今天许多思想家仍奉箴言:

1.绝不对任何没有确认为真的加以接受,只把那些清楚明白的呈现于心智之前。

2.把所考察的难题,尽可能分成细小部分,直到可适于加以圆满解决为止。

3.按照次序引导思想,从最简单、最容易的认识对象开始,逐步上升到对复杂对象的认识。

4.把一切情况尽量列举出来,普遍地加以审视,确信毫无遗漏。

笛卡儿每次碰到疑问都会立刻抛弃原有的假设。作为一个人文主义者,他拒绝接受任何教条,他相信我们唯一可以确定的就是我们的思想。"我思故我在"成了哲学思想最集中的精练表达,同时也是万物存在的基础。

这句话深深扎根于笛卡儿年轻时候的经历。那时,他曾花大量的时间游历——就像一个聪明的旅行家,他总是不断地反思他所经历之事,从中学习并以此为素材写作。他在其作品中提出了处理以后即将出现之问题的方法论。

笛卡儿相信人们唯一可以确定的是他们对自身的所想和所知。他认为我们由感官所体验到的可能都是虚假的。于是,他从零开始,通过怀疑一切,最终重新建立了一个哲学体系。这使笛卡儿坚信只有人类可以思维,自然界中其他万物只能机械地做出应激反应。

Descartes's refusal to accept ideas on faith might have placed him in direct conflict with the powerful forces of the Church.This notion is probably correct.The Church was quick to react with force to any resistance to current dogma.There is no question in some historians' minds that,when he learned about the persecution of Gilileo,Descartes reserved his real thoughts,kept quiet.He delayed publication of his work,the "Treatise of the World." To publish it would have placed him in direct conflict with the Church.The book maintained a Copernican view of the universe,which was in direct conflict with the Church's view.

Historians now believe that Descartes sought safe ground,avoiding taking a public position on certain of his views,a position that would have endangered him.If this view is correct,then one wonders in what direction his thinking,in private,was actually taking him. What brilliant discoveries did this man of genius withhold to protect his life? Whether this analysis is true or not is not important.What is important is that his ideas set the groundwork for other thinkers who followed him to support or refute.

Many refer to him as the father of modern philosophy,one of the most influential thinkers of all time:every thinker who followed Descartes has had to deal with his stance of universal doubt and the methods it provoked.

　　笛卡儿拒绝接受教条的思想很可能使他陷入了与势力强大的教会之间正面的冲突。这一推测极有可能是正确的。教会马上采取行动用武力制止任何对当时教义的反叛。在一些历史学家看来，毫无疑问当笛卡儿得知伽利略如何遭受迫害的时候，他保留了自己的真实想法，而决定保持沉默。他延迟了《论世界》这一作品的发表。因为此书坚持哥白尼的宇宙学说，和教会的地心说背道而驰，出版这部作品将会使他与教会势力针锋相对。

　　现在，历史学家们认为笛卡儿寻找"平安所"，避免了公开宣称其学说所面临的危险。如果这一情况真的属实，那么，有人势必会问他的思想就其本人何以体现。什么样的伟大发现使得这位天才决定保身立命呢？这一分析正确与否并不重要，重要的是，他的思想为后来的思想家们或支持或反对奠定了基础。

　　许多人都把笛卡儿视为"现代哲学之父"，和有史以来最具影响力的思想家之一：继笛卡儿之后的每一个思想家都曾论及过他普遍怀疑的哲学思想，以及这一思想所引出的方法论意义。

Thirty

John Locke:
Two Treatises of Government

Who Was John Locke?

John Locke (1632-1704) was an English philosopher and social theorist who was born in Somerset (near the city of Bristol) into the family of a country lawyer.He attended the prestigious Westminster School in London and later Christ Church at Oxford University.As a student,he read widely but preferred the writings of such modern thinkers as René Descartes to the classics.Eventually,he qualified in medicine.

As a physician,he saved the life of Anthony Ashley Cooper,first Earl of Shaftesbury, which Shaftesbury never forgot; he thereafter acted as Locke's patron.Locke eventually was a minister in the British government.As well,he traveled and wrote extensively.It may be that as a result of Shaftesbury's prompting that Locke composed his *Two Treatises of Government*.

These two treatises defended the Revolution of 1688 (which led the British to overthrow its Catholic ruler James II); as well,they firmly opposed an absolutist political philosophy.Locke's ideas regarding natural rights and government were then considered revolutionary,and,for that reason,his Treatises,when they were published in 1689,were published anonymously.

Two Treatises of Government

Virtually everyone living in the Western world knows that,looking back on our intellectual history,we can identify certain periods in which a particular kind of social and philosophical thought was dominant.Most of us know that the Classical Period (the period of the Greeks and Romans and their many intellectual and artistic accomplishments),was, after the Fall of Rome,followed by a period we now call the Dark Ages,from which nothing very much survives,except perhaps the emergence and domination of the Christian Church. That period is followed by what we now call the Medieval Period or the Middle Ages,in which there is a kind of stirring of intellectual ferment,as the world begins to develop—in its trade,in its social structures,in its formation into nation—states—into the world in which we live now.

And most of us know that the Middle Ages is followed by the Renaissance—a return to a more exuberant life experience,based on a renewal of interest in the example of Greece and Rome,an interest in exploration and new experiences,a flowering of literature and the arts.

We also know that the 19th century is the Age of Romanticism—a period in which a reliance on emotion,on fresh beginnings,held sway.It is also,not surprisingly,a period of revolution—most notable in the United States and in France.In the 20th century and in our own 21st century—we lack the perspective to understand what intellectual notions are paramount; it sometimes seems that all of them exist simultaneously.

But what of the period between the Renaissance and the Romantic Era—that period

30

约翰·洛克
《政府论两篇》

约翰·洛克

约翰·洛克(1632~1704)是英国哲学家和社会理论家,他出生于萨默塞特(靠近布里斯托尔市)的一个乡村律师的家庭。他曾就读于伦敦有名的威斯敏斯特学校,后来加入了牛津大学的基督教会。作为一名学生,他博览群书,但最喜欢读的并不是古典文学,而是像勒内·笛卡儿那样的近代思想家的著作。最终,他决定从事医学研究。

作为内科医生的他,曾救过安东尼·阿什里·库珀和莎夫茨伯里伯爵,令伯爵感激万分,并从此成了洛克的庇护者。洛克最终成为英国政府的一名议会大臣。此外,他还到处游历和撰写文章。或许,正是由于莎夫茨伯里伯爵的支持,他才写下了《政府论两篇》。

这两篇论述都是维护1688年爆发的光荣革命(这场革命领导英国人民推翻崇尚天主教的英王詹姆斯二世的统治);论稿还强烈反对君主专制的政治体制。洛克论及"自然权利"和政府的观点在当时被认为是革命性的,因此,他的《政府论》于1689年被匿名发表。

《政府论两篇》

几乎每一个西方人都知道,回顾一下知识史,我们会发现不同的历史阶段都有其特殊的占主导地位的社会和哲学思想。而大部分人也了解随着罗马帝国的衰败,古典主义时代(指古希腊和古罗马时代,这一时期出现了很多优秀的文艺作品)被"黑暗时代"所取代,这一阶段或许除了基督教会的出台及其统治之外,没有留下任何东西。接下来便是我们现在称作中古时期或中世纪的到来,在此期间,人们萌发已久的聪明才智大放光彩,因为全球在经济贸易方面开始发展,社会结构也日益完善,国家政权逐步形成,整个世界正在朝着我们现在所生活的状态发展。

而且,我们大多数人也知道中世纪之后便是文艺复兴——这场思想文化运动以人们对古希腊和罗马文学经典兴趣的重生为基础,是一次向更加丰富的生活体验的回归,是一种追求探索和新体验的向往,是一次文学和艺术之花的绽放。

我们还知道19世纪是浪漫主义的时代,在这一时期,人们对情感和重新开始的崇尚占了主导地位。同时,称它是一个改革的年代也不足为奇——这一点在美国和法国表现得最为突出。到20世纪以及21世纪,我们却对是何种体现人文精神的主流思想占统治地位缺乏理解;有时,似乎所有的那些思想又同时并存。

然而,处于文艺复兴和浪漫主义时期之间——大概是17世纪中期至18世纪末,是怎

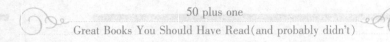

that extends roughly from the middle of the 17th century to the end of the 18th century? Sometimes the 17th century portion of this period is referred to as "The Age of Reason," and the 18th century portion is called "The Age of Enlightenment"—but, just as often, that 150-year stretch is referred to, simply, as The Enlightenment.

Most people have difficulty defining what it was all about.

The Age of Reason is perhaps the better description for this period—for it was in this time that philosophers, intellectuals and other thinkers came to believe and act on the belief that "reason"—the human mind, rather than human emotions—could solve most problems, could provide a basis for how man should live. This notion permeated all aspects of human existence.

Even religion. Most Age of Reason/Enlightenment thinkers would say that religion in the past had been based on revelation—that The Bible is God's word transmitted through his holy servants, that the rules for men's lives are given to us by God, as a result of the interpretations of His priests, that we understand God's will through the actions and examples of His saints. Then, the Reformation took place, with its notion that there was an alternative way of looking at the intervention of God in life; Enlightenment thinkers built on that concept. An Age of Reason philosopher would say God exists in his handiwork—that Nature, the visible world, is God. His rules are those that govern nature; our understanding of Him is through an understanding, via human reason, of those rules.

The primacy of the reason makes sense in human endeavors as well. Whether we are considering art or ethics—the way we live, work or create—reason, not the emotions, is what will take us to an understanding of the world, and from that understanding comes right behavior and right thinking.

It is in this context that John Locke can best be understood. He is a man of the 17th century rather than the 18th century. For a philosopher, he had a very activist life—as a student, as a physician, even as a minister in the British government. Such a life would have been considered entirely appropriate by Locke and his contemporaries. The intellectual should also be a man of action, examining (with his reason) the workings of society and the relations of men and women to the society in which they live.

Although Locke wrote extensively about money and trade-and is very much one of the founders of liberal thinking, whose influence extends to the present day—it is his writings on government, especially in his work *Two Treaties of Government*, that he has been most influential.

Within the time of Locke's life—as a result of the creation of modern countries, with the establishment of trade between countries, with the ascendancy of money as the means of exchange, with the wealth accumulated from foreign exploration and conquest—individual governments became more prominent than they had been before. Although there continued to be monarchies, it was during the Enlightenment that the modern democratic state, ruled by an assembly of elected legislators, came into being.

What, then, Locke asked, is the proper role of government, this entity to which we give so much authority. As well, what is the appropriate role for government to take in relation to those that it governs.

Locke's views will seem familiar to the modern reader—for the reason that they

样一个阶段呢？17世纪这一阶段时常被人们称为"理性主义时代"，18世纪为"启蒙运动的年代"——但是，我们通常简单地把这150年的历史时期统称为"启蒙时代"。

大多数人很难全面地界定这一时期的内涵。

或许，"理性时期"更好地概括了这一阶段的时代特征——因为正是在这段期间，哲学家、知识分子和其他思想家们开始信仰并且验证"理性"——人的理智，而非情感，能够解决大多数问题，并且可以为人们提供生存的依据。这一理念渗透于人们生活的方方面面。

甚至，宗教也是如此。大部分理性/启蒙时代的思想家们都会说宗教在过去是建立在默示基础上的——所谓《圣经》是通过神职人员传授给人们的上帝的旨意，人类生活的法则是上帝赐予的，神父的传教使我们懂得圣徒们的行为和事例都是上帝的意愿。然后，改革应运而生，旨在告诉人们可以用辩证的眼光看待生活中"上帝"的介入；启蒙运动的思想家就以此建立起他们的理念。某个理性时代的哲学家会说上帝存在于他的著作中——大自然，我们可视的世界，就是上帝。上帝的法则支配着自然界；而我们凭借人类的理性思考，通过对其法则的了解认识了上帝。

"理性"的首要地位还在于它使人的努力奋斗变得有意义。无论考虑我们生活中的文化艺术，还是道德规范；劳动，还是创造——理性，而非情感，会让我们了解这个世界，并且这些了解将衍生出正确的行为和思想。

就是在这种背景下，约翰·洛克的思想能够得到很好的诠释。他生于17世纪，而不是18世纪。作为一名哲学家，他拥有一个非常积极的人生——他做过学生，当过内科医生，甚至担任过英国的国会大臣。这样的人生，在洛克及其同时代的人看来，应该是完全合乎时宜的。知识分子就应当负有行动力，用他们的理智去检测社会的运行机制以及男、女性与其生活的现实社会之间的关系问题。

虽然洛克的写作广泛涉及金钱和贸易，并且，在很大程度上，他是自由思想的奠基人之一，其影响一直持续到今天——但他关于政府的著作，特别是他的《政府论两篇》，是其最具影响力的代表作。

在洛克生活的年代——现代国家的创立，伴随着国家之间贸易的开展，作为交换方式的金钱占据了支配地位，财富不断通过海外掠夺和战争聚敛了起来——地方政府的职能变得比以前更为突出。虽然君主政体依然存在，但在启蒙运动期间，经选举产生立法人员组成议会，再由议会掌管的现代民主制政府正日趋形成。

那么，正如洛克所问的那样，我们给予政府这么大的权力，它的适当职能是什么呢？同样，在处理与被统治者之间的关系上，政府应该担当何种作用呢？

对现代的读者来说，洛克的观点并不陌生——因为他的政治信条影响了美利坚合众

influenced the founding of the United States.He argued:We do not simply accept that man must endure some primal form of government—that we are barbarians who must be governed in some way,however inadequately,by the strong and the powerful.Reason says that a government is legitimate only if it receives the consent of the governed.That is,there is a social contract between a government and those that it governs—in which both sides agree about the proper role of government in their lives.That role should be to guarantee,in Locke's formulation,life,liberty and property (a formulation that got changed in America's Declaration of Independence to life,liberty,and the pursuit of happiness).

If such consent was not given—if government was imposed on people or if that government,once created,so much changed that it was no longer reflected the will of the people—then the people being governed had a right to rebel,the right,in other words,to throw out one government and create a new government that did have their consent.

Any American—or indeed anyone who lives in a country that purports to be a democracy—knows this message from the Enlightenment—and should read Locke to see from which man's thinking such an enduring notion has evolved.

There is another value in reading an Enlightenment thinker such as Locke.In the world since the Middle Ages,we have moved from periods in which the reason is imagined to be paramount to periods in which the feelings are imagined to be the clue to a happy life. Sometimes,to modern man,it seems as if such periods,in the past,lasted for a century or more; now,it often seems that periods of intellectual sobriety move to periods of intellectual hedonism within decades (as the 1950s moved to the 1960s; as the 1970s became the 1980s).We should all know the basic principles of either stance—and John Locke provides one of the best cases for the power of reason—one that continues to be felt in every aspect of American life.

国的建立。他认为:我们不能简单地相信人必须接受某种原始形式的统治——相信无论多么不合理,我们就像野蛮人那样,必须受控于来自强大势力的某种形式的管制。"理性"告诉我们一个政府只有赢得被统治者的满意才算是合法的。就是说,在政府和其管辖下的人民之间有一个"社会契约"——双方在有效期内对政府的合法权利达成一致。用洛克的话来说,政府的这项职能应该确保人的生命、自由和财产权(这一表述在美国《独立宣言》中更改为人的生命、自由和追求幸福的权利)。

如果人民的这些权利不能给予满足——政府强加负担于人民,或者它一经建立便改变立场,不再代表人民的意愿——那么,人民就有权起来反抗。换句话说,被统治者享有权利去推翻不代表他们权益的政府,创建一个新的切实代表其利益的政府。

任何一个美国人,或者任何一个确实生活在宣称是民主政体国家的人,都知道这则政治信条始于启蒙运动,并且每个人都该阅读一下洛克的著作去看看人们所探求的这样一则不朽的政治理念是从何演生而来的。

阅读像洛克这样的启蒙思想家的著作还有另外的价值。自中世纪以来,我们已经历了从推崇理性的阶段到把情感想象成为通往幸福生活的途径的时期。对现代人来说,有的时候,似乎这样的历史阶段持续了一个世纪甚至更长时间;现在看来,好像从崇尚保持头脑清醒的时代过渡到情感充盈的时代仅仅经历了几十年的时间(前者从20世纪50~60年代;后者自20世纪70~80年代)。我们都应该了解这两种处世观的基本理念——约翰·洛克就为我们提供了一个最好的展现理性力量的范例——在美国人民的生活中到处都还能感受得到这一影响的存在。

Thirty-one

Sir Isaac Newton: Principia

Who Was Sir Isaac Newton?

Isaac Newton (1642-1727) was an English scientist who has been described as one of the greatest persons in the history of human thought because of his contributions to mathematics,physics,and astronomy.Within a span of 18 months,from 1665 to 1667, Newton developed theories of motion and gravity,discovered the properties of light and color,and invented calculus.

Newton was born on Christmas Day,1642,in Lincolnshire,England.In 1661 he entered Trinity College at Cambridge,but he graduated without distinction.Ironically,Newton returned to Trinity College in 1669 as a professor of mathematics,and 3 years later he was elected to the Royal Society.

Newton developed his theory of gravity during a visit to the countryside,where he had gone to escape the bubonic plague in Cambridge.During this time Newton realized that the same force that attracts an object to earth also keeps the Moon in its orbit.Newton realized that the gravitational force of the Sun holds the planets in their orbits,just as the gravitational force of the Earth attracts the Moon.Nearly 20 years later the English astronomer Edmond Halley convinced Newton to publish these findings.The result was the *Philosophiae Naturalis Principia Mathematica* (*Mathematical Principles of Natural Philosophy*),usually called just the *Principia*.

Newton's discoveries in optics and light were also significant,laying the foundation for the science of spectrum analysis.By passing a beam of sunlight through a prism,Newton discovered that white light is composed of a rainbow band of colors.This discovery led to his invention of a new reflecting telescope that enabled him to see the satellites of Jupiter.

After the publication of *Principia*,Newton began to participate more actively in the public life of his country.In 1689 he became the member of Parliament for Cambridge University.In 1696 he became Warden of the Mint and later Master of the Mint,a position he held until his death.During this time he joined the Royal Society council and became an associate in the French Academy.After serving in Parliament again in 1701,Newton left Cambridge and settled in London.In 1703 he became President of the Royal Society and re-elected to this office every year until his death.In 1705 Queen Anne knighted him.

Principia

The *Philosophiae Naturalis Principia Mathematica,*or *Principia,*is a threevolume work published in 1687.It includes Newton's laws of motion and his law of universal gravitation.During his undergraduate years at Trinity,Newton had studied Nicholas Copernicus's theories about the revolution of the planets as well as Johannes Kepler's evidence that planets move in elliptical orbits around the sun.Newton was also familiar with Galileo's basic theory of dynamics and with the writings of Rene Descartes.All of these sources were instrumental in his development of his laws of basic mechanics as well as

31

艾萨克·牛顿爵士
《原理》

艾萨克·牛顿爵士

艾萨克·牛顿(1642~1727)是一位英国科学家,他在数学、物理学以及天文学方面都做出了突出的贡献,因而被誉为人类思想史上最伟大的人物之一。从1665年到1667年间,仅在短短18个月内,牛顿研究并提出了三大运动定律和万有引力定律,发现了光和色彩的特性,并且开创了微积分学。

1642年的圣诞节这天,牛顿出生在英格兰林肯郡。1661年,他进入剑桥三一学院学习,但直到毕业,他都成绩平平,没有表现出什么过人之处。有趣的是,他于1669年又以数学教授的身份重返三一学院,并且,三年之后他被选举为英国皇家学会的成员。

牛顿是在乡村逗留期间提出了万有引力定律,他本来是去那里躲避剑桥的腺鼠疫,在此期间,他发现吸引物体浮于地球表面的力同样也使得月球按此运行。他还发现太阳作用于行星使其按轨道运行的引力正像是地球之于月球的引力作用。差不多20年之后,英国天文学家埃德蒙·哈雷劝说牛顿发表了这些新发现,其成果都记录在《自然哲学的数学原理》中,通常简称为《原理》。

牛顿在光学方面的发现同样也很重要,为光谱术的建立奠定了基础。他使一束太阳光线穿过一块玻璃三棱镜,结果发现白光是由像彩虹一样的各种彩色光带组成的。这一发现促使他进一步研制出一款新的反射式望远镜,让他观测到了围绕木星的卫星。

在《原理》出版之后,牛顿开始更加积极地参加英国的政府活动。1689年,他被推选为剑桥大学代表,参加英国"国会会议"。1696年,他接受皇家造币厂的监造员一职,之后被任命为皇家造币厂厂长,他担任此职直到他去世。在这段期间,他还加入了英国皇家学会理事会并且成为法国科学院会员。牛顿于1701年再次担任英国下议院议员,之后,他离开剑桥大学,定居伦敦。1703年,他被选为皇家学会主席,并且在每年的换届选举中他都连任此职,直至去世。1705年,他被英国安妮女王封为爵士。

《原理》

《自然哲学的数学原理》或《原理》于1687年出版,全书共分三卷,包含了牛顿的三大运动定律和万有引力定律。当牛顿在剑桥三一学院攻读学士学位的时候,已经学习了尼古拉·哥白尼的关于行星的革新性的理论和约翰尼斯·开普勒关于行星按照椭圆形的轨道环绕太阳运转的论证。牛顿也非常熟悉伽利略的动力学基本理论和勒内·笛卡儿的著作。所有这些知识储备对他提出力学基本原理以及万有引力定律都具有重要的作用。

those of universal gravitation.

In the *Principia* Newton states his three universal laws of motion:

1.Newton's First Law (also known as the Law of Inertia) is that an object at rest tends to stay at rest and that an object in motion tends to stay in motion unless acted upon by an external force.

2.Newton's Second Law is that an applied force equals the rate of change of momentum.

3.Newton's Third Law is that for every action there is an equal and opposite reaction.

Newton was the first person to borrow the Latin word gravitas (weight) for the universal force he would call gravity,and he defined the law of gravitation.He also provided the first analytical calculation of the speed of sound in air.

Although Newton is probably best known for his theories about gravity,his other definitions form the basis of modern dynamics and physics.He began by defining "mass" as the "quantity of matter … that … arises conjointly from its density and magnitude." This formulation led him to develop a definition for "quantity of motion" (momentum) and the principle of inertia,which,in turn allowed him to explore force through the change of momentum of a body.

Newton's rational and logical progression through these definitions compelled other scientists and physicists of his day to accept his theories.Although there are basic omissions in the *Principia* (the dimension of time,for example),Newton's work did lay the foundation of today's basic physics,even though Albert Einstein's theory of relativity in the 20th century superseded some of Newton's findings.

Newton's contributions to science and mathematics are obvious:his laws of motion,his explanation of the earth's gravitational pull,his development of the framework of modern physics and dynamics,and his invention and refinement of calculus fueled the beginning of the scientific revolution of the 17th century.By showing that the motion of planets and other celestial bodies is governed by the same natural laws,Newton was able to prove speculations of earlier scientists,such as Kepler's laws of planetary motion,and establish the Sun as the center of the Earth's universe.His theories have been far-reaching and long-lasting.

Newton also experimented with colors and optics.He showed that white light inherently produced the colors of the spectrum when passing through a prism and that the result was independent of the prism.He concluded that colors remain the same whether they are scattered or transmitted.From these observations he decided that the prevailing refracting telescope would be inaccurate in that it would disperse light into colors.To solve this problem,he invented a reflecting telescope.Newton also developed a theory about the speed of sound in air,and he proposed a law of cooling that described the rate of the cooling of objects when exposed to air.

Newton's most important contribution to science,however,may be his merging of two opposing intellectual trends of 17th century science:the empirical inductive method and the rational deductive method.This synthesis of thought was the basis of the scientific revolution and the beginning of the Enlightenment.By combining both intellectual approaches,Newton provided the groundwork for modern scientific methodology.

在《原理》一书中,牛顿提出了他的三大运动定律:

1. 牛顿第一运动定律:又称为"惯性定律",当物体不受外力作用,或所受合力为零时,总保持静止或匀速直线运动状态,直到受到外力作用为止。

2. 牛顿第二运动定律:物体受力后所得的加速度和其所受的净力(即合力)成正比,和其质量成反比。

3. 牛顿第三运动定律:当两物体相互作用时,存在作用力与反作用力,两者大小相等,方向相反,而且在同一直线上。

牛顿是借用拉丁文字gravitas(重力)来命名"引力"的第一人,他称其为gravity,并且他定义了万有引力定律。此外,他还首次提出了声音在空气中传播的科学计算方法。

虽然,可能牛顿最为著名的是他的万有引力定律,但他所做的其他科学定义为现代动力学和物理学奠定了基础。他首先把"质量"定义为"物质的量…那些…集合它的密度和体积于一体"。这一公式促成牛顿进一步提出了"运动的量"(动量)这一概念和惯性定律,而这一发现又指引他继续探索通过物体动量的变化而产生的力的问题。

牛顿提出的这些科学定义既合乎常理又符合逻辑,使他赢得了同时期其他科学家和物理学家的信服。虽然《原理》中存在疏漏(比如忽略了时间的量度问题),而且,20世纪阿尔伯特·爱因斯坦提出的"相对论"在某些方面超越了他,但牛顿的科学探索确实为今天的基础物理学奠定了基石。

牛顿在科学和数学方面做出的贡献是显著的:他提出了三大运动定律,定义了地心引力,并且发展了现代物理学和动力学的理论框架,他还开创并完善了微积分学,加速了17世纪科学革命的进程。通过展示行星和其他天体的运动是受相同自然法则制约的这一点,他得以证实前辈科学家们的观点,比如像开普勒的行星运动法则,并且,牛顿还使太阳是宇宙的中心这一宇宙观获得了承认。他的理论成就具有广泛而深远的影响。

牛顿还做过色彩现象和光学方面的研究。他证明了当白色光线穿过棱镜的时候,白光本身就形成了光谱的不同色彩,而且,即使不用棱镜这一结果也成立。于是,他确信彩色光线无论是被散射还是折射其特性保持不变。通过这些观测,牛顿得出结论:当时盛行的折射式望远镜并不精确,因为它会把太阳光散射成不同色彩的光线。为了解决这一问题,他发明了反射式望远镜。牛顿还发展了关于声音在空气中传播速度的理论,并且他还提出了冷却定律,阐释了当物体暴露在空气中的时候其冷却的速率问题。

然而,牛顿在科学方面作出的最重要的贡献可能是他把17世纪科学界两种截然相反的思想趋向结合到了一起:即经验主义归纳法和理性主义的演绎法。这种思想的融合为科学革命铺平了道路,并揭开了启蒙运动的序幕。通过综合两种思想方法,牛顿奠定了现代科学方法论的基础。

This kind of intellectual pursuit also influenced the prevailing religious thought of Newton's day. Newton's rational proofs of natural phenomena provided an alternative to the mystical and unsubstantiated claims of Christianity. But that he did so does not mean that Newton did not believe in God. He diligently studied the Scriptures and what most people do not know is that he wrote more about religion than he did about natural science. Newton viewed God as the master creator whose existence could not be denied. God's intervention in earthly affairs was unnecessary; His doing so would be evidence of an imperfection in His creation, and what Newton spent his life proving was that the world operated according to certain natural, eternal and failproof laws.

Subsequent scholars and writers have popularized Newton and his discoveries. The story of Newton's discovering gravity by watching an apple fall from a tree is well known. Yet Newton's accomplishments are of a far wider range. They are summed up by the 18th century English poet Alexander Pope:

Nature and nature's laws lay hid in night;
God said "Let Newton be," and all was light.

　　这一观念同时也影响到了牛顿生活的年代的宗教思想。牛顿对自然现象所做的理性论证为神秘而虚幻的基督教提供了另外的诠释。但是，他这样做并不意味着他不信奉上帝。事实上，牛顿曾努力地学习《圣经》，而且大多数人可能不知道他写的有关宗教的作品比关于自然科学的还要多。牛顿把上帝视为造物主，他认为上帝的存在是不可否认的。上帝并不需要涉足尘世的事情；他之所以这样做证明他的创造还不完美，而牛顿用他的一生证明了世界是按照一定的自然的、永恒且无从证实的法则运转的。

　　后来的学者和作家们已经使牛顿及其伟大发现扬名天下。关于他因为看到苹果落地而发现了地球引力的故事也是家喻户晓。然而，牛顿的成就远不止如此。18世纪英国诗人亚历山大·蒲柏是这样描述牛顿的贡献的：

　　天与天理陷入黑茫；

　　上帝说，让牛顿来！于是光明大放。

Thirty-two

Adam Smith:
The Wealth of Nations

Who Was Adam Smith?

Adam Smith was a Scotsman who lived in the 18th century,a contemporary of the Founding Fathers of the United States (Smith lived from 1723 to 1790; George Washington lived from 1732 to 1799).Unlike the Founding Fathers,or other great men of the 18th century who are now household names,Smith lived a somewhat obscure life.He was,for 12 years,a university professor,then became a tutor to an aristocrat's son,then returned to his birthplace of Kirkcaldy,Scotland,where he devoted himself to his writing for the next 10 years.He then was appointed the Scottish Commissioner of Customs,and went to live with his mother in Edinburgh,and there devoted the rest of his life to his new and rather easy job and to the much more difficult task of writing.Smith was a rather quiet intellectual,not an activist,and yet with one book,*The Wealth of Nations*,he changed the world.

If Karl Marx can be said to have defined and refined communism,Adam Smith can just as surely be credited with having defined and refined capitalism as well.Almost single-handedly,Adam Smith created the academic discipline we now call "economics."

Nothing in his life seems to suggest that it will culminate in such an accomplishment.

Smith studied at the University of Glasgow; later,he went on to Balliol College,Oxford; at both Glasgow and Oxford he studied moral philosophy.That seems a strange discipline for someone who would become one of the world's greatest economists.Yet,all of Smith's views are grounded in moral concerns—economics,for him,is a means of achieving a good life.While a student,Smith developed his passion for liberty,and it is this belief in liberty that grounds all of his economic theory.He became interested in "the progress of opulence," by which he meant the ways in which wealth is accumulated; as well,he thought constantly about what he called "the simple system of natural liberty." His interest was not just in how a man should be allowed to live but also in what would be the most effective and beneficial structures for his labor—both for himself and for the society in which the worker lived.

At the age of 28,Smith was appointed Professor of Logic at the University of Glasgow,then became Professor of Moral Philosophy the following year.Gradually,his lectures changed—he started out by lecturing on ethics and rhetoric; in time,his lectures came to have more and more to do with his ideas about political economy-which,refined, became the basis of his book.

The Wealth of Nations

The Wealth of Nations is perhaps the most influential book on economics ever written.And therein lies an irony.The notions that it offers,revolutionary at the time,are now so much a part of the consciousness and practice of anyone who lives in one of the capitalist democracies that we assume that,in a sense,those ideas are self-evident,that they always existed.That is not the case.Although he often refined and built on the theories of

32

亚当·斯密
《国富论》

亚当·斯密

　　亚当·斯密是苏格兰人,他生于18世纪,和美国的开国元首处在同一时代(斯密生于1723年,1790年逝世;乔治·华盛顿生于1732年,1799年去世)。不像国父们以及18世纪其他著名的伟大人物那样,斯密的生活有些隐秘。他做了12年的大学教授,之后成为一名贵族子弟的私人教师,再后来,他回到他出生的地方苏格兰柯科迪,接下来的10年他在那里全身心地投入写作。之后,他被任命为苏格兰海关监督专员,并搬去爱丁堡和母亲同住,他在那儿重新找了一份较容易做的工作,并继续从事更加艰辛的写作直至去世。斯密并不活跃,他是一个相当内敛的文人,然而,他的《国富论》一书却改变了整个世界。

　　如果我们说卡尔·马克思定义并改进了共产主义理论,那么,亚当·斯密就完全可以被誉为定义和改进资本主义理论的始祖。亚当·斯密几乎是一个人创建了我们当今称之为"经济学"的理论体系。

　　似乎他的一生中并没有什么可以预示他的伟大成就。

　　斯密曾就读于格拉斯哥大学(University of Glasgow),后来,他继续在牛津大学贝列尔学院(Balliol College)求学,在格拉斯哥和牛津期间他一直学习道德哲学。成为一个世界上最伟大的经济学家似乎有些不可思议。然而,斯密的全部观点都是基于对道德的关注——学习经济学的理论,对他来说,只是过上幸福生活的一个途径。当斯密还是学生的时候,他就产生了对自由的热爱,并且正是这一信仰奠定了他的经济学理论的基础。他对"国家财富的增长"颇感兴趣,他认为这便是聚集财富的手段;同时,斯密还不断地思考他称之为"单纯的自然自由体系"的问题。他所强调的不仅仅是人们应该如何被赋予生存的权利,他还关注如何构建人类开展劳动所处的最有效且最有利的社会体系——既针对劳动者本身,又涉及他们所生活的社会。

　　斯密在28岁的时候被聘为格拉斯哥大学的逻辑学教授,第二年又担任了道德哲学的教授。他的课题逐渐发生变化——开始他讲授的是伦理学和修辞学;最后,他的授课内容越来越多地联系到关于政治经济学的观点——这些观点经过修改便成了他著作的基本思想。

《国富论》

　　《国富论》也许是经济学专著中最具影响力的作品。具有讽刺意味的是,他当时所提出的革命性的观点,现在很大程度上融入任何一个生活于资本主义民主制度下的人们的意识和实践中去,以至于我们会设想在某种意义上斯密的观点是不证自明的,并且一直存在着。然而,事实并非如此。虽然斯密经常修正其他思想家的论断,或者以此作为自己

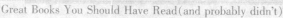

other thinkers,Smith devised ideas that basically we owe to him.

Smith suggested that there should be free markets,not just within individual countries but in the world as a whole; he objected to trade barriers or tariffs of any kind.He believed that a free market—one not restrained by government—was actually beneficial—that people,operating in their own self interest,actually if unconsciously benefited society as a whole—by helping to improve the standard of living of all people.A free market was not,as it sometimes appeared,either chaotic or unrestrained:it regulated itself.An "invisible hand" ("invisible" because most of us are unaware of it) actually contrives to produce the right kind and right amount of goods and services.Say that someone is successfully producing a product.Because of that success,other producers follow.Soon,there are too many of that product in circulation; the price drops below any acceptable profit level,and some producers stop creating that product.If the same demand exists,then this now acceptable amount of product brings with it an acceptable price level.In this way the unfettered market monitors itself.

Smith also rejected the notion that "land" was the single most important determinant of economic activity and wealth; instead,he suggested that "labor" was more important. Another of his ideas was that some tasks are better accomplished if they are divided into component parts,and each worker works on an individual part of the product-what we would now call an assembly line,which is the way that virtually any modern factory or any modern office is organized.Because unfettered markets and unfettered producers could lead to monopolies,Smith saw the government not as the controller of markets but as a refiner of markets.Government should control any tendency to monopolies; as well,it should be a servant of last resort to those who could not educate themselves,learn a skill—or were,for some reason,incapable in participating in free markets.

All of these ideas—now accepted in most of the world,those parts that do not cling to some kind of planned economy—come from this one man.*The Wealth of Nations* should be read by anyone who wishes to know how the modern economic world we all accept as a given actually came into being.If,as someone has said,all philosophy is a footnote to Plato, then it can as justly be said,all economics is a footnote to Adam Smith.

的论据,但我们也承认斯密的确提出了不少他自己的理论观点。

斯密认为市场活动应该是自由的,不仅仅在个别的国家,全世界都该如此;他反对任何形式的贸易壁垒和关税。他相信自由市场不受政府制约,事实上是很有利的,因为那些谋求自己利益的经营者在盈利的同时也不自觉地为整个社会创收,这样就有助于提高全社会人们的生活水平。自由市场有时并不像表面上那样混乱或者毫无秩序,它是会自我调节的。实际上,一只"无形的手"(称其是"无形的"是因为我们大多数人都察觉不到它的存在)会自觉地做出调节,使市场生产出适当种类而且适量的商品和服务。比如,有人成功经营了一种商品,他的成功引起其他的生产商纷纷效仿,不久,流通中出现了过量的同种产品,价格自然随之降到经营者所能承受的限度以下,于是,许多制造商停止继续生产这类产品。如果市场有相同数量的商品需求,那么那些所需产品就会以可接受的价格出售。摆脱束缚的市场就是这样实现自我的调节。

斯密也反对把"土地"视为影响经济活动和财富增长的唯一的最重要的决定因素;相反的,他认为"劳动"更为重要。他的另一观点是如果把某些劳动任务进行分工,让每一个劳动者只负责某一项生产,那么,生产任务将会被更好地完成——我们现在称之为流水装配线,实际上,任何现代化的工厂和办公地点都采用了这种生产组织形式。

由于摆脱限制的市场和生产商可能会形成垄断,斯密认为政府应该发挥改良市场的作用,而不是控制它。政府应该制约任何可能形成垄断的趋势;同时,它还应该帮助那些本身不能从市场活动中总结经验教训的经营者,政府应学会这种技能——否则,因为某一原因,它将无法参与到自由贸易中去。

所有这些观点——现在已被世界大多数人接受,而且这些观点不依附于某种计划经济体制——都源于亚当·斯密。任何想了解我们所处的特定的现代经济世界究竟是如何形成的人都应该读一下《国富论》。倘若像人们所说的那样,全部哲学是诠释柏拉图的注解,那么,我们就可以把整个经济学视为了解亚当·斯密的脚注。

Thirty-three

Thomas Jefferson: Writings

Who Was Thomas Jefferson?

Thomas Jefferson (1743-1826) was born into a wealthy family-his father owned a plantation in Albemarle County,Virginia.At 14,when his father died,Jefferson inherited 5, 000 acres of land and dozens of slaves.Although the plantation was later to become the location of his famous home,Monticello,Jefferson did not really live the life to which he would seem to have been destined.He did not live his life as a wealthy plantation owner.

Educated in the classics,he was enrolled in the College of William and Mary when he was only 16.During his 2 years there,he studied diligently and graduated with honors.He then studied law,and was admitted to the Virginia bar in 1767.Jefferson then went on to become one of the most notable politicians and statesmen that the United States has ever produced,culminating in his election as third President of the United States,an office in which he served for 2 terms.He was also the principal author of the U.S. "Declaration of Independence." After leaving the presidency,Jefferson founded the University of Virginia:it was unaffiliated with any religion,and it allowed students to choose which academic discipline they wanted to study.Both practices were revolutionary at the time.

Writings

All Americans know who Thomas Jefferson was; so do most non-Americans.We know him because he is the author of the "Declaration of Independence." The inception of the Revolutionary War (the war in which the 13 original colonies fought to be free of British rule) really began in the 1760s and 1770s,as relations between Great Britain and its American colonies became increasingly strained.The tension culminated in the battles of Lexington and Concord (small towns near Boston),in which colonists took on the British redcoats—the army of occupation.To discuss the increasingly frayed relations between what the Colonists regarded as the oppressor (Britain) and the oppressed (the Colonists),some of the more prominent Colonists formed the First,then the Second,Continental Congress, which in turn set up a committee to prepare a formal,written statement of grievances.The committee asked one of its members—Thomas Jefferson of Virginia-to write the document, which he did; he consulted other members only for their suggestions.The Congress ratified, and subsequently published his work,the document we now call the "Declaration of Independence," on July 4,1776.Americans regard that date as the birthday of their country,the greatest of secular holidays,and virtually any American can recite by memory the first few words of the Declaration:"When in the course of human events..." Ironically, though appropriately,Jefferson died 50 years later on the 4th of July 1826.

Jefferson's fame is so great as the author of this notable document that we have tended to forget his other accomplishments.They were considerable.As a politician,he served as the second Governor of Virginia (1779-1781),as U.S.Minister to France (1785-1789) as the

托马斯·杰弗逊
《作品集》

托马斯·杰弗逊

托马斯·杰弗逊(1743~1826)出生在一个富裕的家庭,他的父亲在弗吉尼亚的阿尔伯马尔郡拥有一个农场。在杰弗逊14岁的时候,父亲就去世了,他继承了约5 000英亩的土地和数十名黑奴。虽然这个农场后来变成了杰弗逊有名的蒙蒂塞洛庄园,但他并没有真正过看似是命中注定的奢华生活,他不愿做一个富有的农场主。

杰弗逊受过古典学教育,年仅16岁的他就被威廉与玛丽学院(College of William and Mary)录取。在校2年期间,他勤奋好学,并以优异的成绩毕业。后来,他学习法律,1767年,他加入弗吉尼亚律师协会。之后,杰弗逊就成为美国有史以来最著名的政治家之一,当选美国第三任总统使他的事业达到了高峰,并且他连任了两届。此外,他还主编了美国《独立宣言》。

离职之后,杰弗逊创建了弗吉尼亚大学:这所大学是与宗教学说完全无关的高等学院,并且允许学生自由选择自己喜欢的学科,这两点主张在当时是革命性的。

《作品集》

所有美国人都知道托马斯·杰弗逊;国外大多数人也同样如此。他所著的《独立宣言》使他闻名天下。美国大革命(在这场战争中,13个原英属殖民地通过斗争摆脱了英国的统治)真正爆发于18世纪60~70年代,当时英国和其北美的殖民地之间的关系日益紧张起来。矛盾最终激化,爆发了莱克星敦和康科德战役(两个战场都临近波士顿),在那里英国殖民者组织了"红衣军"——占领北美的英国军队。为了商讨应对英国殖民者和受压迫的殖民地人民之间关系不断紧张的形势,北美殖民地人民中一些较为著名的人士组织了第一、第二次大陆会议,接下来还成立了委员会准备起草一份正式的书面抗议。委员会任命其成员——来自弗吉尼亚的托马斯·杰弗逊撰写此文献,杰弗逊接受了这一委任;他请教了其他成员的意见作为参考。国会批准并且接下来出版了他的撰稿,这一文献就是我们现在所称的1776年4月的美国《独立宣言》。美国人民把这一天当做自己祖国的生日和最伟大的非宗教节日,事实上,任何一个美国人都能背诵《宣言》中的前几句"在有关人类事务的发展过程中……"。具有讽刺性的是,50年之后杰弗逊于1826年7月4日逝世。

杰弗逊作为著名的《独立宣言》的作者享有很高的声誉,以至于我们往往忘了他的其他成就。事实上,这些成就也为数不少:作为一位政治家,他于1779年至1781年担任弗吉尼亚的第二任州长;1785年至1789年驻法国大使;1789年至1793年担任首任国务卿;在

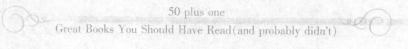

first U.S.Secretary of State (1789-1793) and as the Second Vice-President of the United States,under George Washington (1797-1801),and finally,and most notably,as the third President of the United States,after Washington and John Adams (Jefferson served from 1801 to 1809).In each of these roles,he was an innovator.And often he did the unexpected.

Jefferson is also regarded as the founder of what we now call the Democratic Party.It was a Democratic Party we would not recognize today.Jefferson believed in an agrarian society,one in which power was vested in the States,in which the powers of the Federal government were limited—yet it was during his administration,and at his doing,that the U. S.concluded the Louisiana Purchase,which considerably expanded the size of the United States,essentially paved the way for the United States to become a commercial rather than an agrarian economy,and greatly expanded the powers of the Federal government.Like Lincoln,who is often said to be the first Republican president,Jefferson failed to uphold some of his own most cherished beliefs when he believed that the country's good was at stake.Tax and spend Democrat? Jefferson reduced the country's national debt by half.

Yet,even if we acknowledge that Jefferson is not just the author of what remains to this day the most profound statement of the American consciousness,and even if we agree that he was one of the very greatest of our early national politicians,we have still failed to encompass all that he was.

Jefferson was also a plantation owner,who created Monticello,one of the most beautiful of American presidential homes.He founded the University of Virginia,and,an amateur architect,he made it one of the most stunning and architecturally notable of American institutions of higher learning.He was also a horticulturist,a mathematician,a musician,an inventor and an amateur scientist.In other words,Jefferson was one of the most brilliant men the United States has ever produced.He conformed to the ideal of the Renaissance Man—a notion that had its genesis 2 centuries before he was born—the notion that a well-rounded man was well-versed in a number of subjects,that he had a very many skills,that he was a "complete" individual—a notion that seemed hopeless even in Jefferson's day,much less our own.The concept of individuals as "specialists" in particular subjects was already well established.

Jefferson was a writer for all of his life—from an "Autobiography" to "Notes on the State of Virginia" to the "Declaration" itself to his two State of the Union addresses to Congress.There is no particular magnum opus,however,one that the reader can turn to as Jefferson's "definitive" work.His Writings is a compilation of his various formal and occasional writings throughout his life; it also includes his other public papers and a selection of his letters,some 287 of them in all—it was published by the Library of America in 1984.Though it is not of a piece (it was not written from start to finish as any kind of complete,planned book),it is the most substantial and enduring evidence we have of the quality—the breadth—of the mind of this remarkable man.

In Writings,Jefferson reveals himself to be what his admirers have always known him to be—an ultimately humane man,who regards life with reverence,someone who regards his fellow creatures with generosity and compassion.Writings reminds us of who the best of Americans really was,what he believed and tried to practice,and,in so doing,it provides an example for all of us.

1797年至1801年乔治·华盛顿执政期间,他担当第二任美国副总统;最引人注目的是,继华盛顿和约翰·亚当斯之后,杰弗逊当选第三任美国总统(任期从1801年至1809年)。他担当每一个职务的时候,都例行改革,经常做一些令人意想不到的举措。

杰弗逊被看做是现在我们所称的民主党派的创始人。不过,他所倡导的民主政党和今天的有所不同。杰弗逊崇尚建立一个重农主义的社会,在这一社会中,权力由国家赋予,联邦政府的权力受到制约——然而,就是在他当政期间,政府执行路易斯安纳购地案,此举极大地拓展了美国的疆域,基本上为美国发展商贸经济而非农业铺平了道路,并且也极大地增长了联邦政府的权力。当杰弗逊认为国家的利益面临风险的时候,他也像林肯那样——通常被称作第一位共和党总统,没有固执于自己本人最珍视的信仰。他通过征税偿还国债为国家减少了一半的债务。

然而,即使我们知道杰弗逊不仅仅撰写了至今仍被认为是美国最深刻的觉醒之宣言,并且即便我们认同他是建国初期最伟大的政治家之一,我们还是不甚了解他的全部。

杰弗逊还是一个农场主,他建造了有名的蒙蒂塞洛庄园,那是美国总统住宅中最漂亮的一所。他创建了弗吉尼亚大学,作为一个业余的建筑师,他把学校建成一所美国国内最引人注目且在建筑方面也极为杰出的高级学府。他还是一名园艺学者、数学家、音乐家、发明家和业余的科学家。换句话说,杰弗逊是美国历史上最有才华的人物之一。他完全符合一个"文艺复兴人士"的标准——这一概念源于杰弗逊出生前两个世纪,指的是涉猎多门学科的多才多艺的人,这样的人懂得很多技能,称得上是"全才"——即使是在杰弗逊生活的年代,能够配得起这一称号的希望也是微乎其微,更不用说放在我们当代了。在特定的学科范围内,"专家"这一称呼倒是已经被广泛应用。

杰弗逊一生都在写作——从《自传》到《弗尼吉亚纪实》,到《独立宣言》,再到写给美国国会的两篇《国情咨文》。虽然其中没有大部头的艺术作品,但每一部都被读者视为杰弗逊的"权威"之作。他的《作品集》汇总了他一生中诸多正式和即兴所写的文章;还包括杰弗逊其他的公文和精选的书信,总共287篇。这一《作品集》于1984年被美国图书出版社发行。虽然这一《作品集》没有其他经系统编写而成的作品那样连贯的篇幅,但却是我们所掌握的最确凿且永久的依据来证明这位杰出人物的才干和人格魅力。

《作品集》中展示了杰弗逊是一位完全的慈善家,这一点正像他的敬慕者一直所了解的那样。他认为生命应该被尊重,人们应以宽容和慈悲之心对待自己的同胞。《作品集》让我们回忆起一位真正的杰出的美国人,他的信仰和举措以及他的奋斗历程为我们所有人树立了榜样。

Thirty-four

William Wordsworth: The Prelude

Who Was William Wordsworth?

William Wordsworth (1770-1850),with Samuel Taylor Coleridge,was the poet responsible for launching the Romantic Period in English literature with the publication of their *Lyrical Ballads* in 1798.Their intent was to overturn the pretentiously learned and rigidly conceived poetry of the 18th century Enlightenment.

Born in Cumberland,England,in what the English call the "Lake Country," Wordsworth developed at an early age a love for the countryside and nature.When he was only 8,his world changed—his mother died.Five years later his father died.Wordsworth and his three brothers and sister were raised by different uncles.Many years passed before Wordsworth recovered from the loneliness that followed the loss of his parents and his separation from his brothers and sister.With the assistance of his uncles,he was able to attend St.John's College,Cambridge,from which he graduated in 1791.

Wordsworth married Mary Hutchinson,and they had five children.

Although in later life he was considered a recluse "nature poet," such admirers as the American writer Ralph Waldo Emerson would frequently visit him to talk to him.

The Prelude

William Wordsworth is one of the poets of what we now call the Romantic Period in literature in English.His contemporaries were Coleridge,Keats,Shelley,and Lord Byron. Arguably,though,Wordsworth was the most influential of these poets,for it was his book *Lyrical Ballads*,written in collaboration with Coleridge and published in 1798,that truly launched that movement in literature and thought of the early 19th century that we now call romanticism.

Lyrical Ballads is an act of rebellion against the thought and literature of the century just ending,and the Romantic poets have been seen as rebels ever since.Bohemians,hippies, beats—every generation has a name for the its own romantics and their poetic/social followers.Wordsworth was indeed rebelling against the 18th century.It was the Age of the Enlightenment,and,whatever the licentiousness of the time may have been,it had been a relatively peaceful century in which the primacy of the human mind had gained immense sway.The notion that the greatest thing about man was his mind,a mind that could solve all human dilemmas,was truly entrenched.Its literary expression in poetry was the classical formality of the rhyming couplet.The rationality of the age also took other literary forms— mainly prose,which seemed more appropriate to a rationalist time than did poetry,a time that was emerging from and reacting to the exuberance of the Renaissance.The novel as we now know it was developed,and the essay (never before or since so popular) became a dominant,if not the most dominant,of literary forms.In the poetry of Pope or Dr.Johnson,or in the novels of Fielding,or the essays of Addison and Steele,the rationalist spirit had triumphed.

34

威廉·华兹华斯
《序曲》

威廉·华兹华斯

　　威廉·华兹华斯（1770~1850）和萨缪尔·泰勒·柯勒律治合作共同编写了《抒情歌谣集》，此作于1798年出版，标志着开创了英国文学史上浪漫主义的新纪元。两位作者的创作意图是为了推翻18世纪启蒙运动影响下那些虚饰且构思僵化的诗歌创作。

　　华兹华斯出生在英国的坎伯兰郡，那里被英国人称为"湖畔乡村"。他从小就培养起了对乡村和大自然的热爱。8岁的时候丧母，他的生活因此发生了巨大的变化。5年后，父亲也永远离开了他。华兹华斯和他的三个兄弟一个妹妹分别由不同的叔父抚养长大。多年以后，他才从失去双亲和与同胞兄妹分离的阴影中恢复过来。在叔父的支持下，华兹华斯得以进入剑桥大学圣约翰学院读书，并于1791年毕业。

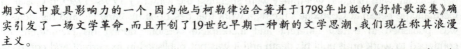

　　华兹华斯与玛丽·胡特金森结婚，并且生了5个孩子。

　　虽然，在以后的日子里，他被认为是过着隐士般的"自然诗人"的生活，但许多像美国作家拉尔夫·瓦尔多·爱默生这样的他的敬慕者也时常造访与他交谈。

《序曲》

　　威廉·华兹华斯是英国文学史上我们称之为浪漫主义时期的代表诗人之一。与他同时代的还有柯勒律治、济慈、雪莱和爵士拜伦。尽管存在争议，但华兹华斯被看做是同时期文人中最具影响力的一个，因为他与柯勒律治合著并于1798年出版的《抒情歌谣集》确实引发了一场文学革命，而且开创了19世纪早期一种新的文学思潮，我们现在称其浪漫主义。

　　《抒情歌谣集》是一场对前一个世纪的思想和文学的反叛，并且自此浪漫主义诗人都被视为叛逆者。波希米亚人、嬉皮士、"垮掉的一代"——每一代人都起出一个名字来称呼他们所生活的时代的浪漫主义者和那些追求浪漫的诗人及社会人士。华兹华斯的确反叛了18世纪，这是一个思想启蒙的时代，无论这一时期多么的放荡不羁，它曾经是相对和平的年代，当时人们的意识形态受到了猛烈的冲击。人类最伟大之处在于他们的思想，且这些思想能够解决人们遇到的所有难题，这一理念在人们头脑中已是根深蒂固，它在诗歌中相应的文学表达就是那些古典且规整的押韵对句。这一时代对理性的表达也呈现出另一种文学样式——主要采用散文体，比起诗歌，这一形式似乎更加适合于理性主义的时代，而这一时代是继文艺复兴之后出现的，同时也反映了文艺复兴时期人们充溢的情感。我们现在所熟悉的小说在当时也开始发展，散文（之前和之后都没有像当时那样盛行）即使没有占支配的地位，也算得上是一种非常重要的文学形式。在蒲伯和约翰逊博士的诗作中，或者菲尔丁的小说、艾迪生以及斯梯尔的散文里，都可以找到理性主义精神的成功示例。

Wordsworth specifically announces in the preface to the *Lyrical Ballads* that he is a rebel.He says that he will write poetry not in the exalted language of his 18th century predecessors but "in the real language of men." Moreover,he appeals to the emotions,not to the mind.Poetry,says Wordsworth in this preface,is the   "spontaneous overflow of powerful feelings...."

It is,however,as much Wordsworth's life as his work that creates the notion of rebel of a peculiarly modern kind—a social rebel who is a bleeding heart,who creates a literature appropriate for that stance.Wordsworth was born in the Lake District,a picturesque district of lakes and verdant hills in the northwest of England.Despite sojourns abroad,and residence for a time in Somerset,near Coleridge,he spent most of his life in this beautiful area,and it figures,as inspiration,in his work.His parents were both dead by the time he was 13,and he and his siblings were separated,raised by different relatives:his childhood was thus both joyful and melancholy.At 17,he went to study in Cambridge,was already a convinced revolutionary and in 1790 he visited revolutionary France and supported the Republican movement because he believed it represented the best hope for mankind.After graduating the next year,he returned for an extended trip around France,met a Frenchwoman,had a child with her,returned to England and a few years later produced the bombshell of the *Lyrical Ballads*.

This early life colors our view of Wordsworth.But,there is another side to the man. Though it,too,conforms to our view of a certain kind of modern rebel.Disillusioned by the Reign or Terror and the rise of Napoleon,Wordsworth turned away from his original radicalism,married and was the father of five children,became a family man; became increasingly conservative in politics and religion; and at the end of his life served as his country's Poet Laureate at the same time that he was the patriarch of his local rural society. The radical had become the pillar of society.

But this,too,is a skewed view of Wordsworth.His sister Dorothy spent a good deal of her adult life with him,and when they were spending the winter of 1798- 1799 in Goslar in Germany,he began,at Coleridge's urging,a work that described his early life and his ideals.It was published in a few different and incomplete versions during his lifetime,but he continued to work on it until his death,and it was not published in its current and complete form until a few months after his deat—his wife named it *The Prelude*,and today we consider it Wordsworth's masterpiece.

The Prelude,which many critics consider the greatest of autobiographies in verse,is a culmination of more than 50 years of intense work—it is also a great poem of human consciousness,taking as its theme "the growth of a poet's mind." In it Wordsworth details the formative events of his childhood and youth,which he presents as universals; as well,he explains his radicalism at the time of the French Revolution.Ironically, *The Prelude* was to have been just that,an introduction to a greater work,The Recluse,a work that Wordsworth never completed.What does remain of that work has been of far less interest to readers of the last 150 years than has *The Prelude*.

It is difficult to imagine Wordsworth intentions—except as he offers them in the introduction to *Lyrical Ballads*,with his emphasis on "powerful feelings." It is obvious that Wordsworth is countering the rationalism of the 18th century with the emotionalism of his

　　华兹华斯特别在《抒情歌谣集》的序言中宣称他是一个叛逆者。他说他不会用18世纪时人们所用的那种矫揉造作的词藻,而是用"人类真正的语言"写作。此外,他更加倾向于感性而非理性。华兹华斯在序言中写道:"诗歌是强烈感情的自然流露……"

　　然而,华兹华斯的人生和他的作品共同诠释了"叛逆"这一对现代人来说尤为特殊的概念——他是这样一个社会"叛逆者",他呕心沥血,为自己的信仰开创了一种合适的文学体裁。华兹华斯出生在湖区,那是英国西北部一个山清水秀的画一般的地方。尽管他曾旅居国外,而且在柯勒律治家附近的萨默塞特住过一阵子,但他大部分时间都呆在这个美丽的湖区,因为这里可以激发他的创作灵感。华兹华斯的父母在他13岁的时候相继去世,他和兄妹几个也被分开,由不同的亲戚抚养,他的童年就是这样既有快乐的时光,又让人感到不幸。他17岁时进入剑桥大学读书,那时他已经开始倾向于革命,1790年他去了正处在革命形势下的法国,并且他支持那里的共和党人的运动,因为他相信这场运动能为人们开创最美好的未来。次年,从剑桥大学毕业以后,他再次重游法国,在那里他结识了一名法国女子,两人生下了一个孩子。后来,他回到英国,几年后便创作出了著名的《抒情歌谣集》。

　　华兹华斯早年的生活为我们提供了了解他本人的丰富的素材。然而,他还有另一面,这一方面也符合我们将他视为现代叛逆者的观点。帝国的专制和暴政以及拿破仑的上台使华兹华斯放弃了最初的激进思想,他结婚,并有了五个孩子,做起了居家的男人,渐渐地他在政治和宗教的态度上也变得保守,他晚年被封为英国"桂冠诗人",同时,他还任当地乡村社区的高层长官。而此时激进的潮流已经成为当时社会的主流。

　　但是,这一方面也是对华兹华斯的一种偏见。华兹华斯的表妹多罗西成年之后的大部分时间都和他一起度过。1798年末至1799年初,他们两人在德国戈斯拉尔过冬,华兹华斯在柯勒律治的催促下开始编写一部描写华兹华斯早年生活和理想的著作。此作品在他有生之年以许多不同且不完整的版本发行,但他一直不断地编写直至去世。在华兹华斯逝世几个月之后,我们现在所看到的这一作品的完整版才得以出版——他的妻子称之为《序曲》,现在被我们视为华兹华斯的代表作品。

　　《序曲》被许多评论家看做是最伟大的诗体自传作品,它是华兹华斯50多年激情写作的精华——其主题是描述"一位诗人思想的成长历程",是一部赞扬人类精神的颂歌。华兹华斯在这一诗作中详细地描述了他童年和青年时代经历的有代表性的事件,将它们呈现得惟妙惟肖犹如大千世界;同时,他还阐明了法国大革命时期他所抱有的激进思想。有趣的是,《序曲》原本只是一部更加伟大之作《隐者》的序言,可惜华兹华斯未能完成此作。而对于上一个半世纪的读者们来说,对这部作品遗留部分的兴趣远远不及《序曲》所达到的效果。

　　除了华兹华斯在《抒情歌谣集》的序言中所提到的注重"强烈的感情"之外,我们很难

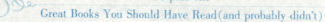
own feelings,and it is easy enough to see in his doing so a reflection of a certain kind of cycle in society and its shifting adherence to certain notions.Thus,in more modern times,the conservatism and complacency of the 1950s is followed by the emotional free-for-all of the 1960s.

Wordsworth is,of course,a polemicist,offering the case for the supremacy of the emotions,for our natural response to nature and the things of this world—for heart over head.But to come up with so simplistic a view of Wordsworth,his life and his work,pre-eminently *The Prelude*,is to sell him short.He may be recommending the contemplation of nature and the events of human existence over the contemplation of the events of a book-but finally he is arguing for an integrated personality,one that depends as much on emotional as mental response to the phenomena of life.

The Prelude is a corrective,but it is a corrective designed to create a more integrated personality—the French Revolution is after all emotion gone mad—and it repays every reader to learn Wordsworth's lesson once again—that the ideal for man is neither mind nor feeling,but an integration of both into a whole personality.

想象他的意图。很显然,华兹华斯是在用他自觉的情感反抗18世纪的理性主义,并且我们也很容易能看得出他追求理想的这一过程反映了某种社会的循环周期,而这一更替遵循某种理念。这样,在更靠近现代的20世纪50年代保守主义和故步自封就被60年代的自由情感主义所取代。

当然,华兹华斯是一个辩论家,他为我们展示了崇尚情感的范例,体现了人类对自然界和世界万物的自然回应——情感胜于理智。但是,相对于华兹华斯的一生及其著作,尤其要提到著名的《序曲》,以上他所提出的这一简单的观点实在微不足道。他可能是在功告人们把思索大自然和人类的存在置于钻研书本知识之上——但是,他最终是在为人类完整的个性辩护,而完整的个性又是依赖于情感和理智的,两个方面缺一不可。

《序曲》是被订正过的,这一订正旨在塑造一个更加完整的个性——毕竟法国大革命是人们在耗尽了所有的情感之后发起的——拿这一作品回报每一位读者,是希望他们能够再次从华兹华斯的身上汲取教训——人类的理想状态既非完全理智,也非完全感性,而是要使两方面融合为一个完整的人格。

Thirty-five

Charles Darwin:
On the Origin of Species

Who Was Charles Darwin?

Charles Darwin (1809-1882),the British naturalist,achieved lasting fame for his theory of evolution or transmutation of species,achieved through natural and sexual selection. Simply stated,his theory proposed that the "best" characteristics of an organism will survive and be passed on to offspring and become the dominant characteristics of the next generation.This theory became popularly known as "The Survival of the Fittest."

Darwin was born in Shropshire,England.As a young man,he went to Edinburgh University to study medicine.While at university,Darwin showed no interest in becoming a physician,but instead he focused his attention primarily on natural biology.In 1827,Darwin transferred to Christ College,Cambridge,to be trained to become a clergyman.

After graduation,opting for a life of neither physician or clergyman,Darwin signed on for a long journey of discovery,a survey of the coast of South America,on the HMS Beagle. Many of his later ideas come from his observations on a trip that eventually lasted for 5 years.

In 1838 he developed his theory of natural selection,but he avoided mentioning it (except to close friends) because he feared he could be severely punished for his ideas.In 1859,he went public with his theory—with his book *On the Origin of Species*.

During Darwin's lifetime,the book went through six editions.In each one there were minor changes; for the sixth edition,he made extensive changes.During most of his later years,Darwin was often incapacitated by illness contracted during his travels.He died in 1882,and was buried in Westminster Abbey in London; he was by then a national celebrity.

On the Origin of Species

The name Darwin (or the term "Darwinisn') has become almost a code word in the consciousness of modern man."Creationists,"as they are now called,subscribe to a literal interpretation of *The Bible*,that God created the world in 6 days,that he rested on the seventh (the day that both Christians and Jews call the Sabbath)—that is,that the universe, particularly life on Earth,has always been as it now is since God created it,that it reveals an "intelligent design," being precisely as God intended.Often concurrent with this view is a belief that the Earth is only thousands of years old,a belief based on various dates that emerge in the stories of ancient peoples that are contained in *The Bible*.

In comparison,Darwinism proposes that the universe,the Earth itself,is very old,that our physical world is constantly changing,that plant life and animal life (including human life) have constantly evolved from simpler beginnings.Thus: man was not created as he currertly exists.He has evolved from simpler creatures that were themselves evolved from even simpler creatures.We would now say that all life goes back to a single cell.

In some ways it seems like an either/or argument—not dissimilar to the flat earth/ round earth controversy of centuries ago.There is a crucial difference between Creationists

35

查尔斯·达尔文
《物种起源》

查尔斯·达尔文

查尔斯·达尔文(1809~1882)是一位英国博物学家,他提出了生物进化或变异理论,指出物种通过自然和两性的选择来实现进化,这一学说为他赢得了不朽的声誉。简言之,他的理论声称:生物体的"最佳"特性将会存活继而传给后代,并成为下一代身上占主导地位的性状。这就是有名的"适者生存"论。

达尔文出生在英国的什罗浦郡。年轻的他进了爱丁堡大学学习医学,在校期间,他无意要成为一名内科医生,反而把主要精力放在了自然生物学上。1827年,达尔文转到剑桥大学基督学院,在那里他接受了专业牧师的培训。

毕业之后,达尔文既不想当内科医生,也不愿做牧师,于是他登记领取失业救济金,并随猎犬号(HMS Beagle)沿着南美洲海岸开始了他长途的探索之旅。他后来的很多想法都是源于此次长达5年的探险。

1838年,他提出了"自然选择"的理论,但是担心会因此受到严厉的制裁,他避免提及这一理论(除了对他自己亲密的朋友)。1859年,他将这一学说公告世人,其著作名为《物种起源》。

在达尔文有生之年,这本书换了六个版本。每个版本都有细微的改动,达尔文在最后一版中作了较大的改动。

后来的大部分时间,达尔文经常在旅途中被疾病缠身,他于1882年去世,被葬在伦敦威斯敏斯特教堂,那时他已经是闻名全国了。

《物种起源》

达尔文这个名字(或"达尔文学说")几乎已经成为现代人意识中的一个代码。"神造论者",就像现在被称呼的那样,信奉的是《圣经》中的阐释,讲述的是上帝六天之内创造了世界,并且在第七天休息(这一天基督教徒和犹太人都称之为安息日)——就是说,整个宇宙,尤其是地球上的生命,自从被上帝创造出来之后一直保持现在的样子,这表明上帝的创造是一个"智慧设计",这也正是上帝造物的意图。通常,还存在另一种观点,认为地球仅仅只有几千年的历史,这一观点是基于《圣经》中出现的讲述古代人民故事的不同时间。

相比之下,达尔文学说则提出宇宙及地球本身存在的历史是非常久远的,我们的物质世界在不断地发生变化,植物和动物体(包括人类)是由较为简单的原始生命不断进化而来的。这就是说,人类并非自创造之初就像现在的样子。他是由低级生物体进化而来,而那些低级生物自身也经历了从更为低级的生物体进化的过程。我们现在可以说所有生命都可追溯到一个单细胞。

从某个角度看,这似乎是一个非此即彼的争论——类似几个世纪以前关于争辩地球

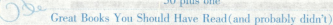
and Darwinists, however—just as there was between flat earth/round earth adherents.

Those who believe in "intelligent design" do so as an act of faith—*The Bible*, such people believe, is literal truth. Those of a more scientific mind (they are not necessarily anti-religion) might ask: Why, if He contains within Himself the universe and time, would God, after a 6-day creation, need to rest? In other words: Isn't *The Bible's* rendering of Creation really poetic, really imaginative? Just a metaphor? In contrast, Darwin himself was a scientist, and *On the Origin of Species* was published after a lifetime of scientific investigation (Darwin was born in 1809; Origin was published in 1859, when he was 50 years old).

For almost all of his adult life, Darwin was a scientist—someone who examines the natural environment in controlled circumstances, then records his conclusions, then tests them again and again, to prove them right—or, if the evidence of testing does not confirm his hypothesis, then to prove them wrong. In all of his investigations and inquiries Darwin did not reject God—he was in his early life a Christian, thereafter and until the end of his life he was an agnostic—he rejected God no more than, later, Einstein did, in proposing his own views of Creation.

Darwin, like Einstein, saw themselves as describing the world created by a higher power, the workings of His creation. Both men would probably say that they were describing a more stupendous Creation than that imagined by the Creationists.

On the Origin of the Species—a book about which it can fairly be said: "It changed the world"—is thus not in any way frivolous, opinionated or flukey—it involves the considered approach of a man who was, by background, by training, and by life-long work in his field, an eminently qualified and gifted natural scientist.

Because the book so changed our views of creation, of the ways in which all life, most particularly human life, evolved into what it is now, it should be read by anyone interested in the world in which we live; the book is surprisingly readable and accessible, even to a non-scientist.

In reading the book, anyone should remember that its conclusions (except to a few scientists) were revolutionary in their time. Darwin was proposing that individual species of life originate through evolutionary change, that this change is sparked by their adapting to the environment in which they live. He calls this process "natural selection," that any organism or characteristics of that organism best able to endure in its environment is the one to survive, that the characteristics of that organism that allowed that survival eventually determine what the species will be like in future (for example: If dark-haired people best survive in hot, sunny climates, then gradually the people who live in that climate will all have dark hair).

Darwin, almost single-handedly, established evolution as the primary explanation of why nature is diversified. A bombshell at the time, and for many years thereafter (evolution was not universally accepted by scientists until the 1920s and 1930s), Darwin's theories, and reverence for his genius, are now accepted by the vast majority of the scientific community—even by most of the world's religious community. All of us—whether we are on Darwin's "side" or not—should know *On the Origin of Species*, the most famous book by one's the world's most famous men.

是平的还是圆的。神造论者和达尔文主义者之间有一个根本的不同,这正如"地平说"和"地圆说"之间存在根本的分歧一样。

那些"智慧设计"的信徒们以此证明他们对其信仰的忠诚,他们相信《圣经》就是文字真理。而那些具有更加科学思想的人(他们不一定反宗教)可能会问:如果上帝自身可以容纳宇宙和时间,那为什么他六天完成创造之后还需要休息?换句话说,《圣经》中对上帝造物的描述是不是太诗意,太具想象色彩了?是否这只是一个比喻呢?相对而言,达尔文本人是一个科学家,并且他经过一生的科学探索写就的《物种起源》最终得以出版(达尔文出生于1809年,《物种起源》于1859年出版,他当时正好50岁)。

达尔文成年之后几乎大部分时间都在做科学研究——在有限的条件下检测自然环境,记下自己的结论,然后反复的验证,以证实它们的正确性;或者,如果检验的证据不能证明其假设合理,那就证实它们是错误的。在达尔文全部的调查研究中,他并未拒绝信奉上帝——事实上,他早年是一名基督教徒,后来直到去世都是一位不可知论者。达尔文没有像之后的爱因斯坦那样完全拒绝信仰上帝,因为爱因斯坦甚至曾提出了他自己的创世观点。

同爱因斯坦一样,达尔文认为他们本身是在描绘由"更高力量"创造而成的世界。两个人可能都会说他们是在描绘一个比神造论者所想象的更为了不起的创造。

我们可以公正地评价《物种起源》这一著作改变了世界——此评价不带有任何的轻率、武断或者侥幸——它是经过仔细考量其作者的背景、科学实践以及终生投身科研工作所做之贡献基础上对这位杰出自然科学家作出的公正评判。

因为这本书在如此大的程度上改变了我们对上帝造物说的看法,同时,论述了所有生命,特别是人类生命发展至今的进化过程,所以每一个对我们生存的世界感兴趣的人都应该读一下这一作品;此书读起来颇为有趣,而且非常易懂,即便对那些不是科学人士的读者也是如此。

在阅读的时候,每个人都应该记得此书的结论在当时是革命性的(除了对少数科学家)。达尔文提出单个的物种都源于生命体的进化演变,这一演变由于生物适应生存的环境而被触发。达尔文称这一过程为"自然选择",每个存活下来的生物体或生命特性都是那些最适应生存环境的部分。而存活下来的生物体的特性将最终决定该物种未来的性状(比如,如果深色毛发的人种最适应炎热、日照强的气候而存活下来,那么,渐渐地生存在这种气候条件下的人都将生有深色的毛发)。

达尔文几乎是在无人帮助的条件下创建了进化论,这是对缤繁多样的自然界作出的首次诠释,在当时以及之后的许多年里引起了很大的震动(进化论直至20世纪20年代到30年代才被科学界普遍接受)。达尔文的学说和人们对他才华的仰慕现在已被科学领域绝大部分人士所认同,甚至也得到了世界宗教界的肯定。我们所有的人——无论是否站在达尔文一边——都应该了解《物种起源》这一世界上最著名的自然科学家所写就的最著名的作品。

Thirty-six

Charles Dickens:
Great Expectations

Who Was Charles Dickens?

Charles Dickens (1812-1870) was a prominent and prolific English writer whose novels,during his lifetime,made him immensely popular on both sides of the Atlantic.His vast appeal to readers has been attributed to his social consciousness and to his literary skill in creating spell-binding and comic novels that were yet very serious in their attacks on injustice,hypocrisy and other social evils of the 19th century.

Born in England into a moderately comfortable family,Dickens received a modest private education.But this way of life ended abruptly when his father was imprisoned for debt,the result of the father's extravagance.Dickens was sent to work at 12 to pay for his lodging and to help support his parents.His family's condition changed a few years later when his father was left a small inheritance,which enabled him to pay off his debts.The family's sudden good fortune did not,however,improve conditions for Dickens.His mother's insistence that he continue working left him very bitter.But it was from his experiences growing up as a working boy that his concern grew for the conditions in which the working class lived,and it was from this experience that the major themes of his stories and novels evolved.

Later,while working as a journalist for the *Morning Chronicle*,he met and married Catherine Hogarth,daughter to the newspaper's music critic.They had 10 children.

Dickens' sharp criticism of the social and economic system of the 19th century in England won him the respect and attention of such radicals as Karl Marx and Friedrich Engels.The writer George Orwell said,"Dickens attacked English institutions with a ferocity that has never since been approached...the very people he attacked have swallowed him so completely that he has become a national institution himself."

Over the years,many writers have been strongly influenced by Dickens,including Thomas Hardy,George Gissing,Samuel Butler,Anne Rice and Tom Wolfe.

Great Expectations

Charles Dickens is one of the few writers,in English or any other language,who has been compared to William Shakespeare.Literary scholars might say that,like Shakespeare, Dickens changed the English language—established new words,new meanings,more than anything else guided the way in which we have come to express ourselves.

But few non-scholars ever think about whether writers have or have not refined our language.In the more popular mind—the mind of the general reader—Shakespeare and Dickens have other things in common.Both come from humble if respectable beginnings, and both had limited educations—which,particularly in the case of Shakespeare,has provoked speculation that he could not possibly have written his plays because he lacked a university education! Both men made slight jogs in their chosen professions:Shakespeare was an actor who became a playwright,who probably never gave up being an actor.Dickens

36

查尔斯·狄更斯
《远大前程》

查尔斯·狄更斯

查尔斯·狄更斯(1812~1870)是一位杰出而多产的英国作家,他一生所创作的小说使其闻名于大西洋两岸。他的作品最吸引人之处源于他的社会阅历以及他在创造引人入胜的喜剧小说方面的才华,而这些小说都是用来批判19世纪的不公正、虚伪和其他的社会阴暗面。

狄更斯出生在英国一个相对窘迫的家庭,从小受到了有限的私人教育,然而,因父亲挥霍无度,全家被迫迁入负债者监狱,以往安稳的生活一下子被打破。狄更斯12岁就被送去做童工以支付租金和补贴家用。后来,他的父亲得到一小笔遗产,并还清了债务,家境曾一度好转。但是,家庭的这次好运并没有使狄更斯的境况得到改善,因为他的母亲坚持让他继续打工,这使他吃尽了苦头。然而,正是做童工的这段成长经历使他开始关注劳工阶层的生活遭遇,并且以此作为他小说创作的主要素材。

后来,狄更斯在做《晨报》的记者的时候认识了这一报社的音乐编辑的女儿凯瑟琳·霍加斯,两人结婚并生下了10个孩子。

狄更斯对19世纪英国社会和经济体制的强烈抨击使他受到了诸多激进人士,比如卡尔·马克思和弗里德里希·恩格斯的敬仰和关注。作家乔治·奥威尔提到"狄更斯对英国社会的抨击其强度是无人能及的,而被他抨击的势力竟如此彻底地吞没了他,使其本身自成一体。"

许多年以来,很多作家都深受狄更斯的影响,包括托马斯·哈代、乔治·吉辛、萨缪尔·巴特勒、安妮·莱斯以及汤姆·沃尔夫。

《远大前程》

在用英语及任何其他语言写作的作家当中,很少有人被拿来与莎士比亚相提并论,而查尔斯·狄更斯就是这少数的其中之一。文学家们可能会说,像莎士比亚一样,狄更斯发展了英语语言,发明了新词,拓展了新的词义,尤为突出的是他促进了现代人的语言表达方式的形成。

然而,对于不是专家学者的人们来说,很少有人会去考虑作家有没有改进我们的语言。大众读者更普遍地认为莎士比亚和狄更斯在其他方面具有相同之处。两人都出身卑微,并且都没有受过充分的教育——尤其是莎士比亚,甚至被人质疑不可能创作出那么伟大的剧作,因为他缺乏正规的大学教育。两人都在选择职业上经历了细微的变动:莎士比亚曾经是一个演员,后来成为一名剧作家,他可能从未放弃过他的表演事业;狄更斯曾撰写特写,后来成为一位小说家,但同样他一生都没间断为一些知名且影响较大的期刊

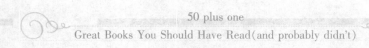
was a journalist who became a novelist,yet also continued reportage for all of his life,writing for a series of popular and influential journals.

Artistically,there are more interesting comparisons:both Shakespeare and Dickens were superb storytellers who created memorable characters,and,making allowances for the difference between 15th and 19th century communications,both men enjoyed great popularity during their lifetimes.Shakespeare was Elizabethan London's most popular playwright; Dickens was,and remains,probably the most popular novelist who ever lived (to this day,everything he wrote remains in print).Although Shakespeare wrote in verse and Dickens wrote in prose,that distinction is not precise.Shakespeare usually writes in blank verse (verse that does not necessarily rhyme); Dickens often,in the midst of prose,writes poetry (his sentences "scan" as progression of some variant of heavy beat/light beat,as sentences in poetry do).Hence,Dickens often sounds Shakespearean.As if to complete the comparison:both men died relatively young,in their 50s,having created an immense body of work that still stuns the world.

Some readers,though,might object to such a comparison.Shakespeare (either reading his plays or seeing them performed) seems "difficult," particularly his language.Dickens,on the other hand,whose language after all is much closer to our own,seems highly accessible. He always tells rollicking good stories in what seems to be down-to-earth language.Nothing could be further from the truth.

Dicken's language is both florid and dense; and,although the use of irony and symbol is hardly unknown in the works of novelists who came before him,Dickens is the master of these modes and devices—and in this he is unique,that many of the true meanings of his novels are unknowable without reference to their symbols.

Dickens's novels,without a deep pondering of his symbolism,are pleasing to readers as stories.That is why so many of his novels have been turned into movies,why a *Christmas Carol* is adapted for the stage,at Christmas,in so many different American cities.But a failure to read Dickens closely,with maximum attention,fails to yield Dickens' deeper meaning and commentary—just as a superficial reading of Shakespeare fails to tell the reader what Shakespeare was trying to convey about human experience.Thus,in a superficial reading,A *Tale of Two Cities* is about an English family caught up in the French revolution,or *King Lear* is the story of a ruler with a couple of ungrateful daughters.

There is,however,one crucial difference between Shakespeare and Dickens: Shakespeare presents,superbly (no one has done it better),the different situations in which humans find themselves-the human desire for power,our propensity to greed,the joys of love (and the impediments to love),but it is extremely difficult for the reader/listener to discover Shakespeare's stance on any of the universal human experiences he portrays. Dickens,conversely,is manifestly religious,believes in a higher power; more important,he believes that good in life ultimately triumphs-as it had in its own.His father had been imprisoned for debt,he himself had worked in an almost unbelievably squalid factory,yet he was the most popular novelist in England,then the world,before he was 30,and that fame and popularity lasted for all of his life.He ardently believed that,if one avoided certain pitfalls,life provided abundant opportunities for self-fulfillment and for happiness.

One of his greatest novels—in its plot,its characterizations,its mastery of language,its

撰写报道。

在文学艺术方面,他们的相同点更为有趣:两人都是一流的叙事高手,他们塑造的人物形象往往给读者留下极为深刻的印象。考虑到15世纪和19世纪人们交流方式上的差异,两者都乐于追求他们各自生活的年代的社会风尚。莎士比亚是伊丽莎白时期伦敦最受欢迎的剧作家;狄更斯曾经且现在仍为文学界最受欢迎的小说家(直到今天,他的所有作品仍在出版)。虽然莎士比亚使用诗体写作,而狄更斯用的是散文体,但差异并不那么严格。莎士比亚通常写无韵诗(这一诗体不要求押韵);而狄更斯经常在散文写作中用到诗体(他的语句在强音和弱音的变换过程中符合诗体的韵律)。这样,狄更斯的小说读起来仿佛莎士比亚的诗作。宛如是要结束这一比较:两人都是在50岁左右的时候较早去世,留下了丰硕的文学成果至今还在影响着世界。

虽然,有的读者可能会反对这样的比较。他们会说:莎士比亚(要么读一下他的戏剧,要么看一下这些剧本的演出)似乎"很难懂",尤其是作者的语言。而狄更斯的语言毕竟更靠近我们现代,极易读懂。他总是用朴实的语言讲述一些诙谐的好听的故事。没有什么比狄更斯的语言更贴近现实的了。

狄更斯的语言既华丽又缜密,虽然在他之前讽刺和象征的写作手法已是人尽皆知,但狄更斯却是运用这些文学形式和技法的艺术大师,并且他的风格独树一帜,如果他的小说中没有象征手法,那么许多作品的真正内涵简直无从揭晓。

狄更斯的小说中不含令人费解的象征主义,所以读者都很乐意将其当做故事来读。这就是为什么他那么多的小说都被拍成了电影,以及为什么在圣诞节的时候美国那么多的城市都把《圣诞欢歌》搬上舞台。但是,若不能下工夫细读狄更斯的作品,就读不出文中的深层含义及作者对现实社会的强烈批判——这就像只是浮浅地阅读莎士比亚的戏剧将无法领会他在作品中有关对人类生活的表达。如此,仅仅粗读一下《双城记》就只能了解有一个英国家庭在法国大革命时期被捕入狱,又或者只略读《李尔王》也就只能知道这是关于一个国王和他几个忘恩负义的女儿之间的故事。

然而,莎士比亚和狄更斯之间有一个重要的区别:莎士比亚用绝妙的笔触(没有人比他更为杰出)呈现给读者人类生活的不同画卷——对权势的奢求、贪婪的倾向、被爱的欢乐(以及其中遇到的阻碍)。但是,读者和听众们却很难发觉莎士比亚本人对他所描绘的人类体验的立场。相反,狄更斯显然带有宗教的色彩,他相信存在"更高力量",更重要的是,他相信生活中善行将最终取得胜利——这本就是天意。他的父亲曾因负债而入狱,他自己也曾在一家令人不齿的工厂做苦工,但是后来他成为英国最受欢迎的小说家,30岁之前就闻名国内外,并且他的声誉及其作品的流行伴其一生。他坚信只要人们避免阴谋圈套,生活中有很多机会让你去实现自我、追求幸福。

就故事情节、人物塑造、语言的推敲以及微妙的象征手法而言,狄更斯最伟大的作品

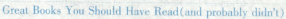

extraordinarily subtle symbolism—is *Great Expectations*.Any of Dickens's novels repays study,but *Great Expectations* shows him at the height of his powers.

Pip,a young orphan,lives with his bitter older sister and her saintly husband,Joe,in the area around Rochester,Kent.He is hired as a companion to an eccentric local rich woman, who was jilted at the altar and thereafter lives in the world of that moment—surrounded by stopped clocks,a rotting wedding cake,wearing a bridal gown now in tatters.Miss Havisham's only other close companion is her adopted daughter,Estella.She is training her to cultivate her beauty and her accomplishments,to tempt men,then break their hearts. Meanwhile Pip becomes an apprentice to Joe,a blacksmith.Miss Havisham pays the fees necessary to reimburse Joe for his training of Pip—but Pip has been entranced by the trappings of money that he has observed in Miss Havisham's ruined and neglected mansion,as he has been entranced (as Miss Havisham intended) by Estella.

In the fourth year of his apprenticeship,he encounters an escaped convict on the marshes near his home—and helps him.

Years later—via a lawyer who also serves as Miss Havisham's lawyer—he learns that he has "great expectations" of wealth,and moves to London to take up the life of a gentleman and to continue his pursuit of Estella,who has been trained only to repulse him and make him miserable.He forgets his best friend Joe,spends too much money,eventually learns that his benefactor is not Miss Havisham (as he had always supposed) but the convict he once helped,now grown rich in Australia.In the end,Pip spends himself into bankruptcy, loses his best and most well-meaning friends,yet he is redeemed by hard work and remorse, by the love of those he has wronged—and by the love of Estella,who,having suffered as Pip has done,comes to understand how she too has thwarted and cheated life.

Within this beautifully constructed novel,Dickens weaves a number of his characteristic themes—but nowhere so intensely and movingly as here.The power of money,or the emotion of greed,to corrupt.The joy of true love; the misery of love thwarted or demeaned. The damage to the human psyche caused by obsession with self; the happiness to be gained by selflessness.The beauty of true friendship,the ways in which such friends can form a life to the good,contrasted with the damage that false friendship can do to any life.Above all,the possibility of redemption,no matter how far we have fallen.

Everyone should re-examine his own humanity by putting himself or herself in the hands of this master,and by reading *Great Expectations*,one of the great documents of the human spirit.

中应当包括《远大前程》。他的任何一部小说都值得研究,但是《远大前程》却体现了狄更斯写作的最高水平。

皮普,从小便成了孤儿,和刻薄的姐姐及虔诚的姐夫乔一起生活在肯特郡的罗切斯特市附近。他被聘请到当地一个富有且有些古怪的妇人家里做陪护,这个老妇人新婚当天被丈夫抛弃,从此便一直生活在回忆里——周围摆满了已经停止的钟表,和已经发霉的婚礼上的蛋糕,穿着破碎不堪的婚纱。哈维汉姆小姐的唯一另外一个伴侣就是她的养女埃斯特拉。哈维汉姆训练她如何打扮以及教她才艺好去引诱男人,然后甩了他们,叫他们痛苦。此时的皮普正在求学于做铁匠的姐夫。哈维汉姆小姐付给乔皮普学徒所需的费用——但是皮普当时已经垂涎于哈维汉姆小姐那所又破又冷清的宅院,同时也迷上了埃斯特拉(正如哈维汉姆小姐所料想的那样)。

在皮普做学徒的第四年,他在他家附近的沼泽地偶然遇到了一个逃犯,并且救了他。

多年以后,皮普从哈维汉姆小姐的律师那里了解到他得到了一笔财产,于是他到伦敦去过上层社会的绅士生活,并继续追求那个受训练只为打击伤害他的埃斯特拉。他把他最好的朋友乔抛到脑后,大肆挥霍度日,结果发现背后资助他的人并不是哈维汉姆小姐(像他一直认为的那样),而是他曾经救过的那个逃犯,当时此人在澳大利亚挣了很多钱。最后,皮普破产,他失去了最善意的好友。但是,他通过努力工作改过自新,得到了曾被他无礼对待的朋友的宽恕,也得到了遭遇与他相同苦楚而最终发觉是在虚度人生的埃斯特拉的爱。

在这部构思微妙的小说当中,狄更斯编进了几个特色的主题,但此处的描写最为深刻且感人——金钱的力量,或是贪婪的秉性所导致的堕落;真爱的欢乐,及爱心受挫或被侮辱之后的痛苦;由于鬼迷心窍给心灵带来的创伤,和由于大公无私所获得的幸福;美好的真挚友情可以使人生充满阳光,而虚情假意对人生带来的只有伤害。而作者最强调的是,无论人们陷得有多么深,都将能够被救赎。

通过阅读《远大前程》这部体现人文精神的伟大著作,每个人都应该把自己置于这位艺术大师的笔下,重新审视一下人性。

Thirty-seven

Karl Marx:
The Communist Manifesto

Who Was Karl Marx?

Karl Marx (1818-1883) and Friedrich Engel wrote one of the most influential and widely read political tracts of the 19th century, *The Communist Manifesto*. Marx distinguished his kind of socialism from that of others by claiming that his version was scientifically based on history regarded objectively.

Born into a Jewish family in Trier, Germany, Marx attended the University of Bonn, where he studied law. His interest, though, was really in philosophy and literature. During his second year, he transferred to the more academically rigorous Friedrich-Wilhelms-University in Berlin. It was here that he began to write poems and essays and consider his own philosophical stance.

Marx's thinking was strongly influenced by Hegel's dialectical method. Ideas, according to Hegel, are formed through an evolutionary process in which a concept leads to a conflict of opposites, which leads to a synthesis, which leads to another conflict of opposites, which leads to another synthesis. This process continues progressively upward until an individual reaches the highest level of awareness.

Marx took this dialectic and applied it to history, society and economics in order to explain the causes and developments in human society. As feudalism evolved into mercantilism, which evolved into capitalism, so will capitalism ultimately evolve into communism, he believed.

In 1842, Marx left university life and became a journalist. Hs political views caused him to clash with the Prussian censors. He moved to France, where he met Friedrich Engels who awakened Marx's interest in the working class and in economics. *The Communist Manifesto* suggests the path to take for the overthrow of capitalism by proletarian revolutionaries. In the Manifesto a course of action is outlined that Marx believes will bring about a classless society.

To achieve communism, the supreme end of a stateless and classless society, a revolutionary government must be organized.

A crucial passage in the Manifesto is this: "When, in the course of development, class distinctions have disappeared, and all production has been concentrated in the hands of a vast association of the whole nation, the public power will lose its political character. Politica! power, properly so called, is merely the organized power of one class for oppressing another."

In the Manifesto the authors write, "The proletarians have nothing to lose but their chains. They have a world to win." The famous political cry of all socialists, which appeared in the Manifesto and on Marx's tombstone in London, is: "Working men of all countries, unite! "

37

卡尔·马克思
《共产党宣言》

卡尔·马克思

    卡尔·马克思(1818~1883)和弗里德里希·恩格斯共同起草了《共产党宣言》,这一19世纪最具影响力、阅读面最广的政治文献。马克思宣称他所倡导的共产主义不同于其他人的,因为他的科学研究是建立在客观考察历史背景基础上的。

    马克思诞生于德国特利尔城的一个犹太家庭。他就读于波恩大学学习法学专业,然而他真正感兴趣的却是哲学和文学,于是,第二年他便转入了位于柏林的宗教学术气氛更浓的弗里德里希-威廉-大学,在那里他开始写诗和散文,并思考他个人的哲学主张。

    马克思的思想深受黑格尔辩证法的影响。黑格尔认为,思想的形成是一个革命的过程,在这一过程中,一种想法导向它与其对立面的冲突,而两者又趋向综合,继而导向了另一个冲突以及下一个综合。这一过程不断向前发展直到某一个体达到意识的最高层次。

    马克思利用这一矛盾思辨的方法并且将其应用于研究历史、社会和经济,以期解释人类社会的形成因素和发展过程。他相信如同人类历史经历了从封建主义发展到商业主义,继而商业主义过渡到资本主义那样,资本主义最终必将发展为共产主义。

    1842年,马克思结束大学生活,开始为报社撰稿。他的政治观点使其陷入了与普鲁士检查当局的激烈冲突之中。后来,他去了法国,在那里结识了弗里德里希·恩格斯,马克思受其影响开始对工人阶级和经济学理论产生兴趣。《共产党宣言》指出了通过无产阶级革命推翻资产阶级统治的革命道路。马克思在《宣言》中庄严宣告要组成全世界无产阶级的同盟。

    为了实现共产主义,这一没有国家、没有阶级的社会最高形式,就必须组织建立一个革命的政府。

    在《共产党宣言》中有一段非常重要的表述:"当阶级差别在发展进程中已经消失而全部生产集中在联合起来的个人的手里的时候,公共权力就失去政治性质。原来意义上的政治权力,仅仅是一个阶级用以压迫另一个阶级的有组织的暴力。"

    作者在《宣言》中写道,"无产者在这个革命中失去的只是锁链。他们获得的将是整个世界。"同时,《宣言》中发出了国际主义的"全世界无产者,联合起来!"这一著名的战斗号召,此箴言被记载在位于伦敦的马克思的墓碑上。

The Communist Manifesto

Virtually any adult who was alive in the 20th century knows something about the life and writings of Karl Marx.He is a famous political and economic philosopher,one of the most famous figures of the 19th century,one whose influence was felt more in the 20th century than in his own time.A Jew who was born in Germany in 1818,Marx spent most of his later adult life in London,where he died in 1883.He produced a great body of work, and almost any educated man or woman has read about his work-and-study vigils in the Reading Room of the British Museum in London,which,in the popular imagination,he seems never to have left.He is buried in Highgate Cemetery in London,a place of pilgrimage for many visitors to that city.Yet,despite this enduring fame,and despite the near legendary quality of his life and his work,many people assume that Marx is now no longer "relevant."

Although the Russian Revolution (the Bolshevik Revolution) of 1917 happened almost 35 years after Marx had died,it was Marx's ideas (and those of his colleague Friedrich Engels) that inspired that revolution and provided the "philosophical" basis for what became the U.S.S.R.(The Soviet Union)—as well as China under Mao,Cuba under Castro,Vietnam under Ho Chi Minh.In the second half of the 20th century,it seemed that half the world was comprised of countries whose economic and political stance and structures were directly influenced by the precepts of Karl Marx.With the decline,then break-up,of the Soviet Union,and the increasingly capitalistic stance of China,it now seems as if only a few third-rate powers still subscribe to,or base their economies and governments on,the notions of Karl Marx.

Although the influence of his ideas has obviously declined,Karl Marx remains an important historic figure whose pronouncements about politics,economics,and the historic class struggle remain potent even today.The historic figures he inspired—the great thinkers such as Lenin or Trotsky or Sartre,the tyrants such as Stalin or Mao—are now far less important than Marx himself,their intellectual mentor.

His great and monumental work is the three-volume Das Kapital (Capital),the first volume of which was published in 1867; the last two volumes were published (supervised by Engels) after Marx's death.Given the complexity of this work,it is usually read only by philosophers and by scholars of politics and economics.The Communist Manifesto (1848), which Marx wrote with Engels,has been much more influential; it provides an excellent and brief introduction to his thought.

Initially,Marx's life and work were in the service of what might now be called liberal causes in the classic,conservative world of 19th century Germany,then France.After a career as a journalist,speaker and revolutionary,and a year after publication of The Communist Manifesto,he moved,at the age of 31,to London—and it is there that he refined his theories.He was no longer welcome in either France or Germany; England provided a much more congenial atmosphere.

Marx is not as harsh and unbending as some people have painted him; he is by no means some kind of monster whose ideas almost destroyed the world.Socialism,after all,in which Marx was a firm believer,is a humane kind of economic organization/government— that everyone should produce as much as he or she can,that all of us should be provided

《共产党宣言》

事实上,任何生活在20世纪的成人都了解一些关于马克思的生平和著作。他是一位著名的政治、经济哲学家,19世纪最著名的人物之一,较之他在他生活的年代的影响他对20世纪造成的影响更为明显。1818年,拥有犹太血统的马克思在德国诞生,他成年以后的大部分时间都在伦敦度过,直到1883年他在那里去世。他创作了大量的作品,并且不论男女几乎每个受过教育的人都知道马克思曾在位于伦敦的英国博物馆阅览室里夜以继日地工作和学习,大家似乎感觉他从未离去。马克思被葬于伦敦的海格特公墓内,很多到伦敦的游客都会来这里拜祭一下。然而,尽管马克思赢得了不朽的声誉,并且他生活和工作环境的艰苦让人难以置信,许多人还是认为他已经"脱离"了我们当今的时代。

虽然,1917年俄国革命(布尔什维克革命)爆发于马克思逝世后差不多35年,但却是他的思想(和他的合作伙伴弗里德里希·恩格斯的思想)唤醒了这次革命并且为后来的苏维埃社会主义共和国联盟(前苏联)——以及毛泽东领导下的中国、卡斯特罗领导下的古巴和胡志明领导下的越南的建立奠定了"哲学"的基础。20世纪的后50年间,似乎世界上一半的国家所建立的经济、政治体制和机构都直接受到了卡尔·马克思理论的影响。随着前苏联的衰退和后来的解体,以及中国日益倡导的中国特色社会主义的发展,现在仍有一部分第三世界的国家继续推崇马克思的政治信条,并且以之为理论基础建立他们的经济制度和政府机构。

尽管马克思主义的影响有明显的下降,但是马克思仍不失为一位重要的历史人物,他关于政治、经济和历史的阶级斗争的言论至今仍占相当的地位。深受马克思主义思想影响的历史人物中包括:伟大的思想家列宁、托洛茨基和萨特,国家元首斯大林和毛泽东。马克思是这些伟人的思想启蒙导师。

马克思写就的不朽的伟大之作即三卷《资本论》,其中第一卷于1867年出版;后两卷在马克思逝世之后(由恩格斯整理)出版。由于此作比较复杂难懂,其读者通常是那些哲学家和政治经济学者。《共产党宣言》(1848)由马克思和恩格斯合作完成,其影响更为深远,这部作品简洁且成功地展现了马克思的政治经济思想。

最初,马克思是在19世纪时期那个古典而保守的德国社会中从事我们今天所称的自由主义事业,后来去了法国,他曾为报社撰写过文章,做过演说,参加过革命党。《共产党宣言》出版后一年,即他31岁的时候搬去了伦敦,在那里修缮了自己的理论,当时马克思已不再受法国和德国的欢迎,而英国却给他提供了更为宽松的环境。

而且,马克思并不像有的人所描绘的那样严苛和固执,他绝不是什么怪物几乎能用自己的思想毁掉整个世界。马克思所深信的共产主义毕竟只是要建立一个人性化的经济组织和政府——让每一个人各尽其职,每个人也应该被充分地给予满足——这样,我们所有人都将过上幸福的生活。从马克思大部分的思想中,我们可以看出,他是一个彻底的人道主义者,他希望让尽可能多的人过上更好的生活。

for—so that we all have a decent life.Marx could be said to be,in much of his thinking,a radical humanist,someone who wished to make the human condition better for as many people as possible.

Socialism proposes that the production of goods and services should be controlled by the state,which will in turn guarantee this central goal of each of us producing to the best of his/her ability,of society's taking care of those who cannot take care of themselves.

What Marx brings to this particular mix—he did not,after all,invent socialism—is the idea that history has been moving to an inevitable time when the state will function for the benefit of all.He argues that there has been a feudal period,in which people sold (or bartered) what they produced as a way of acquiring goods that they needed.As society became more complex,so did its economic systems become more complex,ending in the capitalistic system that we now know—in which comparatively few people (with capital) control the means of production and the benefits from the fruits of the labor of their workers,who have no direct financial connection with the products of their work.Thus,say,a man works an hour to create some household good,a cooking pot for instance.He is paid $10 for that hour's work.Yet the man who owns the factory where he works in turn sells that pot for $30,which involves $10 in profit,a profit that the worker never sees.

Marx argues that this situation is exploitation,that,eventually it leads to incredibly rich factory owners and nearly destitute workers (the owner constantly devises more refined methods of production,often not involving human labor,which in turns leads to unemployment,which in turn means workers will work for less to avoid abject poverty),a situation that must lead to conditions of revolution,in which workers (the "proletariat") will, by fighting for their rights,triumph and establish a new kind of economic system leading to a new kind of government,one in which we are all the "factory owners," sharing the $30 among each other.

That Communism in our time produced such dictators as Stalin and Mao in no way negates Marx's thought; it merely points out that there are tyrants of the left as well as the right,murderers posing as benefactors.

Marx's abiding legacy is not so much a system that has yet to prove workable as an idea that retains its potency to the present time-that in a world that gives lip service to the idea of human equality,our existing economic structures do not allow for such equality; indeed,they work against equality.Whether in the advanced democracies of the West,or the countries of poorest Africa,the division of reward is obviously in no way reflective of any ideal of equality.Marx's lasting accomplishment may not be the system of government and economic structure that evolved from his work—but his forceful reminder that,as human beings,we ought to be able to do better—to erase poverty,to provide healthy and fulfilling lives for all people.

共产主义提倡生产物资和服务应该由国家控制,这将进一步确保每个人的中心目标都集中到最大限度地发挥自身能力上来,同时让那些没有能力自食其力的人也能得到保障。

马克思对"共产主义终究不是他个人凭空创造出来的"这一模糊的说法的解释是——历史已经发展到一个不可逾越的阶段,在这一阶段中,国家将为所有的大众谋福利。他指出人类已经经历了封建主义时期,当时人们出卖(或者交换)他们的产品,以此换取自己所需的物品。随着社会发展更加复杂化,经济体制也随之发展,最终出现了我们今天所知道的资本主义体制,在这一体制下,相对少数的人(拥有资本)控制着生产方式并且从他们所雇用的工人创造的劳动成果中谋利,而工人本身却与自己创造的劳动产品之间没有直接的经济关系。就是说,一个工人劳动一个小时换来的是某种家庭用品,比如一个烹调用的锅。这个工人用一个小时挣了10美元。然而,那个工厂主却以30美元的价格出售那只锅,其中就包含了10美元的利润,而这一利润是这个工人无法看到的。

马克思指出这种情况就是剥削,最终,它将造成工厂主腰缠万贯,而工人们则几乎一贫如洗(工厂主不断地发明更高级的生产手段,通常不占用劳动力,这将进一步导致失业,就意味着工人们为了避免挨饿会以更低的价格出卖劳力),这一境遇必将引发革命,工人们("无产阶级")将通过斗争维护自己的权益,取得胜利,并建立一种新的经济体制,继而形成一个新的国家政府,那时所有的人都是"工厂主",都享有以上提到的"30美元"。

我们现代的共产主义运动造就的斯大林和毛泽东绝对是马克思主义理论的忠实拥护者。不过,也存在一些"左倾"或是"右倾"的独裁分子,打着慈善家的旗号做出一些杀人越货的勾当。

马克思的政党理论现在已经被证明是可行的,但他的不朽功绩更在于他的思想至今仍具有强大的生命力——当今世界高呼"人生而平等",但现有的经济体制根本无平等可言,相反,它们却是在反对平等。无论是在西方高度民主的国家,还是最贫困的非洲国家,人们福利的差距显然反映不出任何理想中的平等。马克思的伟大成就可能并非他在作品中提到的政治、经济体制,而是他强有力的警示:作为人,我们应该能够做到更好——消除贫困,为所有人提供健康而殷实的理想生活。

Thirty-eight

Fyodor Dostoyevsky:
Crime and Punishment

Who Was Fyodor Dostoyevsky?

The Russian author Fyodor Dostoyevsky (1821-1881) made a lasting impression on modern fiction with his profound development of characters and his incisive examination of the political,spiritual and social conditions of Russia during his lifetime.

Because he despised mathematics,Dostoyevsky wasn't a good student at the St. Petersburg Academy of Military Engineering,where he turned his attention instead to literature,especially the works of the French novelist Balzac.In 1846,he published his first short novel,*Poor Folk*,which was well received.

A few years later,Dostoyevsky's world changed for him when he was "linked" to a radical intellectual group that opposed the Tsar.While attending a meeting,acquainting himself with Karl Marx's idea,about which he knew nothing at the time,Dostoyevsky was arrested and sent to Siberia.This experience—his having to live in appalling conditions- caused a significant change in him.Forced to mingle with all classes,Dostoyevsky altered his view of the common man.That view enlarged—he stopped seeing such men as just serfs, now saw them as fully developed human beings.This realization was to alter his writing, freeing it of stereotypes and bigoted caricatures of the lower class.

After his release from prison,Dostoyevsky married and settled in St.Petersburg where he and his older brother published a few literary journals.They were not successful.When his brother and his own wife died,Dostoyevsky became depressed and despondent.He now found himself deeply in debt because of his unsuccessful business ventures and his obligation to provide financial support to his brother's wife and children.He increased his debt by gambling.*Crime and Punishment*,his most famous work,was written in haste to obtain cash to pay his gambling bills.

Crime and Punishment

Russia has produced more than its fair share of important writers,and its greatest novelists are Tolstoy and Dostoevsky.Both lived during the 19th century,and,though they never met,they knew and admired each other's work.Yet,though they wrote about and from within the same milieu,no two writers could be more different.

Tolstoy is the classical master:he re-created the vast panorama of the Napoleonic wars in *War and Peace*.Thomas Mann called it the Russian national epic; the rest of us would probably call it the greatest of historical novels.Then,dazzling in his virtuosity,Tolsoy wrote Anna *Karenina*,in many ways the greatest novel of society,the intimate plot of which could have happened at any time and in any place.

In comparison to the classicism and perfection of Tolstoy,Dostoevsky seems a wild man.He is very much a man of his time and place in history; writes mainly about dysfunctional characters; experiments as a writer with stream of consciousness; offers

38

费奥多尔·陀思妥耶夫斯基
《罪与罚》

费奥多尔·陀思妥耶夫斯基

俄国作家费奥多尔·陀思妥耶夫斯基(1821~1881)因其作品中深入的人物心理刻画和对他所生活的俄国社会的政治、精神及社会状况的敏锐洞察赢得了不朽的声誉,被称为现代派小说的鼻祖。

陀思妥耶夫斯基不屑于学习数学,因此在圣·彼得堡军事工程学院就读期间成绩不甚理想,相反,他对文学极为感兴趣,尤其喜欢法国小说家巴尔扎克的作品。1846年,他出版了自己的第一部短篇小说《穷人》,受到读者的普遍欢迎。

几年之后,陀思妥耶夫斯基因为同反对沙皇专制的激进人士有"牵连",人生从此改变。在出席一次会议的时候,他了解了卡尔·马克思的思想,当时他对此一无所知,但却被捕并被发配到了西伯利亚。在那里极端恶劣的条件让陀思妥耶夫斯基的思想发生了重大的变化。他被强迫与各个阶层的人混在一起的经历改变了他对普通大众的看法。他的观念不断发展——他不再把他们视为简单的农奴,而认为他们是全面发展的人。思想的这一转变也影响了陀思妥耶夫斯基的写作,他摆脱了旧有的对下层社会人们的陈规式描述和那些偏执的讽刺漫画形象。

陀思妥耶夫斯基刑满之后,结婚并在圣·彼得堡定居,在那里他和他的哥哥出版了一些文学期刊,但并未取得成功。在他的哥哥和自己的妻子死后,陀思妥耶夫斯基变得心灰意冷。因为生意亏本并且要承担资助哥哥的妻儿,他发觉自己背上了沉重的债务。又加上他赌博成瘾更加重了负担。为了偿还赌账他较为仓促地完成了《罪与罚》,这部作品成为陀思妥耶夫斯基最著名的作品。

《罪与罚》

俄国孕育了大量的重要作家,其中最伟大的两位小说家是托尔斯泰和陀思妥耶夫斯基。他们都是生活在19世纪,尽管两人并不相识,但他们却互相了解且欣赏彼此的作品。虽然,他们生活在相同的时代,创作的作品也都是反映相同背景的社会状况,但两者之间的差异是任何其他作家无法赶超的。

托尔斯泰是一位古典主义的大师:他在其作品《战争与和平》中重新塑造了拿破仑战争的全貌。托马斯·曼称这部作品是俄国的史诗;其他人可能会将其视为历史小说的最伟大之作。后来,托尔斯泰以其精湛的技艺写下了《安娜·卡列尼娜》,这一作品在很多方面都称得上是最伟大的社会小说,其逼真的情节描写仿佛随时随地都可能会发生。

较之托尔斯泰古典而完美的创作,陀思妥耶夫斯基似乎显得有些粗犷。他切切实实地属于他所生活的年代和地方;他描写的主要是一些有机能障碍的人物;他的创作深受

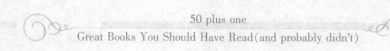

psychological portraits of his characters; and,given these extraordinary innovations,has been a great influence on the writers and philosophers who followed him in a way that Tolstoy has not.One of his characters says:If God does not exist,then anything is allowed; and many of Dostovesky's characters live according to this notion,which seems to the reader to be Dostovesky's own conclusion about life.It's easy to see how such an attitude could be embraced by such writers as Kafka or such existential philosophers as Sartre.

Often this has been the critical view from which Dostoevsky has been approached- as the great if messy and disillusioned innovator who had an almost unbelievably profound effect on 20th century fiction and philosophy.

Some commentators have seen Dostoevsky's fiction as a reflection of his life.He was an orphan by age 18; at that time he was studying at the St.Petersburg Academy of Military Engineering.He studied mathematics,a subject he disliked,and he increasingly turned his attention to literature.At 25,he published his first novel.In his youth,Dostoevsky was a revolutionary hothead,and he was arrested and imprisoned in 1849 (he was 28) for supposedly engaging in revolutionary activity against the tsar.He went to prison,in Siberia, until 1854,then served another 5 years in the Siberian Regiment (a condition of his being released from prison).During this period in his life he abandoned his earlier liberal ideals, became an upholder of traditional Russian values; as well,he became a Christian.He returned to St.Petersburg in 1860,was subsequently devastated both by his wife's death in 1864 and by his brother's subsequent death,as well as by the responsibilities of meeting his own debts and those of his brother's widow and children.Crippled by depression,he began frequenting gambling parlors,the beginning of an addiction to gambling that would plague him for the rest of his life.He spent much of his later life in various gambling spas in Western Europe and in Russia,and died in 1881 of the complications of emphysema.

The events of Dostoevsky's life seem to lend credibility to the notion that his dysfunctional characters,who are inevitably suffering from some kind of addiction-to alcohol, to sex,to gambling,to their own psychological proclivities—that such portrayals,as within St. Petersburg,a city of unbelievable squalor,are really a reflection of a life that,compared to Tolstoy's,was,much of the time,out of control.

Yet such analyses—that he was the Russian wild man whose chaotic but innovative point of view influenced generations to follow and/or that he was a madman whose fiction reflected his own life as jailbird or reprobate—though these analyses are hardly far-fetched- do disservice to the man and his novels.

It is well to remember that his experiences made him a traditionalist.The reality is that he approached the greatest questions of man's existence,did so by inventing,for fiction,new techniques to ask old questions-created,from what he saw around him,the psychological novel,attempted to create complete characters who could ask;who could act out,the eternal questions of man's existence and grope their way to answers.

Crime and Punishment is considered by many people to be Dostoevsky's finest achievement.Such a judgment must be subjective:is it better than *The Brothers Karamazov* or *The Idiot*? Whatever the final verdict,*Crime and Punishment* is a very great novel indeed.

In it,Dostovesky considers the question,borrowed (with his own variants) from the

意识流的影响;着重刻画人物的心理;他的这一重大革新对后来的作家和哲学家们造成了深刻的影响,而在这一方面托尔斯泰也未曾做到。陀思妥耶夫斯基的作品中有一个人物这样说道:如果没有上帝,一切都可以被容许。他作品中的许多人物都以此信条过活,读者们似乎可以感到这就是作者自己的人生总结。而这一理念对作家卡夫卡和仍然在世的哲学家萨特的影响也是显而易见的。

通常,人们对陀思妥耶夫斯基的评论是这样的:他是一位伟大的作家,混乱而醒悟的改革家,他对20世纪的小说和哲学的发展带来了几乎令人难以置信的深刻影响。

有的评论家发现陀思妥耶夫斯基的小说反映了他的一生。他18岁成了孤儿,当时他正在圣·彼得堡军事工程学院学习数学,但是他对此并无兴趣,渐渐地他喜欢上了文学。25岁的时候,他出版了他的第一部小说。陀思妥耶夫斯基年轻的时候拥有革命的激进思想,但因被认为参加了反对沙皇统治的革命活动于1849年被捕入狱(他当时28岁)。他被流放到西伯利亚直到1854年,之后又在西伯利亚兵团服了5年役(出狱之后的另外一个环境)。在这段期间,陀思妥耶夫斯抛弃了早期的自由理想,成为一个俄国传统价值观念的维护者,并且他开始信仰基督教。1860年,他回到圣·彼得堡,结果妻子于1864年去世,哥哥也相继死去,这给陀思妥耶夫斯基的精神造成了强烈的打击。他还背负着沉重的债务同时又要资助哥哥的妻儿。意志消沉的他开始经常出入赌场,他的赌瘾毁掉了他的后半生。他后来的大部分时间一直游荡于西欧和俄国的不同赌场,1881年因肺气肿发作逝世。

陀思妥耶夫斯基的人生经历似乎揭示了他作品中有机能障碍的人物的人生信条,他们都无一避免地苦于某种癖性——嗜酒、沉迷色情、嗜赌,以及他们自己的心理倾向——这些描述,是当时圣·彼得堡,这一肮脏不堪的城市中人们生活的真实写照,托尔斯泰的作品中大部分也是表现人们生活的混乱状态。

然而,诸如说陀思妥耶夫斯基是一个粗野的人,他的混杂但革新的思想影响了后辈的作家;或者说他是个疯子,他的小说反映了他作囚犯或地痞的人生——这些评论虽然都牵强附会,但的确有损于这位作家及其著作。

我们很容易就能想起陀思妥耶夫斯基的经历使他成为一个传统主义者。而事实是他触及了人类生存的最重大的问题,他利用新的写作手法在其作品中创造性地提出那些旧有的问题,借此我们可以看出,作者创作的描写人物心理的小说旨在塑造这样的完整形象,他们探求人类存在的根本问题并付之以行动不断地寻找解决问题的途径。

《罪与罚》被很多人视为陀思妥耶夫斯基的最优秀之作。这一评价也许带有主观性:它比《卡拉马佐夫兄弟》或是《白痴》更好吗?然而,不管定论如何,《罪与罚》确实是一部很伟大的小说。

陀思妥耶夫斯基借用了哲学家尼采的问题(经他自己改动之后)在这一作品中问及

philosopher Nietzsche,of whether or not an ubermensch,a superman,can really exist.It is a question that went on to haunt the 20th century and haunts us still.In Dostovesky's formulation:Are some people of so superior an intellect that the common restraints on mankind-its laws,its taboos—do not apply to them,that they may be allowed to violate those restraints because,in the end,it is their actions,and their actions alone,that advance the cause of civilization and the consciousness of mankind? Readers of 20th century history will instantly recognize the question,because it surfaces in widely disparate circumstances,from the trial in the 1920s of Leopold and Loeb to the coming of Hitler,his concept of the Germans as a race of ubermensch,and it culminates in the horrors of World War II.

Dostoevsky ingeniously reduces this proposition to the banal.His plot is simple: Roskolnikov (though of a good family,capable of working) is a down-and-out perpetual student,who studies/analyzes/obsesses about the chaotic world of St.Petersburg in which he lives.Sick and feverish,he contemplates the possibility that he is an ubermensch,then embraces the idea,then determines that he will randomly murder a somewhat despicable woman money-lender-to rid the world of her kind of vermin,simultaneously to rob her and do good with her money.His real motive? To prove that he can accomplish such an action, that he is above the laws that apply to the ordinary people around him,people trapped by the addictions of drink or gambling or poverty or just the "addiction" of muddled thinking. He commits the murder; it goes wrong.The money-lender's sister comes into the room when he is murdering the money-lender,and he must murder the sister too; in the event,he botches the robbery as well.

Thereafter,he is pursued by Petrovich,a senior police official who knows in his heart that Roskolnikov is the murderer.But,Petrovich never entraps him,instead allows him to dangle in freedom; Roskolnikov,whose guilt plunges him further and further into a kind of mental illness,at last confesses.He has come to know Sonya,a prostitute who has degraded herself to save her family.Roskolnikov is drawn to her (to her goodness,though he doesn't understand at the time that this is the reason for the attraction),and it is to Sonya that he first confesses; it is she who urges him to embrace her Christian faith and to confess to the world.He does confess to Petrovich,is sentenced to prison in Siberia,and Sonya follows him there; she takes up residence in the town where the prison is located.Roskolnikov's spiritual rebirth begins.

The plot is simple—though it is sometimes difficult for readers to focus on that simplicity,so rich is Dostoevsky's portrait of the nether world,the dysfunctional world,of St. Petersburg.Yet within that incredibly rich panorama,his message is also simple:we all suffer. None of us is superior to anyone else; we achieve superiority only by serving others—as Sonya serves her family,as she cares for Roskolnikov's fellow prisoners; and only by loving others better than we love ourselves—as Sonya loves Roskolnikov.

Dostoevsky's message to his own time and to the modern world in which he has had such influence:Be humble,there is moral regeneration possible through suffering; understand that God is infinitely merciful,merciful beyond our comprehension,that only Sonya—only the action of love—is what allows us to live our lives fully.When one considers the horrors that the alternative message has caused,it is obvious that Dostoevsky's message is profound and eternal,one that still reverberates in the modern consciousness.

是否超人在现实生活中真的存在？这一问题到20世纪甚至我们现代都一直存在。用陀思妥耶夫斯基的话说：有没有具备超智慧的人，他们不受像法律、禁忌等人类普遍约束的限制，他们可以被允许打破这些限制，因为最后他们的行为，也只有他们的行为，才能推动人类文明和意识的发展？读过20世纪史的人将会立刻意识到这一问题，因为它展现了一幅广阔而全新的历史画面，从20世纪20年代利奥波德和罗卜的审判直到后来希特勒的出台，希特勒曾把德国人民看做是超凡的种族，结果最终导致了第二次世界大战的爆发。

陀思妥耶夫斯基非常巧妙地避免了这一描述落入俗套。他创作的故事情节相当简单：拉思科里涅珂夫（虽然出生于一个良好的家庭，且具备工作能力）是一名穷困潦倒的学生，他研究/分析/沉醉于他所居住的圣·彼得堡混杂的社会。他生病发着烧苦思冥想的却是自己是否是一个超人，后来他想出了一个主意，决定要随着自己的性子杀掉一个可恶的放高利贷的老太婆，以替天行道，同时抢掠她的财产去做一些善事。那么，主人公的真正动机何在呢？作品中证实他的这一计划得以实现，主人公超越了周围普通人所遵循的律法，而这些人都是深陷诸如嗜酒、赌博、贫困或者精神上的某种"癖好"。主人公杀了人，铸成了大错。当他谋杀那个放高利贷的老女人的时候，她的姐姐碰巧进了房间，而他又不得不把她也杀死；在这一事件中，主人公在抢劫的时候表现得也颇为笨拙。

之后，拉思科里涅珂夫被一个高级警官彼得罗维奇追捕，他心里很清楚拉思科里涅珂夫就是那个谋杀犯。然而，彼得罗维奇并没有给拉思科里涅珂夫设陷阱，反而允许他逍遥法外；拉思科里涅珂夫越来越重的负罪感使他患上了精神病，最终他投案自首。在这中间，他曾认识了索尼娅，她为了救济家庭卖身为娼。拉思科里涅珂夫深深地为她所吸引（因为她的善良，虽然当时男主人公并没有意识到是被她的这一点所打动），并且第一次向索尼娅忏悔。正是她劝拉思科里涅珂夫信仰基督教并向上帝忏悔。他后来向彼得罗维奇自首，并被捕入狱押送至西伯利亚。索尼娅也跟着去了那里，她在监狱所在的镇上住了下来。这样，拉思科里涅珂夫的精神获得了重生。

这部小说的情节非常简单——虽然，有时读者很难捕捉这一"简单"，陀思妥耶夫斯基对圣·彼得堡污秽的下层社会描写得相当深刻。但是，作者笔下这一超凡的描绘当中，寓意也非常简单：我们都在受难。没有谁比别人更高级；我们只有通过为别人付出才能得到提升——像索尼娅为她的家人做出的牺牲，以及她对拉思科里涅珂夫狱友们的关怀；也只有对别人比对自己付出更多的爱——像索尼娅对拉思科里涅珂夫的爱那样，我们才能达到更高的层次。

陀思妥耶夫斯基作品中所暗含的寓意影响了他自己生活的年代以及我们当今世界：保持谦逊，人们的道德就能从苦难中获得重生；应该认识到上帝是无限仁慈的，他的慈悲超越了我们的理解，只有索尼娅——只有爱——才能让我们过上幸福充实的生活。当人们想到这一寓意的反面是多么可怕的时候，很显然，它证明陀思妥耶夫斯基的寓意是深刻而永恒的，它就反映在我们现代人的意识之中。

Thirty-nine

Sigmund Freud:
The Interpretation of Dreams

Who Was Sigmund Freud?

Austrian neurologist and psychiatrist Sigmund Freud (1856-1939), the founder of psychoanalysis, is best known for pioneering ideas that lead to a better understanding of human behavior. These breakthroughs in psychology led all of us to a more comprehensive view of human instincts, anxiety, repression, and defense mechanisms.

Born to Jewish parents in Moravia, Freud lived in Vienna for 80 years. He left after the Nazis occupied Austria in 1937 when he knew that his life, as a Jew, was in danger; he then sought safety in England.

He wrote: "A man like me cannot live without a hobbyhorse, a consuming passion—in Schiller's words, a tyrant. I have found my tyrant, and in his service I know no limits." His tyrant was psychology, and it took him into the dark corners of his patients' minds where he confronted the psychological entanglements of emotions and experiences that shaped their neurotic or psychotic personalities.

Freud studied at the University of Vienna. In 1886, he opened a private practice in Vienna where he began his experiments in psychology, using free association (Freud would say a word of phrase, then allow his patients talk about whatever occurred to them) in order to probe deeply into their minds. It was his belief that the mind contained hidden memories, which once uncovered would release the patient from any anxieties associated with these memories. His reasoning for using free association was that within the information he uncovered through free association some of the crucial memory contributing to the personality disorder would surface. In his probing into the human mind, he discovered that some information was blocked by resistance, which he wasn't always able to counteract. This realization forced him to search for other ways into the repressed regions of the mind. He turned to dreams, which he believed could be "the royal road to a knowledge of the unconscious activities of the mind."

In 1900 he published his book on *The Interpretation of Dreams*. According to Freud, our minds preserve memories and emotions that aren't always known to us. Memories and emotions that exist for us during dreaming appear to us then in disguised form. By considering the fragments of dreams that we remember, it is possible for us to uncover repressed emotions. Freud believed that dreams were wish-fulfillments connected to sexual needs, and nightmares were anxiety attacks that these wish-fulfillments/needs might have caused.

Although his book received a cold response when it was published, Freud still believed that it was a significant breakthrough, and he once wrote, "Insight such as this falls to one's lot but once in a lifetime."

39

西格蒙德·弗洛伊德
《梦的解析》

西格蒙德·弗洛伊德

奥地利神经学专家和精神病学专家西格蒙德·弗洛伊德(1856~1939)是精神分析学的创始人,他为人类更好地了解自己的行为创立了一套理论并因此闻名于世。这些在心理学上的突破让我们所有的人更加综合地看待人类的本能、渴望、压抑和防御的心理机制。

弗洛伊德生于摩拉维亚的一个犹太家庭,在维也纳度过了80年。1937年,纳粹分子占领奥地利之后他知道作为一名犹太人他的处境非常危险,于是他离开那里并前往英国避难。

他写道:"像我这样的人,活着不能没有嗜好,一定要释放自己的激情,用席勒的话说——这是一个暴君。我已经找到了自己的'暴君',并且心甘情愿为之服务。"弗洛伊德的"暴君"就是心理学,这一嗜好使他走进了他的病人们心里黑暗的角落,看到了他们心灵深处的情感纠葛以及形成他们神经和心理机制的个人体验。

弗洛伊德曾就读于维也纳大学。1886年,他在维也纳开办了自己的诊所开始从事临床心理学研究,他应用自由联想的诊疗方法(他先说出一个词,然后让患者想起什么就说什么),由此走进病人的心灵深处发现隐藏的病因。弗洛伊德相信人的大脑都存有一些隐藏的记忆,这些记忆一旦被揭开,患者将从与此记忆相关的焦虑中解放出来。他之所以应用自由联想的治疗方法是因为在这一过程中他发现有些导致患者心理紊乱的关键记忆确实浮现了出来。在弗洛伊德分析人类精神的过程中,他还发现有些信息在获取的时候遇到阻碍,并且不能给以解决。这一发现迫使弗洛伊德开始寻求其他途径去透析患者压抑的内心世界。他转向了对梦的解析,弗洛伊德认为"了解人类潜意识的捷径是:释梦。"

1990年,弗洛伊德出版了他的著作《梦的解析》。按照他的理论,我们的意识中储存着一些记忆和情感是我们自己都没有觉察的,这些记忆和情感在人们的梦中会以伪装的形式出现。通过考察人们留下记忆的梦境的片段,我们可以揭开他们心中被压抑的情感。弗洛伊德认为梦是与人们的性需求有关的欲望的满足,而噩梦则是反映了这些欲望满足/需求所带来的焦虑。

虽然,弗洛伊德的这一作品在出版之后遭到冷落,但他始终相信他的这项研究是一个重大的突破,并且他曾经写道:"这样的真知灼见一生中顶多能撞上一次。"

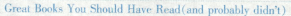

The Interpretation of Dreams

In the late 20th century and early 21st century,the term "Freudian" has become one that almost involves derision.There are good reasons for this state of affairs.The profession of psychologist,which Sigmund Freud was instrumental in creating,now abounds in theories, and Freud's descendants do not necessarily subscribe to those of Freud.Psychiatry has made great strides in supplanting psychology as the scientific discipline devoted to the human mind,mainly because it is a branch of medicine,not of the social sciences.A psychiatrist is a medical doctor—and most psychiatrists now believe that mental disorders are in fact disorders of the brain and nervous system that can be most effectively treated by drugs—not the examination of the "unconscious" that Freud recommended.Even artists and intellectuals tend,these days,to see Freud's analysis of "mind" as more poetic than scientific.

In this context,it is difficult for modern man to comprehend just how influential Sigmund Freud really was in the years after World War I and for decades that followed.It is no exaggeration to say that Freud was regarded as a god,as a person who had almost single-handedly unlocked the mysteries of man's mental existence.

Many words and phrases in common usage come from Freud—Oedipus Complex, defense mechanism,the ego and id,repression,the unconscious,transference.How,anyone might ask,do they all "fit together" into a coherent theory or theories?

Freud's accomplishment was to offer an alternative to the Enlightenment dogma that man knows himself—Descartes's "I think,therefore I am"—the view that any man or woman knows who or she really is.Freud believed—and,as a doctor,he believed that his views were scientifically based—that the psychic dynamic in man is far more complex,that man represses certain wishes or desires (often sexual or violent in nature),represses them in the sense that they became part of man's unconsciousness,not the consciousness with which he lives each day.That mechanism sounds innocent enough—but Freud also believed that all neuroses (that is,all troubling behavior—troubling to both society and to the individual) was the result of this repression,its coming,so to speak,to the surface.

The solution was psychoanalysis—and,indeed,Freud has been called,and deserves to be called,the "Father of Psychoanalysis." Any patient—that is,a person suffering from a debilitating neurosis—can be helped by an objective therapist,who attempts,with the patient,to explore the unconscious.We are all familiar with the picture (it has been the subject of numerous cartoons) of a patient lying prone on a couch,talking about feelings to an objective therapist who sits on a nearby chair,tablet and pen in hand,taking notes,posing seemingly banal questions.Freud's view was that one of the ways that individuals recycle the dynamics of the unconscious was through dreams-and one of his most influential books is *The Interpretation of Dreams*,published in 1901.

Freud believed that the goal of his therapy—psychoanalysis—was to bring "to the surface" repressed thoughts and feelings,to help the patient develop,as a consequence,into a stronger,more self-aware person.The bringing of unconscious thoughts and feelings to consciousness is accomplished by encouraging the patient to talk,often via the method of free association."If I say crocodile,what is the first thought that comes into your head?"-but also by talking about dreams that the patient can remember.It is this methodology that is most clearly explained in *The Interpretation of Dreams*—though,in fact,Freud constantly

《梦的解析》

　　20世纪末21世纪初的时候,一提及"弗洛伊德"这一称谓几乎就会遭到嘲讽。对此我们有合理的解释。弗洛伊德所从事的心理学这一行业如今已经形成了比较成熟的理论,所以弗洛伊德的继承者们不见得都会赞同他的理论。精神病学有了很大程度的发展,作为一门科学,它在解析人类的意识方面已经取代了心理学的地位,原因主要是精神病学本身是医学的一个分支,而不属于社会科学的范畴。一位精神病学专家就是一位医生——并且大多数精神病学家现在都认为精神的紊乱事实上是大脑和神经系统的失控,可以用药物给予最有效的治疗——而不像弗洛伊德所提出的那样要检测患者的"潜意识"。甚至,现代的艺术家和知识分子们都认为弗洛伊德的"精神分析"较之科学性具有更多的诗性色彩。

　　在这样的背景下,对现代人来说,很难理解在一战结束后及后来的几十年中弗洛伊德如何造成了那么深刻的影响。毫不夸张地说,弗洛伊德被看成是一个神,他几乎是靠一个人的力量解开了人类精神存在之谜。

　　弗洛伊德在其理论中普遍应用了诸多术语——俄狄浦斯情结、防御心理机制、自我和本我、抑制、潜意识、转移。人们可能会问,它们是怎样被"整合"编入这个这些有机的理论体系的呢?

　　弗洛伊德的成就是继启蒙运动时期笛卡儿提出的"我思,故我在。"的关于人类了解自身存在的宣言之后提出了另外的学说。他相信——作为一名医生,他认为自己的观点是有科学依据的——人类的精神动力是超级复杂的,人们压抑某种希望或者欲望(通常本质上与性或暴力有关),而压抑之下它们便成了人们潜意识的一部分,而不被人们日常的意识所察觉。这一心理机制听上去似乎很单纯——但是,弗洛伊德同时也认为所有的神经官能症(指一切对社会及个人引起祸患的行为)都是压抑的结果,因此可以说成是压抑的表现。

　　而解决的办法便是进行精神分析——弗洛伊德被人们称为"精神分析学之父",他也的确应该被赋予这一称号。任何一个病人——指患有神经衰弱的人——都可以从一名客观的医生那里得到帮助,这位医生会与患者一起走进病人的潜意识。我们都很熟悉这样的画面(很多漫画都反映了这一点)——一个病人平卧在沙发上,与一位坐在他旁边的客观的医生谈心,医生坐在椅子上,手里拿着药和笔,一边做笔记一边提出一些似乎很乏味的问题。弗洛伊德认为要唤起人们的潜意识,办法之一就是通过释梦——他最有影响力的一部著作《梦的解析》于1901年出版。

　　弗洛伊德认为他所做治疗——精神分析——的目标就是要使病人压抑的思想和情感都"释放"出来,以帮助他们发展成为一个更健康、更自醒的人。而让人们潜意识中的思想和情感显现到意识中来要鼓励他们交流,通常是要通过"自由联想"的方式来实现。比如,这样引导他们——"如果我说鳄鱼,你头脑中最先想到的是什么?"此外,还可以与病人谈论他能够回想起来的梦。《梦的解析》这部作品中非常清楚地阐述了这一治疗方法——事实上,弗洛伊德在他后面的著作中不断地完善了自己的理论。

refined his theories in his subsequent books.

It is a curiosity that,though in many circles he is discredited,Freud goes on being immensely influential up to the present time.There is a perfectly reasonable explanation. Though many psychologists,and certainly most psychiatrists,no longer accept Freudian explanations of all mental phenomena,they accept more than they sometimes realize-as do we all:in a sense,we are all Freud's children.

In his writings and in his lectures,Freud introduced concepts that resonate; broadly speaking,they seem to us to touch on something we know instinctively to be true.Some of Freud's specific theories now seem to many people to be suspect:Do all boys at some point in their maturation have erotic feelings toward their mothers,at the same time that they wish to complete with,even destroy,their fathers (the Oedipus Complex)? And do all boys suppress such feelings? Most people would,now,shake their heads at such a proposition:If anything,it seems a little simple-minded,a little too pat as a means of accounting for a long list of human behavioral difficulties.

But,the central Freud precepts do strike any reader as valid—for example,that we are not completely aware of what we think and that we often act for reasons that have little to do with our conscious thoughts—our own actions often mystify us.Also,most of us know that talking out our thoughts to a neutral third party often clarifies our motives for us.From time to time,we have all had the thought that perhaps our motives and actions are more mysterious than we like to think—that we do not entirely understand ourselves.

It is this questioning that is Freud's greatest legacy—as is the consequence of questioning,that we can become more complete,better functioning men and women by understanding and mastering our unconscious thoughts and desires.

令人好奇的是，虽然在很多文章中弗洛伊德总是受到非议，但直到今天他的影响还是很广泛。在此有一个比较不错的解释：尽管许多心理学家和大多数的精神病学专家拒绝接受弗洛伊德所有关于精神现象的分析，但他们有时候比自己意识中要接纳的多——我们所有人都是如此：在某种意义上，我们都是弗洛伊德的后代。

弗洛伊德在他的作品和讲座中提出的概念引起人们的共鸣；大体上说，这些概念似乎触及某些我们本能地认为正确的东西。弗洛伊德某些专门的理论现在被有些人认为是悬而未决的：真的是所有的男孩在他们成长的某个阶段对其母亲都怀有性的冲动，同时，他们还希望赶走，甚至杀死他们的父亲（所谓的俄狄浦斯情结）吗？并且，所有的男孩真的都会压抑这一感受吗？现在，大多数人都会否认这种说法。因为毕竟这一分析似乎显得头脑有些简单，对于解释人类行为困难的冗长记录显得有点以偏概全。

然而，弗洛伊德理论的核心概念确实得到了所有读者的认可——比如，我们不能完全意识到自己的思想，以及我们经常做出一些我们的意识无法解释的事情——我们自己的行为时常令我们不知所措。此外，我们大多数人都知道对不抱有偏见的第三者说出自己的想法通常可以帮助认清自己的动机。我们往往都会考虑也许我们的动因和行为比我们预想的还要更加难以捉摸——我们并不完全了解自己。

这一问题正是弗洛伊德留给我们的最宝贵的财富——而这一问题的答案将使我们的人格变得更为完整，通过理解和把握我们潜意识中的思想和欲望，我们可以更好的掌控自身。

Forty

Mahatma Gandhi: The Story of My Experiments with Truth

Who Was Mahatma Gandhi?

Mahatma Gandhi (born Mohandas Gandhi:1869-1948) freed India of British rule by inciting his people to civil disobedience and non-violent resistance.His use of "satyagraha" —deliberate,non-violent resistance to tyranny through mass disobedience—has ever since inspired civil-rights movements around the world.In his autobiography,*The Story of My Experiments with Truth*,he clearly states his position on non-violence: "There are many causes I am prepared to die for,but no causes I am prepared to kill for."

Born in a rural area of India untouched by any foreign influences,Gandhi was taught by his mother the Hindu doctrine of "ahisma" (to do good,not harm).This belief,inculcated in him from early childhood,was responsible for his many non-violent acts against oppression. His technique for non-violent resistance (satyagraha) was used to fight against what Gandhi regarded as forms of tyranny—for example,the caste system,excessive taxation,foreign rule.

After receiving a law degree from University College,London,Gandhi returned to India and unsuccessfully attempted to set up a law practice in Bombay.In 1893,he was retained by an Indian firm with offices in Durban,South Africa.His experiences there shaped his future.Horrified by the South African government's blatant disregard of the civil and political rights of its Indian population,Gandhi actively campaigned against these outrages,all the while demanding basic rights for his people.He remained in South Africa for about 20 years; his activities there caused him to be imprisoned many times.The writings of the Russian novelist Leo Tolstoy,the teachings of Christ,and the essays of Henry David Thoreau (especially his *Civil Disobedience*) strongly influenced him.The result of his efforts was that in 1914 the South African government made important concessions to his demands; it recognized Indian marriages and eliminated an Indian poll tax.

Although his fight against racism,colonialism,and violence established Gandhi's reputation internationally,the underlining reason for his actions has been often overlooked. A very religious man,Gandhi attributed his successes to the will of God.It was his desire to grow closer to God through the purity of his deeds—he lived simply,he lived to serve others.Gandhi,who had been subject so much pain in his life,found many answers in Hinduism:"Hinduism as I know it entirely satisfies my soul,fills my whole being."

Gandhi also said this:"What I want to achieve-what I have been striving and pining to achieve…is self-realization,to see God face to face,to attain 'Moksha' (Salvation).I live and move and have my being in pursuit of this goal."

The Story of My Experiments with Truth

No one contemplating the early life of Gandhi would imagine that he would go on to

40

圣雄甘地
《我的对于真理的实践经历》

圣雄甘地

圣雄甘地(出生时名为莫罕达斯·甘地:1869~1948)领导印度人民通过开展国民抵抗和非暴力不合作运动使印度摆脱了英国的统治。他所倡导的"非暴力"——即通过组织大众进行非暴力不合作的运动来抵抗外来的殖民统治,从此也激发了其他殖民地的人们起来为他们的独立而奋斗。在甘地的个人自传《我的对于真理的实践经历》中他清楚地表达了自己的非暴力的立场:"有很多原因让我准备为之付出生命,但没有理由能让我去屠杀生灵。"

甘地出生在印度的一个乡村,那里不受任何外国的影响。他的母亲教给他印度教的信条"非暴力"(要从善,不要伤害)。这一信条从甘地孩童时期就已经根深蒂固,这就是他进行非暴力地反抗压迫的原因。甘地所开展的非暴力的抵抗(satyagraha)都是针对他认为是当局者的暴政的行径——比如,社会等级制度、苛捐杂税以及外国的殖民统治。

甘地在从伦敦大学学院拿到法律学位之后返回印度,并且曾经试图在孟买开创自己的律师事业,但没有成功。1893年,他被位于南非德班市的一家印度公司聘用,在那里的工作经验成就了他以后的事业。甘地看到南非政府公然漠视印度公民的自由和政治权利,很是愤慨,于是他积极地参加反抗歧视的示威活动,同时为印度同胞争取基本的权利。他在南非呆了20年,他的抗议活动曾经使他几次被捕入狱。俄国作家列夫·托尔斯泰的作品、基督教的信条以及亨利·大卫·梭罗的论文(尤其是《论公民的不服从》)对甘地的影响极为深刻。他的努力最终使得南非政府于1914年对其要求做出了重大让步,政府承认印度传统的结婚仪式并且取消对印度人民的人头税。

虽然,甘地反抗种族主义、殖民主义和暴力的努力为他赢得了世界性的声誉,但他开展这些斗争的原因却经常被人们忽视。甘地是一位宗教人士,他把自己的成功归于上帝的旨意。他希望能够通过净化自己的行为变得更加靠近上帝——他过着简朴的生活,并乐于为他人服务。甘地忍受了生活中如此多的痛苦,最终他在印度教信仰中找到了答案:"我发现印度教满足了我的灵魂,充实了我的整个生命。"

此外,甘地还说过:"我想获得的——我一直以来所努力奋斗并渴望的……是实现自我,能够让我和上帝面对面,获得'解脱'(拯救)。我为此而生,并努力朝它迈进,我的存在就是为了实现这一目标。"

《我的对于真理的实践经历》

听一下甘地早年的生活,人们都不会想象得到他将来会成为20世纪最重要的政治和

become one of the most important political and spiritual leaders of the 20th century.Quite the contrary:he seemed destined for a life of obscure failure.

It is important,though,to understand the ways in which he did so.Such a description of Gandhi suggests that he was a firebrand,someone who was the driving force behind a bloody revolution.Yes,he was a revolutionary:such a description is true,but it is only half true.

Gandhi became the apostle,and the embodiment,of "satyagraha"—the resistance to and defeat of tyranny by one group of people over another through a kind of mass civil disobedience that completely avoids violence.His example proved decisive for those leaders of liberation movements who came after him—from Nelson Mandela to Martin Luther King Jr.—to the leaders of liberation movements—from those of women to those of sexual minorities to those of immigrants.All later civil rights and liberation movements took their example from him.

Gandhi defeated the British Raj,was instrumental in gaining independence for his country,using the method of refusing to co-operate with its oppressors.He tells his story in his autobiography,*The Story of My Experiments with Truth*.This title suggests that there was more to his philosophy and method that simple civil disobedience.Gandhi believed that all wars,all destructive times in human history,were aberrations,that again and again the forces of human love and morality eventually win out.Though a life-long Hindu,he believed that all the major religions are forces for good that essentially believe in the same God.He believed,too,that no one who professed allegiance to God could do so and simultaneously ignore the moral demands of human life.That is,unless one practiced the "Golden Rule," there was no way that anyone could claim to be godly or religious.

In his autobiography,as in his life,he offers the radical proposition that the oppressed must live,must behave,in such a way that is more loving,more moral,than the lives of their oppressors.

Gandhi sets out,in *The Story of My Experiences with Truth*,what he regards as the components of a good and moral life.They are these:one must always devote oneself to the discovery of truth (as he said:"The truth is far more powerful than any weapon of mass destruction"); one must avoid violence to achieve worthy ends (though,he adds,if the choice is between cowardice and violence,then he prefers violence); one must live simply; one must strive for what is called "bramacharya"—spiritual and practical unity.That is,unity of the spiritual person with the person who must perform some kind of job,must raise a family, must be a member of society; and we must all embrace faith in God,knowing that at the core of all religions is the desire,the striving for,truth and love.

Gandhi was a great political leader,yes:he did what many people said could not be done.He freed his populous but weak country from the control of a small but very strong country by guiding the Indian people in ways that threatened to destroy the economy that the British had created.But the independence of India (and the subsequent partition of that India into Hindu India and Muslim Pakistan—a move that Gandhi vehemently opposed,and the conflict over which caused him to be assassinated by a Hindu zealot),happened a long time ago in the modern consciousness.His political triumph has now faded.What has not faded is his spiritual legacy—his vision of the "good life" as set out in his autobiography.It is one autobiography that all of us should read-for insight into the mind of one of the great religious leaders of modern times.

精神首领之一,相反,他看上去似乎注定会碌碌无为。

然而,我们很有必要去了解为何对他有如此评价。对甘地的这一描述暗示着他曾是一个煽动者,即极力支持暴力革命的人。是的,他的确是一名革命者:这一评价没错,但只有一半符合事实。

甘地是"非暴力、不合作"的倡导者和实践者——一部分人通过非暴力的、群众性的不合作运动反抗并挫败当局者的暴政。他为后来领导解放运动的领袖树立了榜样——从纳尔逊·曼德拉到马丁·路德·金;深刻影响了妇女解放运动、性别少数人群的维权运动,还有移民的维权运动。所有后来的争取民权的运动和解放运动都借鉴了甘地的例子。

甘地领导印度人民打败了英国的殖民统治,通过开展反抗压迫的不合作运动为他的国家赢得了民族的独立。他在个人自传《我的对于真理的实践经历》中记述了他的故事。这部作品的题目显示出文中包含了甘地个人的哲学思想以及领导不合作运动的方法。他相信一切战争、人类历史上一切的毁灭行为都是反常规的,并且人类爱的力量和道德规范一次次地获得了最终的胜利。虽然甘地终生信仰印度教,但他相信所有主要的宗教都是倡导向善的力量,本质上都是信奉同一个神灵。同时,他也相信人们一方面信仰上帝,同时也不能忽视人类的道德规范。也就是说,如果一个人不能遵守"神旨",他就不能称作是上帝的信徒或者称其有宗教信仰。

就像甘地在生活中实践的那样,他在自传中提出了基本的主张——受压迫的人们必须通过一种比压迫者更加仁爱、更加道德的方式生存、行事。

甘地在《我的对于真理的实践经历》中列出了他所认为是好的、道德的生活标准,它们是:人必须一直献身于追求真理(像他所说的"真理的力量比任何大规模的杀伤性武器都强";人必须避免暴力去实现有价值的目标(虽然,他补充说,如果要在怯弱和暴力之间选择,那么他宁愿选择暴力);人必须简单地生活;人必须努力实现"禁欲"——精神和实践的统一,即人的精神必须和从事某种工作、养家糊口并处身于社会之中的实际达成一致;我们所有人都应该信仰上帝,认识一切宗教的核心都是祈求并努力追求真理和爱。

甘地是一位伟大的政治领袖,的确,他做到了人们认为是不可能做到的事。他通过领导印度人民开展抵抗运动威胁要摧毁英国建立的经济,使一个人口众多的弱国摆脱了一个规模小但实力雄厚的强国的控制。然而,印度的独立(及接下来的印巴分治——此举受到甘地的强烈反对,并且这一冲突导致甘地被一名印度教狂热分子刺杀)在现代人的意识中已经是很久以前的事了。现在,甘地在政治上的胜利已经逝去,而留给我们的是他的精神财富——正如他在自传中描述的关于"美好生活"的观点。这是一部人人都该阅读的自传——以深入了解这位现代伟大的宗教领袖的思想。

Forty-one

Thomas Mann:
The Magic Mountain

Who Was Thomas Mann?

Thomas Mann (1875-1955) is considered the most important German novelist of the 20th century. His writings deal with important political and intellectual concerns in Western society.

Born in Lübeck, Mann studied at the University of Munich, where he prepared for a career in writing. His epic novel *Buddenbrooks* (1901), which is a story about the decline of a family over a period of 4 generations, was largely responsible for his winning the Nobel Prize in Literature in 1929. In this novel, one of his great accomplishments is to dissect the lifestyle of the middle-class. Mann documents this lifestyle through various generations, showing very minor alterations—until the family yields to a modernity that is in conflict with its traditions and is ultimately destroyed.

Mann married Katia Pringsheim, a member of a prominent Jewish family, in 1905. In the early 1930s he began to denounce Nazism in an effort to create a strong resistance among the working class. When the Nazis took power in 1933, he and his family settled in Küsnacht, near Zürich, for safety, and in 1939 they left for America. In 1952, he left America when Senator Joseph McCarthy began his hunt for communist sympathizers, and he moved to Switzerland, where he later died.

During his lifetime Mann was the recipient of numerous awards.

The Magic Mountain

From the humble beginnings of his life, few people could have predicted what Thomas Mann would become. He lived from 1875 to 1955; he was born in Lubeck to a German father, who was a grain merchant, and to a mother who had been born in Brazil. When his father died in 1891, his family moved to Munich where he attended university there, preparing for a career in journalism. Apart from a 2-year stint with an insurance company, he attempted to live by his pen—not in journalism but as a novelist and short story writer. In 1905, he married, he and his wife subsequently had six children (some of whom themselves became famous as adults), and his family continued to live in Munich until 1933. Then, his life became more adventuresome. Because his wife was Jewish, and because he disapproved of the Nazi regime, he moved to Switzerland in that year, then in 1939 the Mann family moved to the United States, where he taught at Princeton University. In 1942, the family moved to Pacific Palisades in California, and lived there until after World War II. In 1944, he became a citizen of the United States, and in 1952, he returned to Switzerland, where he lived until his death; he never lived in Germany again.

Despite this quiet life, which became more exciting only in its last 25 years, when he became a refugee, Thomas Mann was the greatest German novelist and short story writer of the 20th century. His works were widely translated, and were as well known and honored in the United States as in Europe; his fame was worldwide, and his accomplishment was

托马斯·曼

托马斯·曼(1875~1955)被视为20世纪德国最重要的小说家。他的作品涉及西方社会中重要的政治和思想问题。

曼出生于吕贝克,在慕尼黑大学就读并准备当一名作家。他的叙事小说《布登勃洛克一家》(于1901年发表)讲述的是关于一个家庭四代人逐渐落寞的故事,这部作品在1929年为他赢得了诺贝尔文学奖。在这一作品中,曼成功地剖析了中层阶级的生活方式。他记录了几代人的生活方式,展现了其中非常微小的变化——直到这一家庭陷入了传统与现代生活方式之间的激烈冲突,最后以衰败告终。

1905年,曼和出生于有名的犹太家庭的卡蒂亚·普林舍姆结婚。20世纪30年代初期,他开始谴责纳粹主义的行径,并努力组织工人阶级起来反抗。1933年,纳粹分子上台执政,曼和他的家人搬到苏黎世附近的古斯纳特市避难,他们于1939年移居美国。1952年,当参议院议员约瑟夫·麦卡锡提出开始实施逮捕共产主义的拥护者的时候,曼离开美国去了瑞士,后来在那里逝世。

曼一生中获得了诸多奖项。

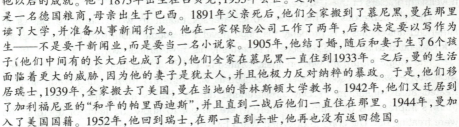

《魔山》

从托马斯·曼早年卑微的生活来看,很少有人能预测得到他以后的成就。他于1875年出生在吕贝克,1955年去世。父亲是一名德国粮商,母亲出生于巴西。1891年父亲死后,他们全家搬到了慕尼黑,曼在那里读了大学,并准备从事新闻行业。他在一家保险公司工作了两年,后来决定要以写作为生——不是要干新闻业,而是要当一名小说家。1905年,他结了婚,随后和妻子生了6个孩子(他们中间有的长大后也成了名),他们全家在慕尼黑一直住到1933年。之后,曼的生活面临着更大的威胁,因为他的妻子是犹太人,并且他极力反对纳粹的暴政。于是,他们移居瑞士,1939年,全家搬去了美国,曼在当地的普林斯顿大学教书。1942年,他们又迁居到了加利福尼亚的"和平的帕里西迪斯",并且直到二战后他们一直住在那里。1944年,曼加入了美国国籍。1952年,他回到瑞士,在那一直到去世,他再也没有返回德国。

曼平静的生活到了他人生的后25年变得漂泊不定。他是德国最伟大的作家和20世纪最伟大的短篇小说家。他的作品被广泛翻译成其他语言,在美国和欧洲国家都深受读者的喜爱。他的声誉响遍全球,1929年他被授予诺贝尔文学奖。但是,除非你去读一下他的

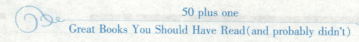

acknowledged by the Nobel Prize in Literature,which was awarded to him in 1929.Yet, unless one has read his books,they seem,from the analysis they provoked,unusual "creatures" to have become world classics.He is often cited for his highly symbolic and often ironic epic novels and novella-length short stories,notable for their insight into the consciousness of the artist and intellectual-artists and intellectuals who are usually European, most often German.

One has only to pose the question:Why isn't there a French or Polish or Italian writer of equal stature,of equal renown,to realize that Thomas Mann must in some way have been unique?

There are several reasons why this is so:

He was pre-eminently a great novelist,a great storyteller.In the sweep and drama of his novels,he is the rival of a Dickens or a Dostoyevsky—also their equal in his mastery of symbolism.He is,as well,master of a variety of prose forms.

The events of his life give resonance to his works.During World War I,he was a conservative; by the 1930s,he had become a liberal,an avowed enemy of the Nazi regime, and subsequently he became a leader of the refugee colony of German intellectuals in the United States.Moreover,he never forgave Germany,refused to live there again after the war—he became a symbol of those Germans who had not succumbed to Hitler.Because his experience—though on a more exalted,more intellectual,plane-mirrored the experience of millions of his fellow Germans,his works became fascinating even to those,especially to those,who had not experienced what being a liberal German,during the horrors of the 1930s and 1940s,had actually meant.

Finally,Mann tries to explain the first half of the 20th century to his readers; it is no exaggeration to say that he attempts to explain all of human history,before the 20th century,as well.No one has done it more brilliantly,from the exquisite novella *Death in Venice* to *Buddenbrooks*,the saga of a family over 3 generations (to an extent,based on his own family history),as brilliant and comprehensive as anything produced by the great novelist/chroniclers of the 19th century.

Though numerous of his short stories are still taught in world literature classes in American universities,it is probably his huge novel *The Magic Mountain* that is generally acknowledged to be his masterpiece; it is certainly his most famous work.

The Magic Mountain was originally written in 1912; it was then a brief novel or long short story—what is usually called a novella.His wife,suffering from a lung complaint,was treated at a sanitarium in Davos,Switzerland during that year,and the novella reflects Mann's impressions of visiting her there,where he got to know the team of doctors who were treating her.The coming of World War I interrupted his work on the book.He returned to it after the war,and,though he uses the same situation,he greatly revised and greatly expanded his book,converting it from a novella to a huge two-volume novel: it was eventually published in 1924.The sanitarium has now become the microcosm of the civilized world and the forces of perversity that caused the disaster of World War I.

His hero,Hans Castorp,goes to visit a friend who has tuberculosis,who is confined to a sanitarium in Davos,where he is hoping to be cured.Ironically,Castorp,during the visit,also develops symptoms of tuberculosis:his symptoms become worse,and in the end he himself

作品,才能领略其中千奇百态的"人物"塑造怎么会被奉为世界经典的。曼通常采用高度的象征手法和讽刺效果创作出一系列的编年史小说以及中短篇小说,这些作品深刻反映了这位艺术大师以及其他文学家和大部分欧洲尤其是德国文人的思想意识。

有人可能会问:"为什么没有一位法国或者波兰或者意大利的作家享有和托马斯·曼同等的地位和声誉呢?他应该是有什么独到之处吧?

原因有以下几点:

曼是一位卓越的小说家、一位伟大的故事大王。他在文章的构思和设置戏剧性场景方面是狄更斯和陀思妥耶夫斯基的竞争对手——同样,他们都是运用象征手法的文学大师。此外,曼还是应用散文体写作的行家。

曼的人生经历在其作品中有相应的体现。一战期间,他是一个保守派;而到了20世纪30年代,他成为公开反对纳粹暴政的革命分子,并且随后成为驻美国的德国人民反对殖民奴役的领袖。另外,他无法宽恕德国政府对他的所作所为,战后他拒绝重返那里——曼成为不屈从于希特勒的众多德国人民的代表。由于他的经历——虽然相对体面而且更加理性,但却真实反映了数百万德国百姓的遭遇。他的作品,尤其对于那些没有亲身感受过享有自由之身的人们来说,是非常有吸引力的,读者可以从其作品中真切地领会20世纪30年代到40年代期间的社会恐怖。

最后,曼力图剖析20世纪的前50年;毫不夸张地说他努力为读者展现了整个的人类历史,当然,其中包括20世纪之前的阶段。从他创作的优秀的中篇小说《威尼斯之死》到描写一个家庭四代人兴衰历程的《布登勃洛克一家》(某种程度上,这一作品是基于作者自己的家史),曼的创作无与伦比,同19世纪伟大的小说家或者编年史撰写者一样,托马斯·曼的作品也是相当卓越和深刻。

虽然托马斯·曼的诸多短篇小说现在仍然被美国的大学拿来在文学课堂上讲授,但他的长篇小说《魔山》被公认为是他的代表作,当然也是其最有名的作品。

《魔山》最早于1912年完成,当时是一部较为通俗的小说或者叫长篇故事——通常被称作中篇小说。曼的妻子因患有肺结核被送去瑞士的达沃斯村的一所疗养院治疗,这部小说就是反映了曼去探望妻子时对疗养院留下的印象,他在那里认清了为他妻子治疗的医生队伍。一战的爆发打断了曼的创作。战后,他又继续拿起了笔,虽然他依然沿用当初的创作背景,但他很大程度上修改并扩展了这一作品,使其从原来的中篇增加到长达两卷的长篇小说,这部作品最终于1924年出版。文中的疗养院现在已经成为整个文明世界的缩影,同时也体现了好战者的偏执最终导致了一战的爆发。

小说中的英雄人物汉斯·卡斯托普去达沃斯的一所疗养院看望患肺结核的朋友。具有讽刺性的是,卡斯托普在此次探望中也染上了肺结核:他的病情越来越重,结果这一呆就是7年。小说的结尾一战爆发,卡斯托普应征入伍。虽然文中没有明说,但暗含的意思却

spends 7 years in the sanitarium.World War I begins at the end of the novel; Castorp is conscripted; and,though this is not said overtly,the implication is that he will be killed on the battlefield.

During his "incarceration," Castorp endlessly talks with,and experiences,both the other patients and their doctors,all of whom are "spokespeople" of some aspect of pre-war and historic European notions,good or bad.The novel is what is usually referred to as a "bildungsroman." That is,a novel in which the hero is educated.In classical literature,a common element of plot has the hero visiting the underworld (the world of death) as a way of understanding (being educated to) the world of life.*In The Magic Mountain* the sanitarium serves the same function,as Mann says,commenting on his novel "One must go through the deep experience of sickness and death to arrive at a higher sanity and health." Simply put:one must experience the sanitarium-both our notions of good and our human notions and practices of evil—to learn how to live.Yet,in the end,Castorp probably dies.A cautionary tale? Probably a more accurate interpretation is that unless more of us are willing to examine our own beliefs,motives and actions,then we will,as a civilization,always end in conflict,war,and destruction.We pick up the pieces,start again,only to end up in the same place.It is too late for Castorp; it is not too late for the reader.

What can be said definitively about Mann was that he was a man of the world,a humanist,someone who believed that a man's life can be valued by how well he upholds the good in human civilization against the forces of barbarism:he believed,as he said,that life should be "led consciously,that is,conscientiously." We should all have read *The Magic Mountain*—to profit by Mann's vision of how man should live in order to create a better world,not a world that inevitably ends.

是主人公将会在战场上牺牲。

　　卡斯托普在"监禁"期间,不断地与其他病人和医生交流,体验在那里的生活,他们不论好坏,所以人都是战前某些领域和历史上欧洲思想观念的"代言人"。这部作品通常被视为是一部"教育小说",即以描述英雄人物的成长过程为主题。在经典文学中,普遍都有这样的情节:一位英雄通过造访地狱(死者的世界)最终明白了(被教化而懂得)人生的真谛。在《魔山》这一作品中疗养院就承担了这一功能,要领会他的作品,正如曼所言,"人们必须经过疾病和死亡的洗礼才能达到心智健全的更高境界。"简单说,即人们必须体验过疗养院里的生活之后——人们好的意识和邪恶的思想及行为——才会知道如何生活。然而,小说最后暗示卡斯托普可能死了。这部作品是否讲述了一则警世的故事呢?可能更确切地说它揭示了这样一个道理:除非我们大部分人都愿意检验自己的信仰、动机和行为,否则,作为文明社会的一员,我们往往会在冲突、战争、毁灭中结束自己的一生。我们振作精神,从头来过,结果发现最终面对的还是相同的结局。对于小说的主人公卡斯托普来说已经为时已晚;但对于读者来说还不算晚。

　　我们可以很肯定地说托马斯·曼属于整个世界,他是一位人文主义者,他相信人生的价值可以由人在此文明时代多大程度上维护正义、反对野蛮来评判:正如曼所言,他认为人生应该"保持清醒,即要有良知"。我们都该读一下《魔山》——去领会托马斯·曼关于人类应该如何做才能创造一个更美好的世界的观点,而不是不可避免地要以恐慌告终。

— Forty-two —

Albert Einstein: Relativity: The Special and General Theory

Who Was Albert Einstein?

The German theoretical physicist Albert Einstein (1879-1955) made important contributions to our understanding of physical reality. The greatest of his conceptions are his theories of relativity, which have become a model, a basis, for every physicist who has followed him. His speculations about energy and its relation to matter led the way to the creation of nuclear power and to the atomic bomb.

Einstein had an ordinary beginning. He was born in southern Germany to middleclass Jewish parents. At 15, he left his prep school and enrolled in the Federal Swiss Polytechnic in Zurich. In 1906 he received his Ph.D. from the University of Zurich. While at the Zurich Polytechnic, he met and fell in love with Mileva Maric, a Serbian physics student. This marriage, though of kindred souls, didn't last long; they divorced in 1919.

Also in that year, at the age of 40, Einstein became world famous, when the British Solar Eclipse Expedition confirmed his theory of general relativity: The gravity of the Sun deflected the stars' light rays exactly as he had predicted. Even today scientists marvel at his discovery.

In 1921, he won the Nobel Prize in Physics.

Einstein used his fame to champion what he believed were important causes- pacifism, Zionism, and liberalism. He once again: "It is important for the common good to foster individuality, for only the individual can produce the new ideas which the community needs for its continuous improvements and requirements."

Relativity: The Special and General Theory

Albert Einstein is almost certainly the most famous person of the 20th century, and his fame endures into the current century. When the 20th century ended, *Time* magazine conducted a poll of its readers and staff to name the "Person of the Century." Einstein won. The runners-up were Franklin Roosevelt and Gandhi. Most people would agree that President Roosevelt rescued his own country from the worst Depression in its history, that he helped save the Free World from destruction by being its most prominent leader in the fight against Germany and Japan in World War II. Equally exalted claims could be made for Gandhi-that all freedom/liberation movements of the 20th/21st centuries begin and end with him, with his example, his actions and his pronouncements. Yet, Einstein beat out these two giants in the *Time* poll.

In a sense, there are two Einsteins—the scientist who 100 years ago published papers in a somewhat obscure scientific journal, scholarly papers having to do with what we now call "relativity" that irrevocably changed the way that man viewed the universe; and as well, there is the famous man, famous for being famous, who resided at Princeton from the

阿尔伯特·爱因斯坦
《相对论：
狭义与广义理论》

阿尔伯特·爱因斯坦

德国理论物理学家阿尔伯特·爱因斯坦(1879~1955)在物理学方面做出了重大贡献。他最伟大的学说就是他提出的相对论，这一理论已成为后来物理学家的典范和研究基础。爱因斯坦关于能量与质量的关系问题的研究为核能以及原子弹的研发开辟了道路。

爱因斯坦出生于德国南部的一个普通的中产阶级犹太家庭。15岁的时候，他完成初级教育，并进入瑞士苏黎世联邦工业大学学习。1906年，他获得了苏黎世大学的博士学位。在大学期间，爱因斯坦认识并爱上了米列娃·马里奇，她是一名物理学专业的塞尔维亚学生。他们的婚姻虽然充满激情，但没有维持太久，两人于1919年离婚。

就在离婚的同一年，即爱因斯坦40岁的时候，他的成就闻名于世，英国的日食观测证实了爱因斯坦的广义相对理论的正确性。正如他所预言的那样，太阳的引力作用造成了星体光线的偏转。甚至直到今天，科学家们还惊叹于爱因斯坦的这一伟大发现。

1921年，爱因斯坦荣获诺贝尔物理学奖。

爱因斯坦利用他的名气开展了他所认为的重大事业——倡导和平主义、犹太复国主义和自由主义。他曾说过："利用公益事业扶持个人发展是非常重要的，因为只有个人才能产生新的观点，而整个社会正是需要借此获得继续发展并满足需求。"

《相对论：狭义与广义理论》

阿尔伯特·爱因斯坦几乎称得上是20世纪最著名的人物，他的声誉一直持续到当代。20世纪末的时候，《时代》杂志曾对其读者和工作人员做过一次民意调查，让他们选出"本世纪的代表人物"，结果爱因斯坦胜出。调查结果中排第二位的是弗兰克林·罗斯福和甘地。大部分人都认同罗斯福总统从美国历史上最严重的危机中挽救了他的国家，并且在反抗德国和日本的第二次世界大战中罗斯福是为世界和平而战的最杰出的领袖之一。甘地本来也有可能获此殊荣——20/21世纪中所有的自由/解放运动都始于甘地并且以他的领导和宣言而告终。然而，爱因斯坦在这次问卷调查中胜过了这两位伟人。

从某种意义上说，有两个爱因斯坦——这位科学家100年前在某份不知名的科学期刊上发表过文章，这些学术论文是关于我们今天所称的"相对论"，而这一理论真正改变了人们的宇宙观；同时，他又是一位名人，因为著名而闻名，他自纳粹分子上台就一直住在普林斯顿直到1955年去世。他洒脱不羁，拥有精灵般迷人的外表，通常相片上的他都是

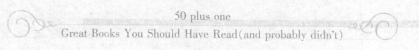

coming of the Nazis until his death in 1955.He was bumbling,elf-like and charming in appearance,usually photographed wearing a moth-eaten sweater (having failed for months to have his hair cut),speaking with a thick German accent.He was,as more than one commentator pronounced,"cuddly." He might have been invented by Hollywood,and,more than any other public figure of his time,he was instantly recognized by the man in the street.

To most people,the latter Einstein is better known than the former Einstein-and most people also know the events of that Einstein's life—that he was the child of an obscure Jewish couple from southern Germany.He was educated at the Zurich Polytechnic,that, though he was a great womanizer in his youth,his romantic attachments were rather bizarre,that he devised his theories about "relativity" while working at a dead-end job at the Patent Office in Bern,Switzerland.Fame was suddenly thrust upon him when his theories were proven in 1919 (nearly 15 years after he published his famous papers).He left Germany when the Nazis came to power and came to reside at the Institute for Advanced Study at Princeton,a research institute/think tank specially created for him,which endures to the present time as one of the great scholarly research centers of the United States.

Because his theories had brought him fame,he was listened to,and it is important to remember in how many ways he was a force for good:Einstein was one of the great moralists of the 20th century,and,in retrospect,we see that he was right about virtually every issue on which he commented.During World War I,he signed an anti-war petition, incurring the great displeasure of the official Germany in which he worked.Later,in response to German anti-Semitism,he became a Zionist,yet at the same time he expressed his concerns about the rights of Arabs in any future Jewish state.Once resident in the United States,he urged America to military action against Hitler at a time when many Americans were isolationists.He helped many Jewish refugees come to the United States when such actions were not popular.He wrote to President Roosevelt , warning him that the Germans could conceivably , given German accomplishments in nuclear physics,create an atomic bomb,and,as a result,Roosevelt created the Manhattan Project,in which American scientists raced to produce the bomb before America's enemies could do so.

Although his theories were largely responsible for the creation of nuclear weapons, Einstein was horrified at what happened at Hiroshima and Nagasaki,and after the war he became a leader in the campaign for a comprehensive ban on nuclear weapons.He denounced Joe McCarthy,opposed the Cold War,and pleaded for an end to bigotry and racism.At that time,America was in a state of Cold War hysteria,and the response of many Americans was to regard him as innocent and naïve.And,to everyone's surprise,he maintained all of his life a belief in God,saying always that part of his life's work was to understand how the Lord had created and formed the universe that he,Einstein,had only described.

A formidable moral figure—yet there is also the other Einstein,the humble genius,the greatest scientific mind in a century in which the greatest scientific discoveries in the history of mankind were made.All the accomplishments of the era,for good or bad,bear his imprint-from nuclear power to the Big Bang to quantum physics to electronics-to,most important,the very structure of the universe.But all of us,50 years after his death,tend to

穿着一件虫蛀了的毛衣(几个月不剪头发),说话带有很重的德国口音。不止一个的评论家说他"随和"。他就像是好莱坞影片中塑造的人物形象,并且较之任何与他同时代的公众人物,爱因斯坦会被街上的行人更快地认出。

在大部分人看来,后一个爱因斯坦比前者更著名,大多数人也了解爱因斯坦的生平——他出生于德国南部一个不知名的犹太家庭,他曾就读于苏黎世联邦工业大学。虽然他在年轻的时候个性风流,但他的浪漫情怀是我们意想不到的。他在位于瑞士伯恩的国家专利局苦心工作的时候提出了他的"相对论"。1919年(差不多在他发表他著名的论文后15年)他的理论得到证实,荣誉一下降临到他身上。在纳粹分子上台之后,他离开德国来到普林斯顿高等研究院,这是一个专门为他建造的研究所,直到今天这里依然是美国著名的高级学术研究中心之一。

因为爱因斯坦的理论成就为他赢得了声誉,人们都愿意听取他的意见,并且我们也很有必要了解他在诸多方面都是代表了正义的力量:爱因斯坦是20世纪最伟大的道德主义者之一,回顾一下,我们可以看出事实上他在每个问题上的见解都是正确的。一战期间,他在反战请愿书上签字,结果招致了他所为之工作的德国当局的不满。后来,爱因斯坦反对德国的反犹太主义支持犹太复国运动。同时,他还非常关心未来犹太国家中阿拉伯人民的权力问题。一移居美国,他看到很多美国人民持孤立主义的态度,于是他便催促美国政府对希特勒的法西斯统治采取军事行动。他还秘密地帮助许多犹太难民迁渡到美国。爱因斯坦致电罗斯福总统,提醒他如果德国在核物理方面研究成功的话德国很可能会研制出原子弹。结果,罗斯福实施启动了曼哈顿计划,在这一行动中美国科学家抢在他们的敌人之前研制出了第一颗原子弹。

虽然爱因斯坦的理论很大程度上推动了核武器的研制,但他对在广岛和长崎投放原子弹的事件极为震惊,并且战后他成为联合抵制使用核武器运动的首领。他谴责乔·麦卡锡的政策,反对冷战,并且要求制止独断主义和种族主义。当时,美国正处于支持冷战的热潮当中,很多美国人都认为爱因斯坦非常幼稚和天真。令所有人吃惊的是,爱因斯坦终生信仰上帝,他宣称他人生的一部分任务就是要去搞清楚上帝是如何创造了宇宙,他自己只是负责描述。

然而,爱因斯坦还有另一面——他是一名彻底的道德主义者,一位谦逊的天才,他的科学探索成就了人类历史上一个最伟大的发现。这一时代的所有成就,不论好坏,都留下了他的印记——从核能的研发到宇宙大爆炸理论,到量子物理学,再到电子理论——最重要的是,他对宇宙构造的发现。但是,我们所有的人,在爱因斯坦逝世50年之后,往往忘

lose the great scientist by contemplating the great moralist,who was right about almost everything.

Yet his scientific genius was remarkable.It seems that,merely by thinking about it,about what troubled him,he came to conclude that the universe was not at all what it seemed—that it "operates" in a way very different from what anyone had thought before.His ideas are presented in full in *Relativity:The Special and General Theory*.Everything he thought or wrote thereafter was basically a footnote to these papers-as indeed is everything else done by the physicists who came after him.Most readers who do not have a scientific background in physics will find the theories presented in his scientific papers tough going-not so much because they are impossible to comprehend but because they ask us to comprehend our surroundings in ways that are foreign and strange to us.It is fair to say that,having read Einstein,almost anyone will require additional help from those hundreds of commentators who have attempted to explain relativity in layman's terms.The reader should not feel daunted in having to seek help.Iit took some of the greatest scientific minds of the last century years and years to understand Einstein's theories,to see the way in which they changed everything we knew,or thought we knew,about the physical laws of the universe.

Basically,Einstein proposes that distance and time are not absolute—as man has imagined from the beginning of time.Only light moves always at the same speed as an "absolute structure." Einstein proposed that gravity,as well as motion,can affect the intervals of time and of space.The gravitational force of a huge mass—for example,a planet—is so powerful that it has the effect of "warping" space and time around it.

Much of Einstein's later life was spent in trying to come up with a comprehensive theory—that which would unite all physical forces in the universe (even though his relativity principle is a fundamental criterion for all physical laws)—a grand "unified theory." He never succeeded,but his work paved the way for others—in ways they might never have imagined.All of us should try to understand him—by trying to read the famous papers,by choosing whatever commentary on those papers makes sense to us—because he can truly be said to have changed the world,and,however dimly,all of us should understand,or try to understand,why.

记了作为一位伟大的科学家之外他还是一名伟大的道德家,他几乎在所有问题上的观点都是正确的。

　　爱因斯坦在科学方面的天赋是卓越的。似乎他仅仅通过思考他所遇到的疑问,便得出结论:宇宙根本不像它表面上那样——它的运行规律并不像之前人们所认为的那样。爱因斯坦的这一观点在《相对论:狭义与广义理论》中有完整的表述。他之后的思想和作品都成为这些理论的有力证明——同样,继他之后的物理学家们也尽其所能地给以有效的论证。大部分不从事物理学研究的读者会发现爱因斯坦论文中所阐释的理论非常难懂——并不是它们本身不能被理解,而是因为这些理论要求我们去理解外界的且对我们来说是陌生的周围环境。可以说,要读完爱因斯坦的著作,几乎每个人都需要借助上百个评论家的帮助,这部分人都曾经用非专业术语解释过爱因斯坦的相对理论。读者们不应该因为要查找这么多资料而退缩。上个世纪伟大的科学家们曾花费很多年的时间去理解爱因斯坦的理论,了解这些理论何以改变了人们的认识和思想,以及关于宇宙的运行规律。

　　爱因斯坦从根本上提出空间和时间不是绝对的——正如人们从最初一直想象的那样。他论证了只有独立于观察者之外的光速是个"常数"。爱因斯坦提出,引力作用和运动会影响时空的间隔。一个巨大物体的引力——比如,一颗行星——它的能量足以"扭曲"周围的空间和时间。

　　爱因斯坦晚年的大部分时间都在尝试提出一种综合性的理论——这一理论将统一宇宙中所有的物理力量(虽然,他的相对论为一切物理学法则提供了一条基本标准)——统一场论。虽然他没有成功,但是他的努力为其他人铺平了道路——这是那些科学家所没有想到的。我们所有人都应该试着了解爱因斯坦,通过阅读他的著名的论文和关于他的理论的评论,这些对我们来说是非常有价值的——因为可以说爱因斯坦改变了整个世界,即使有些难以理解,我们都应该清楚,至少要尝试搞清楚,他何以做到了这一点。

Forty-three

T.S.Eliot:
The Waste Land

Who Was T.S.Eliot

T.S.Eliot (Thomas Stearns Eliot),who lived from 1888 to 1965,had in some ways a very conventional if privileged life.He was born to a rich St.Louis businessman and his teacher/poet wife,and was one of six children.His family's ancestors were from England,and the family had connections in the eastern United States as well.A distant cousin,Charles William Eliot,was President of Harvard University from 1869 to 1909.Eliot himself attended Harvard (he earned his B.A.and M.A.there,and would have earned a Ph.D.if he had shown up for the oral part of his examination),and he spent a year on scholarship at Merton College,Oxford.He was destined for a career as a philosopher at Harvard,having written poetry only as an avocation.

But his life was also unconventional.He decided not to go back for a second year at Merton College,and instead settled in London in 1915.He never returned home to the United States but spent the rest of his life in England.He also married that year but the marriage was unhappy.Both Eliot and his wife suffered from nervous problems.He recovered but she spent the last 10 years of her life in a mental hospital,where she died. Eliot took a job in the foreign accounts department of Lloyds Bank in London,and worked there from 1917 until 1925,when he became a director at the publishers Faber and Faber, where he worked for the remainder of his career.In 1927,he became a British subject and converted to the Anglican religion (the official religion of the United Kingdom).The following year,in one of his books of essays,he describes his position as "classicist in literature,royalist in politics,and anglo-catholic in religion." His last major work of poetry Four Quartets,was published in 1945,and thereafter,for 20 years,he published very little new poetry,though he did continue to write verse plays and essays.In 1957,he married Valerie Fletcher,38 years his junior,who,after his death,became his executor,his editor,and the preserver of his legacy.

The Waste Land

T.S.Eliot had an unusual life,to be sure—but it was also an important one.Forty years after his death it is perhaps difficult for most of us to imagine just how important T.S.Eliot was during his lifetime—or how famous.He wrote critical essays that profoundly influenced a generation of readers and scholars.He wrote poems that still resonate,that most people would agree changed the course of modernist poetry.In 1948,he won the Nobel Prize for Literature; as well,he won most of the exalted literary prizes that England and America offer; and he was given the Order of Merit by the British Government—the highest honor that country confers.But this is most important:it is probably no exaggeration to say that he was the most influential poet in the English language in the 20th century.

What,precisely,was his accomplishment? Considering only the poetry (it is that which will endure); most people have found it complex,though,ironically,it is often written in very

托马斯·斯特恩斯·艾略特
《荒原》

托马斯·斯特恩斯·艾略特

　　托马斯·斯特恩斯·艾略特(1888~1965)的生活传统而优越。他出生于圣路易斯一个富有的商人家庭,母亲是一名诗人,也是他的老师,家里有六个兄妹。艾略特的先祖来自英国,后来移居美国东部。他的远方堂兄查尔斯·威廉·艾略特在1869年至1909年间曾任哈佛大学的校长。艾略特本人也就读于哈佛大学(在那里他获得了文学学士和硕士学位,并且如果他参加口试部分的测试的话,他本来可以拿到博士学位)。他曾获奖学金在牛津大学默顿学院学习一年。艾略特在哈佛就读期间决定要作为一名哲学家开展他的事业,他仅仅把写诗当成是一种业余爱好。

　　然而,艾略特的人生又是非传统的。他决定不回默顿学院进行第二年学习,而是于1915年定居伦敦。他之后一直待在英国,再也没有回过美国。同年,他结了婚,但他的婚姻并不幸福。艾略特和他的妻子都患有神经病,他后来痊愈了,但他的妻子后10年时间却一直待在精神病院里,最后在那里去世。艾略特于1917年到1925年在伦敦的劳埃德银行外汇部工作,后来,他创办了文学评论季刊《标准》,并以此作为自己的副业。1927年,他加入英国国籍和国教(英国官方正式的宗教派别)。第二年,艾略特在他的文章中自称他"在文学上是古典主义者,在政治上是保皇派,在宗教上是英国天主教徒。"他最后一部重要的诗歌作品《四个四重奏》于1945年出版,之后的20年,虽然他也在继续创作诗歌和散文,但很少发表新的诗作。1957年,他与比他小38岁的瓦莱里·弗莱彻尔结婚,在艾略特死后,妻子成为他遗嘱的执行者,并且作为他遗作的编者和遗产的继承人。

《荒原》

　　我们可以肯定,托马斯·斯特恩斯·艾略特的一生是不寻常的,但又是非常有价值的。在他逝世40年之后,也许对于我们大多数人来说很难想象他在他所生活的年代有多么重大的影响——或者说多么著名。他写的评论文章深刻影响了一代读者和专家学者。他的诗歌现在依然可以引起共鸣,大部分人都赞同艾略特改变了现代主义的诗风。1948年,他获得了诺贝尔文学奖;同时,他也荣获了英国和美国颁发的诸多重要的文学奖项;他还被英国政府授予一等功绩勋章——这是英国颁发的最高荣誉奖。然而,最重要的是:我们可以毫不夸张地说艾略特是20世纪创作英文诗歌的作家中最具影响力的一位。

　　那么,具体他取得了哪些成就呢?我们仅仅来看一下他的诗歌创作(它们将一直流传

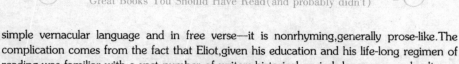
simple vernacular language and in free verse—it is nonrhyming,generally prose-like.The complication comes from the fact that Eliot,given his education and his life-long regimen of reading,was familiar with a vast number of writers,historical periods,languages and cultures. Thus,he may be quoting the Buddha; in the next line he is reproducing the conversation of a London barmaid.These different voices,and the huge range of different allusions,have confused people.

The reader may be reading five lines of language so straight-forward that it seems like prose when,suddenly,there is a quotation from a medieval French poet.

It will be helpful for any reader to remember that Eliot is trying to create,in writing any poem,a synthesis of what has been thought and said throughout human history.

It is also helpful,for any reader coming to Eliot for the first time,to remember this chronology.For convenience,we can say that there are three phases to his poetry: 1) a period in which he expresses the disillusionment of the post World War I period—"the lost generation;" 2) Then there is the period,after his conversion to Anglicanism in 1927,in which he struggles with the intellectual difficulties of religious faith; and 3) Finally,there is a large gap in his writing of nearly 15 years (during which he writes Old Possum's Book of Practical Cats,which in turn,and much later,becomes the Broadway musical "Cats").This period ends with "Four Quartets," the poetic cycle that most critics consider his masterwork,that which sums up all of his beliefs about life and religion,the relation of man to God.

The religious poems of the 2nd and 3rd periods are thrilling.It is impossible to read them without being moved,without examining one's own religious beliefs.But a modern reader might say:this is Eliot's solution to the problem of modern life,but I can be neither a classicist nor a royalist nor a convert to anglo-catholicism.For such a reader,the early works will almost certainly be more rewarding.

The Love Song of J.Alfred Prufrock,composed when Eliot was only 22,is the utterance of a middle-aged man who laments his inability to find anything meaningful in life,even as it is passing him by; he sees no spiritual or mental progress in his life; he is unable to connect,in love,with any other human being.It is one of the most dazzling debuts in our language.His next major poem,published in 1922,when Eliot was still a young man,is The Waste Land.It is one of the literary landmarks of the 20th century.

The Waste Land can best be described as Eliot's vision of the society he knew,a society he regarded as touching bottom—and,indeed,he said,after publishing the poem,that he was feeling his way to a new form,a new style,a new positiveness.Its central image is that of a fisherman (who is also royalty—an Everyman,in other words) fishing for meaning in life.And through a series of allusions to past cultures and to past writers and what they said in other periods of human longing,Eliot offers a definition of the disillusion felt by man in the 1920's.The Waste Land is deeply pessimistic,and un-Christian,and,in its lack of positiveness,deeply non-American.Many critics have called it the "first European poem" written by an American.In the poem,nothing provides solace—not sex,not love,not religion, not the past:God is nowhere to be found; the father of the world is dead; the fisher-king endlessly fishes without "catching" anything.As the last line of the poem says,Everything passeth our understanding.

下去);大多数人都发现艾略特的诗作非常复杂,虽然,有趣的是,诗人采用了简单的白话文和自由诗的形式——这一文体不讲究押韵,一般像散文的风格。艾略特的创作之所以复杂,是源于他所受的教育以及他终生博览群书,熟知大量的作家,了解不同历史时期的背景,懂得多门语言和多种文化。因此,他可能引用佛经的内容,而下一段又会重新设计一组与伦敦吧台女郎的对白。他文中的不同声音和大量的典故,真的会让读者摸不着头脑。

读者可能像阅读散文一样很顺利地读完他的五行诗句,突然,碰到一段引自中世纪法国诗人的诗歌。

最好每位读者都能记得艾略特在写每一篇诗歌的时候都力求创新以实现人类历史上思想和言语的综合表达。

对于第一次阅读艾略特作品的读者来说,记住以下的年代顺序也是非常有帮助的。方便起见,我们可以把他的诗歌创作分为三个阶段:1)这一阶段反映一战后人们思想的幻灭——"迷惘的一代";2)第二阶段是继1927年他加入英国国教之后,参加克服宗教信仰带来的思想困惑的运动;3)在最后一个阶段,他的近15年的诗歌创作出现了一个大的飞跃(在此期间,他写下了《擅长假扮的老猫经》,之后过了很长一段时间被拍成百老汇的音乐剧《猫》)。在这一阶段最后,艾略特创作了《四个四重奏》,被大部分评论家视为他的代表作,这一作品总结了艾略特所有的人生和宗教信条,以及关于人类与上帝的关系的思考。

艾略特在第二和第三阶段所创作的宗教诗歌非常震撼人心。读过的人一定会被其感动,并且也会自觉地检验一下自己的宗教信仰。但是,有的现代读者可能会问:艾略特的作品反映的是他自己处理现代生活问题的方法,而我既不是古典主义者,也不是保皇派或者英国的天主教徒。对于怀有如此疑问的读者,艾略特早期的作品应该会更受欢迎。

艾略特仅在22岁的时候就创作了《普鲁弗洛克的情歌》,记叙了一名中年男子对无力悟到生命真谛而虚度年华的感叹;主人公看不到自己精神或者思想上的进步;他无法用爱心去跟其他人交流。这本书是最耀眼的英文经典作品之一。1922年,年轻的艾略特发表了另外一部重要的诗歌《荒原》,这一作品是20世纪文学史上的一座里程碑。

《荒原》很好地展现了艾略特对他所认识的社会所持有的观点,他把当时的社会视为坠入了深渊——确实,在这一作品发表之后,他说他感受到了通向新形式、新风尚和新希望的道路。诗歌的中心形象是一个渔夫(他出身皇族——同时又是一个普通人)"垂钓"生活的意义。艾略特从之前的历史阶段的文化和作家以及他们的话语中引用了一系列典故,展现了20世纪20年代人们思想的幻灭。《荒原》深刻反映了当时社会的悲凉、基督教信仰的丧失,人们思想的迷惘,此作完全不像美国风格的诗歌。许多评论家称其是由一个美国人创作的"第一部欧洲诗歌"。在文中,根本找不到什么寄托——没有性、没有爱、没有宗教、没有过去;上帝无处可寻;我们的主死了;渔夫——殿下不断地垂钓,但却"一无所获"。正如诗歌最后一行,一切都穿越了我们的理解。

If, as someone has said, the Modern Period begins with World War I—that is, a different world would have emerged after that war than what had been known before it—and if, too, that different world, that world in which we now all live, started in disillusion and personal heartbreak (there is no solace for the human consciousness in the poem), then The Waste Land may well be the most perfect—certainly the most explosive—expression of that beginning in disillusion of the modern period. Everyone should have read it—or should have tried to; and everyone should also remember that Eliot ended the quest that started in disillusion with one of the most positive religious poems in the English language.

Everyone will not of course end in the same place, but all of us know what it is to start any quest from a stance of disillusion, from a feeling of despair. The Waste Land is a great poetic statement of that bleakness that all of us, from time to time, have felt.

　　如果真像有人所说,现代是开始于第一次世界大战——战争之后,一个全新的世界诞生了,但之前人们却是预料不到的——并且,如果这个全新的世界,这个我们现在所生存的世界开始于思想的幻灭和人们的绝望（诗歌中找不到人类精神的寄托）,那么,《荒原》将是最好的——当然,也是最具揭露性的——现代开始阶段人们思想幻灭的表达。每个人都应该读一下这一作品,至少要试着去读;并且每个人都应该记住艾略特用英文创作的这一最具宗教复兴色彩的诗歌解答了对现代初期人们思想幻灭的探究。

　　当然,每个人读完以后的感受是不尽相同的,但是,我们都会领悟到幻灭和绝望之后将意味着重新开始。《荒原》就是这样一首描写当时那种阴郁景象的伟大诗篇,读者都将感受得到其中的荒凉。

Forty--four

George Gamow: The Creation of the Universe

Who Was George Gamow?

George Gamow (his last name is pronounced GAM-off) was born in Odessa, in what is now the Ukraine, in 1904. He trained at both the university in Odessa and subsequently at the University of Leningrad and became a prominent physicist and cosmologist in Russia, much respected by his Russian colleagues for his brilliance in the theoretical physics that he practiced. Although he was allowed to study at Gottingen and at the Theoretical Physics Institute of the University of Copenhagen (with time out to work at the Cavendish Laboratory at Cambridge University), Gamow became disillusioned with the oppressions of the Soviet Union, and he and his wife defected, in Brussels, in 1933, then moved to the United States in 1934. He worked at George Washington University in Washington, D.C., for 20 years, 1934-1954, spent a year at the University of California at Berkeley, 1955-1956, and ended his life's work at the University of Colorado at Boulder, from 1956 until his death in 1968.

The Creation of the Universe

Throughout his life in America Gamow worked with a who's who of the West's most important theoretical physicists; he was responsible for bringing them together in annual symposia. He studied and contributed to our knowledge of such physical phenomena as the nucleus of the atom, the construct of stars, the creation of the elements, the genetic code of life, quantum theory and, most notably, the Big Bang Theory of the origin of the universe. In 1948 with Ralph Alpher, he published a paper, "The Origin of Chemical Elements" that described what came to be known as the Alpher-Bethe-Gamow Theory—a theory proposing, as proof of "Big Bang," the current levels of hydrogen and helium in the universe (thought to make up 99 percent of all matter). Those levels could be explained only as a result of reactions that would have taken place if the Big Bang had actually occurred.

In 1946, too, he postulated the existence and the residual strength of background microwave radiation—again, a phenomenon that could be explained only by Big Bang (his speculation—that is, the existence of microwaves and their likely current strength—was later proved, in 1965). His contributions to this theory, and its refinements, are almost endless.

What is the Big Bang Theory? At its simplest, it holds that at one time, roughly 14 billion years ago, energy and matter were unbelievably condensed and that the "mixture" was almost immeasurably hot. This unimaginable concentration—call it the "original atom" then exploded (at that moment both space and time begin), threw out matter in all directions, which then coalesced into atoms. Which in time, created stars and planets and galaxies and eventually life itself, or just remained undifferentiated matter, all of which constantly retreats (the universe constantly expands) from the original "bang." Does this theory contradict religious belief- specifically, that God created heaven and earth, i.e., that God created the universe? Not necessarily. Most of the world's great religions have

乔治·伽莫夫
《宇宙的诞生》

乔治·伽莫夫

　　乔治·伽莫夫(其姓读作gam-off)1904年出生于敖德萨,该省位于现在的乌克兰。他曾就读于敖德萨大学,后来进了列宁格勒大学学习,并且成为俄国一位杰出的物理学家和天文学家。因其在理论物理学方面的突出贡献,他得到了俄国同行业人士的广泛赞誉。虽然伽莫夫曾被批准进入哥廷根大学和哥本哈根大学的理论物理研究所学习(业余时间在剑桥大学的卡文迪什实验室工作),但是前苏联的压制政策使得这一切化为泡影,1933年,他和妻子趁在布鲁塞尔的机会离开前苏联,1934年,移居美国。直到1954年伽莫夫在位于华盛顿特区的华盛顿大学工作了20年。1955年到1956年他在伯克利加州大学任教一年。从1956年起他在波尔德的科罗拉多大学工作一直到他1968年去世。

《宇宙的诞生》

　　伽莫夫在美国工作期间与西方最著名的物理学家在一起共事,他负责把他们的想法汇总成年度专题论文集。伽莫夫在原子核物理方面、星体的结构、元素的生成机制、生命的遗传密码、量子理论研究上做出了重大贡献,此外,他还提出了最著名的"宇宙大爆炸"学说。1948年,他和拉尔夫·阿尔菲共同发表了题为"大爆炸元素合成"的论文,后来称为"阿尔菲-贝特-伽莫夫理论"——这一理论提出了当前宇宙间存在的氢元素和氦元素的比例(被认为是占所有物质成分的99%),以此来支持"宇宙大爆炸"理论。这些成分的比例只有作为宇宙大爆炸确实发生之后物质间相互作用的结果才能被解释。

　　此外,伽莫夫还于1946年预言宇宙微波背景辐射的存在——再一次,提出这一现象只有以宇宙大爆炸的发生为前提(他的假说——微波及其可能发出的辐射力的存在——后来于1965年得到证实)。伽莫夫提出并改善了这一理论,他在这一方面的贡献是巨大的。

　　如何解释"宇宙大爆炸"理论呢?简单讲,它提出大约在140亿年前宇宙间的能量和物质的密度高得令人难以置信,并且这个"混沌体"的高温几乎无法测量。这一聚集——称作"初始原子"后来爆炸(从那时起,时间和空间便诞生了)向周围喷出物质,这些物质继而合成了原子。之后,形成了星体、行星和银河系,最后便有了生命体,有的物质仍然保持分化不良的状态,所有一切都从"爆炸"后不断地外溢(宇宙在不断扩展)。那么,这一理论是否违背了宗教信仰——尤其是认为上帝创造了天和地,上帝造世说呢?我看不见得。世界上绝大多数的宗教都已经接受了这一理论。比如,教皇皮乌斯七世便是这一理论早期的非常积极的支持者,并且罗马天主教会也承认用"大爆炸理论"解释宇宙的起源有其合

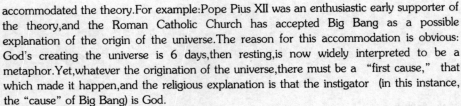

accommodated the theory. For example: Pope Pius XII was an enthusiastic early supporter of the theory, and the Roman Catholic Church has accepted Big Bang as a possible explanation of the origin of the universe. The reason for this accommodation is obvious: God's creating the universe is 6 days, then resting, is now widely interpreted to be a metaphor. Yet, whatever the origination of the universe, there must be a "first cause," that which made it happen, and the religious explanation is that the instigator (in this instance, the "cause" of Big Bang) is God.

Gamow's accomplishment in defining aspects of Big Bang, in other words, is a very substantial—but, with the possible exception of Einstein and his theories of relativity, most of the great advances in science in the 20th century have been collective accomplishments. A very large number of people has been involved in what we now know of the structure of the atom or the components of our universe and, pre-eminently, Big Bang itself. In some ways, almost all of contemporary theoretical physics is an attempt to refine the theory of Big Bang. Although he is sometimes cited as the "Father of Big Bang," that attribution is a mistake, one that only laymen, not other physicists, would make.

Gamow, amazingly, given that he seemed to work 24/7, was also the author of a number of books, and it is for these books that we most remember him today. His accomplishment in these books is substantial, because, in them, he did what many people thought could not be done. He explains in layman's terms some of the most difficult concepts in modern theoretical physics. So successful was he at doing so that Unesco awarded him its Kalinga Prize (for the popularization of science) in 1956. Two of his most famous books-*Mr. Tompkins in Wonderland* in 1940 and *Mr. Tompkins Explores the Atom* in 1945—remain in print to the present day. Cambridge University Press brought out a combined edition of the two books, as *Mr. Tompkins in Paperback*, in the 1990s. In these books, Gamow creates an Everyman, an inquisitive bank clerk, Mr. Tompkins. He puts him through a series of adventures. the result of which is that the difficult principles of relativity and quantum theory are explained in a way that makes sense not just to adults but also to young people.

One, Two, Three...Infinity of 1947 attempts to explain modern science, from biology to crystallography, to the same audience. *Thirty Years That Shook Physics: The Story of Quantum Theory* is perhaps more theoretical but still comprehensible to the lay reader.

These are by no means his only books, and all of them will repay the modern lay reader, providing him or her with insight into the scientific marvels of our time. But it is perhaps *The Creation of the Universe* in 1952 (revised, 1961; reissued, 2004) that all of us should have read. For it is here that Gamow most cogently, most exhaustively, explains the Big Bang Theory (as well as the opposing, "steady state," theory of the universe). Obviously, a half century has passed since he wrote the book, and new discoveries are made about our universe on practically a yearly basis. Yet all of these discoveries are really confirmations of theories well known to Gamow (indeed, many of those theories were devised by him) at the time he wrote his book. For anyone wishing to know the basics of creation—and who does not? *The Creation of the Universe* remains our most comprehensible explanation and, for that reason, perhaps the greatest scientific text, for lay readers, about the modern scientific revolution in physics and about the way that we now view the universe.

理性。这一理论能够得到他们的认同理由很明显:对于上帝用6天时间创造了宇宙万物之后便休息了的说法,现在被普遍看做是一个比喻。但是,无论宇宙从何起源,肯定要有一个"起因"使其发生,而宗教观点认为上帝就是这个引发者(在宗教界看来,这便是"大爆炸"的"起因")。

伽莫夫在提出"大爆炸"理论方面做出了突出的贡献——不过,除了爱因斯坦及其相对论,20世纪在科学上取得的重大进展大部分都是集体智慧的结晶。很多人都参与了原子结构和宇宙构成的研究工作,并且在最著名的"大爆炸"理论的提出上做出了他们的贡献。从某种角度上看,几乎所有现代的物理学专家都试图完善"大爆炸"理论。虽然,伽莫夫有时候被称作"大爆炸理论的始祖",但是这一叫法并不正确,除了外行,专业的物理学家们不会犯这个错误。

令人吃惊的是,伽莫夫写下了24~27部著作,并且这些作品使现代人了解了他。他在这些作品中提出了许多人们认为是不可能做到的事情。伽莫夫用通俗的语言解释了现代物理学中许多最难理解的概念。由于他在普及科学知识方面作出的杰出贡献,1956年,联合国教科文组织为他颁发了卡林伽奖(一个科普奖项)。伽莫夫的两部最著名的作品——《汤普金斯先生身历奇境》(1940)和《汤普金斯先生探索原子世界》(1945)至今仍在印刷出版。90年代的时候,剑桥大学出版社合订了两部作品,题为《物理世界奇遇记》。伽莫夫在书中塑造了一个家喻户晓的人物形象,主人公是一个叫汤普金斯的满怀好奇的银行职员。他游历了一系列的奇境,最终了解了难懂的相对论和量子理论,文中以一种老少皆宜的方式娓娓道来。

1947年,面向普通大众出版了《从一到无穷大》,试图解释整个现代科学,内容涉及从生物学到结晶学。《震惊物理学的三十年:量子理论的故事》或许更理论化一些,但对大众读者来说仍然是通俗易懂的。

伽莫夫的作品远不止以上这些,他所有的著作将出版发行以敬现代读者,让大众都能够了解现代科学的奥秘。但是,1952年出版的《宇宙的诞生》(1961年修订,2004年重新发行)是所有人都应该读一下的。因为在这一作品中,伽莫夫非常详尽非常彻底地阐述了"宇宙大爆炸"理论(同时反驳了"稳恒态"宇宙理论)。很明显,自此书被创作以来已经过了半个世纪,并且每年都会有关宇宙的新的发现。然而,所有的发现事实上都证实了伽莫夫在其作品中提出的著名理论(确实,很多理论都是当时伽莫夫提出的)。对于任何希望了解宇宙起源的人——谁又会不愿了解呢?《宇宙的诞生》以通俗的语言为普通大众展现了现代物理学方面的科学革命以及对宇宙的认识,因此,对大众读者来说,它可能是最伟大的科学著作。

Forty-five

Samuel Beckett: Waiting for Godot

Who Was Samuel Beckett?

The Irish writer Samuel Beckett (1906-1989) wrote plays and stories about the human condition. Though they were sometimes laced with humor, most of his works are deeply pessimistic.

Beckett was born and raised in Dublin. He was athletic, excelled at cricket, and he went on to play successfully for Dublin University. At Trinity College Dublin, he studied Italian and French, as well as English, and later became a lecturer in English in Paris. While there, he was introduced to James Joyce who became both a good friend and an important influence on Beckett's work. In 1929 Beckett published his first work "Dante…Bruno.Vico…Joyce," an essay on Joyce's writing. In 1936 Beckett settled permanently in Paris.

His two-act tragic comedy *Waiting for Godot*, first presented in Paris in 1953, established him as a major international playwright, even though its meaning, and that of his other plays, have been endlessly debated.

Backett received the Nobel Prize for Literature in 1969.

Waiting for Godot

Many critics would claim that Samuel Beckett is the greatest playwright of the 20th century.

He was a true cosmopolitan. Though born and raised in Ireland, he went to live in Paris at the age of 30 and remained there for the rest of his life (he wrote in French, then himself translated his works into English). He was the friend/confidante of the great Irish writer James Joyce, who also spent a good part of his life in Paris and is himself regarded as the most innovative novelist of the 20th century. Beckett was far more diverse in his literary output than was Joyce. Besides a number of plays, Beckett also wrote well-regarded poetry and novels.

But it is his plays, in English, that have had the greatest influence on his times—and it is *Waiting for Godot* that is still regarded as the most important of those plays. It seems to have come from nowhere. He wrote two plays before Godot—one is lost; the other is known only to scholars, because it was never produced or published. Five years later, in 1952, he published *Waiting for Godot*. It was produced on stage in Paris the following year. He translated it into English in 1954, and it was produced in London and New York in 1955-1956. Since then, it has probably been produced at least once by every college drama department in the United States and Europe.

Suddenly, and ever since, the previous unknown Beckett became a household word. Why this acclaim? Because, more than anyone else, Beckett captured and defined an essential part of one aspect of the thought of the last century.

The play, in two acts, is very simple in its plot. In act one the tramps Vladimir and Estragon wait, by the side of a road, for Godot—they have an appointment with him. Pozzo

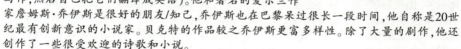

萨缪尔·贝克特
《等待戈多》

萨缪尔·贝克特

　　爱尔兰作家萨缪尔·贝克特(1906~1989)所作的戏剧和小说都是反映人类生活的。虽然,他的作品时而带有幽默情节,但绝大部分都是极具悲观色彩的。

　　贝克特出生于都柏林,并在那里长大。他非常喜欢体育运动,最擅长打板球,在都柏林大学就读期间继续他的爱好,表现也极为优秀。他曾在都柏林三一学院学习意大利语、法语和英语,后来在巴黎高等师范学校任英语语言讲师。在巴黎逗留期间,他经介绍结识了詹姆斯·乔伊斯,两人成为很好的朋友,乔伊斯对贝克特的写作影响非常大。1929年,贝克特发表了他的第一部作品《但丁……布鲁诺·维柯……乔伊斯》,这是一篇关于乔伊斯作品的专题论文。

　　1936年,贝克特定居巴黎。

　　他的两幕悲喜剧《等待戈多》于1953年首次在巴黎面世,这部作品奠定了他跻身于重要的国际性剧作家的基础,即便如此,此剧及其他剧作的意义一直备受争议。

　　1969年,贝克特荣获诺贝尔文学奖。

《等待戈多》

　　许多评论家都声称萨缪尔·贝克特是20世纪最伟大的剧作家。

　　贝克特见多识广,他在爱尔兰出生并在那里长大,30岁的时候移居巴黎,在那里度过了他的余生(他先用法语写作,然后自己把它们翻译成英语)。他和著名的爱尔兰作家詹姆斯·乔伊斯是很好的朋友/知己,乔伊斯也在巴黎呆过很长一段时间,他自称是20世纪最有创新意识的小说家。贝克特的作品较之乔伊斯更富多样性。除了大量的剧作,他还创作了一些很受欢迎的诗歌和小说。

　　但是,贝克特的英文戏剧为他所生活的年代带来了最为深刻的影响——其中《等待戈多》仍然被认为是最重要的一部。从这部作品中我们似乎找不到源头。在此之前作者还创作了两部戏剧——其中一部丢失了;另一部只有学术界才了解,因为此作从未出版发行。5年之后,即1952年,贝克特出版了《等待戈多》。第二年,在巴黎被搬上了舞台。1954年,他将其翻译成英文,1955年到1956年此剧在伦敦和纽约上映。从那以后,可能在每个美国和欧洲国家大学的戏剧学院都要上演至少一次。

　　瞬间,之前不知名的贝克特成为家喻户晓的人物。为什么他会那么备受欢迎呢?因为贝克特超越了所有其他的人,他捕捉并界定了上个世纪人们思想中的一个基本的层面。

　　这部戏剧非常简单,只有两幕剧情。在第一幕中,两个无家可归的流浪汉弗拉基米尔和艾斯特拉冈在路旁等待戈多——他们有预约。波卓和他的仆人乐克出现,并且波卓嘲

and his sidekick Lucky turn up,and Pozzo taunts the two tramps,says that he owns the land on which they wait.They are followed by a boy who announces that Godot will not come today but will almost certainly come tomorrow.The second act is really a repeat of the first, except that,when they arrive,Pozzo has now gone blind,and Lucky is mute.Although the play is interesting when read,and compelling when presented on stage—its language and images are stunning—it is essentially about things not happening.Finally,nothing really happens in the play,according to audience expectations of the "dramatic"—however cleverly it is presented,the play involves futility and inertia.At the conclusion the tramps decide to move on,but the play ends with their doing nothing,just staying where they are.

What does it all mean? The play has been endlessly interpreted,but most people agree that Beckett is dramatizing the tedium,repetition and pointlessness of human life.We deal with provocations,with events,but otherwise all we do is wait for some intervention that does not come—an intervention that will give our lives meaning (by Godot? by God?).

There is a recurring attitude among people of the Western world in the past century that is profoundly pessimistic.There are variants on this notion.Nevertheless,it seems to be the same notion,endlessly repeating itself.The notion has its beginnings,perhaps,with the disaffected intellectuals of late 19th century Russia—the "nihilists." World War I,with its disillusionments (it was a war,its participants came to feel,that had been fought for no purpose other than to enrich Western industrialists),which had in turn produced what the writer Gertrude Stein called the "lost generation," disaffected young people who railed against the world as they found it,lived only for gratification of the senses,believed that everything else in life was "meaningless." After World War II,the disillusionment was felt again-expressed by the "Beat Poets" of the day.And still the malaise continues—in the "live for money" attitudes of the 1980s,or in the rather more universal notions that "God is Dead" (never shows up,is always expected) and that the only way to live life is to regard it as only a chance for self-gratification.

Of course,there has always been,in all of this,a strain of utopian reform—thus the Russian Revolution,also an event of World War I,in which the attitude seems most to have been that if an economic system that benefited everyone could replace one that benefited just a few,then the world would be a better place.Or,a generation or two later,much of the world believed that if the empire created by that revolution could just be destroyed,then the world would be a better place—or if the industrial power structures of the West could be replaced by a system that exalts the individual,then we will all be happy.The century abounds in other such one-change-fits-all solutions.In our own time:If we can just defeat some extremists,if we can just bring democracy to the Middle East,then the world will be a better place,and we will all live happily ever after.

But,despite these activist solutions,the passive solution is simply that life finally is meaningless,that one responds only to events (Pozzo and Lucky),that Godot is never going to arrive.This is the basis of the attitudes of the existentialist philosophers who became so popular after World War II—that,because human life is meaningless,because there are no determinants,because good and evil are simply human constructs,man must,to have any kind of purpose in life,invent himself and decide what gratifies him personally.Otherwise there is no hope—not from society,not from a Supreme Being:we will always be sitting on

笑这两个流浪汉,自称是他们所在的那片土地的主人。之后,一个孩子告诉他们戈多当天不会到,不过第二天很可能会来。第二幕实际上是前一幕的重复,除了当两个流浪汉到那的时候,波卓的眼睛变瞎了,乐克也变聋了。虽然,这部剧作读起来很有趣,并且搬上舞台之后也激起了强烈的反响——它的语言和人物形象都是出人意料的——它基本上是在表达没有发生的事情。最终,就像观众期待的"戏剧效果"那样,剧中的确什么也没有发生。多么巧妙的演绎,这部剧作暗含着一种"无效"和"惯性"。在剧终,两个流浪汉决定继续赶路,但是最后他们就站在原地,什么也没做。

这意味着什么呢?此剧作不断地被人阐释,但是大多数人都认为贝克特是在将人生的乏味、重复和漫无目的戏剧化。我们都在应付生活中的挑衅和事件,但是,此外我们都要等待某种未知的介入——这种介入将给予我们的人生以意义(由戈多?由上帝?)

在上个世纪带有强烈的悲观色彩的西方世界,人们的头脑中都有一种历史重复的思想。这一意识有不同的变体。然而,似乎是同一种观念在不断地重复。也许,这种观念源于19世纪晚期俄国的"思想不满人士"——"虚无主义者"。第一次世界大战造成了人们思想的幻灭(参与这场战争的人开始感觉这场战争毫无意义,只是让西方的工业者获得了暴利),继而产生了作家格楚德·斯泰因笔下的"迷惘的一代",指的是对现实世界不满的青年一代,他们只为情感的满足而活,并且相信除此以外的任何其他事物都"没有意义"。二战以后,这种思想的幻灭再次发生——正如"垮掉一代的诗人"所表达的那样。这种思想的"不自在"继续发展到20世纪80年代的"为金钱而生"的价值观,或者更加通用的"上帝已死"的观念(上帝从未显身,他只存在于人们的意念中),而生活唯一的出路就是把它当成实现自我满足的机会。

当然,一直都有一股理想化的改革张力贯穿其中——像俄国的改革,一战也一样,人们的态度似乎是:如果有一个可以造福全民的经济体制可以取代只为少数人谋利的体制,那么世界将会更加美好。或者,一两代人之后,由革命建成的帝国如果被消灭,那么世界也将更加美好。又或者,如果西方的工业体系能够被有利于个人发展的体系所替代,那么所有人的生活都将更加幸福。这样的解决办法对于以后也是一劳永逸的。对于我们现在所生活的年代来说:如果我们可以打败某些极端分子,为中东地区带去民主,那么整个世界将会更加美好,我们所有的人今后都将过上幸福的生活。

但是,尽管有这些积极的解决方法,令人沮丧的是生活最终变得没有意义,可以看一下剧中波普和乐克的反映,戈多也将永远不会赴约。这是存在主义哲学家们基本的态度,他们在二战以后变得非常流行——因为人生是没有意义的,一切都没有定数,善和恶乃人类的秉性,人要想实现生活的目的,必须塑造自身并且选择什么才是有利于满足自身要求的。否则,社会也好,上帝也罢,都无法带给我们希望:我们只能一直处在别人的领地上,戈多也终将不会来赴与我们的约会。

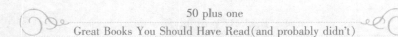
someone else's land,Godot will never keep his appointment with us.

But that somewhat positive approach to life of the existentialists (it assumes,after all, that if life has no cosmic purpose,it can have a personal purpose) is a step or two beyond what Beckett was doing.The great accomplishment of *Waiting for Godot* is that it defines the sense of helplessness,of purposeless,that so many people in the last century have felt. Perhaps they go on to believe in new systems of government or morality.Perhaps they go on to develop new philosophical stances.The expression goes:If you've hit bottom,there is nowhere to go but up.Beckett,in *Waiting for Godot*,more tellingly than in any other modern work,describes what,for modern man,the "bottom" has actually meant.It is this facet of the work that most accounts for its enduring appeal-the beauty of its rendering of the "nothingness" that so many modern men and women have felt.

　　然而,对于那些存在主义者们生活中也有积极的一面(毕竟,假使生活没有大同的目的,那可以以个人为目的),它离贝克特所刻画的剧情只有几步之遥。《等待戈多》之所以伟大在于它定义了上个世纪中人们的无望和漫无目标。也许,他们会继而信仰新的政府体制或道德规范;也许,他们会继续发展出新的哲学观点。可以这样表述:如果你已经坠到谷底,那么你无处再继续下沉,只能上升。贝克特在《等待戈多》中超越了所有其他的现代作品,为现代人描述了"谷底"的真实含义。这一层面正是此剧作不朽的魅力所在——对很多现代人"虚无"的情感世界的完美刻画。

Forty-six

Marshall McLuhan: Understanding Media

Who Was Marshall McLuhan?

The place called "The Global Village" or the expression "The medium is the message" are now so much a part of our contemporary vocabulary that it seems as if they have always been there. But they didn't spring into existence on their own. They come to us from the life's work of Marshall McLuhan, a Canadian scholar and communications theorist who was a Professor of English at the University of Toronto from the end of World War II until 1979 (he died in 1980).

McLuhan was just as ordinary, in demeanor and career, as that description suggests. A native of Alberta, he did a B.A. and M.A. in English at the University of Manitoba, then did his work toward at a Ph.D. at Cambridge University in England. There, he studied with I.A. Richards and F.R. Leavis, two of the great gurus of the New Criticism, which holds that literary works are entities in themselves—standalone art works—that exist without reference to their writer's biographies, that are completely understandable as verbal constructs (edifices made of words). Their thought influenced him—but one can't push that influence too far. McLuhan is really unique. This mild and formerly obscure professor created some of the most influential scholarly works of the 20th century—notably *The Mechanical Bride* (1951), *The Gutenberg Galaxy* (1962), *The Medium Is the Massage* (1967), and, perhaps most notably, *Understanding Media* (1964), works that utterly changed the way in which scholars, but also ordinary men and women, thought about the workings of the media, which have been so integral a part of all of our lives in the years since World War I.

Understanding Media

Ironically, given his popular fame, Marshall McLuhan is actually very complex. His writings have spawned an industry of commentators telling us what he was really talking about—which explanations are often themselves so complex that they require even further explanation. Yet, McLuhan's basic ideas—however he may have chosen to elaborate them—are actually simple and comprehensible to the ordinary reader.

McLuhan starts by saying that different kinds of media have characteristics of their own different from the content that they are actually delivering—hence the "medium is the message" expression. For example: The experience of reading *Gone with the Wind* is different from the experience of seeing the movie of the novel, which in turn would be different from seeing it as a play, as a theatrical presentation. If such a play existed—and all would be different yet again if various people were gathered in the same place, reading the novel on a gigantic television or computer screen. Yet the content is the same; it is the same novel, involving the same characters and scenes and incidents. From these differences in our experience of each medium, McLuhan concludes that different media must convey different messages (different from the content itself), which is another way of saying, as well, that our response must necessarily be different. As the human response is so different, could it not be

马歇尔·麦克卢汉
《理解媒介》

马歇尔·麦克卢汉

"地球村"或者"媒介就是信息"这一表述现在已经被广泛运用于我们现代人的语言，似乎它们原来就一直存在。然而，它们并不是自己冒出来的，而是源自马歇尔·麦克卢汉一生的研究，他是一位加拿大学者，同时也是一名传媒理论家，他自二战结束到1979年期间曾任多伦多大学的英语教授(他于1980年逝世)。

就像人们所描述的那样，麦克卢汉的仪表和他的事业都是朴实的。他出生于亚伯达，在曼尼托巴大学拿到英语文学学士和硕士学位，后来到英国剑桥大学留学，继续攻读博士学位。在那里，麦克卢汉与I.A.瑞恰慈和F.R.利维斯同窗学习，他们两位都是新批评学派的大师，倡导文学作品应该是自身存在的实体——独立于艺术作品——文学作品的存在不应借助作家的自传，它们作为文字建筑(用文字建造的实体)是完全可以被理解的。两人的思想影响了麦克卢汉——但是，这一影响并非长远。麦克卢汉的确是不同凡响的，这位谦和的、往日里并不知名的教授创作了20世纪最具影响力的学术作品——著名的《机器新娘》(1951)，《古腾堡星系》(1962)，《媒介即信息》(1967)，还有最有名的《理解媒介》(1964)，这些作品彻底改变了专家学者和普通百姓对于媒介传播的看法，一战以来它已经成为人们生活中必不可少的一部分。

《理解媒介》

有趣的是，马歇尔·麦克卢汉虽然闻名于世，但他的作品实际上非常复杂，引起很多评论家都来为我们阐释他在作品中表达的含义——而这些阐释本身通常也是很难理解，需要有进一步的解释。不过，麦克卢汉的基本思想——无论多么字斟句酌——事实上对普通读者来说是非常通俗易懂的。

麦克卢汉在作品中一开始便阐述了不同类型的媒介都有其自身的特质，这些特质区别于它们所传播的具体内容——因此，可以说"媒介就是信息"。比如，阅读《飘》这部小说和观看由它所拍成的电影时人们的感受是不同的，而观看这样一部话剧又与戏剧演绎大相径庭。如果真有这样一部话剧——不同的观众聚在同一个地方观看此剧，也许在大型电视屏幕前或者电脑前阅读这部小说，那么一切都会不同。然而，内容却是相同的；都是针对同一部小说，涉及相同的人物、场景和事件。从每个媒介所得到的不同体验中，麦克卢汉总结出不同的媒介必然传播不同的信息(区别于它所承载的内容本身)，也就是说，我们的反应必然是不一样的。人类的反应如此多样，麦克卢汉问道，每个媒介怎么可能没有自己独有的特点呢？

said,McLuhan asks,that each medium has characteristics of its own?

He further differentiates between "hot" media (that which requires very little participation on our part,just the participation of one sense)-for example,the movies.Or "cool" media,that which requires a great deal of participation,because not all facts are provided to us as in a picture book or comic book.

It is one of McLuhan's favorite tenets that our culture was originally,when it emerged from the barbarous to the civilized,aural and visual—the world in which writer/composers such as Homer would have sung or recited their stories to a group of listeners.They responded as if they were a tribe,a collective of people.This was a kind of revolution in culture.The coming of print creates another revolution.Suddenly man is coping with a medium on his own,not collectively,not tribally.This is one of the major revolutions in human experience because the advent of the solitary leads to the concept of specialization, to secularization,even to the notion of sovereign countries,which are a kind of specialization:we are German (i.e.,have the consciousness of Germans) as opposed to we are Chinese (i.e.,have the consciousness of Chinese).

He believes that a third,and perhaps even more dramatic,revolution has taken place in the recent past and continues to the present time.The electronic revolution of the movies, radio,television,and the computer (though McLuhan precedes the world wide web,he anticipates it in all of his writings).Once again,and ironically,considering that most of us imagine these inventions to be great technological advances,he sees us as reverting to the tribe.

His description "The Global Village" has been much bandied about-to mean that the great miracle of modern media technology is that the world has been brought closer together. What McLuhan is saying is not precisely the opposite—but,he is much more pessimistic than most commentators about whether this kind of globalization is a good thing.He is warning that when electronic media replaces visual cultures (by which he means the culture of the printed word),then the tendency will be for mankind to move from individualism,from being "specialists," to a kind of collective identity.It's a very simple step,for him,from that prediction to this:That a world that has a collective identity—that is,one that's a "global village"—has the great potential to become a place where terrorism and totalitarian governments rule.If we are all the same,then we are easy to dominate—as if we were robots.

We need go no further than to contemplate television,in which packaged shows from advanced countries are shown round the world—never more comprehensively than now; or to contemplate the modern internet,which threatens to reduce all media (from books to recordings to movies to letters between individuals) to just one world-accessible single medium,to realize that McLuhan's concerns warrant our attention.

Finally he is saying this—and it is worth our contemplation:Any media technologies have an effect on our thought processes,which in turn affect how we organize ourselves socially.Print technology led to world wars between people who had organized themselves as nationalities or religions,but it also led to what is best in our culture:individualism and democracy.Are we quite sure that we like where the new technologies seem to be leading, which could well be the totalitarian state and,as he says,an atmosphere of constant violence? "Violence,whether spiritual or physical,is a quest for identity and the meaningful. The less identity,the more violence." His warnings are well worth heeding as we head further and further into the third great revolution in media.

他还进一步区分了"热"媒介(指接受者参与程度较低,只需要动用一种感官)——比如电影。而"冷"媒介则需要人们更多的参与其中,因为像图片或者漫画那样,不是所有的信息都直接提供给我们。

麦克卢汉最崇尚的信条之一便是我们的文化在由野蛮发展到文明的最初阶段就是可听可见的——当时像荷马一样的作家们便为一群听众唱出或者吟诵他们的故事。这些听众就像来自一个部落的族民。后来,文化中出现了改革,印刷术的发明造成了另一次重大革新。突然间,人们可以单独面对媒介,不用搞集体形式,也不用像部族人们那样。这是人类体验的一个重要的改革,因为人类独居生活的开始促进了专门化、通俗化,以至主权国家的诞生——我们是德国人(假设受德国社会的意识形态的影响)与我们作为中国人的身份(假设拥有中国社会的思想意识)是截然不同的。

麦克卢汉认为第三次,或许更加戏剧性的改革已经在前不久的历史阶段展开,并且一直持续到现代。在电子领域出现了电影、收音机、电视以及电脑的革命(虽然麦克卢汉生活在网络世界之前,但他在其所有的作品中对此都有预言)。另一点饶有趣味的是,我们大多数人都认为这些发明创造乃是巨大的科技进步的成果,而麦克卢汉则把我们视为是在回归原始部落。

麦克卢汉提出的"地球村"这一概念已经是众所周知——意思是现代传媒技术取得了惊人的进步,世界已经紧密地联系在了一起。麦克卢汉所指代的并非反面的意思——但是,针对全球化是否是一件好事,他比大部分评论家更为悲观。他是在警示一旦电子媒介取代了可视文化(麦克卢汉指的是打印的用文字记载的文化),那么人类往后的趋势便是从个体主义、"专门主义"发展到集体主义的状态。对麦克卢汉来说,很容易从这一预言做出这样的推论:一个集体主义的世界——即"地球村"——极有可能变成一个由恐怖主义和极权主义政府统治的地方。如果我们都保持一致,那么我们将很容易被控制——就像机器人那样。

我们需要停下来认真思考一下电视,这一媒介把发达国家的信息"打包"后一股脑地呈现给全球的观众——从未有过像现代这样的解释力;或者仔细思量一下现代的因特网,它威胁到所有媒介的存在(从书本,到录音磁带,到电影,再到人们之间的书信交流),它只允许唯一的可以博览世界的媒介,使我们意识到麦克卢汉的观点的确给我们提出了警示。

他文中最后的几句话值得我们好好琢磨:任何传媒技术的发展都影响到人们思想的发展,继而影响我们的社会构成。印刷技术导致了世界大战,因为人们之间都形成了自己的民族和宗教,但是它也促进了文化的发展:个人意识和民主政治诞生。我们真的喜欢新科技把我们引向的世界吗?像麦克卢汉所预言,那里很可能充满了极权主义和暴力的气氛。"暴力,无论是在精神上还是肉体上,都将求向存在的身份和意义。越没有自主的身份,暴力就越猖獗。"在我们迈向第三次媒介革命的同时,麦克卢汉的警示值得我们好好地思考一下。

Forty-seven

Alan Turing:
On Computable Numbers

Who Was Alan Turing?

With regard to its stance on homosexuality, Great Britain is now one of the most liberal countries in the world. Homosexuals may serve in the military, they cannot be discriminated against in any commercial and social activities, and they are allowed to form and register domestic partnerships (the near equivalent of heterosexual marriage). Fifty years ago, in the years after the war, the situation was very different: homosexuality was a criminal offense. The scientist and mathematician Alan Turing (he was born in 1912), a homosexual, was arrested in 1952 in Manchester, where he was then a Deputy Director of the Computing Laboratory of the University of Manchester. His offense was that he had been sexually involved with another man. At one time, in 1943-1945, he had been head of Anglo-American efforts to break Axis codes, yet, as a result of his known homosexuality, he had already lost his security clearance. Turing was tried for this latest offense, convicted, and sentenced to forced therapy with estrogen, a misguided attempt on the part of law officials to "neutralize his libido." This barbaric therapy had a disastrous effect on him both emotionally and physically. In 1954, via the dramatic means of injecting an apple with cyanide, then eating the apple, he committed suicide.

His life became the basis of a successful biography by Andrew Hodges, *Alan Turing: The Enigma*, published in 1983. That book provided the inspiration for what became a well-known play by Hugh Whitemore called "Breaking the Code," which was produced in 1986. The title of both the biography and play refers to one of the great accomplishments of Turing's life—as the leader of a team in Britain's Department of Communications during World War II, he was directly responsible for solving ENIGMA, a German machine that produced codes that described Axis military operations, particularly their naval operations in the North Atlantic. "Breaking the code," most military historians agree, lead to the Allied victory in the naval part of the conflict.

On Computable Numbers

The tragedy of the end of Alan Turing's life (he died when he was only 42), and the posthumous fame that the famous biography and play accorded him (the play ran for 2 years, first in London, then in New York). The play drew on the more sensational aspects of Turing's life, have obscured the greatest accomplishment of that life—not that he broke the code but that he was, by any measure, the father of what is perhaps the most influential of all the inventions of modern life—the computer.

In *On Computable Numbers*, a book that he wrote when he was only 24 and just starting his work toward a Ph.D. at Princeton, he discusses, plants the seeds of, everything to which he would devote the remainder of his life—which is no less than the greatest single invention of the 20th century, the one that has most revolutionized modern life, has led to increased communications between businesses and individuals, and may be more responsible

阿兰·图灵
《论可计算数》

阿兰·图灵

提到对同性恋的态度，现代的英国是世界上最自由开明的国家之一。同性恋者可以参军，在任何的经济和社交活动中他们都不能被歧视，并且他们被允许组建和登记家庭伙伴关系(几乎与双性的婚姻关系平等)。50年前，战后的几年中，形式完全不同：同性恋被看做是犯罪行为。作为科学家和数学家的阿兰·图灵(他生于1912年)是一个同性恋者，1952年他在曼彻斯特被捕，当时他正任曼彻斯特大学计算机实验室的副主任。他的罪名是和另外一个男性有不正当关系。1943年到1945年，图灵担任英美密码破译部门的总顾问。然而，因为他同性恋倾向为外界所知，于是被取消了安全特许。图灵接受了审判，并被定罪，他被强行注射荷尔蒙治疗，这是法律官员为"中和他的性欲"而做出的错误的尝试。这项残忍的治疗方法对图灵的身心都造成了毁灭性的影响。1954年，他食用了一个注入氰化物溶液的苹果自杀结束了自己的一生。

安德鲁·哈吉斯为图灵写的一部脍炙人口的传记《谜一样的图灵》于1983年出版。这本书启发了休·怀特摩尔的灵感创作出著名的舞台剧《解密》，此剧于1986年上演。在此，传记和戏剧的题目都揭示了图灵一生中一项重大贡献——二战期间，他担任英国通讯部的带头人，直接负责破译德国军方使用的著名通信密码系统"谜"(ENIGMA)，敌方的这一密码系统尤其用来指挥北大西洋上的作战。绝大多数军事历史学家都认同"破译密码"促成了同盟国海军作战的胜利。

《论可计算数》

阿兰·图灵生命的最后演出了一段悲剧(他去世的时候年仅42岁)，然而，在他逝世以后，记载他一生的著名传记和舞台剧为其赢得了荣誉(这部舞台剧在伦敦和纽约先后上演了两年)。此剧展现了图灵一生中更加不同寻常的一面，而没有强调他所做的巨大成就——不是指他破译了密码，而是说，无论从那一方面评判，他都称得上是现代生活中造成最深刻影响的发明之始祖，这一发明便是电脑。

《论可计算数》是图灵在他24岁的时候写成的，这本书写于他在普林斯顿大学攻读博士学位的开始阶段，他自称这部作品为他后半生所要从事的事业播下了种子——这一著作称得上是20世纪最伟大的个人创造，它最大限度地革新了现代生活，加强了商务和个人之间的交流，并且较之其他的因素这一作品更大程度上促成了现代商业的"全球化"。

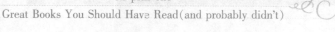

for the "globalization" of modern commerce than any other single factor.

Probably most modern readers—particularly those who are neither scientists nor mathematicians—will not be able to comprehend all of this book:it is enough to skim it,to "dip in"—to glimpse the breadth of Turing's thought—and to realize to what that thought led.

Here are some of the concepts that he later developed:

The Turing Machine is one that would read a series of ones and zeros from a tape.The ones and zeros described the steps that need to happen in order to solve a particular problem/task).A "program," we would now say.The Machine would read each of the steps and perform them in sequence—which brought the machine to the proper answer.This Machine,the concept of which he continued to develop after publication of On Computable Numbers,is essentially today's multi-task digital computer.

In fact,the breaking of the ENIGMA codes during World War II relied on a device, largely developed by Turing,based on his precepts,called COLOSSUS.The brilliance of ENIGMA was that,itself a kind of computer,it constantly changed the codes that the Germans were using.Just as soon as the Allies had deciphered one German code,ENIGMA would change the code,and the Allies work proved useless.COLOSSUS,a precursor of the digital computer,quickly deciphered whatever ENIGMA could devise.

Turing continued his experiments with digital computers after the war—at the National Physical Laboratory—and developed the Automatic Computing Engine (ACE),one of the first attempts to create a true digital computer.In 1950 he developed what is now known as the Turing Test.It consists of asking both a person and a machine (a computer) a series of questions—at the point at which the answers do not differ,the machine may be said to be "intelligent"—and the Turing Test is now seen as the precursor of the concepts of artificial intelligence—as was Turing's article "Intelligent Machinery," which was published after his death,in 1969.

Turing continued his work on an Automatic Digital Machine when he moved to Manchester,where he worked on the Manchester Automatic Digital Machine (MADAM) and created an operating manual for his invention.Turing believed that by the year 2000 computers so sophisticated could be developed that they would in essence replace the human mind.That hasn't happened,but most computer scientists believe it is only a matter of time before such computers exist.

Turing was not only a very great scientist-but also one of the great thinkers about the modern computer,if not the greatest one of all,the one who most deserves the title of its inventor.All of his work,from his mid-20's until his death at 42,has its foundation in what he writes in On Computable Numbers.It is one of the most important scientific documents of the 20th century—one that was destined to change the world in which we live and to cause Turing,now,to be regarded as the Founder of Computer Science.

　　大部分现代读者——尤其是那些既不是科学家又非数学家的人——可能不能完全理解此作品,不过,只要略读就够了,仅仅"浏览一下"就足以领略图灵思想的广博,并理解他的思想对人们的启迪意义。

　　以下是图灵后来提出的一些概念:

　　"图灵机"是一种在纸带上标出一系列编号为1和0的计算模型。这众多的"1"和"0"描述了为了处理某个特定问题或某项任务要实施的步骤。我们现在称之为"程序"。图灵机将读出每一个步骤,并按顺序进行操作——最终机器会得出一个合理的答案。在《论可计算数》出版之后,图灵机继续发展,直到改进为今天的可以处理多重任务的数字电脑。

　　事实上,二战期间成功地破解德军的"谜"(ENIGMA)是靠一台叫"巨人"(COLOSSUS)的装置,而这台设备基本上依赖于图灵的理论。"谜"(ENIGMA)的绝妙之处在于它本身就是一款电脑,可以不断地变换德国军方所使用的密码。而一旦盟军破解了德方其中的一个代码,"谜"就会更改密码,这样盟军的努力就白费了。而"巨人",这个数字电脑的前身,立刻破译了"谜"的"诡计"。

　　战后,图灵在英国国家物理实验室继续他对数字电脑的实验,并发明了自动计算引擎(ACE),这是创制一台真正的数字电脑的首次尝试。1950年,他提出了我们今天所称的"图灵试验"。这个测试包括问一个人和一台机器(电脑)一系列的问题——当两者的回答一致的情况下,这台机器可以说是能"思维"的。"图灵试验"现在被看做是"人工智能"的先驱——图灵的题为"智能装置"的论文在他去世之后的1969年发表。

　　图灵到了曼彻斯特以后继续研制自动计算机,在那里他开发了曼彻斯特自动计算机(MADAM),并且为他的这一发明写了一本操作指南。图灵相信到2000年一定可以制造出更加精密的电脑,那么它们基本上就可以替代人类的智能了。虽然这一天还没有来临,但是大多数电脑专家认为这只是一个时间问题。

　　图灵不仅仅是一名伟大的科学家,他还是关于现代电脑的伟大的思想家之一,就算不是最伟大的一位,他也最有资格获得"计算机之父"的称号。大约从图灵25岁直至去世,他的所有研究工作都是基于他写的《论可计算数》这一著作,这是20世纪最重要的科学文献之一——它改变了我们所生存的世界,并且为图灵赢得了"计算机科学之奠基人"的称号。

Forty-eight

Saul Bellow:
Henderson the Rain King

Who Was Saul Bellow?

Saul Beloow,who had a very long life (he lived from 1915 to 2005) is now widely regarded as one of the two greatest American novelists of the 20th century; the other one is William Faulkner.Bellow,of the two,had the more cosmopolitan life.A Jew,he was born in Canada in what is now a section of Montreal,soon after his parents had emigrated from Russia to Canada.To improve their position,to get better-paid work,his family moved to Chicago when he was 9 years old.Until he moved to Boston when he was nearly 80 years old-to take up a new academic position there—he was always associated with Chicago,and many of his most famous novels are set in that city.Despite his family's very humble start in the Chicago slums,Bellow was a reader who consumed everything he could put his hands on,and he was educated at both the University of Chicago and Northwestern University.For years he was a member (professor) of the highly prestigious Committee of Social Thought at the University of Chicago,one of the greatest of honors bestowed by that university.He spent his life in reading and discussion,was the master of a variety of different subjects,was handsome and elegant in his appearance and demeanor,was an academic among academics at Chicago.In his personal life,he can be said to be one of the few Renaissance Men the 20th century produced.

Yet,if anything,he was even more of a Renaissance Man in his novels than he was in his person.He lived through most of the 20th century,and he tried to convey not so much its events as the psychology of his fellow human beings,whether his subjects were intellectuals,gangsters or frauds.His characters live in panoramic worlds that suggest the teeming milieu of Dickens.He was the master of a peculiarly 20th century "voice," one of his own devising,that ranged from the inflections of the Yiddish to the vernacular of the Chicago streets to the rhythms of jazz to the inflated speech of the most gifted of his colleagues at the University of Chicago.His accomplishment was recognized with the highest honors.He won the Nobel Prize in Literature,as well as,from his own country,the National Medal of the Arts and three National Book Awards.He was one of the few American writers who was as popular in other parts of the world,most notably in Europe,as he was in his own country,and there is some justice in the claim that,for the last half of the 20th century,Bellow was America's voice to the rest of the world.

Henderson the Rain King

Because in his novels he held up a mirror to America,and expressed his vision in a peculiarly American idiom,Saul Bellow is well worth reading.It can fairly be said that any of his novels is worth our attention—for Bellow's unique vision of the world in which we live. His subjects are the isolation of modern man,his separation from anything that would sustain him spiritually,the possibilities,despite these difficulties,of a good and fulfilling life. These are compelling subjects to any modern man or woman who thinks rather than just

索尔·贝娄
《雨王汉德森》

索尔·贝娄

　　索尔·贝娄(1915~2005)度过了很长的一生,现在被广泛誉为除了威廉·福克纳之外的20世纪美国最伟大的两位小说家之一。贝娄相比之下拥有更加丰富的生活经历。他是一名犹太人,出生于现在的加拿大蒙特利尔市,之前他的父母是从俄国移民到这里的。为了提高他们的身份,找到更高收入的工作,在贝娄9岁的时候全家搬到了芝加哥。快80岁的时候,他又移居波士顿,在那里开展一项新的学术事业,至此贝娄一直保持着与芝加哥的联系,并且在他最有名的作品中有很多都是以芝加哥为背景。虽然贝娄的家开始是在芝加哥的贫民窟,但是他尽其所能地博览群书,后来就读于芝加哥大学和西北大学。他曾好几年在芝加哥大学担任教授,并是享有很高声誉的社会思想委员会成员,这是芝加哥大学最高荣誉机构。贝娄一生都在读书和讨论,掌握了若干不同学科的专业知识,他的外貌英俊风度翩翩,是芝加哥学术界的一位资深专家。就他个人生活而言,他称得上是20世纪少有的博学家之一。

　　然而,贝娄在其作品里比在生活中更加显示出了他的博学多才,他的一生贯穿了20世纪的大部分时光,并且他试图在其作品中不单单记述发生的事情,而是更强调刻画与他同时代的人们的心理,不论这些人物形象是知识分子、街头流氓,还是江湖骗子。他塑造的形象所生活的背景类似狄更斯作品中描述的社会环境。贝娄是专门记录20世纪"声音"的大师,他的创作采用了他自己的风格,包含意第绪语发音的曲折变化到芝加哥街头方言,蕴含着爵士乐的节奏,再加上作者在芝加哥大学的天才同事的夸张演说。贝娄的成就享有极高的声誉,他荣获过诺贝尔文学奖,此外,还获得了本国的国家艺术奖和三项国家图书奖。贝娄是极少数的在世界其他国家,尤其是在欧洲,和在自己国家一样备受欢迎的美国作家之一,并且有评论声称在20世纪的后50年间贝娄向世界呐喊出了美国人民的心声。

《雨王汉德森》

　　因为索尔·贝娄在其小说中以一种美国独有的语言风格反映了美国人民的生活,所以他的作品非常值得一读。可以毫不夸张地说,他的每一部小说都值得引起我们的关注——贝娄对我们当今世界有一个独特的视角。他创作的主题是有关现代人的孤立,人们脱离了任何赖以维系的精神支撑,也远离了通向幸福且充实的生活的可能。这些题材对于任何不单纯为了谋生而且有所思想的现代人来说是颇具吸引力的。

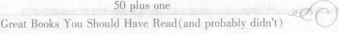
survives.

Some critics would argue that Henderson the Rain King is neither Bellow's most profound nor most popular novel,but it outlines Bellow's characteristic themes in a vivid and understandable manner:

Published in 1959,Henderson explores both the post-war affluence and the postwar disillusionment of the 1950s in America,an affluence and disillusionment that continues to this day.Henderson is a millionaire—and a pig farmer.Thus,he is a representative of a simple man,yet at the same time his riches allow him to have any material possession he desires.In a sense,he is a kind of composite Everyman.But finally he has no desires—he feels lonely,despairing,estranged from the modern world,yet at the same time he searches for some purpose and meaning in his own life—and in modern life itself.Approaching middle age,Henderson feels only desperation,a sense of his own "deadness," a lack of connection with his life or with that of other people.

Henderson decides to make a pilgrimage to Africa,even though he has prejudices against African civilization (as "less advanced" than his own),to see whether a complete change of scene and cultures will cause him in any way to re-examine self and find new meaning in his life.After some misadventures,he arrives in a village that declares him Rain King.The villagers hope that he will soon make it rain,to counteract a drought.He becomes friendly with the king,Dahfu,and together they discuss various issues of life and death.

In these discussions,Henderson comes to a gradual transformation.He comes to believe that life is not so much an inevitable progress to death and decay; it is rather a series of constant rebirths—provided a man is willing to follow certain truths:That the relationship between the spirit and the flesh is a dynamic,not an antagonistic,one (put in different terms—body and soul are not enemies); that any rebirth,or self-transformation,must be accomplished by the human imagination; that rebirth spiritually involves a continual effort throughout our lives; and that love is the goal toward which all human striving should be directed.Our attitude should not be one of despair,a wishing to escape from human life; rather,it should acknowledge the wholeness of all being,and life should involve a constant spiritual growth—to the accomplishment of achieving love.

In the end of the novel,the rain comes,symbolizing rebirth.Yet Bellow leaves purposely vague what that rebirth may be,though Henderson plans,having returned home,to become a doctor—someone who will accomplish his own rebirth by helping others.

Although Bellow was to go on to write many more novels,to great acclaim,it is Henderson the Rain King that gives us the simplest expression of his philosophy of life— and serves as an inspiration to all those who,in modern life,have,like Henderson,reached what they regard as the end of the road.It is one of the more positive literary works of modern times.

有的评论家可能会辩解:虽然《雨王汉德森》既非贝娄的最深刻之作也非他最著名的小说,但是它以一种生动而易于理解的方式体现了作者的个性化主题。

这部作品于1959年出版,文中主人公汉德森体验了战后20世纪50年代美国社会的富足和精神上的幻灭,并且这种物质上富有和精神上幻灭的状态一直持续到今天。人物汉德森既是一个百万富翁,又是一个养猪户。这样,他便代表了一个普通人,然而,他的财富让他可以获得任何他所期望的物质利益,所以从某种意义上说,他是某种"合成"的平常人。但是最终他失去了欲望——他感觉到孤单、绝望,以及跟现代世界的隔绝,不过他同时也在寻求某种目标和生活的意义——现代生活本身。汉德森到了中年只是感觉孤注一掷和自己生命的衰退,缺乏自身以及和其他人的沟通。

于是,汉德森决定去探访非洲,虽然他本身对非洲的文明存有偏见(他认为非洲的文明不如自己社会的发达),他还是想看看环境和文化的彻底改变是否能让他重新审视自身并找到生活的新意。在历经很多磨难之后,他到达了一个村庄,那里的村民称他为"雨王",因为他们希望汉德森将能为那里带去雨水,以解救当时的旱灾。汉德森与当地的国王大富(Dahfu)关系非常好,两人一起谈论生与死的很多人生话题。

在这些谈论中,汉德森的思想逐渐有了转变。他开始相信人生并非只是注定趋于死亡、腐朽;而是一个不断重生的过程——只要你愿意追求真理:精神与肉体的关系是互动的,不是对立的(换句话说,灵与肉并非敌人);任何一次重生,或者思想的转变,必须由人类的想象来完成;精神的重生需要持续一生的努力;爱是所有人应该为之奋斗的目标。我们的人生态度不应该是悲观绝望的,那只是对人生的逃避;而应该持有的态度是认识到存在的完满,并且人生应该不断追求精神上的进步——去实现爱的目标。

小说最后,雨下下来了,这一点象征着"重生"。不过,贝娄故意没有点明重生的是何物,虽然主人公汉德森打算回家之后开始从医——医生将能够通过救治他人获得重生。

虽然,贝娄继这部作品之后写了更多的小说,但《雨王汉德森》以最简单的表达展现了作者的人生哲学,并且作为一个启示,去激发现代生活中所有那些像汉德森一样自认为是走到了生命尽头的人们。这是现代较为积极乐观的文学作品中的一部。

Forty-nine

Nelson Mandela:
The Long Walk to Freedom

Who Is Nelson Mandela?

Looking back at the century just passed,many commentators have said that the 20th century was the bloodiest in human history.It is easy enough to imagine how such a judgment came to be.The first half of the 20th century involved two world wars; the second half involved conflicts between the capitalist West and the communist Soviet Union and China that,in their own way,were just as destructive of human life as the world wars had been.And compared to the tyrants of the past,the despots of the 20th century are now legendary for their mass murders: Hitler killed eight millions Jews and millions more of the peoples of Eastern Europe.They had what they considered rational reasons for the killing-reasons that now seem to us barbarous,as if centuries of civilization had never happened. Other less renown leaders,in positions of power—in Africa,Europe and Asia-engaged in mass murder on a lesser scale.If we think that the killing lessened as the century proceeded, we have only to remember that the horrors of Bosnia happened less than a decade ago.

It is easy,very easy,to be disillusioned about the 20th century-and to wonder whether the 21st century will involve more of the same thing,a fear that is hardly groundless.The century had barely begun when 9/11 occurred,and people in the West realized that they were engaged in a fight to the death with the terrorists.

Yet,in becoming disillusioned,it is easy to forget that there has been another,and very potent,current in 20th century life,which persists to the present—that of the fight for freedom.Whether that fight was embodied by the "underground" fighters in World War II or by the people of the United States who fought for the rights of minorities in the 1960s and 1970s.The fight for human freedom in our time has been as important—and perhaps more significant in the long term—than have the battles that led to human destruction.

This human-freedom movement in the 20th century also produced its notable figures, whether it was Gandhi,inspiring his fellow Indians to fight the British Empire and,through passive resistance and non-violence,to gain freedom for his people as well as to provide a beacon for other colonial peoples.Or,in the United States,Martin Luther King Jr.,inspired by Gandhi and by his own Christianity,to gain civil rights for all Americans.Of all of these life-affirming as opposed to life-destroying leaders,no one gained more famed internationally than Nelson Mandela of South Africa,who was born in that country in 1918.

The Long Walk to Freedom

Whatever the insidiousness of racism,the hatred of one religion for another,or notions of class that have existed in many other countries of the world,these terrible ideas were nowhere enshrined as overt government policy in the way that they were in South Africa-in the policy of "apartheid." Blacks,the majority of the country,were,by law and often violent practice,purposely kept in a subservient position to minority whites (the descendants of early English and Dutch settlers),who controlled the government,commerce and military

纳尔逊·曼德拉
《自由路漫漫》

纳尔逊·曼德拉

回首刚刚逝去的一个世纪，很多评论家都声称在人类历史的长河中20世纪是最血腥的一个世纪。我们很容易想象为何有此评判。20世纪的前半段时间产生了两次世界大战；后半段充满了实行资本主义的西方国家和崇尚共产主义的前苏联以及中国之间的激烈冲突，这样的形势，和爆发世界大战一样，给人类的生活造成了灾难性的影响。比较历史上的暴政，20世纪的独裁者所实施的大屠杀也是骇人听闻的：希特勒杀害了八百万犹太人以及数百万东欧国家的百姓。他们对大屠杀都振振有词——而他们的理由在我们看来是如此野蛮，就好像人类几个世纪的文明不复存在。还有一些不太知名的执政首领——在非洲、欧洲和亚洲——实施过较小规模的屠杀。如果我们以为这样的屠戮随着时间的不断推移有所减少的话，那么我们无论如何都不能忘记不到十年前在波斯尼亚造成的恐慌。

人们往往都会感到20世纪的幻灭——进而担心21世纪是否还会上演更大的悲剧，这一忧虑并非没有道理，21世纪几乎就是开始于"9·11"事件的发生，西方人意识到他们陷入了一场与恐怖分子之间殊死的搏斗。

然而，在幻灭的同时，人们很容易会忘记20世纪还有另外一场强劲的一直持续至今的斗争——为自由而战的斗争。无论这场斗争是在二战期间由"秘密组织"所展开，还是体现于20世纪60~70年代美国人民为争取少数人的权利而进行的斗争。在现代，人们为自由而战的斗争是非常重要的，用长远的眼光来看，或许它们比造成人类浩劫的战争更重大。

20世纪的人类自由运动也造就了一些著名的人物，无论是领导印度人民进行"非暴力不合作"运动反抗英国的殖民统治，最终赢得了民族独立并激发了其他殖民地人民的解放运动的伟大领袖甘地；还是受甘地和基督教义的影响领导美国人民争取民权的领袖马丁·路德·金。在所有这些倡导人权、反对暴力的领导者中，没有人享有比南非领袖纳尔逊·曼德拉更高的世界声誉(他于1918年出生在南非)。

《自由路漫漫》

种族主义所造成的迫害，某一宗教对其他派别的仇视，以及世界上许多国家所崇尚的等级意识，没有哪个地方像南非这样把所有这些可怕的观念完全奉为他们的政府纲领——即"种族隔离"政策。按照法律规定以及强制措施，故意使占这个国家大部分人口的黑人屈从于那些掌管国家政府、经济和军事力量的少数白种人(他们是早期英国和荷兰定居者的后裔)。这些非洲的黑人被禁止从事某种职业，他们被驱赶到少数人住的聚居

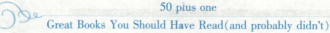

forces of that country.Prevented from holding certain jobs,herded into ghettos away from the pleasant neighborhoods of whites,blacks in South Africa existed essentially as a slave class-in a world in which slavery had been officially abolished.

As a young man,Nelson Mandela,the son,then the ward,of tribal royals,tried the route of passive resistance,moral persuasion and non-violence chosen,too,by Gandhi and King,via the African National Congress,the group that eventually became the most potent force in the anti-apartheid movement.By sheer force of hard work,correspondence courses and attendance at a black university,he managed,with difficulty (he was essentially impoverished, on his own,disenfranchised from his family),to qualify as a lawyer and to try to help his people by providing them with legal advice (usually free).But eventually he came to feel that these actions were accomplishing nothing against the monolith of apartheid.

In the 1950s and 1960s Mandela became instrumental in reviving a stagnant African National Congress and its Youth League,and essentially turned the ANC into a terrorist organization,which fought the government of South Africa in a series of daring and increasingly violent conflicts.

In 1964,at the notorious Rivonia Trial,Mandela was sentenced to life imprisonment for his "crimes against the state;" he served for 27 years,most of it on Robben Island,where he began his autobiography,The Long Walk to Freedom,in 1974.His manuscript was eventually confiscated by prison authorities,but other prisoners had copies,and the manuscript survived.During those 27 years,Mandela became the most famous political prisoner in the world—an inspiration to his own people who refused to allow his legacy to die and a rallying figure for oppressed peoples and their sympathizers around the world who saw him not just as a symbol of anti-apartheid but also as a inspiration for all those people of the 20th century who were fighting oppression in their own societies.Mandela became an international hero,and "Free Mandela" was chanted around the world.

Finally,in 1990,through the intervention of the then president of South Africa,F.W.de Klerk,formerly one of Mandela's great enemies,Mendela was set free.

Together the two men,working together,devised the end of apartheid,and the coming of multi-racial democracy,based on majority rule,in South Africa; and together,they shared the Nobel Peace Prize of 1993.In 1994,Mandela became the first democratically elected president of South Africa,and he served until 1999; he retired in 2000.

After his release from prison in 1990,Mandela returned to his manuscript,completed his book,which was published in 1994 and became an international best-seller.

The Long Walk to Freedom is,of course,Mandela's own story,a memoir of his life,and it includes such poignant details as the necessary estrangement from his family in the service of his country.But it is more than a memoir.It details,as no other work has done,the path to freedom for South Africans.And not just South Africans.Mandela came to feel that the struggle of the blacks of South Africa was the story of all oppressed peoples,that the history of the destruction of oppression in South Africa was the story of the defeat of all oppressions,that his story,and South Africa's story,could inspire other fighters for freedom. In his Nobel acceptance speech,Mandela quotes Martin Luther King Jr.,that humanity can no longer be tragically bound to the starless midnight of racism and war—and sees his struggle (and that of his countryman) as the struggle by all men for "genuine brotherhood and peace." His book has become a kind of monument to that goal.

区,远离白种人所乐以生活的家园,他们过着奴隶般的日子——在一个官方号称已经废除了奴隶制度的世界。

纳尔逊·曼德拉生于一个大酋长家庭,年轻的他选择了走一条消极抵抗、道德规劝以及甘地和马丁·路德·金所采取的非暴力的路线。通过非洲人国民大会的决议,该组织最终成为反种族隔离运动的最强劲的力量。曼德拉努力工作,并在一所为黑人开办的大学攻读函授课程,他克服经济上的困难(离家之后,他几乎身无分文)获得了律师资格,并且努力向他的同胞们提供法律咨询。然而,曼德拉最后发现他的行动对于反抗坚如磐石的种族隔离政策起不到任何作用。

20世纪50~60年代,曼德拉的呼吁有效地唤醒了非洲人国民大会及其青年同盟,使非国大(ANC)基本上成为反抗南非政府的组织机构,展开了一系列勇敢且日趋激烈的暴力冲突。

1964年,在臭名昭著的里冯尼阿审判中,曼德拉被指控犯有"叛国罪"而判为无期徒刑,他在狱中服刑27年,大部分时间是在罗布恩岛上,1974年开始编写自传《自由路漫漫》。他的手稿最后被监狱的长官没收,但是狱中其他的犯人曾抄写过原本,所以草稿被保留下来。在曼德拉服刑的27年间,他成为世界上最著名的政治犯——他激励着那些不愿让他的志愿夭折的南非人民,并且唤醒了受压迫的民族及其在世界范围内的支持者,对于他们来说,曼德拉不仅是领导反种族隔离运动的旗手,而且是20世纪各国反抗压迫的人们的启蒙者。曼德拉成为一名国际英雄人物,"自由曼德拉"的美名也响遍全球。

1990年,曼德拉之前最大的敌人之一,即当时的南非总统F.W.德克勒克出面调停,曼德拉最终被释放。
经过他们两人的共同努力,最后终止了种族隔离政策,迎来了由南非大多数人掌管的多民族民主政治。并且,两人于1993年共同荣获了诺贝尔和平奖。1994年,曼德拉成为第一个由民主选举产生的南非总统,他一直连任到了1999年,并于2000年离退。

1990年,曼德拉获得释放之后又继续进行他的自传编写,完成之后于1994年出版,这一著作成为一部世界性的畅销书。
当然,《自由路漫漫》记述了曼德拉的个人故事,是记载他一生的回忆录,它包含了为了报效祖国曼德拉决意离家的详细情节,令读者深深为之感动。但是,这一自传又不只是一部回忆录,没有其他作品像它一样详细地记述了南非人民争取自由的斗争历程。而且不仅仅是南非人民,曼德拉感到南非黑人所进行的斗争代表了所有受压迫民族的斗争,南非抗击压迫的历史代表了一切推翻压迫的斗争史,他希望他本人的故事以及南非的历史可以唤醒其他民族为自由而战。在曼德拉接受诺贝尔奖的发言中,他提到了马丁·路德·金的例子,他疾呼人道不能再继续悲哀地限制在种族主义和战争的黑暗之中。曼德拉的斗争(以及他的同胞的斗争)可以被视为全人类为"真正的兄弟情谊和和平"而进行的斗争。他的作品已经成为实现这个目标的一座丰碑。

Fifty

Yukio Mishima:
Confessions of a Mask

Who Was Yukio Mishima

Japanese author Yukio Mishima (a pseudonym for Kimitake Hiraoka) was born in Tokyo in 1925 and died there—he committed suicide—in 1970.

Despite his short life,critics have compared him to some of the world's greatest writers—like Stendhal in his precise psychological analyses,like Dostoevsky in his explorations of darkly destructive personalities (*Christian Science Monitor*).

Mishima spent his early years in the care of his grandmother,Natsu,who,though she lived in the same house as his parents,removed him from their care.A woman of aristocratic pretensions,Natsu was sometimes prone to violent outbursts,perhaps (according to some of the commentators on Mishima's life) the result of painful sciatica.Some also blame her for Mishima's fascination with death.While she cared for him,Natsu also disallowed Mishima from engaging in traditional boyhood pursuits:he wasn't allowed to play sports or to fraternize with other boys.Instead,she kept him inside the house,alone or with his female cousins,playing with dolls.A frail boy,he was often ill.

At 12,Natsu returned Mishima to the care of his parents.They,too,provided a strange environment for a young man—his relationship with Shizue,his mother,bordered on the incestuous; his father was brutal,given to raiding Yukio's room and punishing him severely for creating what his father claimed were feminine manuscripts.

Alone,and fond of reading,Yukio devoured the works of such western writers as Oscar Wilde and Rilke,at the same time that he mastered the classics of Japan.He published his first short story while he was still at school.

He was disqualified from military service during World War II,and spent those years in Tokyo.Because his father disapproved of his becoming a writer,Mishima wrote secretly while attending university and later while working at the Government Finance Ministry.His novel *Confessions of a Mask* made him famous overnight,and thereafter he devoted himself to his writings; eventually,he created an extraordinary volume of works in various genres.

After the war,too,he devoted himself to physical training and to para-military activities. On November 25,1970,Mishima led a private militia of his founding in an attempted *coup d'etat*:they seized the office of the commander of Tokyo's headquarters of the Ground Self-Defense Force.The *coup failed*,and Mishima committed suicide.

His biographer and former friend,John Nathan,suggests that Mishima always suspected that his attempt at a *coup* would fail,that he was only using it to fulfill a dream of ritual suicide.Other commentators believe that it was his final and most dramatic attempt to protest against the weakness of modern Japan.

三岛由纪夫
《假面的告白》

三岛由纪夫

日本作家三岛由纪夫(本名平冈公威)于1925年出生于东京,1970年他在此自杀结束了自己的生命。

虽然三岛由纪夫的一生非常短暂,但评论家们都把他视作是世界级最伟大的作家之一——他作品中细致的人物心理分析可以与法国作家司汤达相媲美,在刻画人物阴暗的毁灭性格方面与陀思妥耶夫斯基也有相似之处(引自《基督教科学箴言报》)。

三岛由纪夫早年是在祖母夏子的看护下长大的,她虽然和三岛的父母同住,但却故意不让他们照管三岛。夏子具有日本贵族血统,她时常暴跳如雷,或许(根据有些研究三岛生平的评论家声称)这是因为她患有坐骨神经痛的缘故。也有人指责是她造成了三岛对死亡的迷幻。在夏子照看三岛期间,她不许三岛像传统的男孩子那样过玩乐的童年:三岛被禁止进行体育活动,或者与其他男孩交友。相反,他被祖母单独关在室内,要么就是让他和表姐妹们一起玩布娃娃。童年时期的三岛身体虚弱,并且经常生病。

在三岛12岁的时候,夏子又回到三岛的家里寻求三岛父母的照料。他们为这个少年提供了一种不同寻常的家庭氛围——三岛和母亲倭文重的关系几乎到了乱伦的程度;他的父亲性格粗暴,有时会突然闯进三岛的房间并恶狠狠地揍他一顿,因为他认为三岛尽是乱写一些女性化的玩意儿。

三岛由纪夫个人非常爱好阅读,他博览了大量的像奥斯卡·王尔德和里尔克这样的西方作家的作品,同时也精通日本的古典文学。他还在学校读书的时候就发表了他的第一部短篇小说。

二战期间,三岛因为条件不符没有被征召入伍,这几年的时间他一直待在东京。因为父亲不同意三岛写作,于是他在读大学以及后来在政府财政部工作的时候都是私底下进行创作。他的小说《假面的告白》使其一夜成名,之后他便全身心地投入写作,最终创作了大量的不同文体的作品。

战后,三岛致力于健身并且从事准军事性活动。1970年11月25日,他带领自己的私人武装企图实施计划已久的政变:他们在日本陆上自卫队东京总监部将师团长绑架为人质。政变最终失败,三岛由纪夫切腹自杀。

为三岛编写传记的他的生前的朋友约翰·内森暗示说三岛一直猜测他所策划的政变将会失败,他只是通过这一方式来完成自己所梦想的自杀仪式。其他评论家认为这是三岛最后的也是最具戏剧性的对现代日本国家幻灭的反抗。

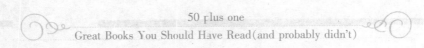

Confessions of a Mask

The circumstances of the death of Yukio Mishima were so spectacular,so bizarre,that even now,more than 35 years later (he died in 1970),mention his name and you're very likely to be given a recitation of the facts of that death—rather than any mention of the accomplishments of his life.

Mishima,with a small group of four of his followers (they had formed a extremist group called Tatenokai—the Shield Society),took over the office of the commandant of the Tokyo headquarters of Japan's Ground Self-Defense Force,where Mishima had undergone basic training,held the commandant,General Mashita,hostage as a means of enforcing their demands,which were essentially that Mishima be allowed to address as many soldiers as could be gathered in the courtyard below the office.He made a speech to them from the commandant's balcony,a speech that could hardly be heard because of the noise of the crowd,the noise of surveillance helicopters overhead.It was intended to rouse them to a *coup* against the government,to restore the Emperor to his rightful place,in effect to re-make Japan into what it had been before World War II (though Mishima's Japan was,to an extent,a Japan of myth).Returning to the inside room after the speech,Mishima committed seppuku-ritual suicide—by plunging a knife into his own stomach,disemboweling himself, then Morita,one of his followers,as prearranged,attempted to decapitate Mishima; he botched the job.Toga,his second,finished off the decapitation of Mishima.Then Morita himself attempted seppuku—and Toga decapitated him too.This double suicide had other ramifications:Morita was widely rumored to be Mishima's lover.

Has there ever been so horrific,so incomprehensible a death,involving a famous writer? Probably not,and that death haunts the public imagination even now,so much so that we tend to forget what Mishima had accomplished,as a writer,in his short life of 45 years.He started writing as a child,and in his lifetime produced 40 novels,20 collections of short stories,20 books of essays and some 20 plays and screenplays.He was three times nominated for a Nobel Prize in Literature,was,obviously,considered a world-class writer, became more familiar to western audiences than any other 20th century Japanese writer, and his last work,the 4-volume novel *Sea of Fertility*,an attempt to capture in fiction the history of 20th century Japan,is widely regarded as a masterpiece.

Yet,given the ritual suicide,the shock it gave the world,we have tended to concentrate on his life—that he was a frail and sickly child,that he was virtually kept prisoner in the family home by his grandmother,that he was a notorious homosexual,and that in his adult life he became obsessed with a strange cult of masculinity of which ritual suicide was a part. Some of this myth is true; most of it is just sufficiently untrue as to be misleading.For example:People who knew him best say that his homosexual liaisons were few and far between; also,he married in 1958,remained married to that woman until his death,and had two children to whom he was devoted.

Confessions of a Mask is a youthful novel (he was only 24 when it was published),and, because it reads as if it must be autobiography,it has become,given the strangeness of his life and death,Mishima's most popular work.It is a novel about a young man growing up in wartime:Mishima was 16 at the time of Pearl Harbor; he could have served in the closing years of World War II,got himself a deferment by lying,spent the war years in bomb-ravaged

《假面的告白》

　　三岛由纪夫的死如此轰动,如此不可思议,直至今日,在他死后35年(他于1970年自杀)人们一提到他的名字就会谈论一系列关于他自杀的真相,而不会涉及他一生所作的成就。

　　三岛带领他组织内的4名成员(他们组建了一个极端组织,起名为"盾会")占领了日本陆上自卫队东京总监部的指挥办公室,由于三岛曾经受过基本的训练,他挟持了指挥上将作为人质,迫使他们允许三岛在指挥办公室楼下集合尽可能多的士兵,之后,三岛在指挥部的阳台上向他们做了一次演说,但因为聚集的人们噪音太大,加上监视他们行踪的直升机也在空中盘旋,他的演讲几乎没有被听到。这则演说是为了呼吁士兵们发动兵变反抗日本政府,恢复天皇的合法地位,重建日本回到二战之前的状态(虽然,某种程度上,三岛头脑中的日本只是一个神化)。三岛讲完退回室内,并按照日本传统仪式切腹自杀——把一把刀刺入自己的腹部,让肠子从伤口流出来。随后,他的一名追随者森田必胜按照事先约定准备为三岛介错,但连砍数次都未能成功,于是,换第二个人古贺浩靖来完成。之后,森田必胜也切腹自杀,并且还是由古贺浩靖为其执行介错。这两起自杀事件有另外的解释:有传闻称森田必胜是三岛的爱慕者。

　　你听说过有哪位著名作家涉及如此骇人听闻的死亡事件吗? 可能没有吧,而三岛的死直到今天还缠绕于公众们的脑海,人们甚至都会忘记他,作为一名作家,在短暂的45年生命中所取得的成就。三岛从孩提时就开始写作,一生创作了40部小说、20册短篇小说合集、20本散文,还有20部戏剧及电影剧本。他曾三次被提名诺贝尔文学奖的评选,显然,他是一位世界级的作家。与20世纪其他的日本作家相比,三岛在西方读者中更为著名,并且他的最后一部四卷小说《丰饶之海》描述了20世纪日本的历史概况,被广泛认为是他的代表作。

　　然而,他的自杀震惊世界,于是我们往往倾向于关注他的人生——他童年时期身体虚弱,常易生病,他事实上是被祖母监禁在家里,他有同性恋的臭名,他成年之后沉迷于对古怪的"男子气结"的崇拜,而自杀便是其中的一部分。但是,这其中有的传言的确属实,而大多数都是虚构且容易引起误导的。比如,了解三岛的人们都说他几乎没有同性恋的迹象,并且说他于1958年结婚,直到他自杀一直保持着与他妻子的婚姻关系,他也尽到了作为两个孩子父亲的义务。

　　《假面的告白》是一部他在年青时代创作的小说(这一作品出版时他年仅24岁),并且因为它读上去很像三岛的自传,充满了他生与死的扑朔迷离,这部小说成为他最著名的作品。小说是关于一个青年在战时的成长经历。珍珠港事件爆发的时候,三岛正好16岁,他本来可以在二战的最后几年时间入伍,但他撒谎推迟了服役的期限,这段期间他待在经受炸弹浩劫的东京。三岛在这部作品的前半部分描述了他逐渐意识到他的性倾向在男

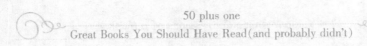
Tokyo. In the first half of the book, he describes the progress toward his acknowledging that his erotic interest is in men; the second half describes his relationship with a woman, Sonoko, for whom he feels a platonic, rather than an sexual, love. From the evidence of this book, readers have concluded that Mishima is confessing to a homosexuality that, given the dictates of Asian society at the time (they persist to the present day), must be hidden behind a "mask." Everything else he contemplates in the book is reduced, by many readers, to just this admission of sexual deviancy.

But that is a very superficial reading of *Confessions of a Mask*. The frail sensitive young man—the man who would become a famous writer—is always playing with, considering, a kind of machismo that at the time seems anachronistic. He idolizes the male body, but in a particular way; it is an idealized body (and, indeed, Mishima thereafter became an obsessive body-builder, transformed himself into his own vision)—the body of a warrior, a throwback to the old samurai class of Japan. Into this mix, there is an aspect of homosexuality that is itself historic—the semi-mythical notion (it persists from Ancient Greece) of warriors who are themselves lovers. As well—drawing on other legends—such warriors are often called upon to make the supreme sacrifice to make a dramatic point, to set an example for the public good.

If these particular notions sound familiar to readers, they should remember that they savor of fascism, of some of the precepts of Nazi Germany—then readers should remember too, though often this is less familiar to us, that Japan was also, in World War II, a fascist, militaristic state, allied with Nazi Germany against the Allies.

The Importance of Mishima

And the lessons for us today? The concept of the superman, from its beginnings in the works of the philosopher Nietzsche, goes on to pervade the thought of the Western world in the 20th century. This concept undergoes sea changes; in the end, it is a corruption of what Nietzsche was actually saying. But the received version goes like this: that there are people who are superior to others, or ethnic groups that are superior to other ethnic groups (think the German view of Jews or any Slavic peoples). As well, it is a superior military class (the S. S.) that will enforce the will of the superior race—who will, if necessary, die for the glory of the Fatherland, to prove both their own nobility and that of their cause.

One of the lessons to be learned in reading *Confessions of a Mask* is that these concepts were not peculiar to the west, that a Japanese man could feel the same way, that such concepts occurred in Japanese society as well in those societies with which we are more familiar. But there is a further lesson here: Mishima wrote most of his works, embarked on his crusade to become a modern samurai, *after* World War II had ended. Japan, with its emperor, with its warrior class, with its industrious, religious and highly educated people (as gifted in their own way as the Germanic classes of central Europe), had in fact lost the war to the superior technology and know—how of the Allies, people regarded by the cultivated Japanese as cultural inferiors. The great cities of Japan, hence its culture, lay in ruins, and in Mishima we find all the resentments of a subjugated people. The difference was that he was writer of genius; he had a voice. More: The response of subjugated peoples is often simply to accept subjugation. In his case, Mishima dreams of renewed glory—of making Japan strong

性身上;后半部分记述了他与一位女士圆子的交往,三岛对她只有单纯的友情而不存在两性之间的爱慕。以此书为依据,读者们得出结论三岛由纪夫是在告白他的同性恋倾向,而迫于亚洲社会的伦理道德观念(这些观念一直持续至今),他必须隐藏在"面具"之后。很多读者都把作品中的其他细节忽略不计,他们关注的只是作者承认了自身有同性恋倾向。

但是,这只能是非常肤浅地阅读《假面的告白》。这个孱弱且敏感的青年——成为一位著名的作家——一直在扮演某种"男子气概",而这在当时似乎已经为时代所不容。他崇拜男性的身体,但是以一种特殊的方式;它们是被美化了的身躯(三岛从此沉迷于健身,希望把自己塑造成他理想中的身躯)——武士的躯体,三岛是一名崇尚日本武士阶层的返祖者。另一方面,同性恋本身也是有其历史渊源的——有一种半神话色彩的观点(可以追溯于古希腊时代)认为武士们之间互相倾慕。同时,还有其他传说声称这些武士经常被命令要做出最大的牺牲以达到某个目标,或者为了实现公众的利益而献身。

倘若读者们已经了解了这些特殊的理念,他们应该会记起法西斯主义以及纳粹德国的某些戒律就包含在内。虽然我们并不熟悉,但读者们还会记起,日本在二战期间也是崇尚法西斯主义,作为一个军国主义国家,它联合纳粹德国发动战争抗击同盟国。

三岛由纪夫的重要地位

我们今天可以从中吸取什么教训呢?"超人"这一概念源自哲学家尼采的作品,后来它继续扩展到20世纪西方世界人们的头脑当中。这个概念历经沧桑变化,最终像尼采所言它实际上象征着堕落。然而,有的观点已经被人们所接受:有些人是比其他人高级的,或者有些种族是比另外的种族高等的(想一下德国人是怎样看待犹太以及斯拉夫民族的)。此外,还有这样的观点:高级的军事阶层(德国纳粹的党卫军)将强制执行高级种族人民的意愿——必要的时候,他们将为"祖国"的荣誉而牺牲,以证明他们及其事业的高贵。

从阅读《假面的告白》中,我们应该学到的一点就是以上所提及的那些意识观念并非西方所特有,日本人也有相同的观念,这些存在于日本社会的思想观念同样出现在我们更加熟悉的社会中。但是,更重要的一个教训是:三岛由纪夫创作了诸多作品,二战结束后,他发动政变希望从中实现当一名现代武士的梦想。而事实上,日本、它的天皇、它的武士阶层、它的勤劳、崇尚宗教且受过高等教育的人民(像欧洲中部的日耳曼民族一样具有天才的素质)在战争中败下阵来——他们输给了高科技和日本所视为是拥有劣等文化的同盟国家。日本繁华的城市及其文化一起湮没在废墟之中。在三岛由纪夫的作品中,我们可以发现他作为战败民族一员所怀有的仇恨。区别就在于他是一位极具天赋的作家;他可以畅所欲言。而且,战败民族通常容易接受妥协,因此,三岛梦想为他的民族恢复荣誉——使日本回到过去以再次实现强盛,恢复以往神圣的天皇制度,以及恢复集美和无私于一身的武士阶层以保卫天皇。

again by reverting to the past,the past of a God-like Emperor,and of a warrior class of beautiful and selfless men who will insure that greatness.

It could be said that many,if not most,20th century intellectuals succumb to nihilism,the view that nothing matters,nothing is of consequence.There is,though,a different current in our times—to spread democracy,to relieve the agonies of the poor and sick,or,in Mishima's vision,to restore a lost (and to an extent mythical) world that was greater than the world in which we live.Mishima,however misguided he may have been,is not the first and he certainly will not be last to have such dreams-and his *Confessions of a Mask* is the perfect expression of a longing for greatness,for nobility,that,even as we enter the 21st century, refuses to die.

如果不是大部分,至少我们可以说有许多20世纪的文人志士倾向于虚无主义,这一观念认为任何事物都不重要,不存在因果联系。然而,我们的现代还流行着另一种趋势——普及民主制度,拯救那些受穷困和疾苦摧残的人们,或者,借用三岛由纪夫的观点,重建逝去的(某种程度上带有神秘色彩)世界,使其建设得比现在我们所生活的世界更加美好。无论三岛由纪夫造成了怎样的误导,他并非第一个也肯定不会是最后一个拥有这样梦想的人——他创作的《假面的告白》完美地展现了他追求伟大和高尚的渴望,即使我们已经步入了拒绝死亡的21世纪,他的教训仍然值得我们借鉴。